C0-BPB-192

Teaching Children & Adolescents with Behavioral Difficulties

An

Educational

Approach

Evelyne Corcos, PH.D.

Tigress Publications
Toronto, Canada

National Library of Canada Cataloguing in Publication

Corcos, Evelyne, 1946-
    Teaching children and adolescents with behavioral difficulties: an educational approach
    / Evelyne Corcos. – 2nd ed.

First ed. published under title: Teaching children with behavioural difficulties.
Includes bibliographical references and index.
ISBN 0-9681526-1-9

    1. Behavior disorders in children. 2. Problem children – Education. I. Title.

LC4801.C67 2003   371.93   C2003-901177-1

Printer: Ricter Web
Book Design & Print Production: MixedMedia, Ann Hibberd
Editor: Nancy Vichert

Copyright © 2003 by Tigress Publications

No part of this book may be reproduced by any mechanical, photographic, or electronic process, or in the form of a phonographic recording, nor may it be stored in a retrieval system, transmitted, or otherwise copied for public or private use, without written permission from the publisher.

Some graphics were produced by Presentation Task Force, a registered trademark of New Vision Technologies, Inc.

Printed in Canada

This book is not only dedicated to my parents Denise Corcos and the late

Salomon Corcos, but also to the late Barbara Brodski, a good friend and

colleague who championed the cause of students with special needs.

Preface

This book is the result of my personal experience as an instructor of a preparatory course for teachers called *Introduction to the Education of Children with Behavioral Exceptionalities*. Over the years, it has become exceedingly difficult to choose an appropriate textbook for the course because, while some books addressing the subject in a comprehensive manner are out of date, others seem limited to a psychological rather than an educational perspective, and a further group lacks a Canadian point of view.

While it is true that many teachers find the psychological perspective intriguing in the available textbooks – because everyone is attracted by explanations of why people behave the way they do – perhaps this fascination is rooted in our desire to understand why *we* behave the way *we* do. Among these same teachers, however, are some who complain about the inappropriateness of therapeutic interventions addressed by the textbooks, especially those designed for clinical settings with low pupil-teacher ratios and varied treatment mandates. As a result of the variable procedures, many teachers find these interventions inapplicable to regular classroom and school contexts. For example, while token economies can be very effective in clinical settings, with their varying staff-to-patient ratios, in the classroom of a typical school, the circumstances often become overwhelming. In some cases, this happens when teachers are required to spend a large part of each day in the calculation and trading of points earned by the children. Another example of an intervention inappropriate in the classroom is the controversial technique of "holding down" an out-of-control child when the goal is to ensure the physical safety of everyone. Although, in treatment centers as well as in some schools, this commonly used strategy is recognized as valid in its clinical setting, teachers in school classrooms feel uncomfortable with the physical restriction of a student.

The challenge of this book, then, is to retain relevant psychological explanations, along with certain treatment interventions, and, in addition, to include strategies peculiar to the classroom setting. To accomplish this aim, a variety of factors unique to the classroom context has been considered, including such elements as, for example, student perceptions and motivations regarding treatment; the mandate and knowledge bases of teachers; and the special challenges of classroom structure and organization.

In every society, school-age children want to be the same as all other children in their age group. Thus, those young students who experience socio-emotional problems often resent the intervention of mental health services or of any resource that sets them apart from their peers: this would be any service not available to and used by all other children. When student behavior has warranted partial or total exclusion from a regular class or school context, the young person often demonstrates a very poor prognosis. Partly, this results from inadequate modeling opportunities, leading to forms of maladaptive behavior; equally often, the unsatisfactory outcome is a factor of segregated settings. Also, however, inappropriate behavior sometimes results from a lack of investment by students in their own recovery. In a few cases, moreover, these students may develop learned helplessness, thereby losing their will to thrive in a normative setting. In consideration of these negative outcomes, it is useful to propose that the classroom is the most natural and obvious context in which to address the social and emotional concerns of children and young adults.

Of very serious concern, too, is my realization that the practices typically adopted for dealing with the social and emotional rehabilitation of children and adolescents are often inherited from procedures originally developed for adults. When a mental health professional – psychiatrist, psychologist, childcare worker, probably a recognized expert within an institution, introduces borrowed procedures into schools, the beliefs and expectations held by the student in a typical school setting may be overlooked. In a relevant instance, "the talking cure" is unsuitable for any child with developing language and metacognitive skills. Another useful example involves Behavior Modification interventions, which although extremely effective in some contexts, may sacrifice long-term educational goals – perhaps becoming a thoughtful person – for more immediate needs such as compliance.

Not only do children and young adults perceive themselves as "students", they are recognized as such by their peers, teachers, and significant others. For this most important reason, the classroom is the most likely place to address socio-emotional issues. In the tradition of John Dewey, this book contends that schools must renew their effort to address the socio-emotional and the socialization needs of students, emphasizing that these approaches must be made in the context which the students themselves find most comfortable.

While the classroom is the most natural setting for socio-emotional intervention, at the same time it is qualitatively different from the situations familiar to many students, whether in one-on-one or small-group contexts in mental health centers and other similar facilities. By contrast, the classroom is a dynamic environment in which events, activities, and learning opportunities flow. In these experimental classrooms, successful teachers, who understand this natural order, have learned to move with the flow, directing rather than opposing or arresting it. As trained professionals, these teachers expect to encounter unexpected situations and crises in the course of each day.

In the classroom, the special conditions always present necessitate "a reflective practitioner" at the helm, a teacher able to anticipate, pre-plan, and evaluate potential scenarios that relate to the events as they occur. During each day, the teacher is able to address the affective, management, and motivational requirements of the group while focusing on the special needs of individual students. Although these elements might appear to make unrealistic demands, this book proposes a framework for promoting the socio-emotional health of students integrated in the existing structure of the classroom.

In Chapters Four to Seven, a model addressing the needs of students as a group is described, along with emphasis on individual needs. This model considers the affective, linguistic, cognitive, and social knowledge requirements of students, detailing the ways in which existing classroom programs can contribute to each student's knowledge base. From a prevention perspective, the model highlights some basic requisites of personal growth and well-being, while, in addition, exploring interventions – suited to the classroom – that can be initiated by teachers when students misbehave. Also are outlined ways of involving not only the school and teachers but also the students and parents as "co-investigators" in discovering creative solutions for students with behavioral difficulties. In responding to the problem of passive compliance, the chapters also emphasizes the development of responsible social behavior, competence, and personal growth.

As a whole, this book chooses to address many types of behavioral difficulties of students from special populations, especially when they are being educated in school settings. It also provides, in this context, information about students who, formerly, attended only treatment programs in non-school locations. In addition, some sections are devoted to the students' socio-emotional needs, providing concrete suggestions for addressing problems in the classroom. Finally, the book aims to impart tips and advice, helpful to teachers, for organizing classrooms in order to optimize socio-emotional and educational goals. To this end, the book deals with common concerns such as ways of ensuring safe and productive field trips and organizing a successful mainstreaming plan.

Focusing on its basic approach, this book has been organized with the teacher in mind, meaning that important information is presented in a manner that makes its intent immediately obvious. In this new edition, too, suggestions made by readers and users of the earlier edition are incorporated. In constructing the various chapters, I have consistently recognized the significance of anecdotes, examples, charts, and models, increased the range of visual presentation to simplify difficult concepts within the information.

I would like to take this opportunity to thank the many teachers who have contributed indirectly to the inspiration for this book. Also, I would like to recognize the late Barbara Brodski, as well as Joe Bellissimo and Margot McLeod, who team-taught courses with me, always providing honest feedback about the relevance of strategies. It is also a pleasure to have the opportunity to acknowledge the contributions of Hella Glinos, Vincent MacNeil, Bill Walkerley, Tracey Hayes, Carolyne Howe, Ginger Howell, and the many other teachers who have graciously permitted me to use their descriptions of real children in actual classroom situations. Finally, I am very grateful to Susan Stowe who volunteered to undertake aspects of the library research; to Judith Wickett for ensuring that the content was user-friendly and for attending to many menial jobs without complaining; to Ann Hibberd and MixedMedia for both the artwork and the production of the book. Finally, a special thanks to my editor, Nancy Vichert, who was unwavering in keeping me on the strait and narrow, and who has sharpened my ability to communicate with an invisible audience.

E.C.

Table of Contents

List of Tables

List of Figures

CHAPTER 1

Introduction

- normality is defined in different ways

- normality is defined differently depending on when and where the individual is

- normality and exceptionality are different sides of the same coin

- social normality is a subjective concept

- major explanations of behavior have historical origins

- the manner in which a behavior is explained determines the way it is treated

Every teacher is familiar with at least one child who, on the one hand, does not appear to "conform" to the social expectations of the classroom or, on the other, because of social or emotional problems, is unable to learn. Often, these children migrate from the regular class to a special one, because their problem behaviors escalate beyond the threshold of tolerance of either the teacher or the other students in the class. A student, for example, who has become violent in anger and frustration, begins to interfere with the learning objectives of the classroom. Such a diversion is accomplished by drawing on teacher attention to deal with the problem situation, while at the same time impacting on the safety needs of classmates. Moreover, when students are placed in special classes for such behavior, they may face an even greater challenge in their journey back to the regular class. Reasons for this unexpected outcome will be explored throughout the book.

It is clear that two considerations remain prominently in the minds of classroom teachers:

- Managing of students with problem behaviors in the context of the regular class

- Helping students in a special class to return to the regular class

To arrive at satisfactory responses to both concerns, a starting point is needed. The adage proposing that the way to change others is to begin by changing oneself is particularly relevant to this discussion. Often, when external pressures are perceived as agents of change, the immediate response is resistance. In cases in which changes appear to occur, a removal of the external pressures usually allows problem individuals to return to the prior inappropriate state. Charlene, as an instance, is still late every morning despite Mr. Kamir's attempt to get her to class on time by using three methods: sending her to the office, charting her behavior, and explaining the importance of punctuality. In contrast, Manfred is punctual, but only as long as Mr. Kamir provides stickers. To effect durable change in these students, it is Mr. Kamir who must first change his attitudes and beliefs about Charlene and Manfred. Mr. Kamir must ask the question: 'Is the problem one of punctuality or of some other factor? Mr. Kamir will need to develop a deeper understanding of these two students' life circumstances. Although it is always difficult for a person to change attitudes and beliefs, even more challenging is the process needed to change behavior. Michael has come to recognize the importance of acquiring effective study strategies in order to boost his grades. Not only has he read all recent books published on this subject, he has also perused a variety of web pages from the Internet directly related to the matter. Although Michael is now an expert on the topic, he remains unable to apply what he has learned. Michael's dilemma is not unlike that of the student who is able to enumerate the problem-solving steps required to accomplish a task, yet is unable to apply them in practice. Similar, too, is the teacher who has internalized classroom management knowledge but remains unable to deal with unruly students. It is safe to conclude that knowledge and practice can exist in a mutually exclusive manner.

Evidently, one can have the knowledge without the practice, but is the reverse also true? It can be shown that working people are required to accomplish many tasks without being aware of the knowledge base they are tapping. Ms. Poulin, for example, was teaching a lesson on algebraic equations. While explaining the concept, she easily switched into an unplanned application to baseball statistics. When asked what prompted her sudden change in direction, she was unable to explain the cause. Often, a teacher cannot detail the knowledge that underlies an action. When questioned, the teacher will usually respond that it seemed to be the "right" thing to do. This means that knowledge and action can co-exist independently even though, when used at the same time, they make effective partners.

In addressing the problems of students with behavioral difficulties, the initial step requires the teacher to change attitudes and beliefs, to acquire the necessary knowledge, and, most importantly, to change personal behavior. In turn, it is a usual expectation that similar processes will effect change in the student. Such a simple answer for such a difficult problem! Other modifications are also pertinent:

1. Additional resources are needed to address the special needs of at-risk students. These range from human resources (lower pupil-teacher ratio, child care workers, etc.) to adequate space (climate controlled classrooms, learning centers, seminar rooms) and finally to learning materials (books, hardware, software, library access).

2. Teachers must be given the opportunity to acquire relevant knowledge about students with special needs and to be familiar with current pedagogy, as well as to understand collaborative and project management.

3. Finally, the student and/or the family must be motivated and committed to change and to work cooperatively with the school.

Without this final ingredient, the family involvement, the process can be severely undermined. Clearly, the many factors associated with the process of helping a child to become "well" are not easily accommodated. Indeed, the task of developing the appropriate intervention plan is very complex.

Sometimes, teachers will bend to administrative and social pressures in order to find immediate solutions when crises occur in the classroom. As a result, they frequently try cookbook approaches, hoping for simple steps to re-establish order. Although such basic procedures sometimes help in the midst of crisis, the goal of such traditional formulae is simplistic. It is meant to make children comply with a teacher's request, a compliance that appears necessary to contain an emergency. The obvious simplicity, however, of such traditional responses suggests how limited are these approaches in establishing the personal social/emotional growth that John Dewey had in mind.

The adoption of a long-term approach, incorporating a social/emotional curriculum, warrants a special perspective. Certainly, the classroom environment is the ideal place in which to learn how to work, share, and collaborate with others; express various emotions in a socially appropriate manner; and perceive one's strengths and weaknesses. Such accomplishments occur while also recognizing personal worth. When teachers complain that certain students do not and will not complete assignments nor follow classroom rules, and that, more importantly, these students are sometimes confrontational, the focus is often entirely on punishing or discouraging such behaviors commonly found in the classroom. If, however, behaviors can be shown to be motivated by feelings, thoughts, and previous actions, as most educators believe, then teachers who focus exclusively on promoting compliance may find themselves frustrated.

Children are people! Like other people they can feel unhappy, afraid, angry, and troubled. Not only are they subject to these emotions, they can also believe that they are unloved; they can be aware that they lack skills; they may even conclude that failure is inevitable. Given the complexity of the student's emotions in this context, it seems irrelevant to focus on traditional concerns like assignment completion, so many other facets being present.

It therefore becomes essential to begin the journey of viewing students as individuals, other humans who live with us for a large part of the day, individuals who need us to create those personalities they are capable of becoming. Such an expectation obligates teachers to acquire knowledge and learn procedures that can provide the needed services for these students. This chapter brings together the many elements required to build a conceptual framework consonant with previously outlined ideals.

First to be examined are the concepts of *normality* and *exceptionality*. In order to produce an objective means of conceptualizing behavior, the concepts of *normality* and *exceptionality* must initially be examined. This important undertaking is essential, because unless the extent and limits of these ideas can be grasped, it will be impossible to identify which students in the classroom require more attention. Also important are those factors influencing a group's ideas about the acceptability of various behaviors and, subsequently, the treatment measures that are generated by such beliefs. As a corollary, it is useful to evaluate definitions of the term *behavioral exceptionality* as recognized by Ministries of Education in Ontario and in several other provinces, as they relate to the needs of children requiring behavioral interventions. Finally, a historical examination of behavioral *normality* and *exceptionality* is presented to illustrate the importance of group values and expectations to behavior and intervention.

Defining Behavioral Exceptionalities

Before it is possible to define *behavioral exceptionality,* the question: "What is normal?" must be examined. The situation is analogous to examining the two sides of a single coin: which comes first? The manner in which *normality* is defined will determine, to a large extent, what *exceptionality* means. Arriving at a definition of *normality*, however, is not an easy task, because of the variety of points of view to consider. Probably, as many perspectives exist as there are people able to create definitions. If, however, each person's unique view of the world were included in the definition of *normality*, the result would be complication rather than clarification. For this reason, three fundamental views of *normality* will be considered: the Medical, the Statistical, and the Social, each of which represents a distinct and independent outlook on the meaning of *normality*.

Medical Normality

When the medical perspective represents the manner in which medicine and other physical sciences conceptualize ideas, it perceives *normality* as a physical condition with objective criteria such as

- the freedom from symptoms of disease

- the presence of normal signs

- the attempt to use absolute values; e.g., "37 degrees Celsius or 98.6 degrees Fahrenheit is the normal temperature, obtained from collecting data on 'healthy' individuals"

At the present time, research efforts are able to indicate recognized medical causes for several conditions previously thought to have social/emotional or environmental sources. For example, schizophrenia, manic-depression, and Tourette syndrome are conditions now known to involve physical causes and/or genetic pre-dispositions associated with the chemistry of the brain. The medical perspective, then, attempts to isolate exceptionality by (a) looking for a "rogue" gene which might be responsible for the condition; (b) pinpointing familial tendencies which demonstrate similar symptoms that may imply physical predisposition; (c) anticipating a normalization of symptoms in response to treatment, either by medication or by other measures directed to physical symptoms.

Statistical Normality

The statistical view of *normality* makes the assumption that human characteristics form a continuum and that, consequently, *normality* is perceived from the perspective of a "distribution" of scores depicted on a normal or Bell curve (see the Curve on p. 6). On the basis of a typical distribution, using standard deviations as units, a *normal* group comprising 67-68% of the population, can be shown as occupying the area between one standard deviation *above* and one standard deviation *below* the mean or average score. Two groups, each making up fourteen percent of the population, are represented by the area between one and two standard deviations *above* and *below* the mean. Finally, two extreme groups located between two and three standard deviations above and below the mean, may represent the most *Exceptional* Statistical *normality*. This perspective, then,

- is based on the notion that human characteristics are normally distributed on a curve

- is implicit in the realization that the normal curve is a statistical and mathematical construction

- is structured so that points on the outer limits of the curve represent atypical or unusual characteristics

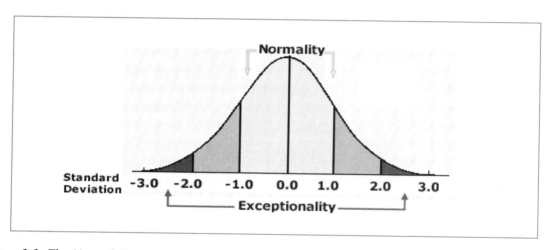

Figure1-1. The Normal Curve

While it is true that physical characteristics such as height, weight, etc., are normally distributed, no compelling evidence exists to indicate that such factors as social behavior and economic status may be viewed in the same way. To determine whether a characteristic is normally distributed, the usual procedure is to collect measurements from a large number of people; then, the number of people within each interval of the measurement scale is recorded; for example, see Figure 2, the curve for height. What is unique to the normal curve is the distribution of cases; e.g., 67% in the middle, etc. Then, on the basis of this graph, it is simple to conclude that people of normal height are 5'7" to 6'3".

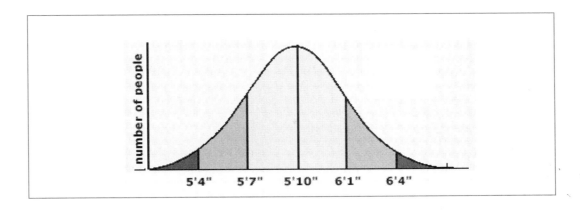

Figure 1-2. **Distribution of Height**

Clearly, this view of *normality* is inappropriate for conceptualizing behavioral exceptionality; because behavior is not normally distributed, the basic assumption cannot be realized.

Social Normality

The social view of *normality* is the perspective commonly adopted by researchers who are evaluating the appropriateness of behavior. In this form of evaluation, the standard of behavior used pertains to those behaviors identified as acceptable – or unacceptable – by a society, a sect, a school, a classroom, or a group. When it is invoked, the code of social **do's** and **don'ts** can be shown to differ, by varying degrees, from one society to another. Interestingly, for example, a North American tourist is less likely to make a social *faux pas* in Europe than in the Far East, although in both societies the traveller is identified as a foreigner. In a culture which differs to a significant level from their own, those from other societies are less likely to be seen as "normal" members. Within any society, smaller variations of acceptability also exist, on the basis of geographical, urban/rural, economic, community, school, cultural, and classroom factors. It is evident, then, that because the acceptability of a behavior is context-dependent, it follows that behaviors deemed acceptable in one classroom – in-seat behavior, language – may be identified as unacceptable, even in other classrooms and in the same school.

The explicit rules that govern a group's behavior are so important that, typically, they are openly discussed, debated, and frequently recorded. For example, each school board has a set of **do's** and **don'ts** for its employees, students, and parents, an outline of regulations of behavior often contained in the printed policies and procedures of the organization. In some cases, these form a printed Code of Behavior.

On a fairly regular basis, children will violate explicit expectations because (a) they are unaware of them; (b) they have forgotten them; or (c) they have chosen to violate them. In such circumstances, parents and teachers, as the primary agents of society, teach and even drill, – look both ways before crossing the street – they reinforce, encourage, and remind children about explicit rules, the ones that matter on a daily basis. Those rules, however, which are implicit, and which are associated with a group's often tacit code of behavior, are more difficult for children to learn, usually because they are acquired by a mysterious process. Not only are these rules never – or almost never – taught, they are rarely discussed. Those young persons as well as adults who learn these rules do so indirectly, perhaps as a function of group membership, but rarely does anyone use spoken words to describe them. It is certain, however, that an implicit rule has probably been violated when the phrase resounds: "You should have known better!"

How and when and where do young people learn the following?

- the appropriate distance to leave between oneself and the other person in the conversation

- the acceptable time interval to wait for someone or for someone to be kept waiting

- the language register to use when speaking to different people

- the appropriate response – laugh, clap, speak, etc., – in various situations

---

Implicit rules which are acquired without conscious attention usually represent tacit (unspoken) knowledge. While it is probable that most people eventually do learn to "know better", it is difficult for them to remember how or when this optimal level was reached. Unfortunately, because the acquisition of such subtle knowledge depends on experience, each person must have the opportunity to spend time in certain contexts in order to acquire the implicit behaviors associated with these situations.

While some children have not had the opportunity to acquire these implicit rules, others, – no matter what their experience – have not learned them. It may be necessary, then, for those adults who recognize the omissions to direct the children's attention to these implicit rules, essentially by making them explicit.

In summary, social *normality*

> - is defined by a group's code of behavior
>
> - recognizes as exceptional any violation of explicit or implicit rules
>
> - considers judgments to be relative to a collective norm
>
> - is relevant to the values of a particular time and space
>
> - is often the least objective view of normality
>
> - is usually over-represented in the diagnosis of behavioral exceptionalities

The subjectivity that so commonly appears in the social perspective results from changing criteria of acceptability. A corollary of this is that the appropriateness of a behavior is a function of the code of behavior being applied to it. This sliding scale creates problems for defining *exceptionality*, meaning that children defined as *exceptional*, by one teacher or school, might be labelled normal by other teachers or schools. An interesting example involves a situation in which the dominant culture defines eye contact as essential between listener and speaker. In such an environment, a child who looks at the floor while the teacher is speaking may be perceived as socially withdrawn or impertinent. But what if the child is acting on the basis of a different set of expectations? Certain cultures associate eye contact with power and/or respect. In such a circumstance, the student may show respect by carefully not looking at the teacher. While it is a truism that social *normality* is less troublesome when applied to homogeneous groups, North Americans (and probably Europeans, now) represent a range of heterogeneous societies. This means that teachers must be mindful of the limitations especially of the social view of *normality*. Because the typical social view of *normality* has become so subjective, measures have been taken to make it more objective. In the next section, three dimensions of behavior are defined in order to achieve this end.

Three Dimensions of Behavior

Evaluating the social acceptability of a behavior is a subjective task because each person in a range of observers – usually teachers – will rate differently the adaptiveness or acceptability of a particular behavior. To minimize personal bias in making observations, in order to optimize consensus among several raters of the same behavior[1], it is helpful to consider additional dimensions of behavior. In this overview, the three dimensions employed will include the quality, frequency, and duration of the behavior.

In any evaluation of *behavioral acceptability*, it is no mystery to discover groups rating behaviors differently on a graded scale. Simple examples show that people usually perceive certain behaviors as qualitatively less acceptable than others. For example, many, although not all groups, would rate killing a group member as highly unacceptable (high quality) and nail biting as less unacceptable (low quality). It may, however, be more difficult to rate cruelty to animals as less or more acceptable than assault of another student.

In a multicultural setting, the problem of rating behavior is compounded when one group, such as the staff, defines a behavior as more unacceptable than does another group, for example, the parents, who will see it as either not unacceptable, less unacceptable, or acceptable. Good examples here would be belching or flatulence. In all classrooms, therefore, teachers and students might agree that hitting a classmate is unacceptable, whereas these same people will vary in their agreement about appropriate noise level.

The acceptability of a behavior is also associated with its frequency: how often does the behavior occur? In certain contexts, behaviors are deemed acceptable only when rare or infrequent. If a student walking to the chalkboard happens to slip and reacts by saying "@%&$!," the teacher may justify the unique occurrence as acceptable in the situation. In sharp contrast, the same words – especially coming from a student in the classroom who punctuates every statement with this language – are likely to be judged unacceptable.

Consider, however, that infrequent behaviors are likely to be acceptable only if their quality is deemed low: some of these might be swearing, lateness, nail biting, lying, etc. In the case of behaviors in the high quality range, a category that includes murder, assault, car theft etc., a one-time occurrence is still recognized as unacceptable, the expectation being that it will be punished.

Finally, it is important to mention duration, focusing on the length of time a behavior is present in the student's repertoire. Not only do teachers and parents usually judge recent behaviors differently from those persisting over time, but the life span of a behavior often provides the impetus for making parents and teachers intervene. A point is reached when observers can no longer tell themselves that the child will outgrow the particular behavior. In addition, because persistent behaviors become age inappropriate (e.g., thumb-sucking, baby-talk), teachers, as well as parents and even peers, become concerned about the social implications for the child.

Almost by definition, persistent behaviors are hard to extinguish because the passage of time reinforces long-standing behavior elements which are absorbed into the young person's self-concept. The behavior becomes integrated into the individual's personal notion, the "Who I am" concept. In addition, a strong association is established between the behavior and the sense of self, and, in more difficult cases, in the way the person is perceived by others. When a child who is asked to complete an assignment silently shrugs, the teacher's willingness to remove demands initially encourages the habit, as does the success implicit in the teacher's habit of turning away in frustration. If the pattern persists over several years, the child accepts a formula: "I'm a person who shrugs silently when someone asks me to do something. That's just me." Eventually, others begin to believe in the status quo: "Don't ask Jerry to do it! Jerry isn't very smart! If you ask him he'll just shrug." At this point, Jerry's behavior becomes very difficult to change: not only is he convinced that the behavior is necessary to his self-image, but now, the established social perception of Jerry will rob him of opportunities to behave differently. During group work, for example, if no one asks him, Jerry has no hope of making a remark or complying with a request.

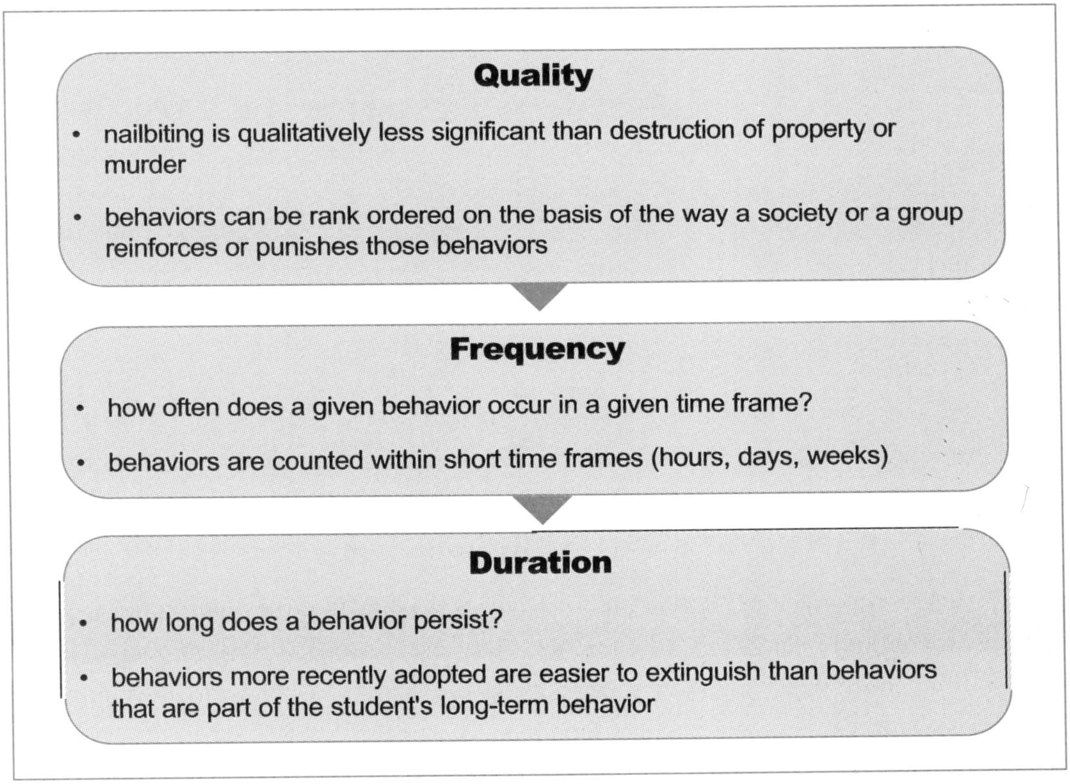

Quality

- nailbiting is qualitatively less significant than destruction of property or murder
- behaviors can be rank ordered on the basis of the way a society or a group reinforces or punishes those behaviors

Frequency

- how often does a given behavior occur in a given time frame?
- behaviors are counted within short time frames (hours, days, weeks)

Duration

- how long does a behavior persist?
- behaviors more recently adopted are easier to extinguish than behaviors that are part of the student's long-term behavior

Figure 1-3. **Three dimensions of behavior**

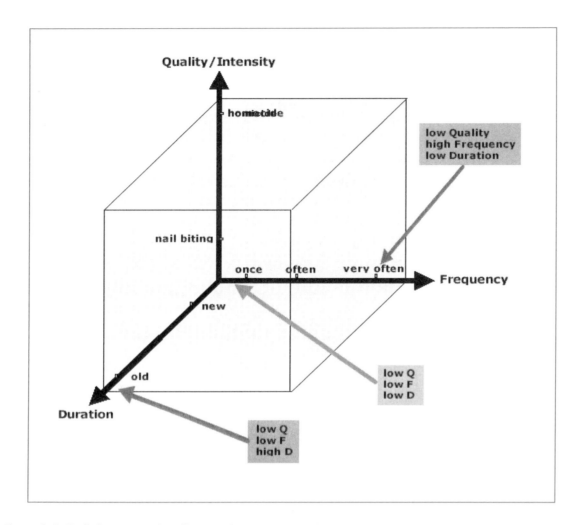

Figure 1-4. Defining exceptionality as a function of quality, frequency, and duration

Figure 1-4 illustrates the interaction of quality, frequency, and duration in evaluating the adaptiveness of a behavior. Note how different levels of each factor interact in identifying highly inappropriate behaviors. In their definitions of students with *behavioral exceptionalities,* Ministries of Education have indirectly included these dimensions of behavior.

Which students have Behavioral Exceptionalities?

Usually, two major types of students with behavioral difficulties can be identified because of such overt characteristics as acting-out, disruptive actions. These are students who interfere with the "flow" of the classroom. The other type of student who may have a *behavioral exceptionality* is reticent or withdrawn, and often invisible.

While disruptive students are easily identified and quickly placed, other 'exceptional' students are often diagnosed only after several years in school. Interestingly, the speed of the identifying process relates to the uncanny ability of disrupters to threaten the status quo of the school. More importantly, not only do they interfere with the learning opportunities of other children, but they are likely to violate the safety needs of students and staff as they demonstrate their personal and educational shortcomings. In some situations, fortunately, the needs of these students are addressed in the regular classroom, but frequently alternative placement must be considered.

The social/emotional issues presented by children with behavioral difficulties are likely to affect all aspects of each student's school life and to influence the home life as well. For this reason, a disruptive child generally receives a disproportionate amount of attention from teachers and administrators, as well as, probably, from parents or care givers. In some cases, a school with a support system is able to buffer the impact of such a student; thus, for a longer time maintaining the disruptive child in the regular classroom. If, however, the teacher is expected to shoulder the responsibility, there is a high probability that the most disruptive students will be placed in special classes.

On the other hand, it is often the case that students who are distant, depressed, or truant are overlooked, and so receive fewer services. What appears to happen is that they remain with the regular class for many years until, finally, their passive – sometimes passive-aggressive – behavior comes to the attention of teachers.

Ministry Definitions

In Canada, because education is a responsibility of provincial governments, the situation exists that only Nova Scotia, New Brunswick, Saskatchewan, Manitoba, Newfoundland, Quebec, and Ontario have enacted laws regarding mandatory special education (Wiener & Siegel, 1992). In the United States, however, where the U. S. Department of Education has national jurisdiction, Public Law 94-142 pertains to all students. The Ministry of Education (Ontario) provides the following definition:

Emotional Disturbance/ Social Maladjustment:

A *learning disorder* characterized by specific behavior problems over such a period of time, and to such a marked degree, as to adversely affect educational performance, and that may be accompanied by one or more of

1. the inability to build or to maintain interpersonal relationships
2. excessive fears or anxieties
3. a tendency to compulsive reaction
4. the inability to learn which cannot be traced to intellectual, sensory, or health factors, or any combination thereof[2]

The U. S. Law, Public Law 94-142, while it provides a definition of *behavioral disorder* similar to that of Ontario, also contains a major difference: whereas socially maladjusted students are included in both the Ontario and Newfoundland definitions, they are excluded in the U. S. definition, being ineligible unless they are also emotionally disturbed.

In Canada, only Nova Scotia and the Northwest Territories have no official definition of *behavioral disorder,* while Saskatchewan, Ontario, Prince Edward Island, and Newfoundland have provincial definitions; the remaining provinces allow modification of the definition only at the school-board level (Dworet & Rathgeber, 1990).

Table 1-1. **Services offered by Provinces/Territories for students with behavioral disorders**

	BC	Alta	Sask	Man	Ont	Que	PEI	NB	NS	Nfld	Ykn	NWT
Special Class	•	•	•	•	•	•		•				
Resource Room	•	•	•	•	•	•	•	•	•	•	•	
Crisis Intervention	•	•		•	•			•		•	•	
Itinerant Teacher	•	•	•	•	•						•	•
Academic Tutoring	•	•	•	•	•		•		•		•	•
Homebound Instruction	•	•	•	•	•		•	•	•		•	•
Guidance Counsellor	•	•	•	•	•		•	•	•	•	•	•
School Social Worker	•	•	•	•		•	•	•	•	•	•	•
School Psychologist	•	•		•	•		•	•	•	•		•
Psychiatric Consultation	•	•	•	•	•		•	•	•	•		•

Legend					
BC	British Columbia	**Ont**	Ontario	**PEI**	Prince Edward Island
Alta	Alberta	**Que**	Quebec	**Ykn**	Yukon
Sask	Saskatchewan	**NB**	New Brunswick	**NWT**	Northwest Territories
Man	Manitoba	**NS**	Nova Scotia		

Factors Affecting Definition and Treatment

In most societies, social views of *normality* are subject to two major types of bias. One of these, the variable known as '**space**', is associated with the way cultures and subcultures, in different geographical locations, adopt distinctive codes of behavior. The second variable is related to qualitative differences; these, when used to evaluate what is judged to be appropriate, are rooted in the dimension of '**time**', and are frequently connected to historical differences. In the next section, a short historical perspective will attempt to demonstrate the effect of cultural values at different points across a time-and-space continuum. Behavior that is deemed to be acceptable or unacceptable can be shown to be determined by locally-held social beliefs. For an educator, it is relevant to consider the impact of such strongly-held beliefs on treatment practices, and, at the same time, to recognize that adopting a treatment practice includes awareness of its inherent social ideology.[3]

Historical Perspective

It is likely that people living in pre-historic times had a sense of socially acceptable *behavior*, an idea of *normality*. Skull remains dating from this period have been found by anthropologists who believe that a primitive form of surgery called *trephining* may have been used in ritualistic treatment for stresses, anxiety, and psychological pain by, possibly, *animistic*[4] people. When spirits invaded an individual, a piece of the cranium was surgically removed to provide an escape route for the invaders trapped in the skull.[5]

As with most treatment interventions, the surgery was successful in some cases (probably those involving cranial pressure), and thus the success was sufficient to continue the practice. While treatment interventions are often maintained as a result of marginal success, recently accepted changes in world view – sometimes involving the development of new beliefs – are responsible for the abandonment of interventions incompatible with the group's new perception of the world.

When early Chinese, Egyptian, and Hebrew people developed a belief in God(s), they subsequently began to blame evil spirits, demons, and possession when they wanted to explain sickness. In the Judaeo-Christian tradition, Biblical sources make numerous references to madness either attributed to Satanic control or experienced as a consequence of moral wrongdoing. As might be expected, those displaying symptoms of illness were treated harshly. Once again, it is evident that the nature of treatment interventions depends on the group's explanatory framework for illness.

In classical times, the Greeks utilized *mysticism* to elevate some mentally aberrant persons to the roles of soothsayers and oracles, while others, less fortunate, were stoned, feared, and hated. When it moved from the domain of religious faith to the realm of medicine, the Hellenic perception of mental illness changed radically. Hippocrates (about 460-351 BC.), known as the father of medicine, because he recorded the first diagnostic description of *melancholia*[6], was interested, first, in finding the causes of *melancholia* and, second, in stressing the physical origins of psychological symptoms. Also relevant to present-day thought is his notion that stress factors in the environment could be associated with psychological symptoms.

Hippocrates believed that people reflected the four principal elements of the universe: *earth*, represented in the body as yellow bile; *water*, as black bile; *fire*, as blood; and *air*, as phlegm or mucus. These assumptions led him to conclude that mental illness resulted when bodily fluids were unbalanced. For example, an excess of black bile would lead to melancholia. By moving away from causes associated with the character or the "goodness" of the person and focusing on physical causes, he was able to probe further for more objective explanations which led subsequently to humane treatment procedures that included massage, calm talking, and water therapy.

The Roman physician, Galen, (130-200 AD) known for his insight about 'treating the illness rather than the symptom, was responsible for promoting ideas about:

> i.   the brain being the center of sensation and the soul
>
> ii.   the role of physical and environmental factors
>
> iii. the relationships between, on the one hand, mental illness and the rational soul, and, on the other hand, the divine and the irrational or animal soul

After the death of Galen, and during the many centuries of the Dark Ages, a general move to demonology and to priests replaced the more scientific physicians. These superstitious practitioners relied on diagnoses based signs of the Devil's presence, which could explain aberrant behavior.

Because of the assumptions held by these new workers, therapies included interventions designed to create discomfort for the resident demons. Very often, however, because the treatments involved fire and/or water, both the devil and the suffering individual perished[7].

During the Renaissance, when the "mind" had become an object of legitimate study, Francis Bacon (1561-1626) argued that some of the mind's characteristics and functions were linked to the body rather than to the spirit. As a result, the mind became the subject of empirical study with researchers using objective methods. During the same era, Juan Luis Vives (1492-1540) suggested that the insane could be restored to sanity by gentle treatment rather than harsh condemnation.

Shortly thereafter, Johann Weyer (1515-1588) became the first physician to specialize in the study of mental illness. Later, René Descartes, (1596-1650) the thinker who reinforced the idea of *Dualism*, the notion that mind and body are separate although interacting entities, identified the pineal gland as the site of their interaction.

By the eighteenth century, major efforts were being directed towards classifying and categorizing mental illness. Franz Josef Gall (1758-1828), believing the brain to play a major role in mental illness, proposed that the patterns of bumps on the cranium were diagnostic characteristics. His theory became the study of Phrenology[8]. In 1775, Johann Caspar Lavater (1741-1801) used the method of observing the facial features and expressions of his patients to diagnose their illnesses.

From a political perspective, part of the ideology which led to the French Revolution was also responsible for changes in the way mental illness was viewed as well as for the creation of some types of medical facilities. Because the newly established notion of "citizen" implied the Stateês responsibility to look after all its people, ill citizens were included in the state's thinking. In one instance, Philippe Pinel, (1745-1826), having inspired the most dramatic hospital reform, allowed some patients who had been locked up in dungeons and caves to see daylight for the first time in years. Subsequently, some of these people were allowed to return to society.

In the new system, appropriately designed hospitals that housed mental patients were run by doctors rather than jailers, and, although conditions were poor in comparison with today's standard, they represented an improvement. Some of these new facilities, although they attempted to provide more humane care than the previous institutions had done, gained so much notoriety that their names were incorporated into the language[9]. In English, "bedlam" a word meaning "uproar", originates from the local pronunciation of the name of the hospital of St. Mary of Bethlehem at Bishopsgate in London. Although this building originally housed a religious order, it was converted to a "lunatic asylum" in 1547. The word "lunatic" itself, was created to describe people whose madness resulted, it was thought, from their gazing too long at the moon - "luna", in Latin.

The changing world order encouraged the development of new forms of therapy. For example, Franz Anton Mesmer (1734-1815) introduced *mesmerism*, a treatment often compared with hypnosis, which was an attempt to restore, inside the patient's body, the balance of magnetic fluid from the universe. In more recent times, Charcot (1825-1893), in addition to putting demonology finally to rest, provided the first physiological explanation of *hysteria*[10]. It was also demonstrated by Charcot that hysterical symptoms could be alleviated with the use of hypnosis (an intervention incorporated in the field of Psychoanalysis by Sigmund Freud). Both Josef Breuer (1842-1925) and Sigmund Freud (1856-1939) developed the "Talking Cure" or *catharsis*[11], while Freud provided the first psychological explanation of neurosis. In addition, his findings gave birth to the First Force in Psychology, the Psychoanalytic View.

Meanwhile, in North America, when John B. Watson (1878-1958) founded the Second Force, the movement known as *Behaviorism*, this uniquely North American perspective discarded all references to *consciousness*, a concept central to Freudian theories. Watson, trained in animal psychology[12], generated fundamental principles of behavior, drawn from his experience with animals, which he believed also applied to humans. He demonstrated that people associate emotions with persons, places, and things encountered in their experiences. These principles of *learning theory,* further developed by Edward Thorndike and B. F. Skinner, explained the role of consequences in strengthening and weakening behavior.

In the period just prior to the Second World War, when European psychology immigrated to North America, disputes in the psychoanalytic camp led Alfred Adler (1870-1937) to create the Third Force in Psychology, Humanism. This new-world view, with its roots in the old world, incorporated North American ideologies. Central to its premise is the concept of personal responsibility in the context of a democratic environment.

In the late nineteen sixties, with the declining influence of the *behavioral* perspective, *information processing* theories began to displace strictly behavioral explanations, with the result that *cognitive psychology* gained prominence. Now the study of *mind* had once again become a legitimate domain of inquiry. Albert Ellis and others explored the way human behavior is influenced by thought.

Summary

In Chapter One, the elusive notion of *normality* is focused on, as a preamble to examining the concept of *Exceptionality*. *Behavioral* difficulties are best explained from the perspective of social *normality* which relies heavily on identifying and meeting the expectation of a given group. The limitations of this definition are outlined, and, to increase objectivity, three dimensions of behavior are presented which allow the teacher to evaluate the inappropriateness of a *behavior*. It is an ongoing and interesting process to compare definitions of *behavioral exceptionalities,* – both those defined by Canadian provincial ministries of education and those within Public Law 94-142 in the United States – and to recognize the contradictions caused by their vagueness. Finally, an overview of the way *behavioral exceptionalities* have been perceived, explained, and treated throughout history reveals the relationships among those factors. In the next chapter, it will be possible to investigate several formal views of *behavior* with the purpose of understanding the different types of interventions used, on a regular basis, in dealing with children who exhibit behavioral difficulties.

Endnotes

[1]   This consensus is often referred to as 'inter-rater reliability' in research articles. As the raters' level of agreement increases, the reliability score approaches 1.00.

[2]   Ministry of Education, Ontario (1984). *Special Education Information Handbook,* Toronto: Ministry of Education, Ontario.

[3]   It is important to conceptualize treatment practices in the context of their ideologies in order to evaluate whether the beliefs and assumptions associated with the intervention match those of the observer/educator.

[4]   **Animism** refers to a world view which holds beliefs about inanimate objects having spirits; for example, the spirit in the wind makes it blow, the spirit in the water makes it flow, etc.

[5]   Blood-letting was used for similar purposes, that is, giving spirits an escape route, in later periods.

[6]   **melancholia** probably referred to a state of depression or unhappiness.

[7]   If the culprit perished when held under water, the death was evidence of innocence. If the unfortunate person survived, demonic possession was confirmed, and, of course the victim was executed.

[8]   Phrenology is a precursor of modern neuropsychology.

[9]   The names of psychiatric hospitals are used in the local language (e.g., In the city of Toronto, an erratic person might be advised to "return to 999 Queen Street", a one-time address of a psychiatric hospital.).

[10]   A condition in which patients suffer physiological symptoms that have with no physical basis, e.g., legs are paralyzed although neurological tests demonstrate that no nerve pathways are damaged.

[11]   from the Greek idea of purging in the tragic dramas.

[12]   The experiments of the Russian, Pavlov, were instrumental in the development of Behaviorism.

CHAPTER 2

The Major Views of Behavioral Exceptionalities

In the previous chapter, three independent notions of normality were developed to demonstrate the conceptualization of Behavioral Exceptionalities. Of these, the best to emerge concentrates on a Social notion of normality. When expressed in an objective form, this concept comprises three variables: quality (intensity), frequency, and duration. Now, in Chapter Two, the chief focus is on the concepts associated with psychopathology - or *behavioral exceptionalities* - developed by the major schools of thought. The seven views to be introduced, which represent explanatory models distinct from each other, are labeled **Paradigms**. According to Kuhn's (1962) definition, a **Paradigm**

- is a set of basic assumptions

- outlines a particular universe of scientific inquiry

- specifies the kinds of concepts that will be regarded as legitimate

- itemizes the methods used to collect or interpret data

As major views of behavioral exceptionalities following criteria outlined by Kuhn (1962), the paradigms describe basic assumptions and provide explanations of the primary concepts, methods, and interventions comprising each view. In addition, the paradigms represent the pillars of a theoretical understanding of behavior and behavioral exceptionalities. Why is theoretical understanding necessary? When creating a positive classroom environment, systems cannot be limited to ensuring student compliance. Rather, the object is to present an entire social curriculum, (e.g., examining the workings of society and social groups); promoting the personal development of students (assisting students to explore their personal goals in order to become actualized individuals); managing a group of individuals who live together for the better part of a day (satisfying classroom expectations); and meeting the aims and objectives of the academic curriculum. Without an understanding of the various concepts and explanations inherent in the paradigms, this book would foster a cookbook approach, concentrating on ingredients rather than outcomes. Although such an approach has advantages it usually promotes only quick fixes. The comprehensive understanding of each student's behavior warrants an examination of the whole person. For this reason, the seven views are presented with the awareness that knowledge of these paradigms will help to clarify the rationale for each of the interventions discussed throughout the book.

Some readers, especially those who have studied Psychology, may have become familiar with elements of the major schools of thought. For these people, Chapter Two will provide a good review, as well as highlighting, in certain sections, the relevance of these concepts to the field of education. Readers less familiar with this information will recognize that, because the major ideas are presented in a relatively concise manner, further reading in textbooks that address these issues in greater detail may be beneficial.

Each view is presented in a format including: a brief description of its historical roots, a summary of its general features, a list of its major concepts, and an explanation of its relevance to education.

An Overview

The paradigms that follow perceive "exceptional behavior" in a distinctive manner. For each view, the basic concept is presented in a one-sentence definition of *exceptional behavior* as it might relate to an educational context. Although none of the paradigms actually adopts the phrase "exceptional behavior", the following definition statements are provided merely as memory ticklers. After a perusal of the chapter, it is interesting to re-read these definitions in order to decide which of the paradigms applies to which of the definitions:

- *Exceptional behavior* is a symptom of deeper and perhaps unconscious conflict.

- *Exceptional behavior* is learned in the same manner and by the same principles as adaptive behavior.

- *Exceptional behavior* is the result of poor self-concept associated with obstacles placed in the way of the individual.

- *Exceptional behavior* is associated with the demands and organization of institutions, especially schools.

- *Exceptional behavior* has a neurological basis.

- *Exceptional behavior* is an outcome of the reciprocal relationship existing between the child and the family, social setting, physical environment, etc.

- *Exceptional behavior* is a result of faulty perceptions and misconceptions.

Each of these statements will provide further meaning during the reading of the seven sections of Chapter Two.

The Psychodynamic View

Because it is the oldest view, the Psychodynamic paradigm represents the *First Force* in Psychology. Apparently, too, it is the view that has the greatest impact on everyday language, as well as on people's understanding of human behavior. Introduced in the nineteenth century by Sigmund Freud, the father of psychiatry, the Psychodynamic view comes equipped with its own vocabulary, consisting of such terms as **ego, schizophrenia, defense mechanism, phallic symbol** and many other equally familiar expressions. Unfortunately, as these terms have seeped into everyday language, they have sometimes acquired new connotations that vary substantially from their original meanings. When someone says, for example, that a person has a big "ego," the words now imply that the individual thus described is arrogant and/or "full of him or herself." Not only is this not the meaning ascribed by the Psychodynamic model, it is contrary to it, suggesting an inappropriate characteristic. Originally, a person with a strong "ego" was thought to enjoy good mental health because, in the personality, ego has a central role in reducing conflict.

General Features:

PSYCHODYNAMIC

- Psychopathology is seen as a quasi-medical "disease."

- Exceptional behavior is the result of unresolved unconscious conflict in the context of the personality and psycho-sexual stages of development.

- The problem originates in the past history of the "patient," and, consequently, early memories are an important domain of inquiry.

- Treatment generally includes catharsis, "the talking cure".

- The purpose of the treatment is to encourage "growth in the patient" as the origin of the problem surfaces. Therapy is, therefore, a long-term procedure.

- Diagnosis and labeling of the patient (e.g. manic depressive) are central to the intervention.

- The role of the therapist is to interpret the patient's experience.

- Psychoanalysis, Play Therapy, Transactional Analysis, Hypnotherapy are some treatment interventions associated with this model.

- Symptoms in the form of observable behavior are not given much weight because they are viewed as expressions of inner conflict.

- Scientific inquiry is conducted mainly in the form of case studies.

23

Included in the concepts associated with the Psychodynamic – sometimes called the Psychoanalytic – view of *behavioral exceptionalities* are Freud's notion of personality, psycho-sexual stages of development, anxiety, and defense mechanisms, ideas that will be discussed in this next section. In recent times, an extension of Freud's views is found in Erikson's *Stages of Man* and *Transactional Analysis.*

Freud's Notion of Personality

In an important idea put forth by Freud, who is the originator of the academic concept of *personality*, he proposes that each individual has a personality comprising three interacting forces: **Id, Ego, and Superego.** Each of these three forces, Freud has said, has a unique character and role to play in creating the personality.

It is Freud's view that Id is fueled by libidinal energy[1], or, as Descartes perceived it, the animal drives and instincts found in people. For this reason, Id is conceptualized as both hedonistic and pleasure seeking, always desiring immediate gratification of its needs.

In contrast to Id, Superego concerns itself with the values and morality of society. While being socialized, especially in the process of being affected by society's forces, the child develops a conscience that places limits on acceptable behavior. In Freud's perspective, Superego's chief role is to consider how the person "ought" to behave.

Given the opposing roles played by Id and Superego, conflict is certain to arise. Ego, created to bring balance to the personality, becomes the mediator attempting to find compromises between the demands, on the one hand, of Id and, on the other, of Superego. Because such compromises are grounded in everyday experience, a strong Ego is necessary to insure the mental health and reality basis of the individual.

When these aspects of the personality are revisited, more recently, in Transactional Analysis and are re-coined, they are transformed into the child (Id), the adult (Ego), and the parent (Superego).

According to Freud's notion of personality, the interaction of the members of the triad – Id, Ego, Superego – implies potential conflict. Again, it is necessary to note that mental health is contingent on a strong Ego, capable of mediating the desires of Id and Superego. This means that "normality" is always threatened when Ego is weak enough to allow either Id or Superego to dominate the personality.

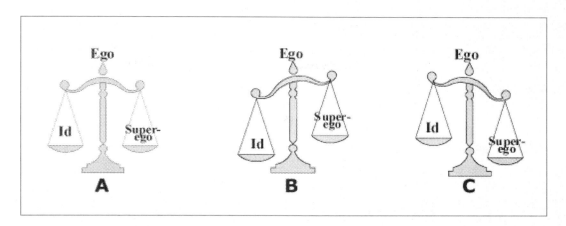

Figure 2-1. Sample scenarios in Freud's concept of the personality.

Important concepts to remember

Id
- consists of libidinal energy
- is self-gratifying, hedonistic, or pleasure-seeking
- desires the immediate satisfaction of primary drives

Ego
- is the mediating force between Id and Superego
- attempts to reach compromises and deal with reality

Superego
- serves as the conscience
- upholds the positive values and morality of the society
- is concerned with how one 'ought' to behave

Anxiety

When Id and Superego overwhelm Ego, with the result that conflict arises in the personality, an internal state known as anxiety is produced. In this model, the Psychodynamic view, the feeling of anxiety that emerges is called, by Newcomer (1980), a form of "psychic pain".

According to the theory, three types of anxiety – Reality, Neurotic, and Moral – form its base. Of course, people feel anxious when their survival is threatened: in a dangerous situation, reality anxiety is an expected and familiar, even beneficial response. If, for example, a person walking on railroad tracks suddenly hears a train whistle, reality anxiety, an adaptive response, will trigger the *fight-or-flight mechanism* provoking the anxious pedestrian to jump off the tracks. In contrast, neurotic and moral anxiety are not reality-based, but, instead, are associated with unconscious personality conflicts. In either case, when Ego is threatened either by Id, in the form of neurotic anxiety, or by Superego, in the guise of moral anxiety, the result will be a feeling of anxiety.

Three Types of Anxiety

1. *Reality Anxiety:* a person is threatened by events in the immediate surroundings, that is, the environment

2. *Neurotic Anxiety:* a person's Id impulses threaten to overwhelm Ego controls

3. *Moral Anxiety:* a person considers engaging in behavior that conflicts with Superego or moral values

---

When Ego is threatened by Id or Superego, it attempts to re-establish equilibrium by responding in one of two coping methods: either by turning to rational measures or by falling back on irrational alternatives. Because personality conflicts are unconscious, the person will find it impossible to respond, in a rational way, to the anxiety: such a process involves conscious awareness. To get around this dilemma, irrational measures called *Defense Mechanisms* are unconsciously elicited to alleviate anxiety.

Defense Mechanisms

In order to cope with the anxiety of the neurotic personality, irrational processes called Defense Mechanisms are employed unconsciously to respond to neurotic and moral anxieties in the individual personality. Because these procedures are *unconscious*, the neurotic person is unaware of drawing on one of the many defense mechanisms to reduce levels of anxiety. In the table below, the behavior associated with each of five different mechanisms is shown. An important aspect of this behavior is that relief from the individual's anxiety will certainly result.

Table 2-1. Defense mechanisms

Defense Mechanism	Behavior
Repression	The person forgets thoughts that are threatening or anxiety-provoking
Projection	The person attributes anxiety-evoking feelings to the actions or intents of others
Sublimation	The person channels 'forbidden' urges into socially acceptable activity
Displacement	The person redirects feelings about one person toward another
Identification	The person assumes the attributes of someone who is perceived as an aggressor and a threat

Psycho-sexual Stages of Development

When Freud outlined concepts of personality, anxiety, and defense mechanisms, he also proposed that **every** individual, in the course of normal maturation, proceeds through specific psycho-sexual stages of development. Because Freud identified each stage of development as representing the gratification of a sexual instinct, the response to his views caused great controversy when they were first revealed.

Freud believed that as each child reaches and experiences a stage of maturation, the possibility of two outcomes emerges: the child might be either successful or unsuccessful in resolving the goals relevant to that stage. In this model, the successful achievement of a stage is associated with good mental health. Conversely, disturbed behavior is expected to result either when a *fixation* is carried forward from an earlier stage of development or when a form of *regression* leads to a more infantile stage. In Table 2-2, the five stages of psychosexual development and their individual central elements are outlined:

Table 2-2. Freud's Psychosexual Stages

Psycho-sexual Stage	Focus
Oral Stage	sucking and biting
Anal Stage	pre-occupation with bowel movements
Phallic Stage	focus on sex organs
Latency	loss of all interest in sex
Genital Stage	advent of sexual maturity

In Freud's view, the role of the parents is central in the child's adjustment or maladjustment. For this reason, parents can arrest their child's growth by being over-controlling in various ways or by blocking the child's need to gratify sexual instincts.

Eriksonês Stages of Man

More recently, in Erikson's theory of stages (1963), his proposal is analogous to Freud's but appears more complete, addressing, as it does, individual issues across the life cycle, from birth to death. In his *Eight Stages of Man,* depicted in Table 2-3, Erikson identifies the critical problems which must be resolved at each stage in order to facilitate the normal development of the personality.

For educators, Erikson's stages are more meaningful than those of earlier thinkers, because they pinpoint developmental challenges in terms of students, while, significantly, for educators and caregivers, they provide insight into possible resolutions of the problems of each stage.

Table 2-3. Erikson's stages

Stage	Time	Resolution
1. Trust *vs.* Mistrust	first year	• achieved by having basic needs met
2. Autonomy *vs.* Doubt and Shame	second year	• attainment of muscular control
3. Initiative *vs.* Guilt	fifth-sixth year	• resolution of the Oedipal crisis which leads to conscience • prerequisite for masculine or feminine initiative
4. Industry *vs.* Inferiority	child at school	• gaining admiration, approval, and affection through achievement
5. Ego Identity *vs.* Identity Diffusion	adolescence	• Ego synthesis • increasing confidence to maintain sameness within the personality
6. Intimacy *vs.* Self-absorption	young adult	• intimacy with another • removing self from fearful situations or people who appear dangerous
7. Generativity *vs.* Stagnation	adult years	• interest in producing, guiding, and laying the foundation for the next generation
8. Integrity *vs.* Despair	late adult	• accepting one's own and only life cycle, and being responsible for the way it has turned out

For educators, the fourth stage – Industry vs. Inferiority – is particularly interesting in that it establishes an important foundation for the child at school. Early school experiences that include mastery, approval, and a sense of belonging may predict, in subsequent classroom activities, both achievement and balanced attitudes.

Contribution to Education

It is most **unlikely** that the Psychoanalytic paradigm will have any direct significance for the educator, because, in this view, personality characteristics are thought to be determined largely by early childhood experiences. In the Psychodynamic view, any damage to the personality, the root cause of behavioral problems, will occur before the child enters school.

According to this view, because "abnormal" behavior is a symptom of unconscious conflict, the child is not held to be responsible for problem behaviors, a proposition that is unacceptable in the classroom. In some cases, however, teachers consider the defense mechanism of *displacement* to be an explanation of hostile feelings directed toward teachers. In such cases, angry feelings about parents (or other significant adults in the child's life) are re-directed or diverted in the direction of the teachers. The same phenomenon, displacement, may explain why some children with behavioral problems appear to relate better either to men or to women, depending on the children's early experiences.

When examining the psychoanalytic view, teachers can expect children's behavior to show inconsistencies, because, in a personality, problem behaviors are symptoms of internal conflict. More important to the educator, however, is the realization that eradicating symptoms, that is, getting rid of problem behavior, especially in the classroom, will not solve the student's problems. Instead, in the prognosis of this model's view, new symptoms will take the place of old ones, until the nature of the underlying conflict is identified and addressed.

Because it so obviously implies that educators cannot intervene to address the causes of behavioral problems with the idea of directly solving them, this paradigm is not attractive to educators. A basic tenet of Psychodynamic thought is that the techniques of psychoanalysis can be implemented only by highly trained individuals who alone can approach unconscious conflicts. Nevertheless, this paradigm offers the educator the following insights: children are driven by their need for immediate gratification (Id); the family and the school play an important role in the socialization of the child, especially as training relates to the development of values, morals, and ethics (Superego); children with behavioral difficulties may be individuals with weak egos that allow Id[2] to overtake the personality. According to these premises, it is possible to surmise that not only teaching children to delay gratification, through reduction of impulsive behavior, but also helping them to find socially acceptable ways to satisfy their needs, through sublimation, may be procedures in keeping with the spirit of this view. Similarly, stages in Erikson's theories may be shown to relate to the development of school-age children. If such links exist, they may provide insight into the challenges such children face and the kinds of environment required for their successful resolution.

The Behaviorist Model

Totally independent of the Psychodynamic view, the Behaviorist model is a uniquely North American approach to the topic. In their attempt to understand human behavior from the perspective of animal – or comparative – psychology, its originators, John Watson and Edward Thorndike, engaged in animal-learning experiments. Subsequently, these two behavioral psychologists developed a framework from which they purported to understand human behavior.

In order to emulate an understanding of human emotion, Watson adapted the seminal theories of Ivan Pavlov, whose initial work involved the digestive processes in dogs. Specifically, Watson was interested in the development of fears and phobias and demonstrated their evolution with the application of Pavlov's classical conditioning process. Thorndike's Law of Effect further revealed the power of consequences in the shaping of everyday behavior. Together, these major directions in Behaviorism reinforced the role of the environment as it affects behavior. Arising partly from this series of findings is the "nature-nurture" controversy, based on the question of whether behavior is more influenced by heredity than by environmental factors.

Right from the start, the Psychodynamic view can be shown to favor the role of "nature" because of the influence of Freud who, being both anatomist and physician, believed in the strength of heredity. In contrast, the Behaviorists, taking the opposite stance, have consistently focused exclusively on the role of the environment, thus developing the "nurture" position as behavior's chief influence.

In order to explain the way the environment shapes the behavior of individuals, Behaviorism proposes two major theories. The first of these, Classical Conditioning, illustrates the manner in which internal states, more commonly called emotions, become associated with environmental events. The second theory, Operant Conditioning, accounts for the strengthening and weakening of behavioral responses. Both of these, however, Classical and Operant conditioning, interact to produce complex behaviors. Unlike the Psychodynamic framework, which is able to explain a person's behavior only after the fact, both behaviorist theories have the capacity to predict future behavior.

Classical Conditioning

When Russian psychologist, Ivan Pavlov (1849-1936), accidentally discovered the basis of Classical Conditioning, he noted that a dog salivating at the sight of food (an unconditioned stimulus), and also continuously hearing a tone (a neutral stimulus), would salivate after many repetitions of simultaneous presentation of the two events. This type of learning – in which an internal state is associated with an external event – depends on establishing a proximate and repeated association between the conditioned stimulus, (the tone), and the unconditioned stimulus, (the food). As a requirement then, Classical Conditioning depends on the temporal proximity, that is, the simultaneous presentation, of the two stimuli to be associated.

In such examples of Classical Conditioning, the learner, that is, the dog, remains unaware of the associations developed between environmental events and internal states. The dog, salivating at the sound of the tone, when tone and food are associated in its mind, has learned that the tone signals the arrival of food. In the event, however, that food without the tone, is consistently presented to the dog, the association begins to weaken until eventually the dog stops salivating at the sound of the tone[3].

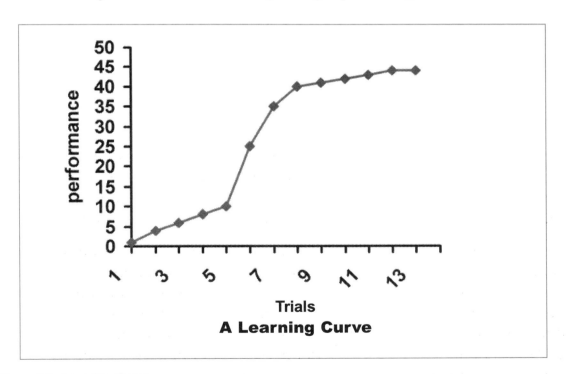

Figure 2-2. Learning Curve

General Features:

BEHAVIORISM

- The model, based on *Learning Theory,* places the emphasis on the way behavior is learned.

- Exceptional behavior is learned and maintained by contingencies (rules describing the relationship between behavior and its consequences).

- This model is interested in the present conditions that impact on the behavior rather than on the past history of the person.

- The model is interested in objective measures of a behavior: how many times did it occur? how often? what preceded it? what followed it? rather than on understanding why it occurred.

- Behaviorists do not find the labeling of a behavior to be useful.

- Treatment is related to the removal of inappropriate behavior (symptoms) and therefore behavioral change rather than growth is emphasized.

- The therapist directs the client (rather than interpreting what the client says) by re-organizing the learning environment and taking complete charge of the treatment.

- Examples of treatment interventions associated with this model include Behavior Therapy, Systematic-Desensitization, Modeling, Behavior Modification, Teacher-directed Instruction.

- Because the intervention focuses exclusively on symptoms, it is individually designed to fit the problems of each student.

- The therapist utilizes learning principles: Classical Conditioning, Operant Conditioning, Modeling.

- Because this model is very compatible with experimental procedures, a great deal of experimental research is available.

- Behaviorism advocates short-term therapy which terminates when the symptoms are removed. As a program, it is efficient and economical because clients can also be treated in groups.

Associated with Behaviorism are key concepts including: Classical Conditioning, Operant Conditioning, and Modeling, each of which is explored in greater depth in the passages immediately following.

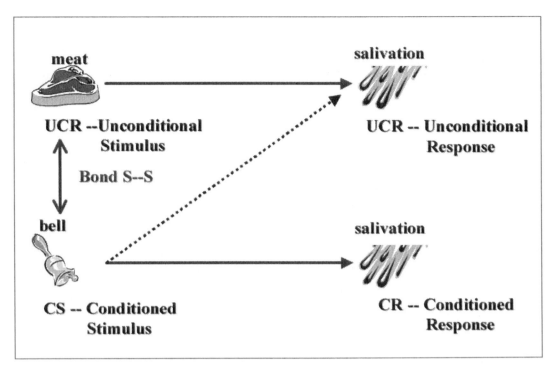

Figure 2-3. Classical Conditioning

J. B. Watson, when he proposed that all behavior is subject to external events, demonstrated in humans the way fear is learned by the same mechanism which induced Pavlov's dogs to perform a salivating response at the sound of a bell. Watson accomplished this task in the now widely-known *Little Albert Experiment.* Devising a procedure similar to Pavlov's, Watson taught Albert, an orphan child, to fear white furry objects when a loud noise triggering a startle response was coupled with the presentation of a white furry rabbit. Pairings of the loud noise and the rabbit were continued until Albert exhibited the fear response even when only the rabbit appeared. Unexpectedly, Albert continued to demonstrate the fear response not only at the appearance of the rabbit but also at the sight of previously neutral stimuli that resembled the rabbit – a stuffed toy, a fur coat, etc. This process of generalization, is shown, subsequently, to account for an increasing number of conditioned responses, although these are often not the objects of the respective primary learning situations. In this process, stimulus generalization, lies the explanation of the way people learn to fear both objects and situations, while not consciously recalling earlier frightening encounters.

Years after Watson's initial *Little Albert Experiment,*[4] his student, Mary Cover Jones, revealed a related process, significant to educators, when she demonstrated that the fear responses present in Watson's subjects could be extinguished by reversing the experimenter's process. Today, the technique known as Systematic-desensitization, used very effectively in the treatment of phobias and fears, continues to utilize Classical Conditioning principles. In Chapter Five, systematic desensitization will be outlined in greater detail.

Operant Conditioning

Two major Stimulus Response theorists, E. L. Thorndike (1874-1949) and B. F. Skinner (1904-1990), studied another learning process known as Operant Conditioning. Drawn to S.R., Stimulus Response, the two theorists focused on behavioral events that occur one after the other rather than simultaneously. Unlike the typical concurrent effect in Classical Conditioning, the *Law of Effect*, first formulated by Thorndike, states: "Behaviors that are rewarded become more frequent, whereas behaviors that are punished become less frequent." When Skinner used the Law of Effect to illustrate the cause/effect relationships existing between behaviors and environmental consequences, he postulated that such a relationship, called a *contingency*, is formulated as an *if-then* statement. A familiar example is: "**If** you do your homework, **then** you may watch your favorite TV program."

Figure 2-4. **The Stimulus-Response Contingency**

Request	do your homework	watch favorite TV program
S	**R**	**S**
Stimulus	**Response**	**Consequence Feedback**

The contingency is **the rule that identifies the cause-effect relationship existing between the response and the consequence.** In a typical instance, the consequence will follow the response, if - and only if - the response is made. The statement "X is contingent on Y" means that X will occur only if Y occurs first. In the classroom, for example, the teacher may arrange for five minutes of free time **to be contingent** on the completion of an independent activity. Such a contingency requires the student to complete the activity in order to obtain the free time. In other words, the free time will be awarded *if and only if* the activity is completed.

Although neither Thorndike nor Skinner worked with human subjects, their findings have provided important concepts that continue to be applied in classrooms to student behavior.

Types of Consequences

Positive Reinforcement

- is a stimulus event

- <u>follows</u> a response

- <u>increases</u> the strength of the response

Melonia,
You've done a
great job on the
characters in
your story!

Will you finish that
assignment! How many
times do I have to say
it before you will do it?
Now get it done!

Negative Reinforcement

- is a stimulus event

- <u>precedes</u> a response and is present until a response is made

- <u>increases</u> the strength of the response

Punishment

- is a stimulus event

- <u>follows </u>a response

- <u>decreases</u> the strength of the response

So, you think that 8 and 6
is equal to 7+7?
Well, that's the wrong
answer. I don't appreciate
your foolishness, missy!

Extinction

- existed in a previous situation using a reinforcer to promote a response

- the same reinforcer now <u>NO LONGER</u> follows a response

- the response is extinguished

In all the previously defined consequences, it is useful to observe that reinforcers increase the strength of a behavior whereas punishers weaken it. As noted earlier, unless behavior continues in association with the consequences that have shaped it, the behavior may revert to the conditions of an earlier state. In cases relating to both classical and operant conditions, *Extinction* is illustrated in the diagram below.

First, it is interesting to consider the idea of Extinction in the case of a classically conditioned response. In Watson's experiment outlined earlier, the association between the noise and the appearance of the rabbit caused Little Albert, subsequently, to fear the rabbit. In the process of *Extinction*, in which old associations are weakened and in which the noise ceases to be heard when the rabbit is present, the rabbit reverts to being a neutral stimulus. This process explains why the passage of time can weaken many developmental fears. (see Childhood fears and anxiety, in Chapter Seven.)

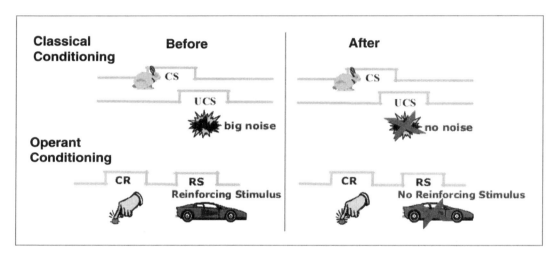

Figure 2-5. The Process of Extinction

As might be imagined, the process of extinction is applicable also in an operant situation. In order to condition a person to push a button for a five-minute ride in a sports car, a contingency between the two events must first be established. Subsequently, if *Extinction* is desired, the contingent relationship between the two events must be severed. If the person is no longer permitted to drive the car, regardless of the number of times the button is pressed, there will very soon be no further pressing of that button (see Figure 4).

What is an Operational Definition?

When an *operational definition* is needed, a concept must be defined on the basis of its outcomes. In a classroom, for instance, when Ms. Zylstra wants to encourage Crystal to strive for task completion, she gives the student, each time she finishes a task, five minutes to work on a puzzle. In summary, the three potential outcomes of this contingency are illustrated below.

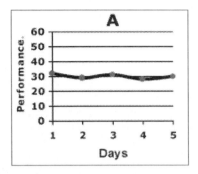 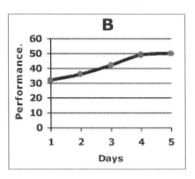 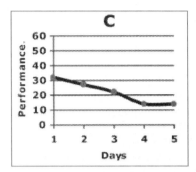

Figure 2-6. **Three Potential Outcomes**

It is interesting to examine the outcome implied by each of the graphs. A look at Graph A indicates that no systematic change in behavior has occurred even though the five-minute puzzle activity for task completion has been given. It is clear, therefore, that the puzzle activity, because it does not affect performance, represents a *neutral stimulus*. Graph B, on the other hand, which indicates an increase in task performance, would suggest to a Behaviorist that the puzzle activity is a *reinforcer*. Graph C, however, illustrates the opposite effect. Here, because the awarding of the puzzle activity for task completion has elicited a decrease in task performance, the puzzle activity is defined as a *punisher*. In summary, the three possible outcomes for the contingency of puzzle activity for task completion illustrate the way Behaviorists perceive consequences: a consequence is defined according to its outcome.

In overview, some key concepts of the Behavioral model indicate that because "maladaptive"[5] behavior is learned, it can subsequently be replaced by new "adaptive" behavior. To accomplish this task, new behavior is taught by organizing or "engineering" sequences of events. Also outlined are the contingencies, that is, the "if–then" relationships that will produce preferred outcomes. When Behaviorists conceptualize students with behavioral disorders or emotional disturbances according to certain criteria, the students are:

- children who do not learn behaviors which will permit a healthy adaptation to their environment

- children who learn maladaptive or non-beneficial behaviors

- children who develop maladaptive behaviors when they are exposed to stressful environmental circumstances that require them to make decisions too difficult for them (Newcomer, 1980.)

What does Extinction have to do with the classroom?

When a child behaves inappropriately to get attention, for instance, when Arielle drops her pencil, Mr. Hsiung looks at her, always suggesting she get back to work. Because an operant conditioning model identifies object-dropping, the inappropriate behavior, as the response and Mr. Hsiung's behavior as the reinforcer, each time Arielle is observed dropping books, erasers, caps, and other objects during independent work periods, Mr. Hsiung responds in a similar manner. According to the Behaviorist model, this pattern indicates that attention is strengthening the behavior. If he wants to reverse this relationship, Mr. Hsiung must no longer respond when Arielle drops an object. If Mr. Hsiung's attention is actually reinforcing Arielle's behavior, the extinction process will successfully reduce the frequency of her object-dropping.

According to the Behaviorist perspective, good mental health requires that students:

  (a) have the ability and the opportunity to learn adaptive behaviors

  (b) experience environments that punish maladaptive behaviors

  (c) permit individuals to discover what is adaptive and what is not

Figure 2-6 incorporates the aspects of both Classical and Operant conditioning that are at play in the context of the classroom. Whereas operant events occur sequentially across time, classical events produce a simultaneous pairing of emotions and internal states along with classroom events as they unfold.

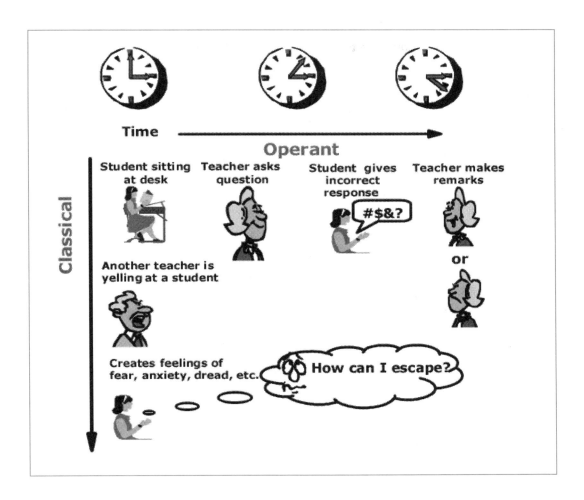

Figure 2-7. Classical and Operant Conditioning in the classroom

Modeling

Albert Bandura examined the role played by *Modeling* – usually described as the imitation of the behavior of others – in learning social behavior. According to his view social behavior is learned: for example, a student develops personal behavior by observing others dealing with social situations and by noticing whether those behaviors are reinforced or punished. Victor, who is new to the school and to his grade 7 classroom, by watching the other students learns the routines and expectations of Mr. Tamir's class. This pattern suggests that contingencies do not need to be experienced directly, because, as can be shown, students will often learn acceptable behavior by seeing in the classroom the types of consequences that follow the behaviors of other students.

More recently, Bandura has further developed the social learning model by his consideration of the impact of *Self-efficacy* on social learning. Defined as people's knowledge of their own capacity to deal with particular situations, self-efficacy is unlike self-confidence in that the latter has further-reaching consequences in comparable situations. Consequently, self-efficacy affects both the students' perception of classroom situations and their motivation to tackle tasks and projects. This capacity can be seen especially in students who perceive themselves as incompetent, as well as in those who evaluate a task as too difficult; sometimes it is also prevalent in those reluctant to engage in classroom situations altogether.

Bandura believes that self-efficacy is able to lead people to specific personal evaluations of their capabilities to deal with a variety of contexts. A correlation is that such personal appraisals can be applied to new situations. This concept implies that, observed in the primary division, a child's classroom performance is able to generate expectations for subsequent performance in the intermediate grades. A careful awareness of the potential for this developing cause-effect relationship is particularly useful for teachers of the early grades. This is the case because so much variability exists in the performance of young children whose nervous systems are still maturing. Matthew, for instance, is not yet able to grip his pencil in a fashion that will allow him to print his name legibly. In contrast, Marika, with her well developed fine motor skills, is able to copy many words quickly and legibly. Ms. Wharton, on the basis of her interaction with the two students, must encourage in both of them positive feelings regarding their self-efficacy.

How well a child expects to accomplish a task is influenced not only by recalling previous accomplishments but also by observing the performance of others – that is, do other students appear to be struggling, unhappy, or having fun? Do teacher and student comments reveal that the task is too hard or too easy? A student's own evaluation will be based on previously experienced internal states – especially such strong feelings as anxiety, frustration, and excitement, emotions that could be experienced at any time before, during, or after the task is or fails to be completed. Self-efficacy judgments will often determine, too, how much effort is to be invested in an activity, while profoundly influencing the student's expectation of success or failure. In Figure 2-8, which illustrates efficacy expectations influencing people's behavior, outcome expectations are shown also to affect the way the student will perceive and consider such external elements as feedback.

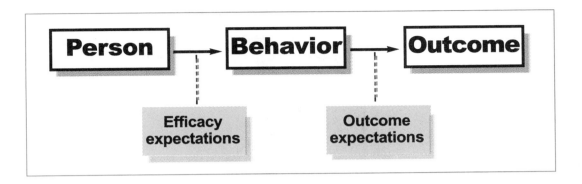

Figure 2-8. Bandura's Self-efficacy Model

Educational Impact

Unlike the Psychodynamic model, the Behavioral model provides an optimistic approach to the treatment of behavioral difficulties. In a context in which the child may be viewed as a victim of inappropriate learning, the Behavioral model emphasizes the role of the teacher in establishing contingencies that will eradicate inappropriate behavior while promoting congenial or cooperative social behavior. Schools must be viewed as natural settings in which behavioral change is made possible in part because of the time factor. If children are spending close to five hours a day in school classrooms, they may be expected to associate the learning of new behaviors with the setting. Not only the clarity, but the specificity and simplicity of the principles proposed by this model make them attractive to educators, especially those in the classroom who will easily be able to adapt and implement their procedures.

The Humanistic View

Associated with Alfred Adler, (1870-1937), the Humanistic model is linked with several other psychiatrists also seriously involved in the Psychodynamic movement. This new model arose, not in Europe, however, but in North America. Perhaps because the Humanistic view has its origins in the New World, it emphasizes a democratic style not only in social relationships but also in other interactions. Also recognizable here are features previously encountered both in the Psychodynamic and in the Behavioral views.

As it relates to Education, the Humanistic paradigm is exemplified in the work of Carl Rogers, Abraham Maslow, Rudolf Dreikurs, and William Glasser.

Carl Rogers

A psychologist most often associated with *client-centered therapy,* Carl Rogers (1902-1987) introduced a new role for the therapist. Unlike the parent figure of the Psychodynamic therapist – the person needed to interpret the patient's internal conflicts – the client-centered therapist works to empower the client to find solutions to these problems. During their interaction, the therapist, behaving as a mirror, guides the client. In the context of the classroom, the Humanist teacher, who becomes a facilitator with the relevant Rogerian qualities,

- possesses integrity, genuineness, and authenticity
- is prizing, accepting, and trusting
- demonstrates empathic understanding

General Features

HUMANISM

- The Humanistic model is influenced both by the Psychodynamic and by the Behaviorist model and therefore some concepts are reminiscent of each.

- "Self-concept" which is an essential feature of the model is associated with the role played by feedback from significant people in an environment.

- This view is concerned with all the events, both past and present, that shape human behavior.

- In this model, it is not important to establish typologies in order to label behavior.

- There is a strong emphasis on the student's growth and development up the hierarchy toward the goal of self-actualization. Maslow's hierarchy of needs is a good referent here.

- Treatment practices include redirecting the individual, assisting that person to attain more rational perceptions, helping the client with the notion of accepting oneself as one actually is.

- Interventions include non-directive therapy: In the *Client-Centered context*, the client is encouraged to express ideas openly, without fear of rejection. The client must draw conclusions regarding the adequacy of personal behavior and make a commitment to change; Dreikur's *Discipline without Tears* and Glasser's *Reality Therapy* and *Control Theory* are useful books here.

- Problems are caused by society or its representatives, such as parents, teachers, significant persons who may obstruct the student's journey toward self-actualization.

- Some formal research exists to expand the basic ideas available.

- The length of therapy is long-term as it is accompanied by procedures that emphasize growth.

Maslow's Hierarchy of Needs

Abraham Maslow (1908-1970) contributed a now-famous list which he called a *hierarchy of needs*. These essential requirements are thought basic to every individual who is developing toward self-actualization. A classroom model of behavior incorporating some of the more important items on Maslow's list of basic needs will be outlined in Chapter Four. In reference to these needs, an important one today, for example, is safety in classrooms, a most pressing requirement. (see Figure 2-9).

Humanists develop safe environments by:

- providing predictable organization and demands
- teaching interactive skills
- recognizing that children have changing safety needs

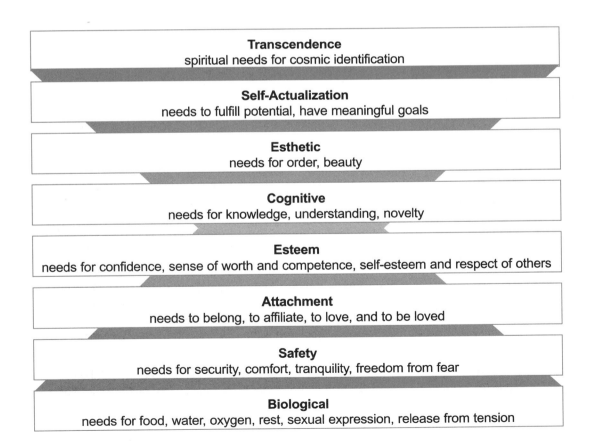

Figure 2-9. Maslow's Hierarchy of Needs

Rudolph Dreikurs

Rudolph Dreikurs (1897-1972) is known for the formulation of the idea of discipline without tears which is described in a book by the same name written with Pearl Cassel in 1972. Dreikurs' procedures are known to reinforce the ideals of the democratic style common in today's schools. Accordingly, a democratic teacher should:

> " have a friendly voice, lead rather than boss, be authoritative rather than autocratic, win cooperation, sell ideas, guide, encourage, be warm, be friendly but firm, be always well prepared, treat pupils with respect, be always impartial, use group instruction well, encourage group discussion, never center out mistakes, mark only correct responses, rotate class monitors weekly." (Dreikurs & Cassel, 1972)

Because Dreikurs believes that competition existing between students has a detrimental effect on self-concept and performance, he emphasizes its avoidance at all cost. In addition, teachers are expected to assist each child to develop into a full social being. As a correlation of this tenet, in some circumstances, it is necessary to put the needs of the group before those of the individual.

In his theory, Dreikurs sees student misbehavior as motivated by four major goals, indicating that if a teacher identifies the goal associated with the inappropriate behavior, the relevant correction procedure will be clear. When a teacher hopes to accomplish this task, it will first be necessary to note personal reactions to the activity of the child. Then, after observing the student's behavior, and clearly ascertaining the goal, the teacher will apply an appropriate corrective procedure.

Goal 1: Attention

When the teacher perceives the child as a nuisance and responds by feeling annoyed, it is because the flow of the classroom has been interfered with, while the teacher's time and attention have been diverted. In many cases, the teacher believes that the child either wants to be noticed or is asking for special consideration. In a typical situation, when a child shows off, clowns around, avoids doing work, and manipulates other students, these activities result from the child's sense of self-worth being associated with attention-getting.

When the child demands attention, Dreikurs believes, the corrective procedure is to ignore the misbehaving child, while, however, concealing personal annoyance. The correlative is that when the teacher gives appropriate attention at another time, it will elicit results more helpful to the student.

Although teachers should not take notice of inappropriate behavior, sometimes, in the context of a classroom, children demand attention because they are unaware of ways to obtain it appropriately. It is often possible for the teacher to dispense such information, while, at the same time, offering suitable prompts to those students who initially need extra support.

Goal 2: Power

When a teacher perceives a child as stubborn, usual reactions would involve a sense of defeat or a perception that personal authority is being challenged. In such an inappropriate situation, a power struggle may ensue. If the child is argumentative, appearing to want to be in charge, the behavior of the child may end in a tantrum or a lie, in fact the opposite of what is wanted.

In such a difficulty, the student's self-worth may depend not only on a desire to take charge, but also on a need to have others do as they are bidden. As a means of correcting this behavior, Dreikurs suggests that the teacher should neither partake in the power struggle nor give in to the student, even if, at the time, such capitulation may seem to be the most expedient course of action.

By recognizing and admitting that the child has power, however, the teacher may be able to devise ways for that power to be exercised. For example, students who are permitted to develop leadership roles may learn negotiating skills as they are required to deal with complex classroom situations.

Goal 3: Revenge

When, as sometimes happens, the teacher perceives a child as vicious, a normal reaction would be to feel deeply hurt, if not outraged by the behavior; in fact, it would be possible for the teacher to so dislike the child as to retaliate in kind by devising inappropriate punishment. In such circumstances, the child may steal, be sullen, or show defiance; may even hurt animals, peers, or adults; and may lash out aggressively, especially if harmed by others. In a situation of this magnitude, the child may also be a sore loser and a potential Young Offender. Sometimes, the child's sense of self-worth has become associated with the need to get even because of having been wronged.

According to Dreikurs, the teacher should neither communicate the idea of outrage nor behave in a hurt manner. Although he suggests that natural consequences should be the result of the child's behavior, Dreikurs cautions that punishment will produce only rebellion. Instead of levying a penalty, the teacher should encourage the class to find ways to help the child feel needed and valuable.

Students associated with this goal behave in a manner deemed more extreme than the behavior described in the other categories. These antics, although not considered serious by the intervention method proposed by Dreikurs, have been known to lead to anti-social and destructive behavior (see Oppositional Defiant, and Conduct Disorders, in Chapter 3).

Goal 4: Display of Inadequacy

In this last scenario, the teacher may experience a sense of helplessness about assisting the child or may even lack a clear idea of what to do. In such circumstances, the child, too, may find the situation hopeless, and, subsequently, may start to behave in a 'stupid' manner. Other possible reactions might be to give up easily, participate infrequently, or even try just to remain alone. By others, students or teachers, the child may be thought to exhibit an inferiority complex, a device some people adopt to mask personal inadequacy.

Even when teachers or students react inappropriately, a child in these circumstances should be encouraged. Optimally, attempts should be made to make the student feel worthwhile, even if this involves providing praise when the formerly difficult student attempts a task. With a student of this demeanor, the teacher should keep disappointment in check while maintaining the motivation to succeed. In a classroom where peer helpers and mentors have been established, such assistants can help to introduce alternate opportunities for success.

Although Dreikurs' model has proved effective as a first line of defense, the notion that behaviors can be neatly compartmentalized into four boxes might be questioned. At best, the Humanistic view is associated with considering the "whole child", but it is important to keep in mind that Dreikurs' typology, in some circumstances, may mislead.

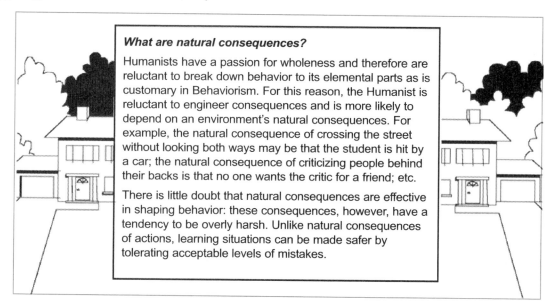

What are natural consequences?

Humanists have a passion for wholeness and therefore are reluctant to break down behavior to its elemental parts as is customary in Behaviorism. For this reason, the Humanist is reluctant to engineer consequences and is more likely to depend on an environment's natural consequences. For example, the natural consequence of crossing the street without looking both ways may be that the student is hit by a car; the natural consequence of criticizing people behind their backs is that no one wants the critic for a friend; etc.

There is little doubt that natural consequences are effective in shaping behavior: these consequences, however, have a tendency to be overly harsh. Unlike natural consequences of actions, learning situations can be made safer by tolerating acceptable levels of mistakes.

William Glasser

In the 1960s, as a means of applying humanistic principles to the classroom, William Glasser's *Reality Theory* was introduced. Like Dreikurs, Glasser encouraged an egalitarian relationship between students and teachers, a contract which encourages negotiations that will result in mutually acceptable classroom behaviors. With the use of contracts and meetings, teacher and students discuss these topics, amiably reaching consensus about the performance conditions both parties will adhere to. When a student fails to meet contract conditions, the teacher is expected, on the one hand, to accept no excuses, but, on the other, to help the student to find ways to meet the agreed obligations.

Identifying his approach as *Reality Therapy*, Glasser, like other humanists, believed that teachers must address a curriculum personally relevant to the student, a curriculum that emphasizes those elements the students consider to be real. More recently, in the 1980s, Glasser further developed his approach when he introduced a new idea: *Control Theory*. Originally, the notion of students' being responsible for their own behavior had been an important principle in Glasser's thesis, but, in this new development, students are expected to have control or influence over the learning itself. In his overview, Glasser suggests that in human beings five basic needs must be satisfied:

- A need to survive
- A need to belong and to love others
- A need for power and influence
- A need to be free to make choices
- A need to play and have fun

While only the first two needs are similar to Maslow's Hierarchy of Needs, Glasser's list does not suggest an order or hierarchy in his five needs. Glasser does claim, however, that the education system fails to meet students' needs when:

- teachers promote competition in the classroom -- a disregard of Need #2
- teachers are totally responsible for student evaluation -- a disregard of Needs #3 and #4
- teachers are chiefly concerned with covering the curriculum -- a disregard of Needs #4 and #5

In essence, Glasser's message is that students can be empowered if they are given the opportunity to make decisions about what takes place in the classroom; to assume such leadership roles as those of mentor and tutor; to promote opportunities for students to become dependent on one another; and to build opportunities for those in the classroom to experience fun and enjoyment.

Educational Impact

As it is often experienced in the child-centered classroom, the impact of the Humanist movement provides stimulation of student potential through imaginative educational opportunities. In addition, because Humanists are deeply committed to democratic principles, they value the creation of an educational climate in which all students have equal opportunities to learn. In humanistic classrooms, teachers develop a variety of ways to teach students how to live in a democratic society. Usually, it is possible for this ideal to be realized when students are given responsibilities and decision-making opportunities, because these will contribute to the operation of the classroom as well as to their own educational experiences.

The Biological View

Taking yet a different perspective, the Biological view perceives behavioral disorders as having roots in the physiology of the brain. Because it is a developing perspective, this one continues to gain ground in the present as scientists unravel the mysteries of the mind through new advances in technology. Among the currently important approaches are CAT scans, MRI, and other imaging techniques. Recently, too, new biological explanations of behavioral and emotional conditions have emerged, including the likelihood that either over-production or under-production of certain neurotransmitters can affect learning. These neurotransmitters, including such brain substances as dopamine and seratonin, among others, facilitate the passage of information between brain cells, also called neurons. Such substances – and others as yet undetected - may be found to create compulsive behavior, hallucinations, and other behaviors previously associated with more complex esoteric causes.

As a consequence of this ongoing research, some pharmacological breakthroughs have occurred, in many cases providing counter substances, able to alter behavior. For example, some persons originally diagnosed as Manic Depressive are now able to have their activities "normalized" by such medications as Lithium, with the result that some individuals once hospitalized are leading rich, productive lives. Given the way chemicals are linked with substance abuse and with mixtures of additives found universally in the food, water, and air imbibed by most people, eventually it may be possible for medicine to explain certain behavioral anomalies.

The story of the "Mad Hatters" exemplifies the contribution of this paradigm: when workers employed in a hat factory, in the nineteenth century, began to demonstrate bizarre behaviors associated at the time with "madness", a systematic analysis was undertaken. After the entire group's symptoms were analyzed, the discovery was made that mercury used in the production of felt hats was the culprit. It was then necessary to re-label as "mercury poisoning" what had been "madness".

The Biological model is concerned with three main lines of investigation:

- Predisposition
- Neurological causes
- Developmental causes

A finding of the recent emphasis on gene research, genetic predisposition is found to relate to the inherent probability of an individual's contracting a disorder. Usually, predisposition in itself is not a sufficient condition, but the interaction of predisposition with environmental factors may produce the disorder. For example, in the family of a student, if there is an inherent tendency toward schizophrenia, other members of the extended family having been diagnosed with the condition, the predisposition is present. Without the appropriate environmental triggers, however, such as unstable home environment, as well as other stressors, the student may have a low probability of affliction. In order to identify a disorder associated with a genetic pre-disposition, researchers usually study individual families to pinpoint the history of affliction. More recently, awareness of these tendencies in genetic systems has elicited an interest among geneticists who wish to isolate and code the "rogue" gene.

Also in biological research, another element involves neurological investigations which examine the chemical functions of the brain. Information relating to levels of neurotransmitters, that is, those chemical agents in the brain as well as the role they play in certain mental disorders, now provides interventions in the form of chemicals which are able to normalize behavior. In addition, the architecture of the brain –in some individuals, certain areas of the brain are found to be larger or smaller than the norm -- has been studied to identify relationships between brain structure and behavior. Finally, through physiological research, tumors existing in particular areas of the brain have been discovered to cause profound changes in behavior.

Also recognized in the field of physiological analysis are causes deemed developmental, related to the maturation of the brain. In some cases, researchers examine prenatal factors such as exposure to environmental agents, among which known toxins are not only second-hand smoke, but also smog and household and industrial chemicals. As scientists probe further into this field, additional findings related to toxicity may include ingestion of agents resulting from substance abuse, diet, medications, etc., as well as disease present in the mother. Scientists are also able to examine factors prevailing at birth, possibly relating to lack of oxygen or similar complications, as well as incidents in the child's development – falls, exposure to toxins, etc. – any of which may explain behavioral anomalies after babyhood.

Unfortunately, while Biological explanations are often deemed more credible than other types of interventions, the same objective standard used to establish them is not always applied in their evaluation. Consider the opposing findings regularly reported in the media, about the benefits or adverse effects on good health of various foods and drugs. Such reports are often conclusions of correlational studies. Scientists interested in causal inferences examine the result of experimental findings and of converging discoveries, rather than outcomes of descriptive studies.

General Features

BIOLOGICAL

- This view is also known as the Physical or Biogenetic Model.

- Biogenetic and organic factors are believed to account for a range of mental and emotional disturbances.

- The problems are expected to arise during the prenatal, peri-natal, and/or postnatal history of mother and child (their physical health is very important).

- Clues to explain the mental health of students are found in the medical history of those students and their families.

- This model is interpreted by analyzing data acquired from observing the physiology of the brain, chemical levels, etc.

- This model represents a true medical perspective; the "disease" notion encourages the utilization of labels to define conditions.

- The goal is to promote *change* in behavior of the "patient." This model attempts, therefore, to 'normalize' and/or *maintain* the condition so that it does not worsen.

- The therapy is directive in that the doctor(s) determines how the condition is to be treated.

- Interventions include medication -- or drug therapies -- as well as diet and surgery.

- The methodology is designed to suit the needs of the patient.

- Problems result from biogenetic make-up, poor nutrition, disease, substance abuse, accidents.

- A large amount of experimental work has been and is generated by this view.

- When it attempts to normalize or maintain a condition, the therapy is usually long-term. Otherwise, when symptoms disappear, treatment is stopped.

Important Concepts

This model, the Biological, has consistently demonstrated that, over time, physiological explanations of behavior will all but replace psychological ones. In addition, the model confirms the important role played by brain function in understanding psychological and behavioral phenomena. In the area of treatment, although many individuals now regularly have medications to treat their conditions, a strong consensus exists that such interventions are more effective when accompanied with therapy, counseling, and other interactive treatments.

Educational Impact

At present, a greater number of children than ever before, diagnosed with behavioral difficulties, are treated on a regular basis with medication. Because of this widespread use of medication, many students who attend school are medicated to such a degree that they are insufficiently alert to engage in academic tasks. Possibly, in the future, to monitor dosages, physicians will require the cooperation of teachers in addition to feedback from the schools.

Knowing that such students are being medicated should NOT deter teachers from implementing classroom interventions in support of treatment. In one instance, Michael takes Rytalin to increase his attention span, and, in addition, Mr. Waldman has introduced an intervention to increase his time on task, by providing short independent projects at first and then systematically increasing the length and difficulty of each activity.

The Sociological View

Interested in explaining human behavior in its relationship with groups, the Sociological view examines the structure and dynamics of social institutions. Unlike the psychological perspective which focuses on the uniqueness of the individual, the sociological perspective evaluates the behavior of individuals primarily in reference to their social groups and to the environments they live in. Logically, then, it is not the intention of this view to explain the behavior of a particular individual.

How do organizations and institutions impact on the general behavior of people? In his book, *Schools Without Failure,* William Glasser applies a sociological perspective when he implies that student failure relates directly to the way schools are organized. One unusual solution involves allowing students, at the start of a program, to decide their grades and then to permit the same students to retake the course – without academic penalty – as often as necessary to obtain the predicted grades. Typical of those researchers who offer sociological solutions, Glasser is proposing a change in the way schools operate. Similarly, Irving Goffman, in his examination of inmate behavior, confirmed that institutionalized individuals develop behaviors directly related to the structure of their environments. Support for this conclusion is provided by social psychologists who propose that, in the context of a group or organization, individuals adopt the "roles" that are ascribed to them.

Important Concepts

Because this model highlights the role played by organizations and social structures in shaping individual behavior, it postulates that whenever school and class demands change, student behavior is altered respectively. In a classroom with well-defined expectations, the same group of students will behave quite differently than they will in a schoolyard operating with very different demands. As current social pressures continue to impact harshly on families, both in the classroom and in the schoolyard, students exhibit relevant stresses.

Educational Impact

Because of a major sociological shift in the conceptualization of schools and their relationship to exceptional children, mandatory special education legislation has become law, at first in the United States and then in most Canadian provinces. With the creation of special services, not only have previously ignored student needs received attention, but, subsequently, resources and intervention have been diverted to this group.

Students diagnosed with severe behavioral difficulties are placed in small classes, taught by highly-trained teachers and child care workers. Not surprisingly, this new environment has been recognized to benefit children with difficulties much more readily than does the regular class, which is rarely conducive to addressing disruptive socio-emotional problems. Because of the noted successes experienced in the special classrooms, the recent government-directed movement to mainstream all exceptional students is regarded by many teachers and other workers as retrograde, a step backwards that has negative results for both regular and exceptional students. Within the teaching profession and the field of education in general, most professionals believe that different organizational options must be made available to permit educators to provide the correct niche for every student. For exceptional students, in this optimal educational climate, educators can select the one that best fits each student.

SOCIOLOGICAL

- The model emphasizes the impact of social forces on individuals.

- The structure of the social environment and the behavior of groups encourage the learning of particular behaviors.

- This view is interested in evaluating the present demands of a situation.

- Although data are collected, this perspective advocates looking for the *meaning* contained in the events.

- This model has developed its own typology and therefore it uses these labels (e.g. *Deviance*) to describe people and conditions.

- The thrust of this view is to effect *change* in social environments.

- The approaches supported by this view are directive.

- Interventions include socializing and re-socializing students, "milieu" therapy, organizational changes, making the system more responsive to individual differences.

- Because it advocates global changes, these changes affect groups rather than single individuals.

- Problems arise as a result of the way a student responds to the social forces of the group, the organization, or the society.

- A great deal of experimental work is available but it is mostly correlational.

- Changes are made very slowly so that, in some cases, solutions are in the very long term (20-30 years).

The Cognitive View

A recent model to emerge is the Cognitive view, an approach which addresses the impact of thinking, knowledge, memory, and problem-solving on human behavior. Interestingly, it has re-legitimized the concept and study of 'Mind', an area of focus ignored by the Behaviorists. As this view has become widely known, many individuals who had once adopted the Behaviorist perspective later shifted to the Cognitivist camp. Of these, a leading example is Albert Bandura, earlier described in connection with Behaviorism. Also associated with the Cognitive view are George Kelly and Albert Ellis. In an overview of Cognitive attitudes, some relevant aspects include: attribution theory and beliefs about ability, as well as the use of inner speech in evaluating, considering, and generating a course of action.

George Kelly

In his development of the Cognitive view, George Kelly (1905-1967) proposed the notion that within the average person reality is constructed using the process employed by scientists who generate theories. In the same manner by which scientists advance hypotheses, people develop expectations that are tested and adjusted, over time, on the basis of their personal experiences.

The notion that anticipation, for example, is able to channel experience can be observed when Marius and Eugene conceptualize the field trip that Mr. Barghava has planned for next month. Whereas Marius happily anticipates the finding of interesting little creatures in the pond water, Eugene feels threatened about being in a strange place, perhaps falling in the water, and certainly getting lost. In this concept, it is clear that each student will construct a separate reality and, in addition, a personal explanation of the workings of the world.

Albert Ellis

Originally a proponent of psychoanalysis, Albert Ellis (1913-) proposes a concept known as Rational Emotive Behavioral Therapy (1957). His "ABC's" address the variables that continue to be important to Cognitivists:

- **A** refers to activating experiences, a set of events that are triggers, including family troubles, unsatisfying work, and early childhood traumas, all or any of which may be the source of an individual's unhappiness.

- **B** alludes to beliefs, focusing on the realization that unhappiness may be maintained when one clings to irrational and self-defeating beliefs.

- **C** relates to consequences of the triggers and beliefs when they manifest themselves as both neurotic symptoms and negative emotions.

In Ellis's view, a number of thinking errors are commonly made by people in everyday life:

- people often ignore the positive events in their lives

- people tend to exaggerate the negative events in their lives

- people habitually overgeneralize their lives' negative events

Finally, Ellis proposed a list of three main irrational beliefs, among many others, commonly held by many people:

- "I must be outstandingly competent, or I am worthless."

- "Others must treat me considerately, or they are absolutely rotten."

- "The world should always give me happiness, or I will die."

What is overgeneralization?

On the basis of a single event or a few experiences, an individual will make sweeping conclusions about people and situations. For example, in this view, all civil servants are self-seeking, every teacher is stupid, and no event can be as interesting as people say. When such individuals attend a program or hear a speech, they have already cynically decided that it will be mediocre. These are the people who begin sentences with, "They say that nothing good will come of this legislation" or "They can't be trusted when they promise to keep the streets clean". A person who overgeneralizes about life circumstance might say, "Nothing good ever happens to me and so there's no point in trying anything new". A young student may say, "The teacher hates me so there's no point in studying for the test".

Important Concepts

Central to the Cognitive view is the idea that individuals perceive a world through senses that successfully filter incoming information – the mind rather than the senses is at work. Such a view implies that what is observed rests not only on the experience but also on the knowledge accepted by the student who will act according to such perceptions. As an overview, it is possible to say of this notion that the irrational beliefs of such students will be the basis for their maladaptive responses.

Educational Impact

Considering the cognitive view, teachers see that a major implication of this situation involves the teaching of appropriate attributions about school success or failure. For example, when students inappropriately blame their lack of intellectual ability to explain failure and, conversely, "good luck" to explain their success, how can the truth be established in the students' eyes?

In response to the problems raised by students' often wrong-headed perceptions, the emphasis on examining mental activity is placed by Cognitive thinkers. This means resolving social and emotional problems, in the classroom, by using problem-solving strategies. As a general rule, this model lends itself not only to the rational examination of behavior but also to the focused use of language activities to mediate. A further use of this approach involves meta-cognitive control as it is applied to regulating and monitoring personal behavior.

General Features

COGNITIVE

- This model has its roots in Information-Processing theories and other theories about the mind.

- This model makes the assumption that students behave in accordance with their belief system or what they know to be true.

- Beliefs are a product of cognitive development and learning (Implicit and Explicit).

- Treatment is based on conditions in the present.

- This view is interested in collecting data (observations) and determining the meaning of such findings.

- The model has not had a typology constructed and therefore labels are not used.

- The object of treatment is change because a change in beliefs leads to a change in behavior and vice-versa.

- This view encourages an understanding of self so that the client can eventually assume the role of therapist.

- Treatment involves both an interpretive and a directive component.

- Interventions include meta-cognitive activities (Awareness), Cognitive Behavior Modifications, conceptual development through language, problem-solving skills, critical analysis (Introspection), rules of evidence, etc.

- Problems are the outcome of misconceptions learned over the course of experience.

- This is a relatively new perspective with a growing body of research.

- The time course of interventions depends on the individual but generally the focus is the short-term solution of a problem. It is expected, however, that the new skills learned by students will become part of their behavioral repertoire.

The Ecological Model

The roots of the Ecological model are perhaps borrowed from Biology where a major consideration is the interdependence of organisms – individuals – and their environment in shaping behavior. Hobbs (1966), however, rebelled against the Psychodynamic notion associating emotional disturbances with disease. By rejecting both individual and group psychotherapies, he argued that such children had learned bad habits from their interaction with the environment. This concept helps to explain that a behavior adaptive in one setting may be perceived as "disturbed" in a different setting.

Project Re-Ed

Project Re-Ed – a structured environment for the Re-education of Emotionally Disturbed children – is prototypical of therapeutic programs. Based on Hobbs' (1969) observations of schools and residential programs, Project Re-Ed has its roots in Scotland and France.

Typically, students reside in their respective residential schools during the week, while spending weekends with their families. In each unit, a group of eight-to-ten students is assigned to a team of three differently focused teacher-counselors:

- a day teacher-counselor charged with developing the academic competence of the student

- a night teacher-counselor responsible for overseeing and nurturing the student's social and emotional competence

- a liaison teacher-counselor dedicated to observing and monitoring the student's place in the ecological system, that is the relationship with family members, school, and community

Re-Ed's philosophy is based on the following twelve tenets:

1. Life is to be lived now

2. Time is an ally

3. Trust is essential

4. Competence makes a difference

5. Symptoms can and should be controlled

6. Cognitive control can be taught

7. Feelings should be nurtured

8. The group is important to children

9. Ceremony and ritual give order, stability, and confidence

10. The body is the armature of the self

11. Communities are important

Important Concepts

In the view that underlies the Re-Ed approach, the importance of addressing behavior in the context in which it occurs is fundamental. In Chapter Nine, an example is given, in which the special class teacher strives to address troublesome situations in their naturally occurring environments. In the particular instance, a student who has difficulty getting along with others at recess is placed in that specific context in order to be shown and to learn new ways of behaving.

Educational Impact

In the Ecological view, the classroom serves as a community that affords the student a medium in which to practice important life lessons. In this environment, many opportunities are available to the student, for incorporating learning that allows reflection as well as the examination of feelings. Finally, in this view, students are consistently directed to be open to cues in the environment which signal appropriateness of individual behaviors.

General Features

ECOLOGICAL

- This view is founded on the therapy community approach which supports the idea that treatment must take place in the student's own environment where problems are encountered.

- Problem behavior occurs when students learn bad habits in the context of their environment.

- The view finds the past and present dynamics of students and their environments as extremely relevant.

- Information, person, behavior, and environment are evaluated for *meaning*.

- This model has no typology and therefore labels are not useful.

- Interventions make certain attempts to re-structure the environment although it is often easier to change the child.

- Project Re-Ed and therapeutic camping are interventions associated with this model.

- The purpose of interventions is to develop the social competence of the student.

- This is model highlights personal experience and therefore behavior is evaluated on the basis of its context. A strong affective component also exists.

- Interventions are offered to individuals and to groups.

Conclusions

In the previous section, each of the views presented is shown to provide a consistent framework. From each of these different viewpoints, the nature of human behavior can be interpreted. Also offered by each of the views is a means to focus on as well as to change "inappropriate" behaviors. It is always important to remember, however, that each separate structure has origins in a specific space and time continuum, and contains, moreover, the limitations and biases of its historical beginnings. What continues to emerge, from a summative standpoint, is the realization that no view exclusively explains all human behavior. Instead, each model can be seen as a unique contribution, offering, in its distinctive way, an understanding of its own part of the solution to the puzzle that is human behavior.

Endnotes

[1]   It is interesting to consider this idea in the context of its historical period, the Victorian era.

[2]   In some cases, Superego takes over.

[3]   The tone is again a *neutral stimulus*. This process, to be discussed later, is known as *extinction*.

[4]   There were many little Alberts, all of them children from the local orphanages.

[5]   Note the use of terms generally associated with animal behavior.

CHAPTER 3

Assessment, Evaluation, and Planning

In Chapter Three, behavioral difficulties are outlined, with emphasis on the way clinicians identify types of problems experienced by children and adolescents as well as adults. Although these practices, which are in use today, have been in existence for decades, many remain within the exclusive domain of clinicians outside the educational context, notably psychiatrists, psychologists, and social workers.

While acknowledging these variables, the chapter's focus is to address the questions, rationales, and decision-making demands faced by any teacher of children with behavioral difficulties, especially in the early stages of the Identification process.

At the outset, Chapter Three examines practices, usually conducted by psychologists and psychiatrists, connected with the formal assessment of behavioral exceptionalities. Associated with such assessments is a range of tools and methodologies to be examined in terms of their specific relevance to educators. Next to be discussed is a set of methods associated with behavioral approaches. Finally, an educational assessment, which concentrates on a student case study, will be outlined in careful detail. Because assessment may be perceived as a system of inquiry driven primarily by the assessor's own questions and queries, the goals of an assessment will be clarified concurrently with the range of questions to be answered.

Formal Assessment

Because this section focuses exclusively on the formal assessment of behavioral exceptionalities, it consequently explores and analyzes fundamental assumptions made by those clinicians who themselves administer the testing materials. Whereas psychologists normally administer an extensive battery of tests designed to examine various aspects of student functioning, for example, sensory, intellectual, etc., a range of tests that concentrate on student conduct are the only ones examined in this section. Also emphasized is the nature of the assessment tests themselves, as well as the clinical criteria applying to them that are contained in the Diagnostic and Statistical Manual of Mental Disorders — Fourth Edition, Text Revised[1].

Although not in a position to administer the tests described in this section, teachers, nevertheless, will have access to reports that describe and interpret them. For this reason, it is useful to have an outline of the ramifications of these results.

Categorization

The process known as "categorization" finds it roots in the idea that clusters of behaviors or symptoms group themselves into behavioral categories. Because certain behaviors are perceived to have a tendency to cluster, they are frequently found manifested in a single individual. For example, past findings have shown that behaviors X, Y, and Z can generally be expected to appear together. This means that when behaviors X and Y are observed, clinicians will have the expectation that behavior Z will also be present. Consider a student who, given a too-difficult task, generally throws down pencil and books: which other behaviors could be anticipated from this student? That the student will be uncooperative, as well as aggressive, can be predicted with a high degree of certainty.

As a result of this concept of categorization, treatment measures can be based on clusters of behaviors rather than on individual behaviors. In addition, implicit assumptions are usually made about causation. A correlation of this view is that a category of behavior may be considered to contain individual behaviors sharing a root cause. Essentially, then, behaviors X, Y, and Z often appear together because, in a cluster, they represent "effects" of the same cause. On the contrary, however, a problem arises with categorization, because it generates expectations which may or may not turn out to be valid. In an example involving Martin, who displays an unusual number of facial tics, an observer might imagine the problem to be symptomatic of Tourette's Syndrome. Upon further investigation, however, after Martin's symptoms are identified as a side effect of his Rytalin medication, they disappear when the dosage is reduced.

As a general practice, when a person's behavior is assigned a category label, based on a few presenting symptoms, all the behaviors associated with the category are expected to manifest themselves. As can easily be imagined, such a generalizing tendency can mislead. A further problem with categorization is that it leaves very little room to provide services to those individuals without the classic clusters of symptoms. When such individuals are children, of course they are less able than adults to access mental health services as well as more likely to be members of classrooms. This group of young people with difficulties may also have few, if any at all, community resources at their disposal.

Among the categories are:

- Phobias
- Attentional Deficit Disorder
- Autism
- Juvenile Delinquency
- Psychosomatic Disorders
- Schizophrenia

Outside the school context, psychologists, psychiatrists, and other clinicians – have access to the American Psychiatric Association Classification System, referred to as DSM (Diagnostic and Statistical Manual of Mental Disorders). Using this manual to identify students, they base their diagnoses on its categories; in addition, these clinicians use the manual to support these same diagnoses. Now in its sixth revision (DSM-I, 1952; DSM-II, 1968; DSM-III, 1980; DSM-III-R, 1987; DSM IV, 1994, DSM-IV-TR, 2000), the manual's newer editions usually contain many more categories than did the earlier range, and, generally, they attempt to provide more objective diagnostic criteria than they were capable of in the past. Sometimes, in fact, the more recent manuals include new categories. What should be remembered, however, is that these categories are likely to be derived more often from clinical practice than from experimental research. Lately, a great deal of controversy has been generated regarding the impact of this information on the validity of the DSM Manual. In one instance, Houts (2002) is not only critical of the increasing number of categories included in the manual, but also suggests that such an expansion does not reflect growth in the understanding of psychopathology.

In the section which follows, the DSM IV-TR categories associated with childhood and adolescence are presented. In later chapters, where they focus on special populations, the criteria attendant on each category will be outlined.

DSM-IV: Disorders usually arising in Childhood and Adolescence

Regularly included in DSM-IV-TR, in sections dealing with childhood and adolescence, are the following groupings:

a. **Mental Retardation**

- mild

- moderate

- severe

- profound

- severity unspecified

b. **Learning Disorders**

- Reading Disorder

- Mathematics Disorder

- Disorder of Written Expression

- Learning Disorder Not Otherwise Specified

  c. Motor Skills Disorder

- Developmental Coordination Disorder

d. **Communication Disorder**

- Expressive Language Disorder

- Phonological Disorder

- Mixed Receptive-Expressive Language Disorder

- Stuttering

- Communication Disorder Not Otherwise Specified

e. **Pervasive Developmental Disorders**

- Asperger's Disorder

- Autistic Disorder

- Childhood Disintegrative Disorder

- Rett's Disorder

- Pervasive Developmental Disorder Not Otherwise Specified

f. **Attention-Deficit and Disruptive Behavior Disorder**

- Attention-Deficit/Hyperactivity Disorder
- Conduct Disorder
- Oppositional Defiant Disorder
- Disruptive Behavior Disorder Not Otherwise Specified

g. **Feeding and Eating Disorders of Infancy or Early Childhood**

- Feeding Disorder of Infancy or Early Childhood
- Pica
- Rumination Disorder

h. **Tic Disorders**

- Chronic Motor or Vocal Tic Disorder
- Tourette's Disorder
- Tic Disorder Not Otherwise Specified

i. **Elimination Disorders**

- Encopresis
- Enuresis

j. **Other Disorders of Infancy, Childhood, or Adolescence**

- Selective Mutism
- Separation Anxiety Disorder
- Reactive Attachment Disorder of Infancy and Early Childhood
- Stereotypic Movement Disorder
- Disorder of Infancy, Childhood, or Adolescence Not Otherwise Specified

In the standard listings of DSM IV, anxiety disorders, identified previously as Overanxious Disorder of Childhood and Avoidant Disorder of Childhood in DSM-III-R, are incorporated in General Anxiety Disorder and Social Phobia. In DSM-IV-TR, moreover, changes are found in categories of Attention-Deficit and Disruptive Behavior Disorder, and in diagnostic criteria of Tourette's.

In the DSM may be found not only identifying categories but also the clinical criteria appropriate for labeling an individual's behavioral anomalies. For example, in Special Education classes, it is not uncommon to have as students a few whom psychologists assign "autistic-like" symptoms. The question must be asked, 'When is a student "autistic" and when is a student "autistic-like"?' In these cases, the difference is usually defined in terms of the DSM category: does the student meet the minimum criteria? If, in fact, all the criteria are met, the student will be labeled "autistic", but, if only a few symptoms are present, the student falls into the borderline "grey" category: "autistic-like".

Before any intervention can be planned and implemented, pressure often exists to label a child, resulting in the use of the "grey" categories. It is not surprising that such information, which may be referred to by the teacher, leads to dubious or equivocal diagnoses. These vague categories imply not only that behaviors are similar to the ones in the DSM category but also that they share a similar root cause. It is probable that either of these assumptions may mislead the intervention process. For this reason, a more useful procedure will avoid the category label, and, instead, simply describe the behaviors: "Antonio does not initiate play with other children and tends to repeat what others say to him."

Traditional Assessment

Several forms of assessment (Martin, 1988) are currently in use, each closely associated with a particular view of behavioral exceptionalities, and, concurrently, based on assumptions supported by that view. Of the three prominent methods of assessment outlined here, the first involves projective techniques (psychodynamic); the second focuses on psychometric methods (statistical approach to psychodynamic categories); while the third concentrates on behavioral approaches. Following these sections, relevant educational ideas will be discussed in relation to the classroom and the school, as well as to identification, placement, and review processes.

Projective Techniques

Projective techniques represent a psychodynamic approach to assessment based on the idea that an individual faced with an unstructured stimulus will make attempts to impose his/her own structure or meaning. In doing so, that individual reveals personality characteristics and the nature of personal conflicts. This explains why a person, strolling on a beautiful sunny day, looks at the fluffy white clouds in the sky and immediately notices elephants, giraffes, and aardvarks. What is not obvious is whether this phenomenon is associated with the personality and its conflicts. Tests considered to be examples of this technique include: the Rorschach Ink Blot Test (Rorschach, 1951), the Thematic Apperception Test (Murray, 1943) (TAT) and the Draw-a-Person Test (Koppitz, 1968, 1984) (DPT). These tests, which are similar in that they present test stimuli with varying degrees of "structure" – from black and white sketches, ink blots, and even a blank page – are able to reveal personality characteristics and conflicts.

It is interesting to observe that projective tests are administered by psychologists and other mental health professionals, rather than by teachers. These are individuals who have received extensive training in the administration and particularly interpretation of such instruments.

The Rorschach

This test, generally given to adults, which is typically associated with the psychodynamic view, is often depicted by the media as the way to assess mental health. Because norms are not generally used, the examiner extrapolates meaningful information from the client's responses in order to render a clinical interpretation. More recently, since the test dates back to 1951, Exner (1986) has developed age norms for children of 5-16 years.

Only psychologists and psychiatrists are allowed to administer the Rorschach which consists of 10 ink blots, half without color. Test administration takes place in two separate sequences: the free association phase and the inquiry phase. As these standardized ink blots are presented, one card at a time, during the free association period, the question is asked: "What do you see?" Traditionally, the examiner records responses verbatim, indicating length of time before the first response and any behaviors that occur, while today, tape recorders facilitate the task. During the inquiry phase, the examiner first reads back the responses and then inquires about the determinants of responses, that is, their location, color, and form, including, in the last, both shape and outline.

The clinician evaluates the responses of the client on the basis of several criteria. Included in this scheme are the number of popular responses, human content, animal elements, original reactions, human details, anatomy characteristics, and sexual content. Also recorded is the number of replies given to each inkblot.

The clinician focusing on these criteria makes judgments based on observations. For example, persons deemed in the obsessive/depressive range generate fewer responses based on the entire inkblot, and are less likely to provide a great deal of detail. In contrast, a person in the obsessive/compulsive grouping will provide responses based on shape, and their descriptions are likely to reveal either good ego strength or poor reality awareness.

The Thematic Apperception Test (TAT)

A test used with both adults and children, the TAT was first introduced by Morgan and Murray (1935). In this instrument, stimuli consist of 30 cards, of which 29 depict scenes of people engaged in various activities, while one is blank. Cards are marked on the back on the basis of their appropriateness for male or female, and for children and adults.

In the standard testing session, cards are presented, one at time, most individuals being shown fewer than 20 cards. In each case, the individual is asked, first, to make up a story about the scene depicted on the respective card, and, second, to state:

- what is happening in the scene
- what the people are thinking or feeling
- what the outcome of the story will be

As the subject speaks, the stories are recorded verbatim, and, while several scoring systems are available (Varble, 1971), these are mainly used in research. In clinical practice the stories are seldom scored, but, rather, are analyzed by the clinician whose interpretation will be based on :

- a consistent theme, such as dependence, aggression, guilt, etc.
- a figure with whom the storyteller identifies, so that questions about the figure may be asked: how adequate is he/she?; is he/she successful?; is he/she easily pushed around? etc.
- the degree to which the story departs from the actual picture; the extent to which stimulus elements, not depicted on the cards, are introduced into the story

The Children's Apperception Test [2] (CAT)

This projective test, which is similar to the TAT described in the previous section, differs in several ways:

- It uses animal rather than human figures
- It assumes that children may identify more readily with animals than with human figures

Because there is no evidence that children identify more readily with animals than with people, and there is very little research on this measure, clinicians usually have little reason to select the CAT over the TAT.

The Draw-A-Person Test (DPT)

Another projective test is the DPT whose instructions are given to the child: "Draw a picture of a person." Once the child has completed the first drawing, the next instruction is, "Draw a person of the opposite sex."

It is assumed that the child will project into the drawings his/her own body image, reflecting the nature of relevant underlying conflicts, anxieties, and other **personality** characteristics.

In connection with this instrument, interpretive guidelines (Machover,1949, 1960) focus on:

- gender – the first figure drawn is the person with whom the child identifies

- placement on the page – usually the upper left indicates anxiety, while the lower half reflects depression

- size – a small figure suggests depression, withdrawal, anxiety, and poor self-concept, while a large one, aggressiveness, grandiosity

- specific content of the drawings – when there is shading or erasure, this may be a conflict indicator with specific location, while excessive detail reflects obsession in cases of strongly detailed eyes, and ears, paranoia may be suggested

Although teachers have employed the DPT to measure visual motor development, its use as a projective measure is the domain exclusively of psychologists and psychiatrists because they have received special training in interpretation.

In summary, the Rorschach, the TAT, and the DPT are the most commonly used projective tests. Each of them provides an unstructured stimulus with the expectation that the individual's perception – revealed through the response – will reflect personality characteristics and conflicts.

Psychometric Tests (Non-Projective)

Unlike projective tests, psychometric tests are designed on the basis of psychometric principles – a statistical approach – applied to clinical categories rooted in the psychodynamic view. The Minnesota Multiphasic Personality Inventory (MMPI), the Personality Inventory for Children (Lachar, 1993) (PIC-2), and the Personality Inventory for Youth (Lachar, 1993) (PIY) are examples of such surveys that are completed by either the child, the parent, or the teacher. Again, these tests are generally given by psychologists and other mental health professionals who have received extensive training in the interpretation of the findings – rather than by teachers.

Psychometrics, a specialty in the domain of psychology, has as its primary focus the construction of tests using statistical methods to ensure validity and reliability. To fully appreciate this method of test construction, several key concepts which exist in psychometrics require definition:

- construct validity

- test validity

- test reliability

Construct validity guarantees that the concepts measured by the test are independent and verifiable. This is an issue when measuring such concepts as creativity and self-perceptions because there is an absence of consensus about the meaning of these concepts. In addition, a question remains about whether they represent a unique abstraction.

Test validity refers to the test measure's ability to achieve what it is intended to measure. If giving a mathematics test, the teacher will be concerned that mathematics rather than, for instance, reading ability, is being measured.

Finally, *Test reliability* warrants that the same phenomenon will be measured each time the test is administered. A clinician giving a math test on Monday expects that, two weeks later, the same math test will still measure the same math skills exactly the same way in, perhaps, a second candidate.

Psychometrics, then, are judged on the basis not only of their construct and test validity but also on the basis of reliability. Unlike projective tests, these are founded on empirical outcomes obtained from test results of a comparison group(s). Essentially, psychometric tests give information about the individual's performance in comparison with the performances of a normative group – other children of the same age, or, possibly, different exceptional groupings.

How is a Psychometric Test Constructed?

Psychometric tests are constructed differently from projective tests because different assumptions are made about what each test is expected to do. Instead of creating tests to provide information about the nature of unconscious conflicts, designers of psychometric tests assign people to clinical categories on the basis of their answers as they are matched to those of people in respective clinical categories.

If a clinician were pretending, for a minute, that it was necessary to construct a psychometric test to identify people with phobias, people who are depressed, and people with attentional deficit disorders, first, it would be important to find sufficiently large groups of people who were – for these purposes – "normal," that is, a control group. A second group of people diagnosed with phobias, depressions, and attention deficit disorders would be in order. Then, it would be appropriate to construct thousands of True or False items:

- Sometimes I am afraid when I'm walking home late at night.

- I eat breakfast every morning.

- People on the bus look at me, etc.

Finally, people in each of the four groups – the "normals," the phobic, the depressed, and those with attentional disorders – would be asked to respond to all the items. Once all responses were collected, items would be categorized in the following manner:

- items that would be rejected:

   ° items answered "True" by all four groups — these items are thrown out because they do not discriminate among the groups

   ° items answered "False" by all four groups — these items are thrown out because they indicate no discrimination among the groups

As expected, this sorting of items would seriously reduce the number of items left to be included in the hypothetical test.

- The items that would be included:
   ° items answered "True" only by the control group
   ° items answered "False" only by the control group
   ° items answered "True" only by the group with phobias
   ° items answered "False" only by the group with phobias
   ° items answered "True" only by the group with depression
   ° items answered "False" only by the group with depression
   ° items answered "True" only by the group with attentional deficits
   ° items answered "False" only by the group with attentional deficits

This psychometric test is designed to compare a subject's responses with one of the three clinical categories: phobia, depression, attention deficit. A person who answered "True" and "False" to the same items answered "True" and "False" by the attentional deficit sample would be labeled as having an attentional deficit.

One of the limitations of surveys and questionnaires of this sort is the possibility that the subject is not providing genuine responses but instead is giving replies that might please the examiner or place the subject in a "better light". The person's honesty is evaluated by small group of items answered "True" or "False" by all four groups. This set of items, included to establish the reliability of a subject's responses, is called a **Lie** scale.

It is evident that psychometric tests have been carefully constructed to provide an objective evaluation – the scoring and interpretation of test results are stable across the various psychometrists who administer them. This is in sharp contrast to projective tests that depend heavily on the expertise of the test administrator and thus are deemed to be subjective.

The Minnesota Multiphasic Personality Inventory (MMPI) [3]

This test, which is given primarily to adults and sometimes to adolescents, is completed by the individual. Its structure parallels that of the Personality Inventory for Children which will be outlined in greater detail in the following section.

The Personality Inventory For Children (PIC-2)

A statistical test, the PIC has as its first intention the collection of observations about a child (K-12) and then the provision of standard scores. The child's performance on the test can readily be compared with a normative sample. In its overall approach, it is very similar to the MMPI, a self-report test mainly for adults, but it differs: the PIC-2 is usually administered to the parents of children 3-16 years (Lachar, 1999). Sometimes, it is also given to the teachers of these children.

In 1989, a major revision of the PIC, which involved re-writing the first 280 of the original items, generated a self-report format known as the Personal Inventory for Youth (PIY). As a result, it is now possible to gather information from parents and teachers[4], as well as from the student, using similar content and style of questions. When evaluating concordance, related to the way each test-taker perceives the student, these items represent important variables.

Originally, the PIC consisted of 600 true/false items to be completed by parents. Then, in 1982, the structure was altered to allow either the first 131, or 280, or 420 items, or all 600 to be completed independently, in order to generate a measure (Lachar, Gdowski & Snyder, 1984). In its most recent revision (Lahar & Gruber, 1995), items with negatively worded statements, such as "My child never had cramps in the legs", to be answered "false" if the condition does not exist, have been removed to eliminate confusion. In addition, the word "parent(s)" is substituted for "mother or father". The results of this last revision and standardization include:

- For parents and sometimes teachers, the PIC-2 consisting of 275 statements, 3 validity scales, 9 scales, and 21 subscales

- For children and youth, the PIY

For the inventory, three validity scales have been designed to detect examples of defensiveness in responding to items:

1. a *lie* scale identifies the situation in which the child is presented in a better than true light

2. a *frequency* scale identifies tendencies, exaggeration, and randomness

3. a *defensiveness* scale identifies the responses shown when the rater is being protective

Both the PIC-2 and PIY consist of nine (9) clinical, or content, scales and 21 subscales, all of which are derived from responses to items. The various scales and subscales provide information about:

1. cognitive impairment
   a. inadequate abilities
   b. poor achievement
   c. developmental delay
2. impulsivity and distractibility
   a. disruptive behavior
   b. fearlessness
3. delinquency
   a. antisocial behavior
   b. dyscontrol
   c. noncompliance
4. family dysfunction
   a. conflict among members
   b. parent maladjustment
5. reality distortions
   a. developmental deviations
   b. hallucinations and delusions

6. somatic concerns
   a. psychosomatic preoccupation
   b. muscular tension and anxiety
7. psychological discomfort
   a. fear and worry
   b. depression
   c. sleep disturbances and preoccupation with death
8. social withdrawal
   a. social introversion
   b. isolation
9. social skills deficits
   a. limited peer status
   b. conflict with peers

For additional information about any of the items as well as about details of these tests, the reader is encouraged to refer to Lachar (1999) and, for information about other tests, to look at Maruish (1999).

In the new revision, previous concerns about collecting data only from parents have been rectified this has been achieved by developing PIY to be completed by the student. Another concern, in three parts, relates to the actual administration of the test: the time taken, the reliance on items that are read, and the nature of the items themselves. These elements have been addressed by reducing the number of items from 600 to 275. In addition, a second profile of eight shortened scales is now available for screening and measuring the effectiveness of interventions.

A major factor to be considered in this and other tests is the student's and/or parent's ability to read and comprehend the items easily. Although the language structure of these items has been revised to make them more readily understood, as mentioned previously, the teacher/assessor should make available the option of having the items read aloud, if it is necessary. A further concern is that, because the test inventory includes descriptions of extreme behaviors, some parents may find certain items upsetting. To avert anxiety, clinicians sometimes warn parents to be aware that not all items will be applicable to all children.

Behavioral Approaches to Assessment

Behavioral approaches to assessment vary greatly from the methods previously outlined because, unlike the procedures used in the other approaches, in these strategies, information about the student is generally gathered in the student's own environment (**naturalistic**), that is, in the place where difficulties actually arise. The methods consist of:

- noting the *inappropriate* behaviors and the setting in which they take place

- rank ordering the behaviors' list in priority on the basis of quality, duration, and frequency

- developing, at the outset, strict definitions of the behaviors to be observed

- counting and charting the target behaviors

- noting the antecedents – listing events which occurred immediately **prior** to the behavior

- noting the consequences – describing what occurs immediately **after** the behavior

From the behavior S-O-R-S model illustrated later in this section, it is evident that the teacher is attempting to understand the behavior on the basis of the elements contained in the operant conditioning model. By identifying the triggers, the student variables, the student response, and the consequences that follow it, the teacher will discover the contingencies and eventually be in a position to predict the student's behavior in a particular context.

Checklists

Although behaviorists encourage direct observation of student behavior as an assessment approach, sometimes, there is a need to rely initially on questionnaires completed by the child, parent, or teacher, to collect as much information as possible about the child's behavior. Examples of such tools, referred to as questionnaires or checklists, include:

- The Revised Problem Behavior Checklist (Quay & Peterson, 1996) consisting of 89 items in six subscales: Conduct Disorders, Socialized Aggression, Attention Problems/Immaturity, Anxiety/Withdrawal, Psychotic Behavior, and Motor Excess.

- The Child Problem Behavior Checklist (Achenbach & Edelbrock, 1991) has approximately 118 items with teacher, parent, youth report, and observation forms. The form for parents has a Hyperactivity Factor, a Social Competence Factor, and several questions to assess the home environment (chores, activities, etc.).

- The Louisville Behavior Checklist (Miller, 1977).

- The Eyberg Child Behavior Inventory (Eyberg & Ross, 1978; and Eyberg, Ross, and Robinson, 1980).

To help parents to identify positive behaviors, a variety of checklists is also available on the Internet [5].

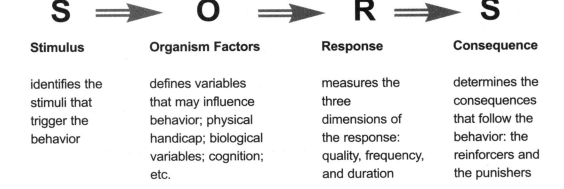

S ⟹	O ⟹	R ⟹	S
Stimulus	**Organism Factors**	**Response**	**Consequence**
identifies the stimuli that trigger the behavior	defines variables that may influence behavior; physical handicap; biological variables; cognition; etc.	measures the three dimensions of the response: quality, frequency, and duration	determines the consequences that follow the behavior: the reinforcers and the punishers

Two Major Behavioral Designs

Traditionally associated with behavioral approaches are two major designs, the Reversal Design and the Multiple Baseline. In each of these two models, the procedure involves the gathering of information about a student in the setting in which the behavior occurs. Subsequently an evaluation of the dynamics of the behavior is elicited in order to generate an intervention. Associated with these behavioral designs are methodologies which may be applied either by teachers or by clinicians. Frequently employed in the research setting, the Reversal Design, for example, is used in situations where ethical standards are not contravened. For reasons to be outlined later, in the school context, the Multiple Baseline is the method most conducive to success. In the following paragraphs, these two designs and their applications are presented.

The Reversal Design (ABAB)

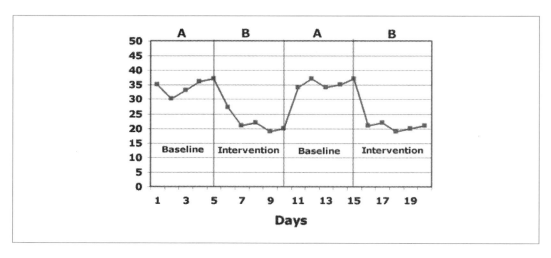

Figure 3 -1. **The ABAB Design**

In this methodology, four distinct time periods are involved, during which data are first collected and, then, subsequently, graphed. Included in these time elements are, at the outset, a *baseline* period which is the space of time when no attempt is made to alter the behavior in any way; the second phase is an *intervention* period, during which treatment is applied.

Hoping to establish a cause/effect relationship between the treatment procedures and the resulting behavioral change, the ABAB design attempts to respond to the question: "Is Treatment A responsible for the behavioral changes which are observed?". In order to deal with this query, the baseline information must first be gathered. Having begun by defining the target behavior, the teacher records each occurrence of that particular behavior over several days. Once a stable rate of responding is recorded, the teacher will first apply an intervention (the B phase) and then observe the results. If the number of occurrences of the target behavior increases, the intervention is seen to be reinforcing the behavior. If the number of occurrences decreases, the intervention – because it serves as a penalty – is punishing and therefore decreasing incidence of the behavior. When, the number of occurrences does not change, however, the intervention can be established as having no effect on the behavior.

During the B phase, that is. the intervention phase, as a result of introducing a new method of interacting with the student, the teacher anticipates one of these three outcomes. Probably, too, the student's behavior will change in the direction that was planned. Finally, in order to ensure that the intervention is indeed responsible for the alteration in the behavior, the teacher, by returning to baseline – the second A phase – will first remove the intervention, and, finally, will re-introduce the intervention – the last B phase. In order to establish cause/effect, the teacher ascertains that the rate of behavior, as expected, returns to the original level during baseline. Then, when treatment is re-applied, there is a return to the rate noted in the first intervention. Because determination of cause/effect relationships allows for model building about the nature of a child's difficulty, and because it also minimizes trial-and-error aspects, it is a very powerful procedure. Instances can be shown, however, that suggest it is not appropriate, even in the research context. If there is a problem, it will probably arise in the third time interval, at the point when the design requires a return to baseline, that is, to the removal of the intervention. At this stage, a risk emerges: either the recently demonstrated behavior may be extinguished or a maladaptive behavior may be promoted, especially if the cause/effect relationship is indeed present. Given the possibility that the behavior in question may be, in an autistic child, either "speaking" or "self-mutilation", it may be necessary to limit the intervention or to stop it. Because these behaviors are of such value clinically, the clinician's ethic will warrant foregoing the firm knowledge that the intervention unequivocally caused the behavior to change. For this important reason, the teacher and the clinical practitioner may, if it is appropriate, limit the design to an AB model, or, instead, may choose the Multiple Baseline Design.

Multiple Baseline Design

Unlike the previous design, which attempts to isolate one target behavior, chosen from a number of behaviors listed in priority order, the Multiple Baseline Design attempts to address several behaviors concurrently. For example, "aggressive" behavior or "on-task" behavior will often be mentioned as if referring to just one behavior, while each of these terms, in fact, represents an entire **cluster of behaviors.**

Because teachers most often mention "on-task" behavior as the type of activity to be promoted in the classroom, this concept should be examined. "On-task" behavior has certain meanings, each of which depends on the observable behaviors that are present when a child is "on task". Some of these are noticeable, for example, when:

- The student is looking at the materials associated with the task

- The student is seated in an appropriately designated area

- The student has all the relevant materials, that is, those required for the task, close at hand (e.g., books, paper, pens, etc.)

- The student produces some output such as writing or answers to questions, etc., relevant to the task's demands

When a *multiple baseline* design is being established, the requirement exists that a cluster of behaviors – such as the group which makes up the on-task behavior – be subdivided into its elemental parts. With this special focus in place, the level of occurrence of each basic behavior may be determined during a baseline period prior to the introduction of an intervention. On the basis of this information, *only one* of these basic behaviors will initially be considered for purposes of intervention.

When focusing on the *multiple baseline* design, the teacher hypothesizes that changing one behavior in the cluster will result in the alteration of the other behaviors. For example, depending on the goal, there could be an increase or decrease in the rate of response, assuming, of course, that all the behaviors in the cluster are interconnected. It follows, then, that if there is no change in the behaviors in the cluster – especially those that are not the focus of an intervention – these behaviors are independent of each other, which means they are not related. The design, therefore, is not only economical, because interventions on a single behavior may also change other related behaviors, but also allows the teacher to discover the relationships between behaviors.

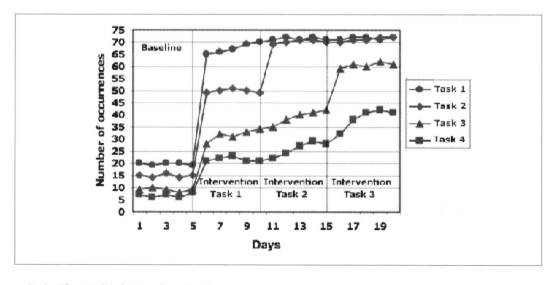

Figure 3 -2. The Multiple Baseline Design

78

More appropriate to the classroom context than the ABAB design, the *multiple baseline* format has some advantages. Here, it should be emphasized that teachers are usually concerned about clusters of behaviors, such as on-task behaviors, cooperative behaviors, sharing behaviors, etc. By allowing teachers to focus on only one behavior at a time, the *multiple baseline* design simplifies the intervention process. This means it provides extra value in that it represents further economy of resources. Such an economy is an essential aspect in a classroom of 30 students, especially if the other behaviors in the cluster are also affected by the intervention.

Summary

Because, as is usually the case, assessment is a process of inquiry motivated by questions, each type of assessment presented so far has attempted to answer questions relevant to its paradigm[6]. Projective techniques, for example, are interested in answering the question: "What unconscious conflicts are involved in this person's behaviors?", while Psychometric tests ask: "What category of behaviors – or form of labeling – is reflected in the way a person perceives him/herself?". On the other hand, when behavioral assessments attempt to identify the contingencies associated with inappropriate behaviors, they are asking, "What causes this behavior and what consequences affect it?" Only when the designs arise from the behavioral paradigm can they be implemented by teachers, whereas the others are regularly administered by psychologists and psychiatrists who are qualified by their professional training.

Educational Assessment

Teachers who approach the task of "inquiry" do so with their own sets of questions: their first concern is probably to determine why a student is behaving inappropriately not only in the classroom, but in the hallways and the school yard. As a correlation, and probably more importantly, the further question is asked: "Why is the student not meeting his/her learning potential?" Far-reaching questions of this sort are usually divided into smaller, more easily answered questions, an initial one of which, focusing on the nature of the student's problem, speaks from an educational perspective: "Is this a primary or a secondary behavior problem?"

Primary versus Secondary Behavioral Problems

Whether the nature of the student's problem is *primary* or *secondary* is a question that addresses and attempts to see the problem from its root cause. A *primary* behavioral exceptionality implies that both the student's behavioral problem and/or the learning disorder stem from social/emotional causes. Following from this idea is that treatment practices, for a primary behavioral problem, will focus on removing or alleviating these social/emotional causes although sometimes the emphasis is on helping the student to learn ways to undermine the strength of their impact. If, however, the problems are deemed to reflect *secondary* causes, then elements other than social/emotional factors are expected to cause the behavioral difficulties. In this instance, the problems may have roots that relate either to intellectual or information-processing factors or to physical causes. It is not uncommon, moreover, that a student defined as having certain exceptionalities will manifest behavioral problems among one or more other consequences of the relevant exceptionality. While social/emotional consequences such as frustration, depression, and persistent anger, among others, are likely to be present, appropriate intervention would involve modifying the factors that cause them. Normally, the teacher may be able to modify the student's secondary behavior problem in order to reduce frustration and depression. Such a result may be a by-product of tailoring learning activities or teaching a set of new skills.

In certain circumstances, however, a behavior problem resulting from secondary causes might require modifications and interventions that will focus primarily on the student's behavior. Such an approach should be taken when:

> - the student's behavioral problems have escalated to the point of overshadowing the primary exceptionality
>
> - the student is reluctant to or refuses to partake in activities
>
> - the student, an adolescent, is involved in peer-group and power issues

Which methods, after all, should a teacher use to judge the severity of a student's behavior? In Chapter One, as a means of evaluating the severity of a behavioral problem, a general model was outlined. In this structure, observations of the quality, frequency, and intensity of behavior demonstrated the methods a teacher could employ to judge its severity. In the section which follows, a specific set of questions is presented that will enable teachers to evaluate severity in classroom contexts.

When a teacher has an awareness of the severity of a student's behavior, there is a chance to ascertain the resources required to address the student's problem. Although, in some cases, teachers find it adequate to make modifications to the student's program within the bounds of the classroom, other situations may be severe enough to need either specialized personnel or other placement prospects. In the inquiry process followed by the teacher, questions are further shaped by the nature of the classroom setting. Unlike the events that occur in clinical settings, classrooms imply that teachers provide instruction to children and adolescents. That these young persons have varying degrees of social and emotional adjustments means that in one classroom there may exist a continuum from some who are very healthy to others who are not at all healthy. A range of questions may be devised, according to the teacher's need to find the severity levels of behavior.

Teacher Judgment of Severity

Intensity	Does the activity disrupt the child's other activities?
Frequency	How often does the behavior occur?
Duration	How long does the behavior last?
Appropriateness	Is the behavior a reasonable response to the situation?
Assessibility of circumstances	Is there an obvious reason for the behavior?
Comparison with the maturity of the other class members	Is the behavior commonly exhibited by some members or all members of the class?
Manageability	Is the behavior influenced by management efforts?
Contagion	Do other children copy the behavior?

Periodically, a teacher will find it necessary to review decisions that may determine suitability of a program. By this means, it will be possible to decide, among three categories, certain useful information: whether a student should be formally identified as having behavioral problems; whether a student's present placement is appropriate; and whether a student still warrants the original program and placement.

In such a survey, answers to the questions cited here will determine whether in-class modifications are likely to be adequate in addressing the needs of the student. If the student's problem has escalated beyond the resources of the regular classroom, a decision may have to be made about interventions external to the classroom. At this stage, a case study is usually compiled for presentation to a treatment group. Often, the next level of referral is a multi-disciplinary team, within the school board itself, responsible for making identification, for deciding on placement, and for reviewing decisions.

Preparation of a Case Study

Once questions about severity are evaluated, if it is decided that the student requires services not available in the regular class, in order to prepare a case study, relevant information will be gathered from a variety of sources possibly by the teacher. The purpose here is the development of a comprehensive overview to integrate information from all available sources, in order to present a view of the "whole" child.

First of all, the starting point should be the several sources of information that are easily accessible: student records; records from teachers who have previously taught the student and are still at the school; remembered knowledge gleaned from teachers no longer at the school who can be telephoned. Here also, valuable information comes from the principal; the school secretary; the parents; and the student. In this careful process, a basic essential is the acquiring of parental permission[7] for the release of material from doctors and psychologists as well as from other professionals, information which may arrive weeks or months later.

Once the inquiry process begins, the teacher is likely to discover that a large amount of information about a given student is available from immediate sources. Unless the gathering process is efficient and economic, however, and the teacher has clear sense of the relevance and location of data, the process can be overwhelming. Directing the process in an orderly manner will identify missing information; for example, a student's vision may not ever have been checked.

In the subsections immediately following, those issues deemed to be important in the initial stages of data collection will be outlined. While this framework is presented primarily for the consideration of teachers, it is by no means all-inclusive. In addition, teachers should recognize the need to personalize the process not only for themselves but also as for each student.

Once a case has been selected for action, the teacher is encouraged to formulate a theory about the student's behavior, which will focus on providing an explanation, while also motivating the gathering of information. At first, this process will ascertain whether sufficient information exists to elicit a workable explanation. When this objective is reached, the scope of the inquiry will be enlarged. Concurrently or very soon, it will be useful to identify potential sources of additional information.

Data Collection

A large amount of information is readily available in school records as well as from personnel who have worked with an individual. By highlighting and outlining useful elements to be found in these sources, the details below will suggest ways in which such data may be meaningful to the case study. In addition, awareness of these elements may assist the teacher to ask further questions whose answers are available in other contexts.

A teacher who is initiating the inquiry process for a student with behavioral problems will find the following categories useful:

Attendance

Examining the pattern of attendance of a student, over several years, can contribute to an understanding of the nature and duration not only of relevant truancy problems but also of possible school phobias. For example, in the life of a child during a particular year, an increase or decrease in school attendance may identify either periods of relative calm and stability or stages of upheaval and crisis. Subsequently, such information can be explored further in both the parent and the student interviews.

Why is regular attendance so important to the socio-emotional welfare of students? When time is conceptualized as a flowing river, it is clear that regular attendance creates opportunities for a series of shared experiences with classmates. A correlation is that such sharing potentially contributes to a sense of group cohesion and belonging. In contrast, an absence of several days from school disrupts this flow of shared experience, making the student susceptible to feelings of alienation. Today, last Monday's best friend is now, several days later, someone else's best friend. For reasons such as this, students often resent leaving the class, even in order to participate in special programs, feeling that important events will occur in their absence.

Mobility

When a family moves several times, from place to place, a number of different schools will necessarily be attended by the student. As may be anticipated, such a pattern has serious implications for the development of social skills, especially in the realm of peer interaction. In a typical pattern, a student is not registered in a given school for enough time to develop long-term relationships. No sooner has the student begun to develop strategies for infiltrating the existing peer group, than the family leaves that school district. Now, faced with another school, a new teacher, unfamiliar classmates, the student is at a severe disadvantage. Also probable is that, during a particular period of time, an increase or decrease in the number of moves made by the family may reflect either a crisis or a form of instability – family separation, divorce, etc.

Also relevant here is, ironically, the opposite situation, the case in which, for several years, the student has remained in the same school. In such a circumstance, it is useful to question whether either the school or the class dynamics may be contributing to the student's maladaptive behavior. Within a given school context, a student will often acquire a role or earn a label which in turn generates expectations about the student's behavior. Trapped into meeting such expectations, for example, identification as the class clown or the school bully, etc., the student is not able to change.

Academic History

Although a student's behavior cannot be deemed to be separate from or independent of the teacher's academic expectations, many other elements may also contribute to student behavior. Among the possible causes of trouble, all or some of family, classroom, teacher, motivation , and peer factors may interact, but how may a teacher disentangle these threads? Beginning to paint the picture requires a look at teachers' comments as well as grades in the student's record.

Age of entry

When forced, for an extended period of time, to be away from their primary care givers, some young children suffer from a separation anxiety. For a variety of reasons, because they may find it difficult to feel safe in the classroom, small children develop feelings which may become precursors to subsequent chronic attendance problems.

Also of importance to the broader attendance picture are maturational factors which frequently contribute to a "poor" beginning. Some children, not yet developmentally ready to tackle certain classroom tasks, seem always to fall short of the expectations both of the teacher and of their parents. If feedback from teachers and parents, as well as from other students, generates anxious internal states in the child, subsequent attitudes to school work, classrooms, school, and teachers may be negatively affected. An example of classical conditioning as blatant as this one will probably be difficult to extinguish, leading as it does to the child's chronic frustration in school experiences.

Date of last vision and/or hearing examination

In any case study, of maximum importance will be information about potentially problematic physical factors, specifically as they relate to a student's difficulty of adjustment. Overlooking such factors can confound, prolong, and cloud an investigation. For this reason, the possibility of problems stemming from physical causes must be investigated, and, if found irrelevant, discounted. When such physical phenomena are present, they must form the basis for re-directing the evaluation.

Often associated with children who have visual and/or hearing challenges, secondary behavioral problems are of major importance. If behavioral problems are found to result from physical disabilities of this kind, then the nature and course of the intervention will be expected to change. For example, in a social situation in which responses depend on paying attention to facial expression, students with visual impairments may be at an unfortunate disadvantage. To cite a different kind of problem, for children with intellectual challenges, social skills involving high-level thinking and reasoning skills, for example moral reasoning, or aspects of altruism, may be problematic. A further consideration involves social skills that rely on receptive and expressive language. This awareness on the part of teachers applies not only to children with innate language problems but also to those with ESL background, (that is, English as a Second Language). In this general grouping may also be found students in the category called "slow learners".

Accounts of injury or disease

In yet another category of health considerations, records of accident and disease must be carefully examined as well as analyzed for their impact on behavior. Cases have been recorded that demonstrate behavioral changes after a student has suffered from a head injury, such as occurs in a fall, a car crash, or a diving accident. In unique situations, radical changes in behavior have resulted from brain tumors. In such circumstances, almost to be expected, physical factors are able to explain the onset of behavioral difficulties.

In other cases, experiences surrounding illness have been seen to affect student behavior. For example, a child's illness and/or lengthy stay in the hospital may explain aspects of the child's perception of self, of the world, of the dynamics in the home, but especially of the role the child plays within the family itself. Commonly, for example, the exceptional student is or becomes the focus of household attention.

Medication

For the assessors who are surveying the entire picture of a student's history, it is important to determine whether the student is taking medication. Because there are side effects associated with most medication, information about each respective drug must be gathered. As a first premise, the teacher-assessor may be able to dissociate the behavior linked to the medication from the student's problems rooted in the 'true' condition. In a typical case, several medications may come into the picture: for example, while one form may be recommended as treatment for a problem, another or several different prescriptions will be required to counteract the negative side effects of the primary drug. When, moreover, the student is taking recreational drugs, the same concerns must be demonstrated by those analyzing the case.

In the world of recreational and therapeutic drugs, addiction, which can take physiological or psychological forms, becomes an issue that must, in any case study, be firmly addressed. When taking

Rytalin, for example, the student may be as convinced as the friend using a street drug that the chemical is responsible not only for the internal state and the behavioral outcomes, but also for any productivity or lack of it. On the other hand, deprived of their chemicals, both students may feel diminished to the point of being unable to function.

Despite concerns associated with the side effects of medication, the relatively small number of students likely to respond to drug therapy must necessarily be referred to physicians (see Chapter Eight).

Methods and strategies used in early literacy development

While student perceptions of school work are related partly to classroom methods and partly to the content of the curriculum presented to students, from the other view, the teacher's standpoint, a proportion of students with behavioral problems will present accompanying academic problems. In view of such complex interactions, the case study being prepared must focus not only on the academic but also on the behavioral problems that need to be addressed.

Because of the realization that school work is profoundly dependent on literacy skills, it is a correlation that student attitudes toward classroom requirements are regularly found to originate in literacy development at its earliest stages. Moreover, associated with the student's long-term feelings and attitudes are the strategies used in those early stages. If, for example, the student has difficulty today with literacy skills, finding out the way reading was originally introduced – in that student's learning history – will provide information about how to proceed. One possibility is that the methodology initially used overlooked the need to present skills the student possibly now needs. On the other hand, the student's feelings about literacy may, by now, have become so negative that an altogether new approach to reading is indicated.

Management system used by previous teachers

It is clear that the way other teachers in the past have dealt with a student, in earlier pupil-teacher relationships, will directly influence the present perception of any teacher by the student. Commonly, the student may define teachers either as caring individuals who try to help students or as adults who push kids around. Any position on this continuum is also possible for the student to hold. At the heart of the matter is the realization that the concept of "teacher", acquired earlier by a student, will be significant to all subsequent student-teacher relationships.

What or who has been successful with this child?

When building a case study, investigators often become so focused on *what went wrong* that *what went right* is often overlooked. Knowing what works is like hitting pay dirt! Thus recovering as much data as possible about past successes will begin to give the diagnosing teacher insight into a different aspect of the student. Such positive information may also serve to reduce the range of trial and error normally used in arriving at an explanation of the student's behavior.

A broad knowledge of the past, especially of the situations and the people who have motivated the child to success, is information suitable for the classroom, ready to be used immediately. For example, if an earlier learning experience shows that computer activities are likely to have positive connotations, some time allowed on the computer can be made contingent on the completion of math work. If a reading problem is a chronic concern, the teacher can designate a "buddy" to read aloud to the student from the social science textbook. When, moreover, ongoing problematic situations persist, the student and the teacher can meet after school to review the accomplishments of the day. These are just a few of the ways in which decisions in the present can influence the structuring of the student's program for immediate use. In the daily context, a certain degree of confidence can be gained in these ways by the teacher who is awaiting completion of the identification process.

Teachers' comments and diagnosis

In the preparation of a case study, teachers' comments recorded in earlier report cards in the student's general file should be read carefully. Initially, reading between the lines will provide useful information about previous teachers' beliefs regarding the root of the student's problems. While it is also important for the teacher reading these records to remain objective, the comments are likely to reveal information about the earlier student-teacher interaction in addition to hinting at causes of behavioral matters.

Also noteworthy in this phase of the investigation is either missing information or incompatible information. As an example, in the earlier report cards, comments may have been made about the child's reading difficulty while nothing was said about the child's visual impairment. In another instance, remarks about a reading problem will be found only in the Grade 4 and Grade 7 reports. An overview of all information, both present and missing, will, of necessity, be considered relevant in the solution of the puzzle.

Formal testing and actions taken

Always, the possibility exists that, sometime in the past when problems seemed severe, formal procedures were initiated for the student. The records of such an analysis will be in the appropriate files. In the setting today, the circumstances surrounding the earlier formal testing must be deemed relevant. Even more essential is the definition of the aims, the focus, and the outcome of that past process. Were recommendations made in the past? Were they implemented? If not, what circumstances prevailed in the decisions made? Sometimes, a family that learns the test results and recommendations from the school, will withdraw the child, moving immediately to a new school in another school board. If such information about past events can be tracked down, it may provide insight into ways of proceeding. It may also save time and effort while avoiding a repetition of the previous pitfalls.

Parent Interview

Despite being in school during a large proportion of their time awake, most children are believed to be strongly affected by the values of their parents. Because such an emphasis exists, in relation to the contribution of the home environment to the child's behavior, and, by extension, the child's mental representation of the world, teachers who plan to treat a child's condition must look positively on the role of the parents. Instead of perceiving parents as the cause of the child's problem, the teacher will actively enlist these caregivers who may serve several informative functions as participants in the child's treatment team. These are their qualifications for such a role:

> - they have known the child longest and therefore have information about the child's history
>
> - they have developed a personal theory about the child's problem that includes facets related to the school's role
>
> - they may be required, as parents, to implement new ways of encouraging their child's behavior at home in order to support treatment measures

Often, because calls from teachers have come to be identified with their child's inappropriate behavior, parents may not be receptive to overtures from teachers. In the passage of time, moreover, the parents may develop certain attitudes and beliefs about themselves, the teachers, and their child. For example, they may feel helpless about affecting change in the child's behavior at school: "What do you expect me to do about it? I'm not there!" Other, underlying attitudes may influence parental hesitation:

> - they may feel responsible for the child's behavior: "The teacher must think I'm a bad parent!"
>
> - they may feel that the teacher is unfair: "Teachers have never liked my child, probably because they don't like people from Antarctica."
>
> - they might feel powerless to affect the child's behavior: "This child is unlike my other children. He will not listen!"

In spite of the kinds of concern indicated by these typical parental comments, the teacher may elicit many useful types of information from parents whose contribution and support will optimize the student's chances for socio-emotional and academic growth.

Culture and language spoken in the home

In every individual family, the culture of the home implies a variety of social values often differing from those of the dominant culture but nevertheless motivating the child. An examination of these may serve to explain relevant behavior, especially if the child is a socialized individual whose implicit, as well as, perhaps, explicit assumptions about the world have been formed outside the dominant culture. In most democratic societies, the culture of any person is officially deemed as valid as the dominant culture. Because of this tenet within the society, the teacher, with the support of parents, may be able to establish which behavioral changes can be hoped for in the child's repertoire. The alternative outcome is a clash that will continue to confuse and torment the student. In an ideal working arrangement, the treatment team may decide to identify the similarities and differences existing in the two cultures, moving on to define, for the child, the expectations of one culture that will be more appropriate than those of the other, according to time/place variables. In addition, the student must be helped to become aware of those cultural values and expectations that are against the law of the new country. Such emphases in analysis and planning, known to the child to be accepted by both parents and teacher, will encourage the child to learn to discriminate. As the child has experience in choosing between cultural expectations and settings from the two sources, relevant details will be reinforced subsequently in each setting[8].

While the role of language in social behavior is often overlooked, it is true that compelling guidelines exist in all cultures, dictating the type of language to be used in specific settings. Referred to by linguists as **registers**, these language customs or terms represent specialized forms of language associated with unique social contexts. Usually, in any language, one form of speech will be employed when talking to babies, pets, and lovers. In most languages, a different form altogether is customarily used with superiors, parents, and older persons. Of course, use of the "baby" register when talking to the "boss" is inappropriate, but because these registers are implicit, children whose first language is not English cannot be expected to acquire appropriate forms simply by modeling. Even native speakers of English sometimes fail to use an appropriate register, as often happens when the traditional emphasis, common in the past, is no longer given to certain language forms. An example of this tendency is the dropping of the "g" in everyday speech , where such casualness is appropriate among peers: "We're goin' to the beach", but Standard English, as represented in the classroom, expects the "g" to be spoken. For speakers of English, the use of appropriate registers is an adaptive skill to be patiently acquired for use in relationships, in school, and in the work place.

Also an important part of language-awareness, especially for the ESL[9] student, is the aspect of language called **pragmatics**[10]. In this context-dependent form of oral language, the intention and message of the speaker are extrapolated not only from spoken words but also from the speaker's body language as well as the immediate circumstances. Ignoring the context – that is, what else is going on at the time – makes the meaning of the message ambiguous. For example, during a quiet tutorial, when Mr. Mortezavi, the math teacher, says, "Mark, close the door!" the intended message, aside from its literal meaning could be, "I'm going to tell you something that no one else should hear, while an equally useful meaning could be, "It's too noisy outside in the hall."

In many daily situations, ESL students, and, in some cases, students with learning disabilities, are also easily confused by idiomatic expressions; for example, "It rained cats and dogs" as well as by irony and jokes[11]. Although it is not possible to forewarn newcomers about each kind of language ambiguity, somehow students must be made aware not only that these forms exist but, more importantly, that their meaning is not literal. When outlining such concerns as these, a teacher can clearly demonstrate how important a role language plays in social interactions.

Perception and expectations of the child

Whether as a loser, as a black-sheep, or possibly as an angel who is always picked on, the way parents perceive their child affects both the child's treatment by others and the child's self perception. Because people behave in accordance with their perceptions – as the Cognitive view holds – these personally held perceptions, if they can be discovered and talked about, may shed some light on the student's behavior.

When typical parental expectations are overheard, they often include such comments as "He'll drop out of school when he is sixteen" or "She'll be a brain surgeon", indicating future choices that the child may choose to adopt or rebel against. While children's self-image and self-concept are known to be shaped largely by parental values and expectations, both children and adolescents will appear to test and reject them, eventually, however, incorporating them, with maturity, into their own value systems.

Routines

While many students live in fairly regimented home situations, others, from day to day, experience very few rules or notice examples of constancy. Often, the daily running of the household may shed some light on the child's reaction not only to the structure of the classroom but also to other school settings. For example, Kayhan may come from a home in which constant and regimented routines are maintained, while Stefana's home is unpredictable, especially in terms of bedtimes, mealtimes, chores, etc. Because of being predisposed by these environments, Kayhan may find he has not developed the skills needed to structure proceedings in an unstructured classroom. While he will find the lack of discipline difficult to handle, Stefana, in contrast, when she is enrolled in a very traditional, structured classroom, may rebel. For her, all efforts to limit her in any way will be resisted, as she is not accustomed to stringent controls. In both these instances in which problems result for the child, the culprit is a mis-match between home and classroom. When inappropriate behavior results, an observant and knowledgeable teacher may recognize what is at the heart of the predicament[12].

Developmental milestones

When assessors are building a picture of the influences on a student's behavior, information from family members relating to the development of walking, talking, toilet training, etc. is important. Especially useful for the identification of slow motor development and language problems, these elements provide knowledge about the child's learning history as well as revealing data about early parent-child relationships.

Disease and trauma

Always a good source of detail about early childhood stages, parents are usually aware of diseases or trauma in the family's health history, enabling them to explain aspects of the student's behavior. In a list of such elements, allergies, head injuries, and operations, among other health considerations, would be helpful to know about.

Interaction with family members

In the world of learning to get along with other human beings, within the framework of a pecking order, the family provides the initial context. By exploring typical interactions of the student with parents, other adults, and siblings, the teacher-assessor will be able to evaluate the way knowledge of social mores, values, and expectations has been inculcated. Not uncommonly, students will replicate home-learned styles of interaction in the classroom, and, in some cases, will displace feelings intended for family members, diverting them to teachers and peers. Observing the way parents treat their child will pattern the child's initial concept of adult-child relationship, a notion which incorporates a larger information package. Included are the ways the student fits into the family organization, especially relating to chores and other responsibilities. In addition, it is valuable to learn about methods used to cause the student to comply with and contribute to the family expectations and setting; for example, knowing what happens when the student violates a family rule will enlighten the teacher about how to react to similar classroom aberrations.

Child's after-school activities, hobbies

In order to obtain a complete profile of the student, any activities that are engaged in outside school should be examined. Does the child, before and after school, have contact either with adults or with other children? Or, from the other perspective, is this student usually engaged in such a solitary activity as watching TV?

Broadly accepted, the belief is that contact by children with other children of the same age, that is, their peers, helps to promote social interactions and, subsequently, to increase feelings of belonging. If a particular student has an established social network, assessors will be helped by becoming familiar with the goals and values of that social group. To understand the student's behavior, it is also important to define what is meant by "a good influence" and then to ask whether this particular group could be said to serve that function.

Health: diet, sleep, vision, hearing, dental condition, etc.

As a means of rounding off the picture of the total student, assessors will find it useful to explore the health condition of the student, a process which may indicate whether there is appropriate parental involvement. In the household environment, for instance, parent awareness can range from pre-occupation to neglect. Knowledge that relevant health information presents no profound difficulties will allow the teacher to dismiss physical problems as the basis of the student's behavior. When a child is experiencing school difficulties, however, periodic vision and hearing examinations are essential because such a large part of the day is spent in both reading and listening. Because dental examinations, too, are basic to the individual's well-being, helping parents access support services, as well as scheduling and financing, may become necessary. As is obvious from generally accepted medical advice, the nature of diet and sleep impacts everyone's life, but especially the lives of the young, on a daily basis. In order to learn, children must receive adequate nutrition as well as sleep, two elements carefully noted in Maslow's hierarchy of needs. Exploring solutions to support parent initiatives on these two fronts is an important early step in addressing the student's problems.

The Student Interview

In the same way that parents have a contribution to make to the student's program, the young person will also be expected to adopt an active role; without this support, any change is likely to be superficial. For this reason, the student must assume responsibility for constructive change in three major ways: by being willing to provide vital personal information; by verbalizing or writing or dictating a list of personal goals and aspirations; and, finally, by showing co-operation through an investment in the program designed by the treatment team.

A student who is perceived to be taking responsibility for personal recovery must be empowered through two aspects of the team's activities: first, by being granted a voice in the accumulation of information; and second, by being made a participant in the decision-making process.

Best and worst subjects

Because the student has feelings and beliefs regarding different aspects of the curriculum, it is important to know what the individual defines as best or worst subjects, placing the others along a continuum. While sometimes revealing curricular strengths, weaknesses, and interests, such data may also demonstrate the compatibility of teachers with the immediate needs of the student. Usually, students tend to like activities that they themselves perceive as simple while habitually tending to dislike frustrating activities. What one student finds easy, another may be unable to grasp, so varied are learning capabilities and styles. When some activities seem too difficult[13], students will often choose to try those which they can share with people they like.

Perceptions, expectations, and explanations of personal problem

When setting up a structure of information for a case study, it is important for the teacher to empathize with the student in order to develop a coherent theory to explain behavioral difficulties. This leap is accomplished by the teacher's developing insight into the ways in which the student sees and understands the world. Also important for the teacher, at this stage, is focusing on a range of the student's own interior picture: a self perception of personal role(s); an awareness of any known goals; and a knowledge of hopes and aspirations. In order for the assessor to build a picture of this range of emotional data, the student might be asked such questions as:

- "What makes it hard for you to follow the expectations of the classroom?"

- "Why is it difficult to complete the work that you are assigned?"

- "If you had something important to learn, what would be the best way to do it?"

- "If you had something to do that you really cared about, how would you go about doing it?"

- "What do you expect to happen if you don't change your behavior?"

- "What do you see yourself doing when you grow up?"

- "If you could change anything about your life, what would you change?"

- "If you could change anything in the school or in the classroom, what would you change?"

- "If you had a friend with the same thoughts, feelings, and behavior as yours, what advice would you give your friend?"

- "Why do people treat you the way they do?"

- "What or who makes you happy?"

- "What would be the most effective way to help you change your behavior?"

- Who are the students in the class that you would prefer to have working with you on an assignment? What do you like about these students?

- Other, similar questions may be devised to add to the list.

Interaction with family members

When both sets of responses about household interaction are available, that is, those of the student commenting about family members and those of the parents speaking about the student, they will show some differences. For example, while the parents may believe that the child gets along well with siblings, the student may feel bullied by those same siblings. Comparing responses may also provide clues about parents or students who are sometimes "faking good", that is, providing for the teacher a set of contrived responses of ideal parents or children. In interview situations, teachers should be expecting such responses, when both parents and students want to make a good impression. As a corollary, the parents may also be observing the teacher, watching for examples of behaviors reported at home by students [14].

Management techniques in the home

When this group of questions is asked, the responses of the student should be compared with those of the parents to ascertain the degree of agreement between the two. Because student perceptions often differ greatly from those of parents, both sets of responses should be carefully recorded. For example, parents may believe that confining children to their bedrooms is an effective punishment for inappropriate behavior, while the student may reveal that behaving inappropriately is the only way of escaping a typical uncomfortable situation.

After-school activities and hobbies

In the process of questioning, differences between responses of students and those of parents are to be expected; for example, although parents may believe that, after school, the student is doing homework, in fact the child is speaking on the phone with friends or playing video games.

Diet: favorite foods etc.

In any conversations between assessors and family members, parents and their child may also differ in their reports about diet. While at school, students often trade lunches, discarding fruit and milk in favor of candy, bags of potato chips, French fries with gravy, and soft drinks. Most importantly, students who are subject to forms of mild food intolerances and even known allergies may, when away from home, find themselves reluctant to avoid the foods that disagree with them. In some cases, such practices may impact the student's health condition, and, subsequently, behavior.

Sleep: nightmares, insomnia etc.

In interviews, students may sometimes reveal details of poor sleeping habits, nightmares, night terrors, and other relevant information, data which may relate to the student's pre-occupation with a personal problem, and, more importantly, such material may shed light on aspects of classroom behavior, such as listlessness, apathy, agitation, etc.

As part of the broader medical picture, poor sleeping habits may be shown to relate to physical problems and/or high levels of anxiety. In order to rule out the possibility that the student has a sleep disorder, a physician should be consulted. On the other hand, by learning relaxation techniques, the student may engage in procedures for a reduction of anxiety. If this tack is successful, the student may begin to experience restful sleep.

Health concerns

Now and then, students complain of physical concerns, sometimes but not always related to their psychological difficulties; for example, anxiety may disrupt the child's feeling of well-being. In some circumstances, these complaints may suggest the possibility of abuse. On the basis of the assessor's recommendation, all health concerns should be referred, immediately, by the parents, to a physician. In situations in which parents are reluctant to seek medical advice, the teacher must refer the case to the principal and the treatment team.

What modifications should be made to the student's program?

In conversations with the teacher, the student must be prompted to suggest possible changes that not only will make the classroom or school situation ultimately more bearable but also will provide for personal growth. Such changes may pertain, among other elements, to student autonomy, choice of classroom activities, seating arrangement, order and length of activities, and student-teacher interaction.

Summary

Although the data collection may appear to be long and tedious process, its onset should be seen in context: the assessment is triggered when the student fails to respond to known interventions. In addition, its purpose is to develop a profile of the "whole" child. Outlined in the table below are the three steps associated with data collection:

Table 3-1. **Sources of information at the teacher's disposal**

SOURCES OF INFORMATION
Student School Records
Reports stored in files at the School Board level
Conversations with the student's previous teachers
Parent Interview
Student Interview
The Teacher's own observations and interactions with the student

Having identified the available sources of information, the process of gathering the relevant data involves three steps outlined in the Table 3-2 below.

Table 3-2. Three steps in Data Collection

DATA COLLECTION
Gather all relevant information
Identify information still needed
Arrange for collection of further information

Thinking and Planning

When special education teachers think about students, they imagine them as individuals with strengths and weaknesses as well as with unique histories, goals, and mental representations of the world. Based on this assumption, a systematic approach to curriculum planning for the student involves a host of factors.

Table 3-3. Steps involved in Thinking and Planning

THINKING AND PLANNING
Review all the information
Generate the best explanation based on this information
Establish goals and objectives
Create learning environments

On the basis of informational data gathered, the teacher reaches a stage at which the information starts to tell a story and even to paint a picture of the student. At this moment, the teacher begins to imagine the forces operating at different settings in the student's life. Before coherence is achieved, teachers commonly begin to generate hypotheses and then to examine the accumulated data to support or reject such hypotheses. For example, when Ms. Budd begins to suspect that Shanta has a learning disability, she will review the information to pinpoint evidence of her supposition. In some cases, whether a broad base of information is or is not available, teachers may choose to test directly. Ms. Budd may therefore decide to refer Shanta for psycho-educational testing. In another situation, if information about Marty's concepts relating to money is not available, Mr. Nunez will take Marty to the store. There, it is possible to interact with him as he uses a five-dollar bill to purchase the items on a list. Although the on-going investigation will have been generating a series of explanations, continuing interaction with the student usually will lead to further modification, and, over time, to refinement of the theory of what lies behind the student's behavior.

In attempting to arrive at an explanation of a given student's behavior, often a teacher chooses to compare strategies with those employed by other teachers to satisfy the first two stages of the Thinking and Planning process outlined in Table 3-3.

Writing Behavioral Objectives

The writing of behavioral objectives constitutes the third phase of the Thinking and Planning process outlined in Table 3-3. It is always easier to write behavioral objectives directly related to an instructional sequence or a unit of curriculum than those with a behavioral component. In addition, such issues as improving self-concept, learning cooperation, and developing sociability are exceedingly difficult to address, not only because these concepts are abstract, but also because the behaviors associated with them are not immediately obvious. For these complex reasons, the teacher may need to arrive at an operational definition of self-concept before attempting to write behavioral objectives to address, for example, "the improvement of Moesha's self-concept."

Further complicating the difficulties regarding the writing of objectives are those related to terminology. For example, many educators use the words "goals" and "objectives' interchangeably, but, when used in the context of planning a student's program, these two words imply different meanings. To insure consistency, assessors will find it useful to adopt the following definitions: A *goal* is a statement of intention to achieve a specific end, regardless of whether that end is ever attained. To demonstrate this aspect, a good example might be to observe someone whose intention it is to win the lottery. Although this goal has no assurance of being met, millions of people adopt it, and, in order to reach it, generate objectives. Recognizing that an *objective* describes the means to accomplish the goal, potential winners describe the steps to be taken to maximize the accomplishment of that goal. Clearly, then, *objectives* outline *how* or *what* must be done at each stage. To win the lottery, a person needs:

- to know how to get to a store where lottery tickets are sold

- to earn money so that some can be spent on buying tickets

- to know how to budget money so that rent, food, etc. are paid first

- to buy lottery tickets

- to learn to read numbers

- to check tickets to see if there is a match, etc.

In order to fulfill the intention of the goal, these behaviors can then be formulated into **objectives** specifically adapted to reflect an individual's level of competence in the behavior implied by the objective. For example, if the buyer of a lottery ticket already knows how to read numbers, that objective need not be listed. Typically, the writing of objectives will include the following steps:

- identifying by name the learner on whom the objective will focus

- indicating the observable behavior to be undertaken and/or accomplished

- identifying the conditions in which the behavior is to be observed

- pinpointing the acceptable standard of behavior to be reached before the objective is clearly met

When behaviors relate to abstract topics like self-concept or self-esteem, more difficulty is experienced in order to conceptualize these ideas in behavioral terms. To make the process easier, the teacher might outline behaviors exhibited regularly by a person with a good self-concept by way of comparison with those of the one in possession of a poor self-concept. By focusing on the two types of behavior, the teacher will be able to state in concrete terms the contents of the objectives. In such an exercise, however, it is necessary to avoid the "Why can't you be more like Rupert" syndrome; probably the idealized person remains anonymous, represented only by characteristics.

For example, Ms. Costello has determined that the goal of Sanjay's program is to improve his self-concept, and because she has ascertained that students with good self-concept volunteer more answers in class, the focus is on concrete behavior rather than on speculating that good self-concept increases risk-taking. Initially, the chief objective in Sanjay's program might be to have him volunteer more answers during Math class, his favorite subject, because Ms. Costello's second intention is to increase the number of positive remarks Sanjay may hope to receive both from her and from his classroom peers. The following list of objectives illustrates the way Ms. Costello will outline Sanjay's program:

1. *Sanjay should complete his math assignment independently during the math-seatwork period.* If he has not completed the work, he will be unable to provide answers and, most probably, he will not volunteer at all.

2. *Sanjay should raise his hand, demonstrating willingness to volunteer an answer, at least once, during the evaluation period following the math seatwork.*

3. *Sanjay, during the evaluation period, should first keep count each time he raises his hand to volunteer an answer; second, he should record the results. At the end of the evaluation period, he will bring his tally to be signed by the teacher.* Ms. Costello wants Sanjay to be aware of how often he is willing to volunteer a response so that he may learn to obtain satisfaction from behavior, even though he can't be called on each time. In addition, when the two of them discuss his record-keeping, this interaction gives an opportunity for Ms. Costello and Sanjay to establish a natural, frequent contact.

4. *During the evaluation period, Sanjay is advised to respond "Thank you", after each compliment given to him by his teacher.* This objective is added because it is evident that Sanjay has been having difficulty using or knowing the appropriate words to say after being complimented.

As Sanjay becomes more proficient in satisfying the four objectives, each expectation expressed in the objectives will be modified until it approximates the behavior of his classmates; that is, the point at which Sanjay volunteers as many answers as most of the students in his class. Only then will a new set of objectives be considered[15].

Individualized Education Plan (IEP)

A document written in the course of the Special Education process, the Individualized Education Plan (IEP), is based on United States legislation: PL 94-142 which requires the completion of an IEP. In Ontario, on the other hand, the Amendment to the Education Act makes no such stipulation. In each local school board, however, teachers may be required to fill out IEPs. While each board has its own name for this form, the procedure insures accountability in the planning and evaluating of a student's individual program. Wherever it is devised, a student's IEP, therefore, is unique to the individual student's needs.

In every school, each teacher is encouraged to obtain IEP-type forms from the local school board and to check for the presence of essential stipulations, most of which are regularly included:

- A statement of annual goals and of the short-term objectives for achieving those goals

- A statement of services to be provided along with an outline of the extent of regular programming

- A starting date and an estimate of the expected duration of those services

- A set of evaluation procedures to monitor progress, accompanied by the criteria for their use, on an annual basis, at the very least. From day to day, teachers usually adhere to programs involving short-term objectives, prepared for weekly or monthly schedules, that is, for units much shorter than a year. As these are met, the results are filed in the IEP folder[16]

Conclusion

In this chapter issues relating to assessment, evaluation, and planning are presented. Initially, emphasis is placed on assessment procedures and tests, especially those typically used by psychologists to identify socio-emotional problems. Subsequently, having shifted to the information-gathering strategies of a teacher preparing a case study, the chapter's focus outlines a problem-solving process including the following stages:

- gathering information from school records and personnel

- obtaining further information from parents and/or caregivers and from the student

- generating hypotheses as well as finding information to support or reject them

- identifying potential sources of missing information

- compiling a theory that explains most of the information

- planning a classroom intervention

In addition to outlining essential goals and objectives, this chapter has defined the requirements for presenting a student to an IPRC[17]. As a further stage in the structuring of an assessment, the chapter details the procedures for setting up an Individualized Education Plan, or IEP, and presenting its evaluation criteria.

What is left to accomplish is the actual creation of learning environments tailored to address the goals and objectives identified for the student. The next four chapters will be dedicated to this aim.

Endnotes

[1] Mental Health facilities are most efficient in dealing with clients who meet the diagnostic criteria of clinical categories, and, therefore, clients who are difficult to categorize may not be able to access appropriate services. Note that the same condition exists when the client's symptoms are not sufficiently severe.

[2] Bellak. & Bellak (1949).

[3] Colligan, Osborne, Swenson, & Offord (1983).

[4] Lachar (1999) describes the Student Behavior Survey (SBS), designed specifically to examine aspects of classroom behavior and to be completed by teachers.

[5] Check http://www.printablechecklists.com/, for a household chores, parenting and other checklists.

[6] See Chapter One for an explanation of 'paradigm' and an overview of the major paradigms in the mental health field.

[7] Parental permission must be obtained in writing. In a school, the principal usually has the appropriate form.

[8] The clash of cultural expectations has a troubling effect on adolescents.

[9] English as a Second Language.

[10] Registers and pragmatics will be discussed in greater detail in the chapter dealing with Behavior, Language, and Literacy.

[11] Note that children with communication disabilities share these language and behavioral problems.

[12] Questions regarding the level of structure in the classroom will be discussed in Chapter Four.

[13] For a more detailed discussion, see Chapter Four, *Increasing Student Motivation*.

[14] A student's comments to parents about a teacher can often create a misleading image of the teacher.

[15] Note that such a process resembles the Multiple Baseline Design described earlier in this chapter.

[16] Examples of weekly and monthly plans are included at the end of Chapter Four.

[17] The Identification, Placement, and Review Committee.

CHAPTER 4

A Model of Behavior in the Classroom

While the idea may be surprising to some, the teaching of behavioral students does not just mean developing methods to control student behavior, while incidentally building strategies for presenting the curriculum. In reality, the creation of a successful learning environment for these students goes outward, beyond the walls of the classroom. In the world experienced by the student, the learning environment includes such factors as the structure of the institution – whether school or treatment center –, the relationships of personnel to both students and one another, the level of parental participation, and the attitudes of the students themselves. In any discussion of the range of methods for teaching behavioral students, these factors, in addition to management and curricular issues, will be essential.

Although the reader will realize that some of the ideas presented here are also applicable to the regular classroom, the thrust of this chapter touches specifically on issues relevant to the special education teacher of a segregated behavioral class and to the use of the resource classroom. When teachers in regular classrooms, moreover, are given adequate support to implement some of the notions outlined here, many types of prevention will be accomplished: this idea could be called the underlying thesis of these pages. In the context of the entire school, however, such forms of support, in their application to the regular stream, are usually perceived only as specific parts of the role played only by the teacher of a segregated behavioral class. Sometimes, if there is not such a teacher in the school, the role is adopted by the vice-principal, who may feel that meeting the needs of all students in the regular classroom, while not only the most beneficial alternative to finding a segregated setting, is still the most economical option.

In the previous chapter, assessment and planning issues were addressed; in the present chapter and the two that follow, the process of intervention will be examined. Once student difficulties are identified, what can be done within the classroom to promote the pro-social behavior and academic success of the student? First, however, it is essential to consider the various environments where students with behavioral difficulties are likely to be found.

Different Behavioral Environments

Students with behavioral problems appear in a variety of educational settings. In Figure 4-1, such environments are shown, typically, to range from regular classrooms to residential care locations. In fact, however, the large proportion of students displaying behavioral difficulties will be registered in the regular classrooms, where, as mentioned previously, early intervention is most effective. While the students remain in regular classes, not only will the problems be less severe but the students are less likely to be stigmatized. If, however, the classroom teacher is unable to provide the necessary intervention, then consultants or itinerant[1] teachers may become involved. When a particular student requires more frequent interaction, especially if academic problems emerge, a resource teacher will withdraw the student for periods of time in order to achieve academic goals and objectives. In the case where a specialized setting is required, the student may spend part of a day or an entire day in a segregated special education classroom. There, in a controlled, small environment, a behavioral teacher and perhaps a child care worker will strive to introduce and exercise behavioral goals and objectives. In some situations, students will require heavier treatment components available in day programs of treatment centers. In these environments, the primary focus is an attempt to stabilize the socio-emotional well-being of students who, at this point, cannot function in normative settings. Finally, for the student whose problems are such that residential care is required, a milieu away from both parents and regular classroom will be needed to address the individual's emotional health.

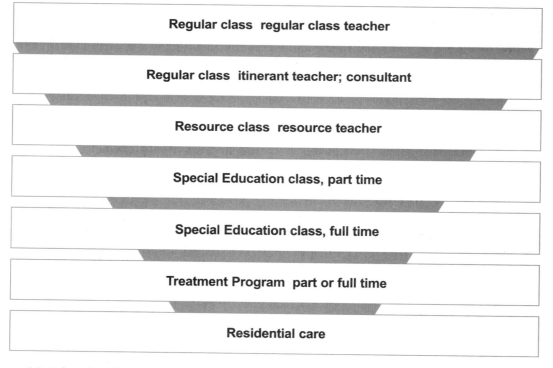

Figure 4-1. Educational Settings where Children with Behavioral Difficulties are Accommodated.

In the section which follows, it is appropriate to consider the segregated classroom, also called the behavioral class, where students unable to function in the regular class will undoubtedly be placed, with the hope that such a move will provide a range of necessary remedies.

Teachers of Behavioral Classrooms and Child Care Workers

Because they usually employ staff members who may not be teachers, but who work with the students, behavioral classrooms are different from regular classrooms. Traditionally, teachers in their classrooms have been and expect to be autonomous. Recently, however, mandatory Special Education legislation has opened the door to teaching assistants who regularly play subordinate roles in classrooms. Initially, because they did not bring specialized training into these settings, their subordinate placements were appropriate. Even more recently, however, because of their community college training, a new group of child care workers, who differ from other teaching assistants, have been introduced into the behavioral classroom. For these workers, in courses that involve learning to interact with children in behavioral classes, their training makes available clinical experience usually acquired in other settings such as group homes, residential treatment centers, etc. From their first appearance in classrooms, these child care workers have expected to be treated as partners, equals of the supervising teachers.

Having both teacher and child worker overseeing a classroom, and, at the same time, having students perceive this arrangement, provides advantages for some of the wilier among them. Similar to the situation experienced by children whose parents bicker in their home, a contending teacher and child care worker usually create an **unsafe** environment for students. By learning to play one adult against the other, the students will take advantage until "The inmates are running the asylum." In order that the two are perceived by the students as a team, both the teacher and the child care worker should consider that:

- Traditionally, according to professional protocol when in the company of students, each adult must support the role of the other.

- Frequently, in order to establish a common philosophy, as well as to define each person's role in the classroom, the two persons must find opportunities not only for holding dialogues but also for providing feedback.

- Before aberrant events have a chance to emerge, regular discussions about ways of coping with potentially troublesome situations or with possible student crises should be scheduled.

- Also arranged and rostered in advance will be an ongoing series of conversations about policies and procedures, especially those relating to treatment team meetings as well as to plans of action which will be implemented in **crisis** situations.

Because continuing communication is critical in a situation in which two parties are mutually responsible, the teacher and the child care worker must speak regularly with each other to create the **safe** environment needed by the students.

In the following section, a model of needs is outlined, emphasizing the relevant educational setting. Compiled using many of the concepts associated with the paradigms discussed in Chapter Two, this model considers the creation of the kind of positive learning environment which allows students to "become the best that they can be."

A Model of Needs

If a positive learning environment is to be created, why is a model required? While the "bricks" and "mortar" of the major paradigms, outlined in detail in Chapter Two, are generic ideas, they lack the actual patterns provided by specific contexts. In some cases, because the paradigms evolved within therapeutic situations, they will be out of sync with the classroom environment. For this reason, a teacher might find it useful to undertake the construction of a model specifically addressing the socio-emotional needs of classroom students. With such a model, a classroom environment can be devised in which students are happily and actively engaged in intentional learning. Only when inappropriate or maladaptive behaviors are reduced, will pro-social behavior and personal growth be able to be introduced and continue to be encouraged.

In the classroom, when the teacher wonders how to deal with the misbehavior of a certain student, usually new strategies are needed to make the student comply with the subsequent request. Commonly, in classrooms, compliance is achieved either with threats or with bribes. In situations in which teachers threaten any one of a series of penalties, for example, the student will go to the principal's office; will not go on the field trip; or will not participate in art class, physical education, and/or after-school sports – the overriding strategy is to suspend any activity the student may enjoy. In contrast, compliant students receive special attention, are given extra classroom duties, and are asked to take messages to other teachers. When students are compliant, that is, when the teacher has supreme control over their behavior, the result is obedient students.

Although certain teachers, in attempting to gain compliance, will achieve some success with many students, a few, unfortunately, will fail to accept responsibility for their behavior. While a paradox, it is true, moreover, that responsible behavior is not learned in an oppressive environment. Only when convinced that they ultimately make the choice – to behave in a particular manner – do students, sometimes reluctantly, learn to accept the consequences of their behavior. The corollary is that learning to be responsible is connected first with the young person's developing a feeling of empowerment, and, subsequently, with a growing awareness of the nature of self-control.

Before the presentation of specific interventions to address individual needs of particular students, certain classroom essentials will be outlined so that teachers may generate individual programs. In Figure 4.2, on page 109, these classroom elements are illustrated.

Basic Needs

In the model depicted in Figure 4.2, three basic needs of students are identified. Labeled "affective", they are rooted in the way a student "feels" in the classroom. Before teachers can expect students to attend to school-related activities, these needs – and there must be confirmation – have to be met:

1. **to feel safe,** that is, free from such adverse actions as harm, abuse, and ridicule.

2. **to feel prized,** including the right to have access to such positive forms of response as rewards, compliments, and recognition.

3. **to feel some control** over actions; for example, to develop the ability to perceive one's role in a series of events as well as to show a willingness to accept the consequences of actions.

The first two elements – safety and prizing – are based on Maslow's hierarchy of needs, while the third – empowerment – is related to Glasser's control theory[2]. Because they involve the way a student should be able to **feel** in the classroom, these elements are defined as *affective needs*. In this structure of requirements, then, the task of the teacher is to create a classroom environment in which students feel safe, know themselves to be prized, and perceive their own individual empowerment.

Obviously, if feeling safe is a fundamental requirement, a student, on the way to school, who is physically threatened by bullies, will not associate school with secure and confident emotions. Such bullying, more commonly experienced than adults often realize, frequently involves younger or smaller children who are picked on in the school yard, in the hallway, in the washrooms, or at any time when adults, especially teachers, are not directly watching or listening. In addition, feelings of fear, that often have their origins in other environments, may interfere with classroom activities. In some situations, students will have fearful emotions because they continue to be physically and/or sexually abused by parents, siblings, other relatives, coaches, or neighbors. In yet other circumstances, emotional abuse occurs when peers or adults ridicule or make sarcastic remarks that motivate the student to *escape* or to avoid an activity altogether.

In front of teachers and peers, making a mistake is still considered one of the most embarrassing and anxiety-producing situations for a student, with the result that an individual may develop an entire behavioral repertoire to deal with not knowing information that is asked for or with being unsure of a response. Among typical student responses are: avoiding eye contact, pretending to do some other important-looking task, and/or creating diversions. For many students in the classroom, negative feelings associated with giving incorrect responses are sufficient cause to undermine feelings of safety[3].

In summary, when students do not feel safe in the classroom, they will probably experience negative affective responses. Included in these reactions are fear, dread – also called anticipatory anxiety – and generalized anxiety. If students anticipate these feelings, they usually react by avoiding or escaping unsafe environments. According to Seligman, in special situations, especially if the student is repeatedly prevented from fleeing, the young person will develop a learned helplessness.

In addition to having a need to feel safe, students must feel prized; that is, they must believe that significant others – especially parents and teachers – not only care for them and worry about them, but also have expectations for them. More importantly, students require behavioral confirmation of these bonds through activities that decrease the emotional distance between adult and child. Types of activities that provide such bonds might involve a teacher describing personal experiences from student days. Because students generally thrive on adult attention, even though they sometimes misbehave in order to get it, some of them will begin to feel elements of emotional closeness with teachers when, in safe environments, those teachers direct more personal attention toward them.

A truism that must be emphasized is that all students will have equal opportunities to access rewards, compliments, special attention, and other positive elements because good teachers will make sure this happens. Unfortunately, those students who lack academic difficulties – the "bright" students, or the "compliant" students – frequently obtain the compliments, the encouragement, and the rewards of free time. Because of this customary behavior, the teacher's criteria should be modified with the hope that each student will feel "special". Some children, because of earlier school experiences in regular classrooms, may complain of unfairness when a child with a behavioral exceptionality receives a smaller or easier workload. In any classroom, students can learn to understand that, as in the handicapping system in golf, the situation is fair only when all students have equal access to rewards. Obviously, by making encouragement contingent upon personal improvement, the teacher can constructively accomplish this feat. Using this criterion, with its focus upon individual development, the teacher may display or show praise for a student's work that demonstrates an advance. Emphasizing a different element, the teacher may nominate a "student of the week" to focus on quality of work done, quantity of homework completed, or improvement in social behavior.

Approximately five hours each day will be spent with their teachers and classmates, a notable portion of any student's life. In this large portion of the student's waking hours, feelings of safety and of being prized will both influence a sense of belonging to the class community and impact significantly on self perception. The resulting sense of belonging is particularly strong in students whose lives outside their schools are unstable or whose homes are experiencing personal crises.

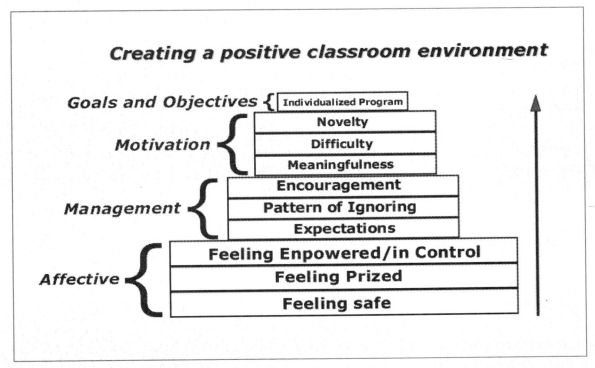

Figure 4-2. **Creating a Positive Classroom Environment**

Because of the individual desire to experience a sense of control over at least some of the events in the immediate context, the third focus addresses this concern. Usually identified in the affective portion of the model, the focus relates to people's need to understand or predict, in a small degree, what happens. In an interesting way, this need is integral to the development of a strong *ego*. Students who are diagnosed with Attention Disorder, for example, while they often behave as though they are driven, usually report that their actions were not purposeful. Such students, apparently, have no sense of being responsible for their actions. When these students' adverse behavior is punished, their own perception – of not being responsible – suggests that penalties result from the teacher's personal dislike. At no time do they perceive retribution as the logical consequence of their behavior. Not only depressed individuals but also students with learned helplessness are able to believe that because of lack of control over their destiny, they must indeed be powerless to effect changes in their lives.

When a classroom is organized around the goal of obtaining the compliance of the students, the teacher will find it difficult to fulfill the other need: that of encouraging students to establish control over their lives and behavior. As a direct correlation of this truth, a student attempting to exercise control may be perceived – by other students and/or by the teacher – as rebellious or unsocialized. Soon, as power struggles develop between teacher and student, it is easy to recognize these dynamics as having their origins outside classrooms. In fact, such conflicts are very prevalent in the family context where distribution of power is more one-sided, but, regardless of the setting, the student will recognize the familiar desire to achieve control through any available measure.

In the classroom context, students who discover ways to establish control over classroom situations are a familiar phenomenon. Usually, the method is simply to refuse to do what the teacher requests. When a student with a personal agenda becomes defiant, because the teacher insists that classrooms expectations be met, the teacher quite logically considers the rebel to be aggressive and dangerous. At this juncture, the common response is either to re-assert power or to demand that the student leave the classroom. On each side, that of the teacher and that of the student, saving face in front of the class may be an element in the power struggle.

When the student's self-perception involves power and control, resentment of authority figures will be strong. What is to be done? By accepting the student's need for a measure of control, the teacher will be able to dispense with the initial reaction: "How dare this student act this way to me?" Instead, the query becomes: "Why is this student or that other one indulging in such behavior?" In response to this question, a number of possibilities may include, for example: one student, upon finding the work too difficult, is attempting to hide this realization from classmates; a second student, perhaps feeling oppressed by the number of classroom rules and expectations, feels those structures have no personal relevance; a third individual has become so preoccupied by personal issues that these have overwhelmed daily life and taken precedence over the seemingly petty expectations of the classroom; a fourth student, in a commonly experienced situation, feels persecuted by teachers and other students in the class; in another typical scenario, yet a fifth student experiences the exertion of power only in the classroom, while in other situations, including the one at home, this same student sees that no show of aggression is successful; for each type of conflict, another student may be the symbol, and so the list may be extended.

An interesting category of student, intent on gaining power and control over situations in the classroom, is one who frequently utilizes knowledge of social conventions. Generally considered passive-aggressive – because the meaning of each action is shrouded – this student, characteristically, will compliment the teacher to camouflage a scheme that may set off an aggressive student; will, instead, tattle about the misbehavior of others; will sometimes submit work completed by another student; will boldly take credit for the accomplishments of someone else; will sneakily deny involvement in misbehavior; etc. In any analysis of classroom politics, this student can be seen to be seeking power without indulging in the messiness of power struggle.

When perceiving certain individuals as vulnerable, the bully recognizes the benefits to be derived from power activities. This student, moreover, is usually experienced in respecting obvious authority, that is, in deferring to the individual who holds the cards. Meanwhile, anyone lacking authority becomes the victim of the bully: a younger child, an animal, a smaller student, or a bigger student who is certain not to retaliate. Behavior usually associated with bullies includes one or more of coercion, threats, taunts, extortion, as well as hurt, each of which the bully has probably experienced at the hands of a more successful bully and/or has observed in action.

In the world of the classroom and schoolyard, while the need for power and control is weakest in empowered and comfortable students, it is strongest in students who feel powerless and out of control. An interesting correlation is that those students who are depressed – and, typically, many of these have acquired learned helplessness – have abandoned any prospect of meeting their need for even minimal control. How then can students be assisted to feel the beginnings of empowerment? While most students recognize the pecking order existing in any milieu, they also focus their attentions on their own world, learning to model individual activities and personalities not only on those of parents, teachers, and siblings, but on media figures.

In a democratic society, concepts of power and control are very different from those in other political systems. In the Canadian scene, it is interesting to note, many students who have emigrated from more totalitarian nations are attempting to find their way. As Dreikurs has pointed out, schools, by encouraging responsible behavior in a context that provides an ever-wider range of choices, must take on the challenge of teaching students about democracy. Within this milieu, the teacher, source of political example, must insist that students recognize and accept the consequences of every choice and every action. This major factor, focusing as it does on personal control and responsibility, is directed to cognitive and social issues. In its deepest implication, student awareness of this syndrome extends beyond merely knowing which behaviors are rewarded and which are punished. In answering the question: "How do responsible people behave?", both teacher and student become aware of the essential point about acting in a responsible manner. First, all individuals require knowledge about the structures that make society work, the ways people relate, and the manner in which people perceive themselves and their actions. Such an awareness may also include the acquisition of specialized skills, an example of which is the importance of *the language to be used when defending oneself.* While the need for empowerment may express itself initially as a feeling, if change is to occur, the necessary elements of thinking and reasoning must follow. The three affective needs described in Figure 4-2 – to feel safe, to know oneself prized, and to exercise at least some control over the things that happen – identify the internal states requisite to optimizing conditions in a classroom environment, enabling learning to take place. In correctional settings, approximately 75% of young offenders are diagnosed as exhibiting some forms of learning difficulty. Such a stern statistic should motivate those who structure classrooms to provide safe environments which both prize students and offer them ways to develop ideas of personal responsibility. As such notions are internalized within the students and, ultimately, within the school structures, they will become sturdy foundations for formal learning.

Classroom Management

In the second tier of the model illustrated in Figure 4-2, issues relating to classroom infrastructures are addressed. Very much like an orchestra conductor, the teacher creates and oversees a system of order that directs the flow of activity in the classroom. At the outset, establishment of firm classroom management implies rules and expectations to protect not only the safety of all students in the class, but also of the teacher. Meanwhile, a second element investigates ways and means of increasing the amounts of both praise and reward, as well as encouragement available to all students. In a third aspect of this outline, methods are introduced to help the teacher discourage actions incompatible with classroom expectations while bringing out in the students those behaviors that exemplify positive qualities.

Expectations

Because rules and expectations are integral to the fabric of any society, students should be made aware of both the **explicit**, that is, stated, and the **implicit**, or unstated, rules that regulate the behavior of individuals at work and at play. By exploring the intention of rules, teachers may group them on the basis of their ultimate purpose. Observably, the social rules, expectations, and conventions of a democratic society begin by satisfying the three basic needs discussed in the classroom model: to keep people safe, to give them a sense of belonging, and to regulate the ways in which power is exercised.

Although they are usually printed in law books, traffic manuals, and *The Bible*, among other codified sources, explicit expectations imply stated rules and conventions often found more readily in the policies and procedures of an institution. Sometimes, of course, the most basic expectations are not in writing, but pass by word of mouth within a group, a family, or a community. In the context of a school, such explicit expectations exist in a variety of school documents as well as in the folklore of certain classrooms or school divisions. Stories are always passed along to the younger students who are about to experience changes warned about in the intermediate division, in high school, or in university. In matters relating to legal behavior, traditionally a person who has committed a crime is not considered innocent simply because of ignorance of a given law. Students in schools, usually aware of most of the structures, are nonetheless often unwittingly guilty of an infraction.

When, however, an explicit expectation is violated, it is possible that the student:

- is unaware of the expectation
- is aware of it but has forgotten it
- is aware but has chosen to violate the expectation

Maury may go inside the teacher's desk to help himself to markers. Because he engages in the same behavior when he helps himself to pencils from his Dad's desk, he may be unaware that he must first ask permission from the teacher. Ms. Mahta makes him aware of the expectation, at first drawing his attention to the difference in the two contexts, and then carefully makes a point of complimenting him when, on subsequent occasion, he properly asks permission.

In a different case, Sanjay has previously been requested by Ms. Mahta to ask to borrow his classmates' materials rather than rifle through their desks. When he is in search of an eraser, he helps himself to one from Abby's desk. When Abby complains, Sanjay responds "Oh I'm sorry; I forgot! Can you please lend me an eraser?" Abby's initial response reminds Sanjay of the expectation which in turn triggers the appropriate behavior. When, the next time, he uses the correct procedure, perhaps he can be praised for remembering. At some stage, however, a discussion may ensue among his classmates about personal responsibility versus prompts: what is required to make this expectation part of Sanjay's behavioral repertoire?

Because of the timing element, as well as a distinct awareness on the part of the culprit, this last situation is qualitatively different from the previous two because Victoria is aware that she must ask permission to borrow Tina's book. Nevertheless, Victoria waits for her to leave the classroom before helping herself to it, because, after all, she wants the book which Tina has refused to lend. In addressing the three examples in the foregoing paragraph, a teacher, a student, or a group of students will realize that stating the expectation is a first viable step in informing the student of its existence. Whereas such an intervention may be sufficient to modify Maury's behavior, Sanjay may also require several reminders before he internalizes the expectation. In Victoria's case, it is evident that some power and control issues are involved. In choosing to violate expectations to suit her purposes, she is implicitly demanding a more substantive intervention. In these situations, however, teasing and irony may play a role: a student may consider the rule itself and the flouting of it to be an amusing ploy. The seriousness, then, of the expectations surrounding private property – even an eraser – becomes the focus of the learning experience.

Because implicit expectations, anywhere in society, but especially in the classroom, are neither stated in written form nor announced by word of mouth, it is unclear how a person actually learns about them. What is evident, however, is that only after spending an extended amount of time in school, both in the classroom and with classmates, will a student acquire a sense of which forms of implicit behavior are acceptable. For example, while the appropriate time interval for being late for lessons might differ from class to class, teacher to teacher, year to year, only a small variation in what students define as lateness exists in these circumstances[4]. Interestingly, in the absence of conscious cues and discussion, students nevertheless share similar parameters in their idea of lateness. Teachers, however, usually have more definite views about tardiness, especially when it is repeated.

As previously suggested, one part of a student's behavioral repertoire is composed of procedural knowledge, that is, knowledge that remains implicit unless an effort is made to describe and examine it. In most cases, procedural knowledge is acquired through experience, by-passing linguistic routes. In arriving in school 3 minutes late for his first class, Matthew may be required to obtain a late slip from the office before being allowed in class. What he learns on his own, without prompting, and without personal awareness, is Mr. Hayashi's unwillingness to overlook an arrival three to five minutes after the bell.

In the broad range of settings where people coexist, however, to ensure that individual needs are met, explicit rules and expectations should be the norm. When relevant cases present themselves, even implicit expectations need to be discussed and stated. For this reason, the class should participate in formulating a set of explicit procedures that will help to guide the behavior of students in the classroom. In addition to encouraging the group to define regulations for individual and group student behavior, teachers must involve the students in finding ways to ensure the smooth running of the day-to-day classroom activities. Not only does such a shared program build on the students' understanding of democratic procedure, it enables each individual in the classroom to know the procedures about such disparate things as: acquiring new supplies; returning to class after an absence; excusing oneself; welcoming a new student into the class; and many similar situations.

If it happens, on the other hand, that a student violates implicit rules, steps should be taken to discuss them in order to make them explicit. Among useful guidelines available to both teachers and students, the following list is a beginning:

- ensuring that classroom expectations facilitate management, while contributing to the well-being of everyone

- limiting the number of expectations to a brief set, preferably of five, but no greater than seven

- stating each expectation clearly enough that it is seen to be fair and readily acceptable

- formulating expectations in positive terms, assuring that the desired behavior is implied while still imparting useful information to students

- avoiding phrases which identify undesirable behaviors, by stating their positive counterparts

- outlining, whenever possible, expectations that include a group of behaviors rather than individual behaviors; for example, polite behavior

- providing concrete examples of acceptable behaviors which, while associated with expectations, relate to abstract concepts; for example, cooperation

- involving students in the actual development and revision of lists of expectations, in order to create a vested interest

- Using an authoritative rather than autocratic style; that is, while the teacher does not relinquish responsibility, the students are involved in discussing the issues that directly affect them.

Pattern of Ignoring

It is a fact of classroom tradition to have a general tendency to overlook the appropriate behavior of compliant students, while attending to students who are indulging in inappropriate behavior. Although counter-intuitive, the teacher's response to inappropriate behavior often has the effect of encouraging and maintaining such antics because adult attention is a premium reinforcer. When certain students have a strong need for teacher attention, they will risk behaving inappropriately to get it. In a classic study, in which students were observed frequently leaving their seats, the teacher responded regularly, asking each in turn to sit down. It soon became evident that the number of times each student stood up approximately equaled the number of times that student was asked to sit down[5]. In their search for attention, students may stand up in order to hear the teacher's request that they sit down; some will chatter only to hear the teacher asking them to stop; others, in expectation of a mild reprimand, will make funny faces at the most critical point of the lesson just so that others will laugh.

As soon as the expectations in the classroom are identified and recognized by all students, the classroom teacher must make an overt effort to respond only to those students not behaving in the explicitly described manner. Along with this decision goes the understanding that any action which threatens the safety needs of the class – or the teacher – is NEVER ignored. When it becomes obvious to the students that previously reinforced negative behaviors will be ignored, the behavioral process known as extinction will be perceived to be consistently in force. At the outset, however, the teacher will expect the severity of the adverse behavior to increase. As the teacher, consistently, makes no response, the student, wondering why, immediately begins to formulate and test a string of hypotheses: maybe I was not loud enough; maybe the teacher did not see me; etc. To reduce and then eliminate speculation, the teacher may efficiently explain the new rules of the game.

In a typical classroom situation, Giselle insists on making remarks to Adele while Mrs. Abernathy is presenting a new math concept. When Mrs. Abernathy asks Giselle to pay attention to the lesson, Giselle will, first of all, adopt a sheepish facial expression, then keep quiet for a few minutes, and soon will go back to the previous annoying behavior. To extinguish Giselle's behavior, Mrs. Abernathy has decided on a planned ignoring strategy. Before implementing it, however, she discreetly outlines the following elements with Giselle:

- the reasons why such interruptions are counterproductive to everyone concerned.

- the various methods that she has earlier tried to implement to modify Giselle's behavior.

- the fact that no longer will Giselle be asked to be quiet; moreover, students sitting next to her are in agreement about ignoring her remarks.

- the assurance that Giselle will not interpret this action as a power confrontation, i.e., "act of war". Mrs. Abernathy not only recognizes the need to be social with classmates, but will release some time just for talk, contingent on Giselle's being quiet during teaching presentations. Perhaps, if Giselle keeps a record of her quiet behavior, she and Mrs. Abernathy will examine it after class.

Praise and Encouragement

While praise and encouragement are generally believed to be powerful modifiers of behavior, a few simple words of encouragement from a teacher have been acknowledged to change the entire course of a student's achievement. In spite of the often demonstrated effectiveness of positive comments and friendly remarks, teachers, traditionally, are more likely to remark about the varieties of student violations of expectations than to comment favorably about effort and accomplishment. In defense of this custom, teachers themselves received similar feedback from teachers and parents during their own student years. In view of what really works, it cannot be too strongly emphasized that praise, encouragement, and feedback are critical in the early stages of learning. Not only is this true of both teacher expectations and the day-to-day operation of the classroom, it is also clear that the more friendly and positive verbal comments a teacher makes when expectations are met, the more these expectations will be met again.

Aside from acknowledging the positive expectations, both praise and encouragement serve other important functions. In an environment where the focus is explicitly on positive outcomes, rather than on the dangers of failure, students feel safe, able to associate positive internal states with the teacher. Very soon, this outward-looking energy extends to classmates, the classroom, the school, and, among other places, the curriculum. In this context as in several others, students will gravitate to people and situations that are pleasurable.

But what about modeling? As has been shown in many ways, teachers realize students will imitate their behavior. When, for example, effort, achievement, and perseverance are acknowledged through praise and encouragement, the students themselves adopt similar patterns of perceiving, recognizing, and emulating such behavior. As a result, students often gain respect from classmates and from other teachers who are likely to value such a perspective.

Summary

The three essential procedures for dealing with general classroom management require the teacher to:

1. **Specify Expectations**

   - In making rules explicit, the teacher conveys to students the list of expectations that will prompt appropriate or desirable behavior.

2. **Pattern of Ignoring**

   - By ignoring undesirable behavior, Ms. O'Connor discourages it through lack of attention. Instead, her positive response is cued to desirable activity. In a typical example, although Maria is walking about aimlessly, the teacher ignores her but focuses on Helmut working at his desk. Soon, Ms. O'Connor walks towards him, looks at his notebook, and compliments him on the intentional involvement in his work. In a carefully structured classroom, the teacher does not encourage misbehavior by giving it attention. Instead, negative actions can be used to encourage an incompatible but positive behavior.

3. **Encourage:**

   - When the teacher encourages behavior, the positive nature of such action should be underscored by giving attention. As well, teachers may indulge briefly in complimenting, recognizing, and rewarding with free time or other forms of reinforcement.

Increasing Student Motivation

In the sections immediately preceding, some methods are outlined by which teachers lay down certain foundations. The idea emphasized first that students could be comfortable in their environment and second that each classroom could be smooth running. Now, the concern is to demonstrate the way an atmosphere can be generated in which students will be motivated to tackle academic work. A widely held view is that much inappropriate behavior exhibited in classrooms is in reaction to the content and presentation of the curriculum. To add to the problem, maladaptive behaviors are often associated with poor motivation. In coming to productive terms with the problem of classroom motivation, the third tier in the model illustrated in Figure 4-2 identifies three factors that often play roles:

- **meaningfulness:** the identifiable level of personal relevance between the student and the content of the curriculum

- **difficulty:** the level of difficulty found in concepts, vocabulary, and other elements

- **novelty:** the level of familiarity detectable in the presentation, content, and activities

As they are experienced in combination, the three levels will raise or decrease a student's motivation to engage in a particular learning activity. Because of the importance of each one, the three will be considered individually as well as in combination with the other two in order to demonstrate their effect on student motivation.

Meaningfulness

The idea of making an aspect of curriculum personally relevant to students is one of the most difficult challenges facing educators. On the other hand, every teacher knows that the most fundamental part of motivation is meaningfulness of what students learn. For younger and less experienced learners, before they can truly embrace the learning process, they need to recognize the way the curriculum material relates to their world. When introducing new curriculum units, teachers must first convince students that the curriculum is not simply an arbitrary construct. In a further stretch of their imaginations, the teacher must make them believe that there is a purpose in learning about, for instance, the explorers of the new world, the difference between an antonym and a homonym, or the procedure for adding fractions. When the typical students are made aware of the many destinations afforded by the learning process, they will maintain not only a natural curiosity but also a desire to explore along with an intrinsic motivation. In this time-warp, teachers will be able to find ways to demonstrate how the curriculum is relevant to what are still those students' unstated future goals. In fact, of course, many students come to cherish knowledge for its own sake, readily accepting the outlandish requirements of the curricula presented to them.

To judge the way the curriculum relates to the class, the teacher invests time and effort in order to become acquainted, one by one, with each student. Possibly, during the first month of the academic year, the teacher will hope to accomplish this goal, at the same time evaluating students' competence in different areas of the curriculum. For this purpose, tasks and activities can be devised to elicit a pattern revealing the personal goals and aspirations of each student.

In a typical behavioral class the teacher has an unusual advantage in the matter of motivating students because, already included in the curriculum, are many relevant elements which focus on appropriate, student-centered topics. Because one of these might involve such a typical student concern as exploring relationships, a good opening for the teacher might be, "How do you get other students to like you?" Of universal concern – feelings – are very important, too. Here, the teacher might ask, "How do you control your temper?" As another area causing chronic difficulty is related to reactions, a good question would be: "What is the appropriate reaction to the remark: "$%#&"?" Because most students are familiar with problems related to social skills, they will be ready for new approaches. An appropriate opening question might be, "What do you do if your best friend starts hanging around with someone else?" Of course, there are many equally suitable topics; sometimes the students themselves will suggest good ones. Usually, such basic topics as these will be taken up readily by students whose social and conversational skills are somewhat or very developed. On the other hand, an interesting challenge for the teacher is to elicit participation from shy students who, prior to this conversation, may not have engaged in opinion sharing.

Difficulty

When students perceive a task as either too difficult or too easy, they may react with misbehavior, and, very soon, they will find ways to avoid it. For example, because she makes so many mistakes on her assignments, Marika believes that Math is a difficult subject. Recently, after asking her parents to help with Math homework, as she had feared, they said they found Math to be difficult. Now Marika believes her Mathematics problems are the result of inheriting poor Math genes. What is often evident in the classroom is that the inherent difficulty of a task is magnified by the student's perception of troublesome elements. When a teacher begins, therefore, to estimate the amount and quality of work needed in a curriculum plan for students, it will be important to consider the entire picture, one that will include students' potential responses to an assigned task.

A strong relationship is known to exist between the enjoyment experienced and the amount of effort a student invests in an activity. Although Alfred loves to converse and to answer questions about stories read in class, when the time comes to write answers in his notebook, he can't find his notebook, wants to be excused, or does whatever it takes to have Mr. Solomon send him to the office. Especially because he writes more slowly than others, while his hand often cramps before the task is completed, Alfred's weakness relates to the amount of effort involved in composing the written component of the task. While Alfred is candid about his dislike of activities that include written components, the overriding question is whether Mr. Solomon will find a way to reduce Alfred's effort level, at the same time satisfying the instructional objectives of the curriculum.

Every student has a unique threshold of effort, which, combined with other factors, may help to ensure the successful completion of a task. If, prior to completing the task, personal effort is required that exceeds the threshold, the student is faced with alternatives: to lower expectations or to abandon the task. Each of these options will diminish the enjoyment level of the activity as well as lowering the student's learning quotient in that unit of the curriculum.

As a result of previous success or failure with similar activities, each student will develop an effort threshold that is personally appropriate. When there is a history of trouble, moreover, before undertaking a task, the student will be predisposed to make effort judgments. On the basis of these considerations, the student will decide whether or not to tackle the task. Following negative effort judgments, when a lack of productivity dogs the student, the foundation of the habit of procrastination may be firmly established.

If effort can be seen as paralleling a physical force, it is easier to understand how such effort will affect achievement. Newton's laws of motion explain that the amount of force required to move an object at rest is much greater than that required to maintain an object in motion; for example, it usually takes several people pushing a car to get the car moving, while maintaining the motion is easy for a single person. A similar law seems to hold true for a student faced with a new project, because more effort is needed to start the project than to continue a project once begun. When any intervention is being designed to increase task completion, it must include initiation strategies to help the student. From the student's point of view, then, it is clear that difficulty affects motivation when the teacher plans an activity without considering the student's knowledge and skill levels. Similarly, a negative result will also emerge when, on the basis of prior negative experience, the student prejudges the activity as too difficult. Finally, when the amount of mental energy needed to undertake the project is above the student's effort threshold, motivation to complete the task will decrease accordingly.

Novelty

While the degree of novelty in the presentation and content of an activity may positively affect student motivation, the corollary is that extremely novel situations sometimes bewilder, rendering the student incapable of identifying the requirements of the task. In contrast, overly familiar situations may bore, making the student unwilling to become involved. A classroom of students may respond to a particular blend of novelty/familiarity that depends on the quality of the activity.

Teaching a new concept or skill necessitates that when the teacher plans to offer an unfamiliar activity, its presentation, structure, and product should be known to the students. In such a situation, when only the content is new, students are free and encouraged to invest effort in learning the unknown concept and/or skill. In Figure 4-3, a task is illustrated in terms of its presentation, the mental activities required to complete it, and the manner in which the product of the task is expressed. For example, if the teacher reads a story to Sepehr, to evaluate his language comprehension, the mode of presentation involves acoustical information to be processed by him. For the teacher to form an evaluation, the mental activities must include procedures associated with understanding language. As to the method of assessment, it must indicate an awareness that he has understood the story. Also, it may require Sepehr to retell it aloud, in his own words, to draw a picture, to word process an outline, or to type a list of the themes.

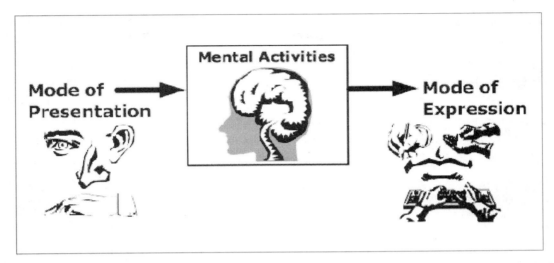

Figure 4-3. **The Structure of a Task**

Once the student has demonstrated an initial understanding of a given idea or procedure, the teacher may construct a variety of activities designed to reinforce that concept. In order to strengthen the learning process, each subsequent activity is made systematically more challenging, as the difficulty and novelty levels of the task are increased. Modes of presentation and expression, as well as types of mental activities, are varied, with the purpose of thoroughly reinforcing the concept and/or skill. In addition, as the students personally experience the task, motivation will be enhanced as will the transfer of knowledge to the new situation.

Because it is difficult to transfer knowledge learned in an earlier situation to a current one, the teacher has to insure variation in the context of reinforcement activities[7] – especially the ones that involve altering the modes of presentation and expression. Transfer of knowledge occurs when the student can apply the newly acquired data to a current situation that differs from experiences encountered during the learning set. For example, in a unit on friendship, the students are able to discuss characteristics of a good friend; to read stories about friends involved in different situations; to examine procedures for making friends; and to investigate other activities connected with the idea of friendship. Mr. Champlain is able to observe transfer of the unfamiliar knowledge when, in the schoolyard, he witnesses Margot introducing herself to a new student as a means of practicing the fresh skills and, perhaps, of acquiring a new friend.

Balancing Meaningfulness, Difficulty, and Novelty

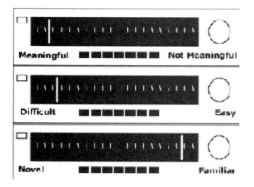

For a particular student, the ideal level of motivation is achieved by coordinating a balance of task meaningfulness, difficulty, and novelty. For example, in a situation where a task is meaningful – in that it serves to help the individual to meet a personal goal – the student will continue to be motivated even when the task is quite difficult or even sufficiently familiar to be boring. In a typical case, Yannick is willing not only to read an anatomy textbook containing difficult words, but also to write a two-page composition on the subject of sexually-transmitted diseases. The reason is simple – this information is personally relevant.

Motivation may also increase when, although the content of the task is both very difficult and **not** particularly relevant to students' experiences, it is presented in an unusual and novel manner. For example, a computer environment[8] like LOGO has made the acquisition of certain cognitive skills possible, although each student must invest substantial effort while unable, immediately, to see the direct relevance of such skills to personal or learning situations.

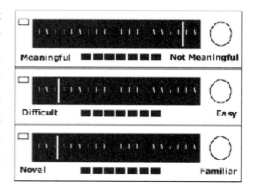

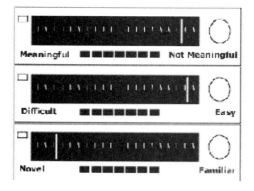

When the task is easy but not particularly meaningful, a novel environment also motivates the student. Using their computers, many people, both young and old, spend inordinate amounts of time learning to play solitaire, poker, chess, and battleship games, activities which, without the computer, they might not pursue. When some computer procedures or pastimes become sufficiently familiar and even routine, usually the amount of time spent playing the games decreases.

Summary

Usually, teachers who are designing curricular activities try to remain aware of relevance of the literary or scientific content to student experience. Such a relationship or parallel will often be achieved by requiring students to transfer an aspect of newly-acquired knowledge to real-life situations. The transition may be facilitated by asking such questions as: "How could this information be used to help a person solve a problem in everyday life?" Each teacher will consider that individual differences in requisite knowledge and skill are exhibited by students ready to undertake an activity. A teacher who is devising curriculum units will be assisted by asking such silent questions as this useful one: "What knowledge and skill must the student possess in order to complete this activity?" Finally, as teachers continue to create learning activities, they must monitor the levels of novelty involved so that, as the students gain mastery, the novelty level may regularly be increased.

Individualized Programs

In contrast to the focus in earlier sections, in which the idea of addressing the fundamental needs of **all** students was outlined, here, individual programs are devised that focus on the unique needs of the individual student. At the point when the teacher and the individual student discuss personal goals and objectives, it is expected that the classroom is already organized to meet the affective, management, and motivational needs of each of them. As a result of the positive climate now existing in the classroom, the teacher has been able to override much that is negative. In ruling out the potential appearance of many classroom elements normally contributing to the misbehavior of students, the teacher can now concentrate on every student's needs as these arise.

Usually agreed upon by educators is the idea that, fundamentally, the educational process involves preparing each student to become a lifelong learner, one who is capable of producing desired personal outcomes. For this reason, the positive classroom is designed to encourage, in the course of each day, a sense of personal responsibility to be gained as the student's goals and objectives are integrated into the curriculum. Guiding students in the context of individual programs involves certain fundamental conditions, each of which is presented in Figure 4-4.

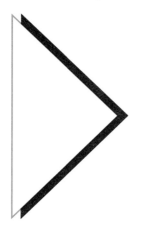

Individualized Programs:

Programs specific to the needs of the individual should promote

GOALS RELATED TO RESPONSIBILITY

- each student can develop the power to choose personal types of behavior

- the individual can learn to accept the consequences of behavior

GOALS OF THE LEARNER

- the individual can determine what to derive from learning situations

GOALS FOCUSSED ON SOCIAL CONTACT:

- each person will be given opporftunities to interact with peers

Figure 4-4. **Conditions of an Individualized Program**

In the process of organizing an individualized program – carefully focused on the specific needs of the student – the teacher must closely monitor both the details and the processes to assure that they maximize student responsibility for a successful outcome. To achieve this individualized structure successfully, the teacher will involve the student not only in the planning, execution, and evaluation phases, but also in any discussion of the consequences of meeting goals and objectives.

Helping students learn how to establish personal goals and objectives is one of the most empowering techniques that a teacher can impart. In the majority of advertised programs that promise to teach people how to become successful – rich, happy, in charge, etc. – this "secret" component is included, because establishing goals, in addition to being an empowering process, provides the learner with a sense of direction. Taking the time to establish goals and objectives is analogous with constructing a road map to pinpoint a destination as well as with making plans regarding ways to accomplish the journey. This process affords the student a sense of control: "I've decided that I want to pass the written half of my driver's test and so I need to get the booklets, read them, study them, take practice tests, etc.". In becoming aware of a project's stages and overview, the student is also able to acquire a sense of accomplishment: "I made the decision; I planned it; and I did it."

When students are encouraged to think about an aim that is personally relevant and then to plan how to achieve such a goal, they become active rather than passive participants. Given the opportunity to decide what is important in their lives, in the process of compiling goals, they discover ways to access the things they want. As a result of formulated objectives, they enter a learning process that provides a personal awareness of how things are accomplished. When these skills relate to real life situations, they influence the self confidence of the learner. The student starts to make things happen instead of allowing them to be imposed. Learning to define personal goals and objectives allows the student to use the many aspects of education – both within and beyond the limitations of the classroom – as instruments to meet individual needs.

In teaching students to personalize their learning, teachers will recognize, on the basis of priorities, that variable performance expectations are associated with the completion of tasks. Figure 4-5 demonstrates some of the goals learners adopt as they complete different activities.

On the basis of personal priorities, students often will decide that, in order to get them out of the way, certain tasks need to be completed as quickly as possible. Through experience, a student may learn to realize that instead of engaging in a lot of energy and time-draining activities designed to escape doing a task, the more effective strategy is **just to do it!** Few people find the daily grind of washing dishes, making beds, and taking out trash to be spiritual experiences, but, nonetheless, this work must **be done.** To complete such tasks, an individual has to begin to think differently about them, instead of using avoidance.

In contrast, achieving other goals may involve more personal satisfaction as well as meeting a particular objective; for example, a situation exists in which a person must follow instructions to put together a TV stand. If the goal is just to get the stand made, in all likelihood, when the job is finished, either the parts will not fit together or the completed stand will not hold the TV. In such a case, the individual must begin again, this time by interacting differently with the task. Very soon, the need for guidelines to be followed becomes apparent if the goal is the successful completion of the task. When the various stages have been followed, with close reference to the instructions, the person obtains from the entire experience a sense of having learned something about putting things together. Finally, certain activities are undertaken because they have some personal relevance to the student. When something special is involved for the individual, tasks warrant careful treatment in the way they are completed. In this unique situation, the learner determines that the completion of the activity will provide information or procedures linked to personal need. Now, the goal is not only to get the process completed while learning something new, but also to integrate this new information into the individual's personal knowledge. This attitude about the achievement of a goal is evident in students who first of all complete the task but then extend it by going to the library to seek further information. When engaged in a new interest of this kind, the student may also discuss the project with others, even deciding to study the subject in greater depth. Subsequently, a variety of mental activities, derived during the completion of the task, will be applied to comprehend the new information. At each stage of the process, in order to compare and synthesize the new procedures with existing knowledge, the student is engaged not only in practical activity but in thinking. Although teachers are interested in developing learning situations which will encourage students to devise loftier learning goals, the true situation in most classrooms is that tremendous emphasis is placed on "getting done!" For this reason, care should be taken to teach the idea of not focussing exclusively on one learning goal. Rather, students should be encouraged to evaluate each task in relation to a variety of factors and to set or alter the goal until it approximates most appropriately the needs of the specific activity. For example, if a series of illustrations is being planned, perhaps a plan for a park, the student may alter the goals – originally standardized photographs – and instead create drawings that vary according to size, shape, color, and number, depending on the suitability of these categories to the topic.

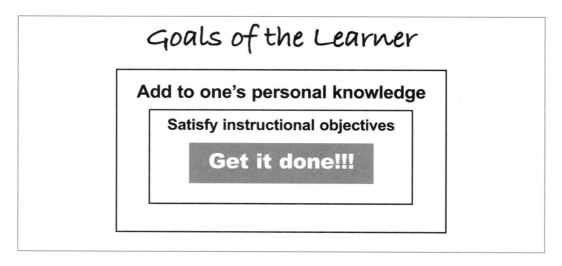

Figure 4-5. **Goals of the Learner**

Individualized programs strive systematically, as much as is feasible, to shift personal responsibility for learning to the student. In addition, they encourage each student to focus on individual tasks, when examining personal learning goals. Most importantly, such programs maximize students' chances of interacting with their peer groups, a fundamental requirement for any behavioral program whose goal is to develop social skills. Inevitably, a peer group provides several opportunities: first, social skills are acquired by observing people interacting in various situations and by having to offer ideas and suggestions; second, the feedback of others, occurring in a friendly interactive atmosphere, frequently shapes behavior. Like a comedian who first observes human behavior, then writes jokes, and finally tests the repertoire with various audiences, students become adaptive as a direct result of the feedback of people around them.

If students are isolated or, in some cases, surrounded by children and teachers not representative of the school community, they cannot fully become adaptive. Although, sometimes, in order to address more serious behavioral problems, it may be necessary to segregate some students in special classes, the teacher will continue to organize normative situations that allow each student to test learning in a social context. For example, a personal goal for the usually segregated student might be to go on a field trip with a small group of students registered in a regular class. Working together, the student and the teacher will plan the objectives necessary to accomplish the goal. As a corollary, the basis for evaluating each student's social learning progress will be focused on the appropriateness of behavior. In general, accurate evaluation of every student's progress typically involves observing each one in social situations that are not only age-relevant but also context-appropriate.

Issues addressed by individualized programs

Up to this point, the focus has been on outlining an individualized program, that is, on establishing goals and objectives while insuring that the process

> - extends the student's awareness of responsibility
> - highlights different intentions associated with the completion of each task
> - maximizes opportunities for social interaction and living.

Now, the task – illustrated in Figure 4-6 – remains to identify the content of the individual program. In structuring this unit, or one that is similar, the teacher will consider behavior, focusing on the several domains of knowledge associated with it. Included in these realms of knowledge are those related not only to the emotions but also to the development of skills for expressing feelings in socially appropriate ways. In addition, knowledge about language becomes important, as do understanding and awareness which foster the comprehension of behavior. An example of such an area of learning would involve recognizing cause-effect relationships, the nature of problem solving, or another basic strategy. A final focus would be on knowledge about living in a social milieu. When setting up projects of this kind, teachers should examine other potential sources of knowledge – especially those appropriate to the needs and skills of the individual student.

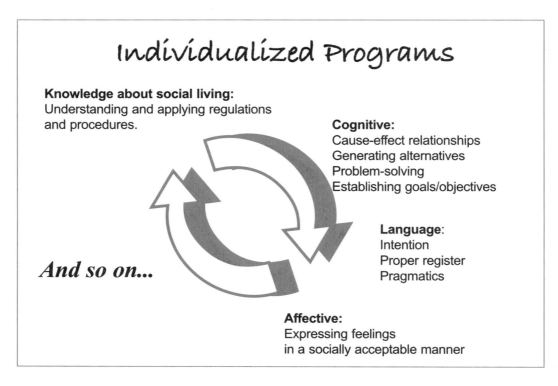

Figure 4-6. **Concerns of the Individualized Program**

Summary

A model of needs is designed by taking psychological premises and applying them to the classroom context. In order to create a positive classroom environment, the first three stages outline and identify issues dealing with affective, management, and motivational issues to be addressed classroom-wide; in the final stage – personal goals and objectives – the suggestions touch on a student's unique requirements and questions.

The affective needs, those related to the student's emotions when in the classroom, include the fundamental condition of feeling safe and experiencing a sense of belonging, as well as of becoming empowered and in control. Management needs, those that ensure the smooth running of the class, identify the necessity for clear expectations. In this connection, a pattern of ignoring inappropriate behavior is established for the purpose of encouraging pro-social behavior. Motivational needs, those relating to academic output, identify the task variables: meaningfulness, difficulty, and novelty. Individually and together, these variables impact on the potential level of students' energy and effort to be invested in learning activities.

In the final level of the model, personal goals and objectives are shown to relate directly to the needs of the individual in the context of the classroom. Often, in circumstances of this kind, students will require individualized programs. In the following chapter, concentration will be on elements and domains that contribute to the need for individualized programs.

Endnotes

[1] Travelling from school to school, an itinerant teacher has intensive training to work with individuals requiring specialized service.

[2] The seminal work of both Maslow and Glasser is outlined in Chapter Two.

[3] The section on interventions includes a discussion of ways in which errors can be transformed into learning opportunities.

[4] Initially, students from other cultures have difficulty with implicit expectations, although they would not experience such problems in their own families.

[5] This is an excellent example of the criticism trap described later in this Chapter Six.

[6] See Appendix 1 for examples of student activities.

[7] Reinforcement activities refer to a series of tasks used to practice a new concept in a number of applications.

[8] Not only are computer environments novel, they can also include meaningful experiences. Some examples are: SimCity, Zoo Tycoon, and other simulation games of this kind.

CHAPTER 5

Application of the
Model of Needs to Individualized Programs

In Chapter Four, a model of needs was presented. Arranged in a pyramid, the model depicted affective needs as the foundation; these were followed by management and motivational needs, and were then topped by individualized programs. In applying this model to the classroom situation, the teacher will see that it provides the necessary structure to create a positive atmosphere. Within this environment, both social and academic learning will be fostered, with the first four levels directed towards meeting group needs. Designed to respond to the unique demands of each student considered separately, the last level is planned as an individualized program. When the teacher believes, however, that the whole class would benefit from examining the same issues, similar themes can be integrated into academic subjects to reach the entire class.

In the sections which follow, general issues are outlined, relating to the construction of individualized programs. In some cases, subsequently, these may be considered appropriate for class-wide presentation.

Affective Issues

When students are beginning to learn ways of expressing feelings in a socially appropriate manner, they face an important challenge. This task is difficult because cues from the environment are not easily interpreted. Often, too, some people's reactions prompt students to believe that certain feelings are best repressed. When, frustrated, Yvonne might be reprimanded for shouting and throwing books, no query is made about the emotions that fueled her behavioral display. After Yvonne has been punished, she will no longer throw her books; less commendable is the realization that she will also learn to bury her frustration.

Some teachers, especially those who subscribe exclusively to the behavioral view, may incorrectly assume that Yvonne's problem has been adequately addressed once she no longer shouts or tears and throws her books. In fact, Yvonne's feelings have not disappeared, and, if the principles of classical conditioning are to be believed, these emotions may unwittingly become associated with various factors in her environment. Not only is it possible, for example, that her feelings of anger and frustration may surface each time she walks into the classroom, but those same emotions may arise as she enters the school or simply sees her teacher or classmates. Even when Yvonne works in a group, the partly repressed emotions may be paramount. Although the teacher might find it expedient simply to modify Yvonne's behavior, if a more profound and long-term form of assistance is to be brought to her situation, her feelings and the sources of her frustration must also be addressed.

Rooted as they are in emotions and their expression, many issues involve a domain of knowledge that may still need to be acquired by the student. Included in this realm are acquisition of the knowledge and procedures to:

- discern internal states or emotions

- label internal states or emotions

- identify emotions associated with the facial expressions and body language of others

- recognize emotions associated with the tone and language of others

- verify emotional triggers

- choose emotional responses that are appropriate to a social or educational context

Younger students – as well as some adolescents and adults – have difficulty distinguishing among varied emotions. After all, these often hidden feelings are not physiological but psychological phenomena. In addition, various types of feelings are capable of generating similar or identical physiological consequences; for example, increases in heart rate, blood pressure etc., with the result that the feedback received from the body is not helpful in identifying the specific emotion being experienced. Upon close examination, however, it is possible to see that individuals learn to label and notice subtle features, especially the distinctive characteristics that differentiate between groups of emotions such as anger, frustration, disappointment. In most cases, this kind of learning is accomplished vicariously – acquired indirectly from experience – rather than empirically. When children appear who have been unable to learn to distinguish these emotions, structured learning activities should be designed with the objective of teaching them directly, through role playing as well as books, television, and videos.

Although students may be capable of recognizing and labeling personal emotions, they must also learn to identify the emotions felt by others – a useful objective in social situations. Usually, such identification will be achieved by having those students learn to infer feelings, once the visual and auditory cues have been perceived. For example, certain facial expressions (see Figure 5-1) and specific tones of voice – in non-conversational situations – help to ascertain and appreciate the emotions felt by others. Because both body language and sounds take many forms, students who appear not to attend to or perceive such cues may require structured activities that will provide practical learning opportunities. A student who cuts out from a magazine a range of faces expressing various emotions may then mount these on poster board, label them, and then outline the identifying methods by which those labels were established. Such pinpointing is a useful and worthwhile beginning for students who have not learned to discern the emotions of others.

Figure 5-1. **Some facial expressions associated with internal states**

Not only in the classroom, but also in the playground at recess, Buffy has difficulty expressing her feelings in a socially appropriate manner. In Figure 5-2, related to Buffy's individualized program, a series of objectives is outlined, with the expectation that she will learn these skills. Such a set of goals is easily incorporated in Buffy's Individual Educational Plan.

Goal: Learning to express feelings in a socially appropriate manner

Objectives:

1. When shown pictures of different facial expressions, Buffy is able to name the emotions associated with them.

2. When asked to listen to statements made in different tones of voice, Buffy is able to name the emotions implied by the speaker.

3. When requested to, Buffy is able to make a series of facial expressions appropriate to the emotions named by her teacher.

4. When appropriately cued, Buffy is able to produce a verbal response using a tone of voice appropriate to the emotions named by her teacher.

Figure 5-2. **A sample set of objectives for a student learning to express feelings in a socially appropriate manner**

In learning to establish personal control over emotions, the student must identify the triggers that precede emotional outbursts. For example, once Yvonne is able to discriminate, separating her anger from other negative feelings, she must also learn to pinpoint the nature of the conditions or situations that usually precipitate the anger. In the classroom, the teacher might encourage her to keep a log of the date, time, and context of her emotional outbursts, as well as a note of the conditions prevailing before, during, and following the event. In order to understand why these outbursts occur, Ms. Papoulos and Yvonne could then discuss the information in the log, focusing on the triggers, ultimately being able – together – to resolve the problem. It becomes evident to Yvonne and her teacher, after their examination of the log in Figure 5-3 that the problem centers upon writing tasks.

YVONNE'S LOG

	Before	During	After
Language Arts	TEACHR ASKD TO WRIT ANSERS TO QUESTNS	I GOT MAD END THRW MY BOOK	TECHR SNT ME TO TIME OUT CHIR
Social Studies	I WUZ WERKING IN A GROUP AND MRCIA SAID WHY DOES'NT YVONNE WRITE THE NOTE	I RIPD UP THE PAPER AND THRW IT AT MARCIA.	I HAD TO SIT BY MYSELF AT THE BECK TABLE.
Math	CAME TO CLASS LATE AND ASKD MARY FOR PENCIL	PUSHED MARY	NOTHNG

Figure 5-3. Yvonne's log

Yvonne's frustration with writing tasks is genuine, partly because she is a terrible speller but also because she has learned that no course of action open to her is adaptive. If she writes sentences using only the words she knows how to spell, the other students make fun of her "babyish" statements. If, on the other hand, she attempts to write more complex sentences, she loses valuable time with the dictionary, looking up the spelling of each hard word. Often of course, she is unable to find the word she is seeking. In the first instance – using the easy words – she feels ashamed and incompetent; while, in the second situation – the dictionary option – she becomes angry and frustrated.

To respond to this complex situation, Ms. Papoulos and Yvonne will come up with a plan that includes not only an immediate procedure but also a long-term course of action. Presently, Yvonne will know instinctively to consult with her teacher each time a writing component is implied in an assignment. Depending on the nature of the activity, Ms Papoulos will modify it. She may begin by requiring Yvonne to dictate an answer orally; to use a personal dictionary[1]; or to illustrate her thoughts. From a classical conditioning perspective, this procedure is able to extinguish the association between writing demands and the habitual negative responses. Each time Yvonne is faced with a writing activity, the alteration in emotional level will be demonstrated, because she no longer feels angry and frustrated. Instead, she is now able to be relaxed and confident, knowing that her teacher will modify the irksome element in the activity and that she – Yvonne – is able to decide when such help is needed.

In addition to presenting these adaptive ideas, Ms. Papoulos will also design a program to address Yvonne's spelling difficulties. Such a procedure may include Yvonne's attending a resource period with a special education teacher for 30 minutes a day. Yet another option would involve completing a set of programmed learning activities, focusing on spelling procedures with the help of a peer tutor. As Yvonne acquires spelling skills and appropriate access to knowledge, she will feel more confident about completing the written component of classroom activities. With time, the source of her frustration will be eliminated.

Although Yvonne's log makes evident that her feelings and behavior are usually triggered by the writing demands, emotional triggers will not always be so obvious or as readily identified. This is especially true when the emotional response is generalized to the present situation; that is, the source of the immediate outburst is not the object of the original classical conditioning but simply resembles the conditioned target. Now that the original target – which has provoked the emotional response – is long forgotten, how can the teacher and the student be expected to intervene? While Sarangan experiences explosive tantrums at different times of the day, despite attempts to log observations, his teachers have difficulty in pinpointing a stable cause of the behavior. Because many aspects appear to vary each time Sarangan has an outburst, Mr. Hassan and Ms. Martinez are uncertain of how to proceed.

Although the cause of the behavior is elusive, if observations of Sarangan's actions and appearance can be made several minutes before the outburst itself, they will indicate that certain responses are common to each episode. Most notably, Sarangan's voice increases in pitch and volume as he draws closer to losing control. Focusing on this observation, Sarangan and his teacher are able to establish a program to be initiated by noting the changes in his voice. Because Sarangan is familiar with relaxation techniques, as soon as his voice begins to increase in pitch and volume, he is asked to go to the quiet area where he may put on his relaxation tape, as has been previously agreed. Not only does this intervention abort the sequence of behavior that has inevitably led to his outbursts, but the reduction in outbursts is instrumental in extinguishing the emotional response. At the same time, Sarangan has found greater opportunity for engaging in behavior both encouraged and approved by his teacher.

Figure 5-4. Series of events leading to an emotional outburst.

Figure 5-4 illustrates events observed to occur before an emotional outburst. Usually perceived to happen in a predictable pattern, the sequence may readily be derived from student and teacher observations. Because Yves has a high frequency of angry outbursts, Mr. Gorlik is prompted to establish an individualized program for him. Before creating this specialized outline, Mr. Gorlik and Yves attempt to pinpoint and record all the stages that lead to each outburst. Once discrete behaviors are identified, the plan is to intervene in an early phase of the pattern, while the student, Yves, is still able to make rational versus emotional decisions. In their investigation, both teacher and student have recognized that an early cue is the way Yves – almost as a precursor to an eventual explosion – begins to invade the personal space of his classmates. At the outset, Yves and Mr. Gorlik will discuss and clarify the procedures to be put in place when Yves begins to move closer to other students. For example, classmates will communicate to Yves that he is uncomfortably close, at which point he will be either cued to move towards or will direct himself to a quiet classroom area equipped with earphones and tapes of relaxing music that he himself has chosen. A timer, to be set by him to five minutes, will signal his return to join the class. At an early stage, it is important that Yves memorize the details relating to what Mr. Gorlik and/or his classmates will do or say – a signal, a phrase – and what the student, Yves, will do to respond. Also to be established are the procedures which will follow the event, the most important of which are evaluation, annotation, and further discussion. From the start of the procedure, both Yves and Mr. Gorlik will chart various aspects of each event, manipulating variables with the intention of reducing – and eventually eliminating – his outbursts.

In reaction to feelings of anger, Guerrero (1994) identified four typical responses on the basis both of their directness and of their threatening features:

1. assertive responses which are direct and non-threatening; for example, Tiffany calmly discusses her angry thoughts and feelings with Alyssa and Peter

2. aggressive responses which are direct and threatening; for example, Mario is arguing with Kurt and in the process is slamming his fist on the desk

3. passive-aggressive responses which are indirect and threatening; for example, Marta, who is angry with Fred, gives him cold and dirty looks, all the while ignoring the other students in the class

4. non-assertive denial responses which are indirect and non-threatening; for example, Solly, who has just had an altercation with Sam, reacts by becoming quiet and walking away from him

To familiarize students with the range of anger responses and their appropriateness, the teacher might devise an individualized program focusing on the types of contexts that would make each of the four potential responses adaptive.

So far, in this chapter, the analysis involves only explosive situations in which anger and frustration are examined. The result of teachers' often stated concerns about difficulties arising in the classroom, this emphasis is directed especially to those teachers who are learning to deal with such problems, although others may find it instructive. In common among the concerned teachers is the realization that remaining confident becomes difficult during explosive moments. But negative emotions are not the only ones that are hard to deal with openly.

Another great difficulty for students – and ultimately for their teachers – is the expression of positive feelings such as love and affection in a socially appropriate manner. For example, Marcus, in grade one, generalizes behavior learned at home among his parents and siblings, transferring it to the classroom. Whenever Marcus feels warmly toward classmates, he wants to kiss them to show his affection. A further aspect of this problem, in which feelings are shown inappropriately, is demonstrated by the adolescent student in the classroom who begins to have romantic feelings for another student, knowing nothing, however, about how to share this discovery with the object of that adoration. First, twelve-year old Victor pinches Mariel's arm and then fourteen-year old Vicky whispers to her girlfriends about her affection for Robbie. In response to their giggling and glances, Robbie reacts in embarrassment. In both cases, however, expressions of positive emotions are causing distress to the recipients.

It will be a useful insight to teachers that researchers have noted gender differences in the emotions of expression. Brody (1985, 2000) concludes that boys inhibit emotional expression when it uses words and facial expression; the exceptions are anger and contempt, both of which flow freely, outwardly directed. In contrast, while girls will express positive, warm emotions through words and facial expressions, they will make an exception for negative emotions – such as anger – which they learn to inhibit. Not only is this phenomenon affected by age, but also, the boys' level of a wide range of expressiveness decreases with age, whereas, when girls age, only the expression of negative affect decreases.

Attempting to learn about the expression of emotions such as sadness, jealousy, and envy can also become the basis of individualized programs. Here, too, gender differences are clearly demonstrated, shaped not only by biological and evolutionary factors but also by socialization variables put into place by parents when a child is born. For example, on the basis of empirical research, parents discuss emotions much more readily with girls than with boys, and, from the earliest infancy of these girls, they try to evoke more facial expression. Also, when telling stories from picture books, for example, parents generate different scripts for their preschool sons than for their daughters of the same age. With daughters, fathers more commonly use emotion words such as "happy", "sad", "love", whereas mothers use fewer anger words, such as "mad" and "hate". When a child falls and gets hurt, Fivush (1989) reports, mothers will inquire about the emotional state of daughters: "How much does it hurt?", but, with sons, will comment on the action, "Did you fall down and go boom?"[2]

An interesting experiment[3] which highlights gender differences in adult interpretation of children's emotion, entails the observation of an infant's behavior. In the experiment, half the observers believed the infant was a girl, while the other half thought it was a boy. On the basis of the infant's emotional display, observers described the boy's emotion as anger, whereas the girl's was identified as fear. When thinking about this dichotomy, a teacher will probably plan to use dimensions other than gender in interpreting the emotional state of a student.

In regard to sadness and depression, studies suggest that boys and girls also differ in their responses. Whereas boys, in order to distract themselves and to avoid facing their feelings, are more likely to act out by becoming defiant and mischievous, girls are more likely to internalize – "I hate myself!" – and reach out to others for comfort. As can be observed, these varied findings demonstrate why it is often difficult for a teacher to ascertain the true emotion felt by the student in order to be able to help the child deal with the problems arising from it..

An emotional state often associated with the behavior of other persons, jealousy requires special focus. When Sylvia, in Grade 3, observes Monica speaking to Chantal, she experiences a painful emotion triggered by the perception of a potential rivalry. Given that Monica is her best friend, Sylvia is suspicious, and, close to the surface of her feelings is the implicit expectation that interactions other than with her are not allowed. Fifteen-year old Mischa experiences the same emotion when Rolanda, his steady girlfriend, takes time to explain the homework assignment to Curtis. Unlike Sylvia, who might respond by telling Monica that they are no longer best friends, Mischa may embarrass Rolanda either by screaming at her in front of others, or worse, becoming physically abusive[4]. In Mischa's case, the thought of losing her, triggered by his feelings of possessiveness toward Rolanda, places him in emotional distress. The way he chooses to respond will invoke various responses: first, a self-evaluation that will perhaps lead him to understand the basis for his feelings; then, more likely, a perception that her behavior is a betrayal. Within seconds, Mischa either storms out, vowing never to see Rolanda again, or, if issues of power are involved, he lashes out verbally or physically at Rolanda, with the intention of modifying her behavior.

Further along the list of the famous Deadly Sins, is envy which strikes when someone else has possessions that a person would like to have but is unable to access. Although Myrna would love to wear the designer clothes that Sharon is seen in, her family is unable to afford such extravagances. For Myrna, feelings of envy are short-lived, however, because she replaces them with daydreams about her future plans involving a good education, a terrific job, and, especially, lots of money to buy a beautiful wardrobe. Francis, on the other hand, would like to wear the sports T-shirts and the athletic shoes often paraded by Jamal. Because Francis feels entitled to have these things, he decides to bully Jamal into giving them to him; he is even willing to steal them when the opportunity presents itself. Being locked into his envy, Francis has not considered that, like Jamal, he could obtain an after-school job that would allow him to purchase the desired objects.

When devising individualized plans, the teacher may be aware of many targets created by negative consequences or states of emotional distress. In overview, the outcome may be refreshingly positive, especially when uncontrolled student behavior associated with emotional responses is shown to be alterable. The success of such a plan is assured, founded, as the plan is, on a blend of student contribution and teacher direction rather than based on a Band-Aid solution.

Language Issues

It is not unusual to find that the more physically aggressive students in the class – those who push, slap, pinch, poke, or hit other children – are also likely to have weak language skills. Interestingly, this sub-group often includes not only some students who speak English as a Second Language but also those who may have a language disability, a hearing challenge, or autism. Also part of this noticeable element are slow learners, developmentally challenged individuals, and those whose cultures or subcultures place less value on language skills than does the dominant culture. Often, such overly assertive students represent environments in which "children should be seen and not heard".

Language skill, which serves many important functions in social interactions, is able to:

- facilitate the communication of specific needs and intentions; for example, "I am hungry". or "I am leaving the class to go to the washroom".

- replace non-verbal behavioral actions that are socially unacceptable; for example, instead of hitting a student who won't let him play, Ben is able to express verbally his displeasure: "Who says I can't?"

- raise an individual's level of empowerment when used for personal defense; for example, Margot had a humorous comeback to Sarangan's nasty remark: "Sure, Sarangan, and you look like a fish!"

- permit reflection concerning appropriate behavior when individuals – faced with decisions about what to do next – take the time not only to think about different courses of action but also to examine the probable consequences of each; for instance, Olivia says to herself, "If I hit him, Ms. Rostov will isolate me".

- promote group membership between individuals who speak the same language, dialect, or language register. The negative side of this may, of course, lead to exclusionary modes of behavior.

- facilitate social interaction when distinct language patterns are used to communicate with parents, teachers, and fellow students; a common trait among students is the habit of saying "Please" when that has been established as a cultural marker. While newcomers may find "the magic word" unfamiliar, they quickly become aware of its importance in the classroom.

Because the major goal of language is the communication of the speaker's intentions, a student who lacks sufficient language skill to accomplish this goal may revert to the use of gestures and other non-verbal behaviors. In this circumstance, the weak speaker grabs a desirable toy to play with or pushes a classmate out of the way in order to pass. In short, students with speech limitations must inevitably experience frustration, anger, and feelings of isolation when they either cannot make their wants and desires known to teachers and classmates or fail to understand what others are saying. When Marianne, a language-disabled student, does not understand Mrs. Wyandotte's explanation of the activity to be completed by lunch hour, she looks around at first. Seeing that some students are drawing pictures, she too sketches for a few minutes, but then, taking a toy from her bag, begins to play. Suddenly, Mrs. Wyandotte, now at her desk, is screaming about something, but Marianne is unable to understand the cause of her teacher's displeasure. When the verbal part of the incident is over, certain now that Mrs. Wyandotte does not like her, Marianne throws down her toy, tears her papers, and begins to cry. When diagnosing the entire event, the teacher will be obliged to consider the possibility that student misbehavior may at times be related to language issues.

In this situation, an evident corollary is that students unable to communicate verbally either their thoughts or their feelings are likely to fall back on inappropriate non-verbal means. In truth, Marianne resorts to throwing objects, tearing her work, and crying because of her inability to say to Mrs. Wyandotte, "Why are you picking on me?" or "I drew a picture". or "You've hurt my feelings". As soon as students are able to develop appropriate language skills, they replace unsuitable non-verbal behaviors with more acceptable verbal remarks; for example, when Franco accidentally steps on Marty's new running shoe, Marty , who previously would have hit Franco, now will only swear at him. Eventually, when his language skills develop enough for him to understand Franco's apology, Marty will realize that an accident has happened.

When spoken language provides people with the means to defend themselves in ways that are socially appropriate, it becomes empowering. Recently, Tony, a new Canadian, has been attending a behavioral class. Because he is too disruptive to remain in the regular class, his teacher has arranged this transfer for part of each day. Specifically, his inability during recess to respond verbally to taunting remarks made by a small group of students has led to physical fights. Viewing things from a distance, the teachers on yard duty were aware only that Tony ran after students, wrestled them to the ground, and hit them. Each time Tony was sent to the office – as frequently occurred – he always promised to be better-behaved the following day. While Tony's sincerity regularly encouraged the vice-principal to give him another chance, eventually he was suspended during recess from the schoolyard. In Tony's behavioral class, where, as a custom, students are able to raise personal problems for the group's input during the arts and crafts session, he decides to ask for help. By questioning Tony, the group discovers some very pertinent facts about what first triggered Tony's anger. When Ramon and Knute called him "Stupid", for instance, Tony, who was unable to respond verbally while still saving face, simply hit them. In the ensuing discussion, the group suggests that instead of hitting Ramon and Knute, Tony develop a sufficiently tough but neutral phrase to use verbally. When the other students provide several choices of repartee, Tony vetoes each, finally settling for: "You can't know everything". As a follow up, subsequent classes involve role-playing situations in which, when his classmates taunt him with "You're stupid! You go to the dummy class!" Tony practices his response: "You can't know everything". No longer perceiving himself as a victim, Tony now has a comeback which makes him feel "just as smart as the other boys".

For the student with behavior problems, another important linguistic ploy involves the development of phrasing to explain program modifications, in particular those comments directed to the peer group. By being able to understand and explain to others the nature of individualized needs, the student is empowered and, as a personal advocate, can relinquish the role of "victim". Characteristically, fellow students often make embarrassing and hurtful remarks about a student who leaves the class to go to another program, uses alternate textbooks, or is given activities that differ from those being pursued by the rest of the class. Especially strong attacks are reserved for simple-looking textbooks. Inevitably, these situations have emotional consequences for the student who has been judged behavioral; almost certainly this is a child who is likely to use inappropriate means to resolve conflicts. In some cases, a group of offending students will go to great lengths to trigger awkward responses in challenged students: it is probable that they derive sadistic pleasure from such situations. For this reason, behavioral students must be given language skills to circumvent potential hurt, anger, and scape-goating. When Leonard is asked by some classmates, for instance, why he is seeing a psychologist, an unpleasant situation is almost inevitable until Leonard calmly explains "He is helping me to learn how to control my anger". Unexpectedly, the intrusive students accept Leonard's simple but positive explanation.

Interestingly, language skills can, on the one hand, provide a student with a feeling of group membership or, on the other hand, encourage a sense of isolation. When students are new immigrants, still unable to speak English, they may be reassured by the presence of others whose first language is the same. While it often may be difficult for the teacher to understand the sub-group's motivation for continuing to speak in the first language when there are opportunities to communicate in English, sometimes the explanation is simple. When speaking in their own first language, at least from time to time, the newcomers are enabled to poke fun at or insult other children in the class. In this informal group activity, newcomers find a means to feel safe and empowered in what may sometimes be a frightening situation. In the classroom, however, the single new immigrant student who finds no compatriots, is likely to feel the isolation that arises, first, from not understanding what others are saying and, second, from the inability to communicate needs or interests. In a few classrooms, an unusual but cruel situation exists in which newcomers are given buddies, mentors who speak both the first language and English. Here, a danger emerges when these translators become overbearing and bossy, because of their power over the recently arrived immigrants.

It is interesting to realize that a student who does not speak the language of the dominant culture is not the only one whose feelings of membership or isolation will be associated with language. Yet another group – those who communicate by means of American Sign Language – face similar problems but are able to communicate. Because of the unique situation in which many hearing-impaired students find themselves, it is difficult for teachers to understand why certain educators – in particular, those who promote "total communication" – fail to recognize how empowering the acquisition of ASL can be for the student with a hearing challenge. Through ASL training, the linguistically disabled student becomes a fully involved part of a non-hearing subculture. For the language-disabled student – this serious point cannot be overstressed – only isolation will result unless the school develops individualized programs targeting language and social skills

When examining the importance of the role of language and group membership, teachers are made aware of small groups of people who speak the same language but share specialized vocabulary, phraseology, inflection, and language patterns. Often, such variation is evident in people who, while speaking English, come from different countries, from different regions of a single country, from different age groups, and/or from different socio-economic backgrounds. Not many years ago, newcomers from Scotland and Jamaica were treated as ESL[5] students, although their first language was English. In these situations, the students' accents and language patterns were sufficiently different from local Standard English to convince educators that ESL programs would be appropriate. Given such conditions, how would any of these students feel about such placement?

Although language is central in communication with others, it also serves important cognitive functions when used to communicate with the self. Vygotsky, who was fascinated by the role of both overt and covert speech in directing human behavior and thought, shows that as students integrate developing language skill with thinking, they accomplish feats such as solving problems, reducing impulsivity by considering the consequences of action, soothing fears, etc. *Language mediation* – what Vygotsky refers to as "inner speech" – while driving the problem-solving process, also enhances performance. Apparently, when people experience inaudible speech in the mind's ear, they perceive it as synonymous with thinking – "I hear myself thinking." Faced with difficult situations or tough problems, people often resort to speaking aloud to facilitate the process. When, for example, still at home and late for school, Gina is unable to find her books, she questions herself aloud: "Where did I go first when I got home from school yesterday? And after that? Where do I usually put my books?" And so she continues. If Gina is still unable to find her books, she can generate questions about her thinking process; for example, "This tack is not working; can I do this differently?" By exploring the ways by which she can retrieve from her memory the location of her books, Gina is acquiring metacognitive knowledge.

In yet another context, language mediation is used by students to evaluate performance. Here, however, the types of personal statements made can augment or hinder achievement. A good instance is Marika, who when she has difficulty with Math problems, always says to herself, "I can never do this", or "I'm really stupid". Characteristically, Marika makes such comments when faced with any Math task. In response, part of her individualized program is structured carefully to transform these self-statements to more productive ones. Clearly, then, in addition to being useful in problem-solving situations, the "inner" language, especially when it motivates and evaluates performance, is an important factor in the education equation. Ultimately, this realization means that a teacher can utilize "think-aloud"[6] protocols to examine the usually silent comments of the student who is completing a task.

According to reliable pedagogic scholarship, language mediation is central to thinking style. As they mature and their language skills develop, children progress slowly from an impulsive to a reflective thinking style. In a theory outlined by Luria, the famous Soviet psychologist, the transition from impulse to reflection begins when the student is approximately seven years old, the age at which most children are able to establish a one-to-one correspondence between language and action. Around that age, for instance, students who are counting aloud will solve simple math problems by pointing to coins. How many coins will Jared put in his piggy bank? "One", drops a coin, "two", drops a coin, "three", drops a coin, "four", drops a coin, "five", completes the set. At this point, Jared will have put five coins in the piggy bank. While some five- and six-year olds are still unable to coordinate the counting with the dropping of the coins – or although able to accomplish the task will forget the last number counted – they might count "One, two, three, four" for the first coin and "five, six, seven, eight" for the second, and so on.

Behavior known as "*impulsivity*" involves impetuous responses that are rarely appropriate: Giles appears compelled to blurt out an incorrect answer before Mr. Montand has a chance to complete the question. This same style is evident in his written work: Giles writes the first thought that comes to mind when writing answers to reading comprehension questions. In contrast, Moira takes her time to consider all aspects of Mr. Montand's question in order to arrive at an appropriate response. For the child with behavior difficulties, a necessary element in any response would be the development of a reflective style. Such an addition to the personality would enable the individual to examine and evaluate behavior, to generate other potential ways of behaving, to consider the consequences of actions, and to choose, research, and execute behaviors appropriate to the context. Under the guidance of Mr. Montand, Giles may be able to start to build such a program, thus setting himself on the road to both reflection and more appropriate responses.

When teachers draw on language theory, they discover that a learner's memory capabilities are supported by language because of the process by which experience is labeled. By means of this labeling procedure, the information is further encoded to make it more memorable. In addition, a great deal of the data that students must remember is language-based. As a direct correlation – because the information is processed at the meaning level – students possessing good language skills are able to remember not only longer instructions, but also such elements as the rules of the game and how to respond to telephone calls when on office duty, as well as other useful data. Conversely, because students whose language skills are weak typically do not label their experiences, they process verbal information at a surface rather than a deeper-meaning level. For this reason, in order to avoid behavioral problems, the teacher must ensure that the most important aspect of a verbal command is found in the first four or five words in the sentence. A good

additional rule is to keep instructions brief. Further modifications to be made by the teacher will include an educational program with increased language stimulation – greater exposure to language forms and vocabulary as well as interactive participation in discussion and drama, along with other forms of oral expression. When language difficulties affect behavior, the teacher should consider interventions that will generate language scripts – imaginary dialogues – to help the student to deal with linguistic demands in problematic situations.

When the subject of language is being analyzed, **"meta-linguistic awareness"** is the term used to describe knowledge acquired about language – its form, its history, its use, and, inevitably, its appropriateness. Over millennia, different civilizations developed not only unique spoken *languages* but also, in some cases, elaborate writing systems. In addition, within each language, regional, economic, and historical variables have produced *dialects, creoles, and pidgins*. Less obvious, but of importance to successful communication, is the existence of registers: language forms that vary according to context, listener, and intention.

Registers – language variations that are context-dependent – always require that the speaker, on the basis of cues from the situation, will decide which are the appropriate language patterns to be used. In regular speech, several registers are available: the baby-talk register – the manner in which older persons speak to infants – is appropriate not only when spoken to babies, but also when used to address pets, a spouse, or a sweetheart; similarly, the locker room language, a coarser register, is suitable in the change room, primarily with individuals of the same sex. Interestingly, someone driving on the highway may employ this register when travelling alone, especially if cut off by another driver. Finally, the way people speak to a prospective client or employer is not only very carefully structured but possesses a tone qualitatively different from tones used in other situations.

In everyday contexts, social interactions require a knowledge of registers as well as the means to decide which one is suitable to a given situation. Among young persons in particular, this meta-linguistic awareness is frequently lacking, for example, in many students with behavioral difficulties as well as in young children who have yet to develop it and in language-disabled students. Among the members of another group – newcomers who are in the process of acquiring English as a second language – such specialized knowledge remains elusive for a long time after their arrival. In a school context, the teaching of necessary linguistic nuances is important as part of the development of social propriety, but, for a number of social and pedagogical reasons, accomplishing the task is very difficult. Achieved by most people through observation and experience, these registers are implicit in communication, but while they are never taught directly, they are also rarely discussed. Because language registers are not as evident in daily conversation as they were in the past, many students today may have difficulty not only learning about the existence of these aspects of language, but also acquiring them. As societal mores change, however, and become more flexible, so do these social expectations about language patterns. At present, when speaking with peers, although people tend to employ language patterns that are less formal than those used in earlier decades, it is evident that "the-customer-is-always-right" register is gaining prominence. As many young people are trained by fast-food chains, a smile and the phrase "Would you like fries with that?" might become standard usage, as could "Yo, Man!"

Generally, when teachers are working with students who have behavioral difficulties, the role of appropriate language skills is not considered to any important degree. When focusing on students of the kind described in this section, however, many behavioral interventions require a new focus. If students are being taught to cope in the world, emphasis must be placed not only on the student's language skills, but also on the ability to communicate personal intentions, while attempting to understand the intentions of others. In summary, moreover, this aspect of social interaction may be recognized as fertile ground for teacher intervention.

Cognitive Issues

In addition to consistently focusing on affective and language issues, the teacher of students with behavioral difficulties must consider that cognitive factors, too, will contribute to inappropriate behavior. This is observed in students who are sometimes unable:

- to recognize the cause-effect relationships existing between personal behavior and its usual consequences

- to evaluate personal behavior and the behavior of others

- to generate alternative ways of behaving

- to find ways to solve personal problems

- to imagine future goals and to plan for them

Although a minor controversy persists about whether cognitive skill or language skill is the first to develop in infants, most experts concur that both unfold in similar fashion – in definable stages. Because three-year old Kwabena is not expected to match the cognitive level of ten-year old Matthew, their social behavior will be judged differently. In the event that both children are thought responsible for the disappearance of an object, the two are held accountable, but in varying ways. Tiny Kwabena is not perceived as having "stolen" the object because, developmentally, he is still unable to comprehend the concept of "mine" and "yours".

At ten, Matthew, who is expected to differentiate among levels of ownership, is, therefore, held responsible for the anti-social act. In this situation, accountability is associated with cognitive ability in that Matthew has the level of skill and knowledge to evaluate the situation. For example, he might think, "This object does not belong to me". Also, he may make decisions; for instance, "When the owner put this in the garbage can, he may or may nor have intended to relinquish title to it. Usually, though, the thing in the trash is thrown away".

Generally, individual differences in cognitive development suggest that factors other than age may also determine levels of social responsibility. Furthermore, because developmentally challenged students are not capable of making certain types of decisions, they may not be held accountable for some manifestations of anti-social behavior. In particular situations, too, a student – who is sufficiently capable intellectually but temporarily emotionally distraught – may be deemed incapable of rational evaluation. The age of the student, as well as both cognitive and emotional functioning, can be factors that limit rational judgment. When evaluating the personal responsibility of an offender, a teacher should therefore consider, separately or together, all three elements.

When the role of cognitive issues in behavior is being defined, the first question for consideration is: "What is thinking?" Although this is a seemingly easy query that should elicit simple responses, it soon becomes evident that several answers are available. Such answers will include those traditionally provided by Behaviorists and Gestaltists, two groups known to differ radically in their points of view. More recently, however, but equally important, are the multifaceted responses offered by Cognitivists.

Generally speaking, Behaviorists define thinking as learning by reinforcement. Faced with a problem situation, a person will have certain response tendencies, created by previous conditioning; of necessity, these will determine what is tried first. When asked why she is leaving the school grounds, Tara, quickly scrambling for an explanation, gives the one that first pops into her head. Because it has been used successfully on previous occasions, she says brightly, "I have a dental appointment". If the reaction to the initial gambit proves unsatisfactory, that attempt will be followed by other responses, in a trial-and-error pattern. When Mr. Quinn challenges her story, Tara indicates that her excuse note has been left at home, and, because both parents are at work, she is unable to access it. Usually, solutions are guided first by previously practiced responses. Soon after, comes the Law of Effect which proposes that rewarded responses increase in strength. In Tara's case, if Mr. Quinn accepts her explanation, it immediately becomes one that she will use again. Because of their success, these positive responses become prominent in the student's behavioral repertoire. If a teacher is reasoning within this *associationist*[7] perspective, thinking will be defined as new combinations of strengthened reactions, usually organized in a response hierarchy. When Tara evaluates her behavior, her false explanations for leaving the school grounds will include all those previously used successfully. In addition, it can be assumed that these will be ordered in terms of priority – which to use first, followed by others less certain of success, and on down the list.

In contrast, Gestaltists conceptualize thinking from a perceptual point of view; that is, they reconstruct the problem in order to look at it differently. Believing that the mind imposes order or structure on all incoming information, these theorists argue that thinkers obtain solutions by insight, a process that involves re-arranging elements of the problem in a new way. In the story about Tara who is looking for a way to skip classes, her initial plan is just to walk out the door, but upon noticing Mr. Quinn in her path, she is so focused on finding a way out of the school that all other routes appear inaccessible. Here, Tara has a flash of insight: "What if I have a legitimate reason for leaving the building?" At this moment, Tara produces the dental appointment explanation, a successful pretext that eventually leads her out of the school. As long as Tara perceives her difficulty in terms of finding an escape route, the solution is not evident. Only when the problem is redefined in terms of an acceptable reason for leaving school does the solution appear.

In their exploration of thinking from several angles, Cognitivists relate all thought to the process of conceptualizing ideas:

- as hypothesis testing – inductive reasoning

- as logically drawing conclusions – deductive reasoning

- as a search for a solution path

- as a series of mental operations

- as striving for meaning – Schema Theory

- as a search of semantic memory – answering questions

- as a learnable skill – creativity training

- as influenced by experience – expert problem solving

- as based on analogues, models, and examples – analogical reasoning

By examining each of these ways to conceptualize thinking, the teacher will be able to see its relevance in understanding student behavior.

Thinking as hypothesis testing

Of major importance to people who view thinking as means of testing a hypothesis, concept learning is basic because concepts are thought to be the building blocks of cognitive activities. When students have learned rules for classifying objects and/or ideas from their daily experiences, they are able to assign objects to categories. For example, given a series of objects, as in Figure 5-5, Sharon not only can correctly identify the item worn on the head, but also can assign the name "hat" to this category. The general rule she is applying is, "If it is worn on the head, it's a hat."

Figure 5-5. **A series of objects including one worn on the head**

 On the basis of feedback received each time she labels an object "hat", Sharon will eventually discern both the relevant and the irrelevant characteristics of "hatness". Very soon, she will be able to conclude that when Sebastian wears a pot on his head it is not called a hat. In addition, she will deduce that variables like color and size are irrelevant, while other features, as, in Figure 5-6, are distinctive. Finally, Sharon realizes that a "cap" is a type of hat.

Figure 5-6. **A series of objects, all worn on the head.**

Similarly, because people often extrapolate rules or concepts about behavior from their experiences, many students learn that "polite" behavior includes important features. Among these are respect for other people – especially in forms that are acceptable in the context of the situation – helpfulness, appropriate language, and many others. Moreover, some students will become aware, as a result of repeated experiences with events labeled as "polite", that irrelevant features such as the time of the day or the identity of the person are unimportant to the classification. When students are involved in normal activities, concepts may be acquired in a manner such as the one described above, but what is still to be achieved is the evaluation, in everyday experience, of the newly learned concept by means of hypothesis testing. In the context of the classroom, this process can, at first, be made explicit, and then, subsequently, encouraged, in the following manner:

- providing an example and asking the student to judge whether it is an instance of the rule; for example, Ms Angibeau may say to the class, "If Jason were to grab a ruler from Alberto's desk, without asking to borrow it, is that an example of polite behavior?"

- asking students to identify the features used to categorize instances and non-instances of the rule; using the previous example, Ms. Angibeau will ask, "What aspect of Jason's behavior made you conclude that his action was not polite?"

- applying the concept to a new situation; for example, Ms. Angibeau will inquire, "If Jason wanted to be polite, what would he do and say to Alberto when hoping to borrow his ruler?"

In classrooms whose teachers ask students to think about rules, the procedures outlined here are customary. If, for instance, directing his query to the whole class, Mr. Fayed asks, "What's the rule about what to do when you don't know how to start your work?" Of course, this experienced teacher knows that having students recite rules will be a ploy of insufficient strength to reinforce concept learning. Hypothesis testing, however, encourages the cognitive examination of concepts. In order to achieve this end, Mr. Fayed requires his students to contemplate the following:

- "Is this situation an example of the concept in question?" *Do I sometimes find myself in a situation where I need help in starting my work?*

- "What characteristics of the situation cause me to conclude that it exemplifies the concept?" *I have read the instructions and I have no idea what I should do first.*

- "How do I change this situation which is a non-instance to an instance of the concept?" *I will start by asking my classmate to explain to me what is required; then I will be able to begin doing my work.*

- Other similar questions may be devised.

A variety of games can be generated by teachers and students – even in senior classes – to strengthen the acquisition of key concepts.

Thinking as drawing conclusions

When someone is thinking, the process may also involve analyzing pieces of existing information in order to draw logical conclusions. A famous example relates to the adventures of the fictional detective, Sherlock Holmes, whose method typifies this cognitive process of deductive reasoning. On the basis of very few clues – usually tiny details overlooked by everyone else – Holmes is always able to recreate an entire murder scene. When deductive reasoning is employed, some of the mental operations will include: isolating a concept and breaking it down into its elemental parts; observing the similarities and differences that exist between two events; giving the proper weight to a clue, that is, concluding that one piece of information is more important than another; and generating a conclusion on the basis of the way a few distinctive pieces of information lead to a clear outcome.

In questions of social behavior, when observations can be based on a few clues drawn not only from the context of a situation, but also from the body language of a person, deductive reasoning is particularly relevant in reaching assumptions about people's internal states. As soon as Jared enters the class, he runs eagerly to Sean to report that his hockey team has won the championship. Although the class is unusually quiet, and Sean is huddled in the corner, his hand over his face, Jared screams out his news. As he approaches, of course he is startled when Sean kicks him. The truth emerges that Jared, focused on his own news, overlooks the signals present in the classroom which could alert him to delay his news-telling. By recognizing the familiar cues as he walks in, Jared might realize that the class is recovering from a crisis situation involving Sean. Many such social situations occur on a daily basis, each requiring attention to contextual clues to help participants determine how to proceed. While some students are, or become, carefully adept at "reading" other people and situations, others find such an interpretive task very difficult or remain unaware that anything is expected of them. Social competence is enhanced by making students able to recognize situational clues that promote greater understanding of social contexts. For many students, further training can be achieved by focusing on those contexts available in classroom situations, as well as in literature, videos, films, and television programs, among other sources. While watching a television program about the challenges faced by Ticia, a character in the story, Mr. Frankl might ask: "What clues lead you to believe that Ticia is contemplating running away from home?" By having students observe personal interactions in social contexts, then showing them how to isolate certain elements, and finally training them to predict the relevance of cues, teachers can lead the group to become more adept at both recognizing certain cues and then using them to adjust personal behavior.

Thinking as a search for a solution path

In their quest to understand thinking, some Cognitivists have generated computer simulations of human behavior which they then frame in their search for a solution path that progresses towards a goal. In this process, thinking is equated with a sequence of mental operations or internal states which lead, usually, to a solution to the particular problem. To change the problem from one state to another involves making moves that the problem-solver deems valid. To apply this notion to problem-solving, it is interesting to consider the problem of transferring the three rings, illustrated in Figure 5-7, from their position on the first peg to their destination on the third peg, with the proviso that a smaller ring can be placed only on top of a larger ring. After this notion has been transferred to a social context, the teacher will find Marty's dilemma worth observing: Marty has just discovered that Brad is wearing a pair of running shoes identical to the ones that have gone missing from his locker. Given that Brad is the school's bully, the question must be posed: how does Marty find out if the shoes are his? More to the point, if they belong to him, how does he recover them? Certain moves are not advisable to Marty – for example, confronting Brad – and so, if the problem is to be solved with as few adverse consequences as possible, he has to be sure to proceed only in ways that are acceptable in and appropriate to his social context.

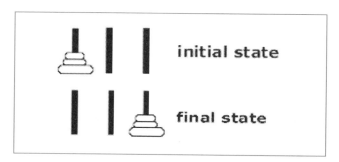

Figure 5-7. **The initial and final states of the rings on the peg problem**

How do Cognitivists build simulations of human behavior? They do so by doing the following:

- collecting think-aloud protocols[8] from people who might be able to solve the problem

- analyzing these protocols

- describing the mental processes used to arrive at various solutions

- generating these mental processes in a computer program

- testing to see how closely the computer can match the protocol performance

- concluding the program if the match is close

- making revisions if the match is not close

Although the actual generating of a computer simulation is of no direct interest to the teacher, very similar procedures can be applied to solving social problems. Earlier, an outline was given of an individualized program designed for Tony, the ESL student who defended himself with his fists when he could not fight back with words. To apply the computer simulation procedure, Tony, when caught in a name-calling situation, will gather important information by observing the behavior of other students who are defending themselves. Later, Tony will obtain think-aloud protocols from each student; that is, he will ask them to describe verbally the, of course, purely mental thoughts they can recollect from the process of finding a solution. By examining the similarities and differences inherent in the other students' situations, Tony is able to get a feeling for the way mental operations can be successful in solving his problem. In the next stage, he will create a personal program to match his goal, later trying it out in an actual situation. Finally, Tony will revise his outline, depending on whether or not it succeeds in solving his difficulty.

Thinking as a series of mental operations

When the idea of thought processes is being examined, one theory that is popular conceptualizes thinking as a series of independent mental operations. In the 1890s, Donders, along with other researchers, attempted to extrapolate and define the basic mental operations associated with perception. The focus was, for example, on response to the presence of a single stimulus or on the discrimination between two stimuli, with the idea of defining all operations that comprise cognitive tasks. Eventually, it was believed, a catalogue would be established, listing all these building blocks of thought. Such a notion as this structuralist view of thinking is somewhat consistent with Bloom's (1956) *Taxonomy*[9], a priority list of educational objectives often used by teachers to introduce a cognitive dimension to curriculum.

According to Bloom's *Taxonomy*, educational tasks may be ordered in six levels of cognitive complexity, from simplest to most complex: *knowledge, comprehension, application, analysis, synthesis, evaluation,* each of which makes specific cognitive demands on the thinker. When students are asked, for example, to recall and/or recognize information, the level called *knowledge* is drawn on. Looked at in a social context, this level would be apparent when Mr. Fortino asks Ruweida to recite the set of five classroom expectations or expects Amahl to state the three things to be done when he feels someone is threatening him. On the other hand, the *comprehension* level of Bloom's *Taxonomy* involves cognitive activity associated with extracting meaning from situations. In the classroom, this process will be usefully illustrated when Paul and Stavros are asked to give their version of what occurred after an altercation in the school yard. Bloom's higher levels also propose independent cognitive expectations: *application* requires that, for example, a student be ready to apply to a new situation what has been learned in an earlier one. In a formal individualized program designed by Ms. Bullock, Shanti has learned the various ways to greet adults and classmates in appropriate situations. As proof of her accomplishment, Shanti will demonstrate her *application* skills when, in the school yard, she generates a suitable greeting for Ms. Maura, the principal.

Further along the scale, Bloom's cognitive skill analysis involves dividing a situation into its elementary components. For example, is Izzy able to isolate the individual steps that have led him, successfully, to obtain his part-time job at Old Navy? Here are the stages he will recall:

- finding the advertised job by reading the classified section in the paper

- writing a job résumé; then having Mr. Wincott read it and offer suggestions

- typing the résumé, making positive changes, and printing it in a well-designed presentation

- sending the résumé to the appropriate address

- accepting a phone call for an interview; copying date and time into a personal calendar

- practicing interview skills with his classmates

- identifying his wardrobe for the interview; ensuring that it is clean and pressed

- other stages as needed

In personal and social contexts, analysis skills are important because, as in Izzy's case, these skills allow the individual to examine experience in its elemental parts. In such an examination, the person can evaluate the relevance of each component to the final goal.

At the next step, the cognitive skill synthesis asks that many basic elements be blended to form one higher concept. When given a series of behavioral instances, is the class able to identify that these are aspects of the concept of honesty[10]?

Finally, the skill of evaluation, which warrants that objective judgments be made about the situation in question, is fundamental to a person's ability to learn from experience. Because personal experience is a subjective phenomenon, the ability to examine it objectively, that is, as if it pertained to someone else, allows the individual a unique perspective that will contribute to necessary positive changes.

Thinking as striving for meaning

For some theorists, the role of meaning is of central importance in thought processes. In the context of thinking, the so-called *Schema* theory[11] not only supports this position but attempts to describe the process of understanding in a very precise manner.

First introduced by Bartlett in 1932, schemas are mental representations derived from past experiences. Implied in this idea is the belief that what is remembered is influenced by what is already known. Thus, in many ways, schemas structure and influence perception. In Chapter Three, this idea was pivotal to projective testing as examiners expected each client to generate a story on the basis of inkblots, pictures, and even blank cards. Similarly, on a summer's day, people who look up at the clouds often see an entire animal menagerie, an activity resulting from expectations created by previously learned thought structures. In another situation, if Ms. Mortedella, observing Marianne and Judith from her window, notes that the two are seated on the grass surrounded by books, she may conclude that they are studying. It is interesting to question why she evokes a "studying" schema, rather than a "picnicking" or "playing hooky" schema. Obviously, then, schema theory suggests not only that meaning is imposed on situations, but also that the nature of the meaning will depend on the past experience of the person doing the imposing.

By extending schema theory to the social context, the teacher demonstrates to the students ways of interpreting situations on the basis of their prior knowledge about similar contexts. In one instance, because Alice remembers always being laughed at by her classmates when answering questions about the story being read, she has incorporated this idea into her classroom schema – expectations about what occurs in the classroom. As a result, Alice will not answer questions in class, although she really likes her teacher, Ms. Silverstein. Many schemas created by previous school experiences dictate the way a student will interpret subsequent events in the classroom, school, recess, cafeteria, and even in other places. Because such schemas are constructed from direct experience and also from vicarious knowledge found in stories and in the recounted experiences of others, they create profound patterns in students' memories. If classroom discussions about various schemas are held in non-threatening circumstances, the confessed details may reveal intriguing notions that will explain many behavioral responses. Usually, long-held schemas are altered by subsequent experiences, and, for example, a schema regarding "restaurants" in four-year old Lisa, who usually eats out at Tasty Bears, will be differ significantly from the schema of ten-year old Rhonda whose family often dines at an Oriental Buffet. In contrast, Rhonda's experience will be quite different from that of Rachelle, also ten years old, whose family rarely if ever eats in public places, because of religious convictions. Rachelle fears the freedom of the buffet because of her certainty that some foods are taboo. When travelling in unfamiliar parts of the world, people are often surprised to find that their "restaurant" schema does not match that of the local folk. The depth and breadth of the schema will be seen to correlate with the richness of the experience.

Thinking as a memory search

In a theory similar to the view that equates *concept learning* with thinking, certain Cognitivists propose that problem-solving relies on the way knowledge is organized in memory. Because of the manner in which memory is structured, asking questions is fundamental to problem solving. As a corollary, both searching and retrieving meaningful information from memory are very important. A further implication can be perceived: when problem solvers are answering questions, they reveal variations in their methods of storing and processing knowledge.

Writing in 1984, authors Scardemelia, Bereiter, & Steinbach devised a way of helping students engaged in the writing process. In an overview of their method, it is clear that they provide potential questions for writers to consider when expanding and/or re-working ideas on paper. In an analogous situation, unrelated to writing modes, a similar model can be applied to various classroom circumstances. Alfred, a high school student whose time- management problems interfere with his school performance, is helped by his teacher. Mr. Janta, who wants to prompt better behavior, works with Alfred to identify a set of target questions that Alfred can ask himself. When Alfred, on Tuesday, for example, enters the school before classes begin, he starts his day by asking himself the prepared questions and hazarding some answers:

- What day is it today? *The schedule varies: is it Day Two?*

- What materials will I need? *For art? For math? For phys. ed?*

- What assignments am I expected to submit today? *Is the role-playing one ready?*

- Are there special events scheduled for today that I should prepare for? *Maybe my clean gym shorts are still in the dryer.*

- Each student will have a personal list of queries and also replies.

If Alfred is concerned that he may not remember his start-of-the-day questions, he can record them on an index card. When the card is filed with others containing typical questions, Alfred must remember not only where they are but also the need to refer to them. Other notations on cards might include a list of "what to do when":

- I don't know what to do

- I'm ill and preparing to go home

- I'm studying for a test

- I've left a book at home

- I've forgotten my note about the dentist's appointment

- other notes about similar contexts

For Alfred, the questions are meaningful, especially because, with the help of Mr. Janta, his teacher, and also his study group, *he* generated them. In the process of asking and answering his sets of questions and notes, Alfred is learning to organize his behavior.

Thinking as a learnable skill

In the 1930s and 1940s, the notion that thinking is a learnable skill began to be affirmed by people in industry who promoted creativity training. Arising from this movement, three sets of strategies have emerged: Crawford's *attribute listing*, Osborn's *brainstorming*, and Gordon's *synectics*, each one intended to make companies more competitive.

In the first of these procedures, Crawford's *attribute listing*, the critical attributes of a product were initially itemized; this stage was followed by a list of potential modifications to be made to each attribute. Then, suggestions were advanced by the participants to show how certain of these attributes could be applied to other objects or products. Ultimately, the object was the production of new and better hybrid products. In the series of three techniques, the second, Osborn's *brainstorming*, involved group problem solving, with each member of the team required not only to produce a great number of original ideas, but also – in a criticism-free context – to combine and improve the suggested ideas. In that context, people believed, such an environment would remove the limitations the mind places on thinking at the time when ideas are judged before their release from the mind. The final technique of the three – Gordon's (1961) *synectics* – encouraged the problem-solvers first to find links in apparently unrelated elements of notions and ideas and then to make analogies among them.

To date, research does not support the effectiveness of these three techniques, while ongoing evaluations of brainstorming, a procedure still used in classrooms, are also not promising. Taylor, Berry, and Block (1958) demonstrate that, working separately, four people generate more novel ideas than do four people working as a group: this finding is replicated by several experiments. In a further breakthrough, Weisskopf-Joelson and Eliseo (1961) are able to show that brainstorming is more productive when practical rather than unusual ideas are being generated. Finally, Weisberg (1986) concludes that brainstorming, as a method of increasing creative thinking, is not effective. While, this finding should not discourage the use of the brainstorming technique in the classroom, it may encourage the teacher to consider its purpose. By challenging students to problem solve together, might the teacher be promoting group cohesion? By experiencing a criticism-free context, will students in a group session be encouraged to contribute ideas and suggestions?

When a classroom teacher examines creativity training, the major obstacle associated with its implementation is the notion of "creativity" itself. Because the idea of creativity is difficult to define, procedures that claim to promote it or evaluate its results remain very elusive. In the context of the classroom, traditionally, creativity training usually focuses on promoting cognitive activity that will result in one or more novel solutions to a problem. In a typical example, students are asked to re-arrange classroom furniture or to find new uses for a cup. Given this pattern, founded as it is in mechanical activities, can students be taught how to generate new ideas or hypotheses? It is evident that the personal meaningfulness (or its lack) of the activity will determine the level of mental energy and investment contributed by group members.

When focusing on the teachable aspects of problem solving, some researchers demonstrate not only that "good habits of mind" exist but also that learning certain subjects – typically, Latin and geometry – may enhance thinking in other subject areas. More recently, in an attempt to teach thinking skills, researchers have been introducing a range of cognitive programs. Of these, Feuerstein's (1980) *Instrumental Enrichment* and de Bono's (1985) *CoRT Thinking Program* are briefly considered here, because they are two most readily used in classrooms.

Of these two ideas, the first, *Instrumental Enrichment* (IE), looks at thinking as a dynamic process learnable by students when taught by teachers who have received in-depth instruction. In the IE program, fifteen units of paper-and-pencil tasks are presented, all of them perceptual and non-verbal in nature. In one unit, for example, illustrated in Figure 5-8, a series of dots must be connected to form geometric figures. Each of the fifteen tasks, ranging in difficulty from simple to complex, is first completed individually and then discussed with the teacher as well as with other students. In overview, this teacher-student interaction provides *mediated learning experiences* that focus closely on the mental activities involved in the completion of each task.

Throughout the process, students learn a variety of problem-solving skills, including, for example, analyzing a problem into parts, generating hypotheses, and examining temporal relationships, as well as other useful procedures. For maximum effectiveness, the program is administered three to four times a week, an hour at a time, for two to three years.

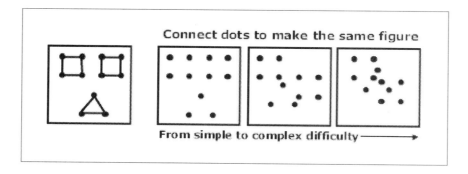

Figure 5-8. **Example of connecting-the-dots task in IE.**

Although Feuerstein (1980) states that the performance of adolescents in special education classes improves if they receive IE training for two years, students who do not undergo training demonstrate no similar progress. Publishing in 1986, Chance reports that the program contains two serious limitations: first, the large investment of time involved in the program appears not to produce immediate gains; a second drawback is that students learn to solve only types of problems similar to the ones included in the program. This latter limitation focuses attention on the lack of *transfer*[12], a problem common to many learning experiences. Although willing to master the skills inherent in a task, students are often disinclined to apply the same skills in new situations.

Treatment of Ideas (PMI):

Deliberately examining ideas for good, bad, or interesting points, instead of immediately accepting or rejecting them

Objectives (AGO):

Selecting and defining objectives: not only being clear about one's own aims but also understanding those of others

Alternatives (APC):

Generating new alternatives and choices instead of feeling confined to the obvious ones

Figure 5-9. **Example of target skills in the CoRT program**

A second type of cognitive approach, called de Bono's Cognitive Research Trust (CoRT) program, is used most often with children between the ages of nine and twelve. Consisting of six units of ten lessons each, it is structured to give each segment a series of steps:

- At first, the teacher describes the specific thinking skill outlined in the lesson; (see Figure 1-9); then examples are provided.

- For a few minutes, small groups of students work on practice problems. In turn, each group reports on its progress; then, the teacher leads a discussion focused on the usefulness of the skill.

- Within each group, the students discuss the principles that relate to the respective skill.

- Finally, the students participate in a project involving the skill.

Unlike the demands of IE, which depend on the presentation of geometric forms and puzzles, CoRT's typical projects involve practical and real-world problems.

Although, according de Bono (1985), in the last fifteen years, the CoRT program has been implemented in 5000 classrooms, in a range of ten countries, a lack of well-designed studies to evaluate its claims continues to pose a serious problem. Moreover, after the lapse of time, supporting evidence, in the form of testimonials, is provided mainly by de Bono himself.

What is evident in both techniques is the importance of the role, in verbal discussions, of language used by both teacher and classmates. In this series of valuable exchanges, language is used to objectify, examine, and evaluate aspects of problem-solving that are usually implicit. In the process of making explicit the mental events associated with problem solving, a learning experience occurs that is of great benefit to students who are unaware that such events even exist. For those students who do use inner speech to direct behavior, this process gives maximum reinforcement.

Thinking as influenced by experience

Are thinking skills influenced by experience? Some researchers believe the differences which exist, in the processes of problem solving, between the novice and the expert should be carefully examined. By asking. "How do experts think?", the novice may glean critical information about the skills to be developed. In fact, experts are demonstrated to have very specific knowledge about their respective domains of learning rather than to possess better general cognitive skills. In addition, as a result of years of involvement in a field, a specialist has, of necessity, acquired a specific vocabulary.

In any attempt to study the field of expert knowledge, the findings will be segmented by knowledge-specific research. To elucidate, it is believed that mathematicians approach problems differently from either historians, psychologists, and physicians or from representatives of other scholarly fields. As a result, those researchers who evaluate expert performance do so in particular domains of knowledge, each with its relevant strategies or necessary preferences. Thus, in this context, a general view of the role of thinking in knowledge acquisition remains elusive.

In their early work, Chase and Simon (1973), in a comparison of the performances of novice and expert chess players, found that while the experts lacked better memories of each chess piece's placement, they had a compensatory spatial vocabulary of board positions that allowed their memories a greater *chunking*[13] capacity. Transferring this concept to education, the work of Carl Bereiter and Marlene Scardamalia is analogous. At the outset, they propose that educational objectives attempt to incorporate the knowledge-specific strategies of experts. In the teaching of mathematics, for instance, the curriculum must include mental activities associated with the manner in which mathematicians approach problems. Similarly, in teaching writing skills, the instructor would begin with the basic strategies of description and narration.

Can experts in the many social contexts be identified for the purpose of studying their performances? Probably, such an idea can be extended to include the context that focuses on social issues. At this stage, social expertise may have to be subdivided into roles – for example, group leaders, good friends, supportive group members, etc. In addition, building a specific vocabulary to describe emotions, attitudes, and types of social behavior may be a good beginning for the student interested in developing social expertise. Although in this area a lot of research is still in process, students can be encouraged to read about, recognize, and seek out the performance of experts as a function of developing their learning and cognitive skills.

Thinking as based on analogues, models, and examples

As a final aspect of the topic of problem-solving in the classroom, the use of *analogues, models,* and *examples* provides a fundamental service. With these elements, when a problem situation is at hand, the problem-solver is encouraged to relate what was learned in a previous problem-solving context. The first of these, an *analogue*, is involved when a problem in a story line or structure is similar to but not the same as another problem. On the other hand, a *model* focuses on the way the workings of a system may be analogous to processes in another structure. An *example* – the third element – involves applying the solution procedure from a solved problem to the elements of challenge in a new problem.

Typically, examples form the basis of most teaching exercises. Focusing, first, on the example of computing that 4 X 3 = 12, and then using an array constructed on a checker board, Marco applies the technique to compute 5 X 2 (see Figure 5-10.)

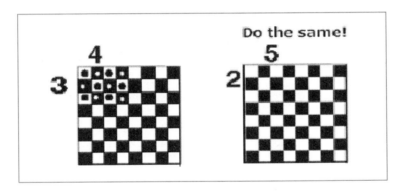

Figure 5-10. learning by example.

When teachers present examples, models, and analogues in order to simplify the learning of concepts, they encourage students to relate new knowledge to previous forms and contexts of learning. As a corollary, students who are required to provide examples, models, and analogues of newly-learned concepts are able to demonstrate the depth and breadth of their learning. When this advantage is realized, students may wish to learn to use techniques such as these to monitor personal understanding.

The Importance of Context

To be initiated when students encounter problem situations, thinking skills – especially when associated with social behavior – are generally conceptualized as a series of fixed sequential steps. For example, in the 1980s and 1990s, many school-wide programs dealing with conflict resolution appeared to show levels of success with "normal" students asked to apply the former framework to various new situations. In these positive situations, both students and teachers recognized the need to address cognitive issues by providing a general framework to accomplish certain behavior goals.

When used with students who have behavior difficulties, these procedures may fall short in their relation to the overall goal of teaching thinking skills. Probably, this happens because, traditionally, the idea of thinking skills seems to include the notion that such processes are independent of their context. In the real world experienced by the student, the mental processes occur in combination with the context of the situation and are not separate.

When factors related to context are neglected, and before solutions to the new problem are looked at, the manner in which the learned skill will be applied in the new context must be altered.

The dimensions associated with context include:

- relevance or personal meaningfulness:

  A math problem that both involves addition with "carrying" and uses money to represent numbers will be conceptualized differently from one in which the units are megahertz. Similarly, an argument with a fellow student who is a long-time friend entails different factors, very separate from those in a spat with an acquaintance.

- familiarity of the presentation of the information:

  This element includes the familiarity of the language, the format, the examples, the models, and the analogues. In a multicultural classroom, for example, levels of respect or traditions of mannerly behavior depend on a wide range of variables, many of them non-transferable. Ms. Vichert has some adult students unable to address her by her first name – they insist on "Miss Nancy" – and others whose address habits are of the "hey you" variety.

- domain of knowledge:

  The same goal, when applied to two varying domains of knowledge, leads to two or more different thought processes, a particularly important consideration if the student is required to explore beyond the information given. An obvious example is in the reading domain: decoding a history textbook involves mental processes very different from those used in learning from a science textbook. What may be deemed relevant or irrelevant will vary enormously from the descriptive subject to the analytic one.

- the problem-solver:

  Individual personality and experiential characteristics figure prominently in the way people choose to solve problems, especially those that arise in a social context. While one person may feel that the best way is to "jump in with both feet", another may be more reticent. In social contexts, an example could be shown in which a certain type of personality leads some people to want to discuss a misunderstanding close to the moment when it happens; for others, letter-writing is the only option.

For teachers who are looking for ways to examine and validate thinking processes, an obvious danger can be seen here: a program which advocates the application of a general formula will probably promote thinking as a series of de-contextualized steps. In real life, problem solving is not accomplished in one straightforward manner; rather, many variations abound.

Clearly, students with behavioral difficulties are not instinctive problem-solvers, first, because frequently they lack the objectivity required to view a situation separately from personal experience. The second reason is that, usually, they are resistant to change, a characteristic unwillingness to adopt new patterns of behavior that may relate to a safety issue. Trying new ways of behaving is somewhat like trying on new clothes to see how they fit and look: a certain amount of courage is required to remove a comfortable outfit in order to sample styles and colors more daring and unfamiliar. "Will I look silly?" "Will people laugh at me?" "Will people think that I am weak?" are typical of the questions asked by a person who lacks confidence. It is clear that thinking skills play a major role in social behavior, with the corollary that classrooms can offer unique opportunities for the solving of social and personal problems. Given the full range of available approaches, teachers are encouraged to provide to students the tools that will help them cope in the many social contexts they will experience.

Social Living Issues

Generally, students respond to topics that relate to developing social competencies, to understanding themselves and other people, and to discovering how society works. Because teachers, usually, are hard pressed to cover the intended curriculum, unless a crisis presents itself, little time can be invested in these issues. When June and Paola's bickering divides the class into two camps, overshadowing scheduled classroom activities, Ms. Palmer finally involves the class in a discussion designed to examine the attributes of "friendship". Unless the social issues that remain important to different ages are addressed, some students may become preoccupied enough to ignore the classroom curriculum – the three Rs, for example.

In an attempt to elicit a range of issues that concern children in grades five and six, teachers were asked to present to their classes an exercise in which students pretended to write letters to Ann Landers[14]. They sent their letters instead to a fictional person, Marina, after the teacher briefly explained that such letters generally request help in solving problems. At the outset, students not only were advised to use pseudonyms, but also were warned not to expect replies because this was a "pretend" exercise. Subsequently, teachers reported, first, that students were quite motivated to complete the task, but second, that the kinds of issues raised by this age group were astounding and surprising. Presented and reviewed here are a few letters that vividly illustrate student concerns.

Dear Marina,
I have many problems but the most serious is about my family. My parents are getting divorced and my mother has another boyfriend. His name is Dave. Dave gives me a lot of things but I don't think I am ready yet. What do you think? Please answer back!!
Yours truly
Dingbat.

In the first of these letters, from Dingbat, the student raises several issues that are central to his life: initially, the dissolution of his family and his new relationship with Dave. In his letter, the second theme to emerge is the guilt associated with liking and accepting Dave, while the third element – which is found between the lines – is an unstated concern about the way this new relationship impacts on Dingbat's relationship with his Dad.

As the reader detects, just below the surface of the letter, the turmoil experienced by Dingbat is typical of the anxiety of many students. While surviving such an ordeal as this, children come to recognize that because their parents are so preoccupied — or are sometimes very distressed — there is no one to deal with their profoundly hurt feelings or to field their questions. Characteristically, young persons often must suffer in silence.

In the findings of such research projects as this one, students are shown to be very interested in issues dealing with family problems and divorce-related situations. In the letter of a second student, it becomes clear that as society becomes ever more heterogeneous, students' curiosity is provoked by differences in family values, especially when these contrast to those of the dominant culture. For example, in one classroom, the children come from some families with very regimented households, while, in other homes, the parents are very flexible. How will students react to these differences?

In Miss Gloomy's letter, the young writer touches on children's universal plight: "Why can't I do what my friends are doing?" To respond to a student's puzzlement, some teachers will provide classroom opportunities when questions arise about confusing family expectations. In addition, as the case opens up, it is clear that Miss Gloomy has concerns about the way she is treated by her parents in contrast to the way her brother is treated. If her perception is accurate, her family may tacitly be advocating a traditional role for women. In the ensuing discussion, the truth emerges that Miss Gloomy faces the dilemma of one day reconciling her family's expectations with those of the dominant culture.

Because Miss Gloomy's family is probably frightened by news stories of delinquent young women who do as

Dear Marina
I am a 11 year old girl, I have this with my parents and my brother. My parents think I am old enough to clean the whole house by my self and I am the only one in the whole class who doesn't play outside on the weekend
For example, It is Sunday, 2 of my friends phoned to go tobogganing I had to say no because I had to clean the house while my brother was at a hockey game for 1 whole day! than that Sunday night my mom said "tomorrow after school you have to come home and dust!" Have you ever had this problem? Please answer back!
From, Miss Gloomy

they please, they may be using housework projects as a means to keep her away from students who could "corrupt" her. How is Miss Gloomy to solve her problem? On the one hand, of course, students must learn to recognize that some problems may have no immediate solution. On the other hand, far-reaching benefits are derived from the chance to express feelings. If it emerges, in the discussion, that fellow students have similar issues with their parents, useful information will have been exchanged that could help troubled young people. This would be the case, too, with other, equally-distressing conflicts.

Not only family-focus topics are revealed in such a spate of letter-writing, but other kinds of concern involve such school-related issues as, for example, feelings of "belonging" or anxiety about schoolwork. In the adjacent letter – untitled and unsigned – the writer conveys deeply-felt sentiments. Possibly, the anonymous writer is a student placed in a Special Education program, away from the home school, or a student recently moved to a new school. Despite the limited writing skill, the student's brief note conveys feelings of isolation and rejection. Is it possible that, previously, this student has been perceived by the teacher either as withdrawn or even as uncooperative?

> I have a roblem with my whole class everybody wants me to go back to my old school because they don't like me

Dear Marina

I am an eleven year old and I go to Lajoie Devivre School. We are doing science projects now and I am doing it on Aspirin, how does it affect children. I am pretty worried because I get embarrassed when I bring in a piece of junk. So to make it better I copy. And I don't think it's good because I have trouble reading and trying to put it in my own words. So that's my problem. I would like you to answer back.

Yours truly,

Coppercatter.

Another school-related problem is evident in the letter of Coppycatter who describes his desire to submit work that meets both the standards of his teacher and the critical gaze of his peers. Obviously aware that his methods are inadequate and perhaps dishonest, he nevertheless knows that, in the present instructional unit, aspects of project completion are emphasized. In addition, he is fully aware of the need to synthesize, as smoothly as possible, information obtained from diverse sources.

Because Coppycatter is ashamed not only of his product but also of his problem, he communicates his dilemma only through an anonymous channel. Such a breakthrough as this reveals, though, that students may be reluctant to bring certain issues to their teachers' attention, even such concerns as relate directly to the classroom context. For this reason, the classroom should offer students a variety of "safe" opportunities to address sensitive issues. For example, when the computer replaces identifiable handwriting, traditionally a teacher's sleuthing tool, confidentiality is definitely assured.

Emotional Safety

Only when emotional safety can be assured, in the context of educational opportunity, should students within the classroom be permitted to explore personal problems. Such an important maxim as this must be respected primarily because the teacher's mandate excludes the provision of either emotional counseling or therapy. To maximize emotional safety, a teacher must assure that issues initially instigated by a personal problem will be addressed objectively by a group or by the whole class. Rarely if ever should any discussion focus on the individual who must remain anonymous. In this way, then, Dingbat's problem may become the catalyst for a classroom unit dealing with different types of families. Another method of developing learning units, this time in language arts, would be to set up a media project about a family in which the parents are considering divorce. In yet a different unit, one that deals with multi-cultural issues, the family's activities could be involved or the aspect of sexism could provide a societal underpinning in the curriculum unit. In either case, Miss Gloomy's anonymous data could be implemented for detail. Always a valuable classroom device, drama that allows for subtle learning experiences may capture themes of the isolation and loneliness experienced when a character moves to a different school. Focusing on such archetypal happenings in the life of one student who moves to a new town – or to another country – may capture the essence of the anonymous writer's experience while providing a universal learning event. Finally, to deal with another topic, the teacher may present a unit of instruction that explores the steps involved in completing a project. Here, hints could be provided about the means of amassing material and then adapting it into one's own words, procedures that might help solve Coppycatter's plagiarism problem.

To recapitulate, when teachers are planning units of instruction based on social living issues, students are – in themselves – the most appropriate source of information. Although the needs of individual students will form the basis of such a curriculum, it must be implemented either within a group or in the class as a whole. Of course, the students whose written letters originally motivated these learning opportunities should never be identified. Just by chance, however, a student may recognize some of the anonymous details and spill the beans, and, while every attempt is made to keep identities secret and to protect confidentiality, the potential for attention-getting may induce some students to reveal their authorship.

Misconceptions

When a curriculum is being planned to address issues in social living, the teacher must first identify and then focus on clarifying students' basic misconceptions. In a range of children, representing various ages and backgrounds, misconceptions may be harbored which could – if not "altered" – skew their understanding of social living. For example, some children who conceptualize "caring" perceive it as a finite substance with the result that someone who "cares" for one person will, they believe, have less care to give to another or others.

Particularly damaging to the learning process is a typical student notion about the way young persons conceptualize errors and mistakes. Related to this concept is the habit of some adults, who, in their zeal to teach new behavior, encourage the belief that – at all costs ——mistakes are to be avoided. When Marta brought her science note to Mr. Pachuk, he first underlined in red the words she had misspelled and then told her the material was missing important information. As a result, Marta felt humiliated, ashamed, and "stupid", and because, for her, making errors was involved with negative feelings, Marta wanted to avoid the error-laden work altogether. Reluctant to make mistakes, many students ultimately avoid doing the work: Marta considered this option.

What is the "truth" about errors? Students should not reject the error-and-correction process because, through it, they chronicle the acquisition and fine-tuning of newly-presented ideas. Hard to accept, but essential, is the realization that mistakes are a necessary component in the learning process. In the 1970s, Eric Houghton referred to errors as "learning opportunities." How, then, does an error become a learning opportunity? One answer is that the benefit of an error lies in directing the attention of students and teachers to future forms of learning and teaching. In Marta's case, by examining her spelling errors – but not treating them as sins – Mr. Pachuk can plan supplementary activities to teach the word-attack skills she has not yet mastered. As a follow-up, by questioning her subtly about the omissions in her notes, he may be able to emphasize for her other attributes of the relevant science concepts and thereby lead her to find her way. Although students should learn to invest their best effort in completing each task, they may also be encouraged to welcome errors as learning opportunities, positive ways of introducing new types of knowledge.

Misbehavior on the part of students is sometimes motivated by misconceptions – incomplete or faulty ideas. Shortly after Majel's mother has given her twenty dollars to pick up groceries on her way home from school, Christine, prior to the noon hour, steals the money from Majel's desk and is seen spending it at the convenience store. Because Majel happens to be in the store at the same time, Christine generously buys her a treat. When Majel reports the theft to Ms. Fortino, who begins an investigation of the incident, all the evidence implicates Christine. Regardless of the mounting case against Christine, Majel refuses to believe that the suspect, who is her friend and who has bought her candy, can have stolen from her. Possibly, because Majel has an incomplete or faulty conception of "friend", attempts are made to provide learning occasions – by, for example, examining the concept in literature – to remediate her tendency to reach erroneous conclusions.

Abstract Issues

When devising a curriculum to deal with issues of social living, the teacher must also outline and help students to investigate the major abstract concepts – honesty, democracy, fairness, justice, friendship, love, etc. – that should be understood before they are fully applied to behavior. While it is commonly assumed that students learn about these ideals as a function of experience, if not of home training, the truth is that social expectations today are not as homogeneous as in previous times, and, therefore, it is more difficult than in past times for many children to acquire appropriate or adequate awareness. In addition, with increased exposure to the media, students are often faced with competing notions of social living – for example, while certain characters in videos and films, as well as sports celebrities, commit anti-social acts without apparent negative consequences, other people are punished for what appears to be far less serious behavior. For the impressionable student, what understanding is gained or what misconception will be derived from such experiences?

Another important aspect of social living involves the choices of behavior students will be expected to make. Generally, in most societies – in accordance with local conventions – members are encouraged to behave in a righteous manner. Traditionally, although parents have been held responsible for teaching moral behavior, the school, as a social institution, – and, by extension, the classroom – also has an obligation to encourage conventional behavior, for example, by encouraging students to evaluate the honesty, lawfulness, and morality of behavior, both in themselves as individuals and in others. Moral development was studied by Kohlberg (1969) who first proposed three major developmental stages that paralleled the child's cognitive maturation:

- *preconventional level*
  While children are still egocentric, they comply with social expectations in order to avoid punishment. Generally motivated by reward and penalty, children at this stage will swap favors or use people to get what they want.

- *conventional level*
  The person not only conforms to personal and social expectations but also identifies with people who represent an established order. Good behavior is motivated by the show of approval received from those whom the child tries to please. An orientation towards authority and fixed rules is also evident.

- *postconventional, autonomous, or principled level*
  The individual at this stage attempts – independently – to define moral values as separate from the authority of the group. Examination of individual rights leads, at first, to an understanding of the relativity of personal values; it then progresses to the development of a universal perspective as well as to the establishing of ethical principles.

Kohlberg produced an assessment tool – found in Porter and Taylor (1972) – that evaluates a student's level of moral development. Based on a set of questions about a moral dilemma contained in a story, the resulting evaluation comes from the student's responses regarding the ethical and moral issues. The main plot of Victor Hugo's *Les Misérables* is a good example of the type of stories used in Kohlberg's assessment. In the series of questions, moral probing takes place: when Jean Valjean was convicted of stealing a loaf of bread to feed his family, was the court justified? Was his theft reasonable? Was Valjean a good person? Were the courts fair in sending him to prison? Would you have done the same thing? How much is the society at fault when starving people have to steal?

In many classrooms, and across curricula, opportunities arise, that are able to form the basis for discussions of moral behavior: was Christopher Columbus justified in annihilating the indigenous people of Hispaniola? Should scientists use animals in research? Should each person be held responsible for maintaining the health of his or her body? Which character would you choose as your mentor in the novel *The Lord of the Flies?*

Kohlberg's work has been criticized for promoting a view of morality that requires reasoning and notions of justice as the primary means to evaluate behavior. An alternative conception – offered by Gilligan (1977) – introduces an *ethics of care*, based on a female perspective concerned with ideas of supervision and responsibility for others rather than with ideas of justice. In the major phases of this development, offered to parallel Kohlberg's, the concept tends to place strong emphasis on the care-giving perspective. Her three stages of moral development – advancing from selfish to social or conventional morality and, finally, to post-conventional or principled morality – are based on the procedure by which women learn to tend to their own interests and to the interests of others. According to Gilligan, perhaps women hesitate to make judgments about others' behavior because they perceive the complexities of relationships more readily than men do.

Individualized programs and the problem of transfer

In their studies in the world of behavioral learning, educators often use the words "transfer" and "generalize" interchangeably. In the behaviorist tradition, however, where both ideas originate, they are given distinct meanings. The first of these, "transfer", refers to the fitting application of old knowledge to a new learning situation. For example, Jarek has previously learned the concept of multiplication with the use of checkerboard arrays like the ones pictured in Figure 5-10. When he is able to calculate the amount of carpeting needed in his bedroom, Jared has "transferred" his knowledge of multiplication to a practical application. In contrast, "generalization" refers, within the process, to responding to a new situation in the same manner as to an old one, overlooking the inherent differences. After learning to say the word "No!", two-year-old Jessica responds "No!" to every question asked. Similarly, Pernell adds the numbers on his worksheet regardless of the subtraction sign that precedes some questions. When Pernell fails to discern that the questions are different, the teacher will implement strategies to promote "transfer" rather than "generalization."

Because they are strongly connected with the context in which they are learned, skills as well as many other types of knowledge, are easily seen to be non-transferable. In fact, the lack of *transfer* may be one of the most pervasive problems in learning and teaching. Unless the teacher targets *transfer* of knowledge as an objective of the learning activity, many students will find it difficult or impossible to dissociate newly acquired information from the accompanying circumstance. Outlined here are certain teaching components that may facilitate the transfer of knowledge, according to teachers' chosen procedures:

- Present a skill or concept using several different contexts — among teachers, a tendency exists to teach component skills within a single learning activity. Today, Ms. Modena is teaching her grade 5 class about the concept of greeting another person, presenting examples of behavior in several settings: children greeting parents as they arrive home; students greeting teachers and principal in the hallways and school yard; students greeting each other at the movies. By demonstrating "greeting" behavior in several situations, Ms. Modena now asks her students to think of examples in new settings.

- Vary the relevant and irrelevant information within each learning situation. Because all the examples provided by Ms. Modena illustrate greeting behavior, she can direct students to attend to the similarities and differences contained in each situation with the intention of tagging the relevant information associated with "greetings".

- Create bridges between contexts by asking students to identify the old knowledge to be applied to each new task. When Ms. Modena requests that the class generate new examples of "greeting" behavior", she asks them to consider what they know about such behavior and how this knowledge applies to their examples.

- Test the learning of a skill or concept in a brand-new context. Once she believes that her students have a grasp of the essence of the concept "greeting", Ms.Modena now tests the depth of their understanding by presenting new instances and non-instances of greeting behavior, requiring students not only to decide whether each is an example of greeting behavior but also to explain their decisions.

- Apply the adage "practice makes perfect" – stay with skill or concept longer than an introductory period, in order to insure mastery. Although she feels confident that her class has grasped the concept of "greetings", Ms. Modena will quiz them about new "greeting" opportunities that may present themselves in the class, in literature, in videos, and in other media.

- Have students discuss mental and behavioral aspects of the task rather than focusing on concern with the "right" answer. Not only is Ms. Modena slow to accept a correct labeling of a greeting instance, but also she requires each student to explain the information leading to the conclusion that an instance of "greeting" behavior has occurred or is required.

By incorporating these suggestions, the teacher will find it increasingly likely that students will acquire a thorough understanding of the concept in question. As well, most students will be capable of applying and recognizing the concept in unusual and novel contexts.

Important to the discussion is a final note about concept acquisition. In education, it is interesting to look at the contrast between the manner in which ideas and behavior are vicariously learned and the way they are traditionally taught. When concepts are taught, first, a definition is presented, along with its characteristics. Then, students are directed to identify these concepts as they emerge in experiences, often in the context of classroom exercises. In everyday situations, however, concepts are acquired in a reverse process. Here, various instances of a concept are encountered, and, by unconsciously attending to certain repeating characteristics, a student will recognize a pattern.

In order to create concepts and ideas, the Semantic Memory[16] functions to isolate experiences that are similar. In the classroom, the process can be mimicked by, at first, presenting several scenarios and then, asking students to identify their similarities and differences. Teachers should be cautioned, however, that some students with behavioral difficulties may not acquire concepts vicariously with this "discovery" method. Is it possible that they are not attending to the relevant characteristics contained in situations, often the case with students who either have attentional problems or who are preoccupied by other thoughts?

To encourage concept learning, the teacher should try to incorporate both the traditional and the discovery methods in a curricular unit. Which to apply first will depend on the individual differences of students: the teacher may be well advised to experiment beforehand with the method chosen to be introduced first.

Summary

In this chapter, the focus is primarily on the varying content of individualized programs designed specifically to address the needs of students. For a context in which an individual's need is more safely dealt with anonymously, a curricular unit of study will be appropriate if it isolates themes to be considered by the entire class. Also included are relevant classroom topics involving age-related challenges as well as interests appropriate to a social curriculum.

In the categories outlined, the three major ones dealt with were the emotional, cognitive, and social aspects of living. Suggestions included various ways in which such topics can be incorporated in the context of individualized programs as well as in classroom units of instruction. The upcoming material, in Chapter Six, will focus on the planning of individual educational programs for students with socio-emotional difficulties.

Endnotes

[1] A personal dictionary consists of lists of words the student is likely to use, printed by the student as they appear in various assignments. Usually, these words are written in alphabetic groupings, in an easily accessed part of the notebook. Because of being – usually – confident about the initial letter of the word, the student can readily find the appropriate section in the list, copy the word, and mentally reinforce memory of the spelling.

[2] See Guerrero & Reiter, 1998.

[3] see Condry & Condry (1976).

[4] The National Film Board of Canada video, *A Love that Kills,* is recounted by Dawna Spears, mother of Monica, a young woman murdered by a boyfriend. In adolescent classes, this video is an effective means of introducing for discussion the issue of emotional distress.

[5] English as a Second Language.

[6] Such protocols will be discussed in the next section, but for further information see Bereiter and Scardamalia (1983).

[7] Associationism supports the idea that thoughts are connected to experience by association, and, for this reason, contiguity, that is, temporal proximity, is an important factor in this process.

[8] A think-aloud protocol records the mental processes involved at the different stages of problem solving. Usually, the solution to the problem emerges from the problem-solver's verbal description of those stages.

[9] See Winzer (1995).

[10] See Chapter 6.

[11] Gestalt psychology also emphasizes the importance of meaning in thought processes.

[12] Transfer is the process by which knowledge derived from one experience is applied to a new experience that varies in at least one element.

[13] Chunking refers to a memory process involving units of information. When the size of the unit is increased, more information is encoded without exceeding the capacity of the memory system. For example, a student unable to read will encode the word "magician" as eight different letters while readers encode the word as a single unit.

[14] Ann Landers was a newspaper columnist who provided advice to readers who sent her letters describing personal problems.

[15] When Eric Houghton was part of the faculty of York University, Toronto, Canada, during the 1970s, he lectured extensively on "Precision Teaching", a behavioral tool initiated by Ogden Linsley (see Houghton, 1971).

[16] Both Semantic and Episodic memories are involved in learning from experience. Information processed by Semantic Memory is evaluated for its sameness – there are, for instance, similarities in the various situations that involve greeting people. By contrast, Episodic Memory, responsible for the autobiographical encoding of experience, tags differences as salient information; for example, not only is September 11, 2001, remembered because a unique event was experienced, but individuals are also able to recall, by association, mundane, usually forgettable, autobiographical details that occurred on the same day.

CHAPTER 6

Planning for Students with Socio-emotional Needs

While, in previous chapters, the comments have focused on general topics, in Chapter Six, the intention is to target individual educational plans for specific students. In the design of these, the context is that of the Model for creating a positive learning environment. At the outset, some general programming strategies are presented in relation to the major objectives of the model; then, actual examples, generated by teachers, illustrate their application. It is also the intention of this chapter to reveal questions teachers might pose as they design and create intervention plans for students. Before reading this section, the reader may, by way of review, choose to consult Chapter Three's overview of strategies for assessment, evaluation, and planning.

Although the overall strategies presented here are illustrative, they should not be perceived as all-inclusive. To emphasize that each plan is generated to meet the unique needs of an individual student, within the context of the classroom or another environment, a range of examples is given. The corollary is, however, that each plan is as unique as the student for whom it is prepared. Other plans for other individuals could be equally personally directed.

Basic Needs

Safety

At the foundation of creating a positive learning environment is the emphasis on safety. Without it, the fearful and defensive student remains vulnerable. Of course, a basic concern about physical threats to personal safety might leave the student preoccupied and therefore unconcerned with the learning objectives of classroom tasks. Equally important, however, are the consequences of a lack of emotional safety, a situation which may be less obvious. When teachers are occupied exclusively with the academic curricula, they may be oblivious to the all-important and fundamental need: emotional safety. In the sections that follow, issues relating to both physical and emotional needs of students are outlined.

Physical

In order to cope, and, subsequently, to learn, children need to feel safe from physical harm. As an evaluation of society will demonstrate, threats to safety may come from many sources both outside and inside school, yet all can impact – inside the classroom – the learning behavior of the student. Across a wide spectrum, physical abuse can take place at home, from parents, siblings, other family members; in the community it can come from neighbors, bullies on the street, and gang members; on the way to school, harm can come from classmates as well as from strangers; in the schoolyard, a student may be hurt by teachers and fellow students; in the classroom, the student can receive types of harm from teachers and peers. Regardless of the source of physical abuse, even if it has come from the pupil's own home, its impact may be felt in the classroom.

When the teacher suspects the safety needs of a student are threatened at home – perhaps the situation is that the student is covered in bruises or reports what appear to be too many unfortunate accidents, – then the individual plan might include advising the principal, referring the problem to the Guidance Department or consulting a representative of the Children's Aid Society[1]. If dealing with an older student, the teacher – through the social worker, if one is available – may provide names and telephone numbers of support groups. In another case, the teacher may facilitate contact with an appropriate agency, especially if the student has decided to leave home.

Sometimes, problems are difficult to solve because they lead to a Catch-22 situation for the student. Marek, who is earning failing marks in his grade eleven courses, has sought the advice of a guidance counselor to whom he has spoken freely about his personal problems. Not only is Marek responsible for looking after his two younger siblings, but he must also care for his two alcoholic parents. During each day, he must shop, cook meals, and clean the house. After an evening of his parents' drinking, he must endure their abuse while attempting to protect his small brother and sister. Once the parents pass out, he must ready the unconscious parents for bed, washing them and changing their clothing. Then, Marek must try to put them to bed. Although Marek has considered leaving home, he is unwilling to abandon his siblings. For a young adolescent, the crisis time has come: he can neither ignore the abuse nor continue to cope with it. For this complex problem, Guidance Counsellor, Mr. Fuqua, needs to enlist the help of a multi-disciplinary team who will generate solutions to try to alleviate Marek's problem. Of course, it is also possible that Marek will be unwilling to accept a suggested course of action and will therefore continue in his present circumstance, eventually dropping out of school.

When the case involves a child's safety being threatened in the community or on the way to school, the teacher might consider contacting not only the parents or guardians but also the police. In order to determine ways of handling the immediate needs of a given problem, the teacher may suggest a self-defense course to help the student to develop some confidence, while in another case, the difficulty may be addressed in class, in a broader context, by assigning such a project as *Making the Streets Safe*. Broadening the scope still further, teachers could also encourage students to invite police representatives, neighbors, or members of community organizations to present information packages that will lead to a "safety" plan for the neighborhood. By giving students an opportunity to talk about the issues and perhaps generate concrete solutions, the teacher encourages pro-action and empowerment.

The Gang phenomenon

In some communities, gangs try both to enlist willing members and to terrorize non-compliant children and adolescents. When parents become aware of these activities, they are concerned not only for their children's safety but also about the apparent increase of gang activity: thefts, violence, muggings. To grapple with this issue, it is important to examine and understand the gang phenomenon. Not only in humans but also in other primate species, "It's unattached males – packs of adolescent primates or lonely single adults – who get into trouble and cause trouble,..."[2] This kind of peer group formation is one of the expected outcomes of adolescence. In recent years, female gangs have sprung up in parts of North America, one, in British Columbia, being notorious for killing an "outsider". Female gangs are, however, less common than male gangs and, usually, less violent.

What is the purpose of forming groups? People join groups as a means of achieving a goal that could not be achieved when acting alone. Unlike "aggregates", which consist of people present at the same time and in the same place without forming a unit, – people standing at a bus stop or students listening to a lecture – a group meets certain characteristics[3]. It is interesting to examine these elements as they exist in a gang.

- *sharing of a common goal*

  People join the "Snake" gang to meet their affective needs: to feel safe, to feel prized, and to feel empowered. To an insider, or to an observer who may be an adult, the gang can be seen and understood as a pseudo-family. Very possibly, the "Snake" gang satisfies the needs of many children and adolescents in this relatively poor community of families. Commonly, here, parents work long hours, leaving their offspring alone for the greater part of the day. In the affluent part of the city, however, the same phenomenon will be observed: here, as well, young people, both boys and girls, also left unsupervised, form cliques and groupings, even gangs.

- *interdependence*

  When Enos is attacked by a rival gang, all the members of the "Snake" gang are outraged; they plot revenge. This attack affects not only Enos, but also the rest of the "Snake" gang members.

- *interpersonal interaction*

  Because the "Snake" gang consists of members who regularly interact with one another, they are quite different from an audience of strangers who share a couple of hours watching the same movie. Knowing each other's habits and backgrounds, as well as experiencing activities together, bonds the group.

- *perception of membership*

  All "Snake" members are aware of the gang's goals and are proud of belonging to the gang. The strength of membership is often displayed in their uniforms, tattoos, colors, jewelry, piercing, and other markers.

- *structured relationships*

  In the "Snake" gang, established norms and expectations have developed. For example, gang loyalty, demonstrated by not divulging the activities of the group, is a central tenet. At the same time, individuals have established roles to play – leader, counselor, enforcer, etc.

- *mutual influence*

  Enos, in speaking to another "Snake" member, Marvin, has convinced him to "cut class" in order to carry out some gang business. Although Marvin is at first reluctant, he is swayed into compliance.

- *motivation*

  Members of the "Snake" gang praise both Enos for encouraging Marvin to skip school and Marvin for agreeing to go along with Enos' plan. In addition, members are regularly able to derive strength from the gang because it allows them to satisfy personal needs: closeness, bonding, companionship, friendship, shared interests. Not all gangs are anti-social, but, clearly, the repetitive nature of such bonding reinforces group cohesion.

Given the value of gang membership, it should not be surprising that youngsters who may have been victimized in their community will choose to satisfy safety needs by joining a group, clique, or gang.

Yet it should not be the gang phenomenon but rather its norms and expectations which form the basis for adult concern. Does the gang encourage illegal or maladaptive behavior? By discussing – in the classroom – the nature of groups and gangs of all types, the teacher is addressing not only a topic of personal relevance to students but also one that will impact importantly on personal decisions and behavior.

If a safety problem exists in the school, – within the building or inside the classrooms – the principal, in conjunction with the faculty, must develop administrative policies outlining procedures for handling aggressive behavior. At first, it is helpful to establish a feeling of safety in the classroom by publishing the policy. Then, the teacher can strengthen the sense of security, during class discussions, by demonstrating to students that the new procedure is being consistently implemented. A side effect might be that crime-prone students will become aware of potential alternatives and deterrents to violence, abuse, etc. In a Grade 8 class, all the students agree that Serena is one of the most powerful individuals. Not only is she a "Queen Bee" who rules the hive, but Serena has also been known to beat up a few of the boys. Although she is responsible for very little overt physical violence, Serena's covert threats have undermined the feeling of safety in many students. Should school policy target only aggressive and violent behavior? What about threats? By incorporating policies and procedures to address threatening behavior, a school is able to intervene before a bully has a chance to exert violence and before another student is, consequently, physically abused.

When the danger of abuse seems likely to become active in the classroom, the teacher should make students aware of the existing school policy and should discuss with students the way feelings of danger may be detected and examined. Also important is the students' awareness of the need to feel safe: they eventually must learn to report malicious and dangerous activities, even though the code of honor among the young seems to forbid such revelations.

Emotional

While physical problems of students are often more readily detected, all students must be able to feel safe from emotional abuse. Not only is such abuse often experienced at home, from parents, siblings, and other family members, it can also derive from the community: from neighbors, adults or youth in the street, bullies in the schoolyard, as well as from teachers and students. Even in the classroom, emotional abuse can exist, perceived to be caused by teachers and peers.

If the trouble presents itself at home, the teacher – for the purpose of discussion and exploration - might consider choosing literature that shows a child-and-parent perspective. Within a classroom discussion, students might be encouraged to identify ways in which characters can respond to emotional abuse either by defusing such situations or by finding alternative ways to be safe. For example, Florence, a character in a story, is upset and sometimes frightened when, on occasion, her Dad comes home from work in any angry mood in which he is likely to scream and yell and also to find fault with everything she does. As she responds emotionally, her crying makes matters worse. What advice would the various class members give Florence? Perhaps by considering the reasons for his being upset, she might discover that his anger is work-related. Possibly, this knowledge would help her to feel better, knowing that she is not the source of it. Can she imagine that by approaching him when he is calm, she might speak to him about her feelings? Can her Mother help?

When the problems are coming from peers, on the other hand, students may be encouraged to write and role-play scripts that introduce language to use in response to verbal abuse. In addition, the entire class may benefit from presenting playlets or skits whose thematic objective is to develop empathic skills, communications that send to the hurting person a clear message: "I understand what you say and I feel deeply about your situation." To acquire such skills, students must be encouraged to reflect on the content and feeling of the situation, to personalize the event. In adopting such awareness and personalizing it, a student must pretend that the character is one's own sibling or a close friend. Then the attempt must be made to self-disclose feelings experienced in a similar situation. By this means, the outsider learns to interpret the various aspects of the activity; for instance, the individual is being victimized because of wearing a pair of glasses and so the role player imagines: "I think I felt the same way when ..", giving new meaning to the event. In such small dramas, students learn to feel the pain inflicted by name-calling as well as by other hurtful contexts. In summary, then, classroom expectations should include the overt presentation, in a range of settings, of specific provisions related to the respectful treatment of class members, and, by extension, to other members of society.

As an instance of possible emotional abuse that occurs when children regularly deal with several teachers – a very common arrangement in rotary programs – students may complain to one teacher that verbal abuse is perpetrated by another. In these circumstances, students may learn to recognize not only that each individual teacher will have a unique approach, but that relevant teacher-style is associated with classroom expectations. Again, literature, video, or film may be used as a medium, first to explore such issues, and then to discuss, as a group, different ways to solve specific problems. In conjunction with the topic of verbal abuse, it is important that teachers avoid forms of ridicule or sarcasm, and even certain types of irony, when attempting to control student behavior. From all reported data, these techniques have been found as hurtful as physical abuse, if not – permanently – more harmful.

Prizing

Often, researchers have emphasized the importance of types of positive feedback received by students from teachers and peers. According to such evidence, it seems clear that a sense of being prized may result from this form of positive response. It must be noted, however, that positive feedback does not refer to showering a child with compliments but rather to the manner in which people respond to student behavior; for example, when Ms. Henriques returns Suzanne's exam, she focuses, in her comment, on the idea that the young pupil has improved her performance. Rather than harp on the grade – 6 out of 10 – the teacher emphasizes the positive element, the improvement over an earlier grade.

In class, from the teacher

To augment a student's feelings of being prized, the teacher may choose to stress one (or more) positive aspects of classroom performance among which may be a focus on:

- what the student has learned as opposed to what still needs to be learned
- ways in which the student has improved instead of on the grade obtained
- the amount of effort invested in the task rather than the grade achieved
- methods the student might use to arrive at better performance on the next test, in place of noting present lack of accomplishment

In addition, prizing includes perceiving and recognizing the unique qualities of a student. Because of the need to deal with normal classroom pressures, a teacher may focus on and define a child merely by academic performance, but when students are engaged in a variety of events, interests, and accomplishments, in and out of school, such co-curricular activities and achievements also define and further elucidate who they are. In the morning following his hockey game, Ken beamed proudly as he reported to his classmates that their teacher, Ms. Kosmitzki, had attended the game. Through the teacher's recognition of and participation in these additional dimensions, the students, particularly the non-academic ones, will feel prized.

Although Cannis, a student with behavioral difficulties, may be reluctant to accept Mr. Che's intervention, the teacher has the option to approach the student in a non-threatening way, by talking about pets, television programs, or another general topic, eventually asking "Cannis, shall I help you with this work while I'm here?" In such a careful intervention, the student/teacher contact achieves a new meaning as well as, for the student, a special feeling.

In the context of a busy classroom, the teacher may have difficulty directing positive statements to a particular student. Given such circumstances, the teacher, in order to reinforce the element of prizing, must find innovative ways to accomplish this all-important task; for example:

> • plan to identify and state one positive aspect of the student's performance during each class
>
> • focus on five students during each class and tactfully rotate the attention

In class, from peers

To respond to the prizing needs of a student with behavioral difficulties, the teacher should elicit the contribution of the peer group, a goal which may be accomplished in several ways:

> • first, because the peer group is likely to imitate adult attitudes and methods, the teacher must examine and modify personal behavior. When hoping to test student perception, the teacher should ask one of the class members to "pretend" to be the teacher – an eye-opening exercise
>
> • then, the teacher must find ways of highlighting the strengths of the particular student to the entire group, thereby helping classmates to adopt a more balanced view of the individual's traits
>
> • finally, by providing opportunities for the class to learn this process, the teacher must encourage students to make positive statements to and about each other; for example, Mr. Hunt suggests that each class member state one positive element about the person to the right. When Mark describes the way Marty often shares an orange with him, Mr. Hunt congratulates Marty on his generosity

On assignments

Because – for many students – academic performance is possibly the primary aspect of school life, feeling prized correlates with classroom accomplishment. For this reason, when preparing an individualized plan for a student experiencing academic difficulty, the teacher must implement the idea of presenting errors as learning opportunities. In asking a series of critical questions about self-performance, some of which may be devised by class members in discussion, the student may be helped to become aware of the potential for improvement:

- Did I do as well as I expected to?

- What did I learn from completing this task?

- What concepts require new ways of learning?

- What changes must I make?

- other such questions may emerge

Traditionally, in education studies, when they are shown to be aware that more than one solution may be found to each problem, students will be more positive about their school work than those offered only the "right"/"wrong" perspective. In a typical instance, a student who embarks on a particular solution path will reveal to the teacher new aspects of the student's cognitive framework, and, if permitted to continue, the student may feel prized when allowed to follow through, rather than be interrupted and re-directed. The path, while it may not lead to a solution, will ultimately encourage student initiative. In one example, when made uneasy by having to structure a short story, Lisa writes a very simple dialogue, almost a play, about bigotry in the classroom. Because Lisa has only to make up the conversations and can easily reveal the hidden prejudices of the characters as they speak, her teacher, Ms. Martynek, has a chance to find out that Lisa has serious views about racism. Later, Lisa can begin to learn about short-story structures.

Extra attention: mentor or peer-tutor

Often, when a student requires more attention than is available from the teacher, the assigning of a "buddy" may be appropriate. In such an arrangement, when the teacher's close attention is unavailable, the student having problems may receive feedback on performance or answers to questions. For the one who is given a "buddy", another important function emerges – status in the perception of the peer group is enhanced. "Popularity" is a commodity which appears to rub off; when Raoul's "buddy" happens to be the most popular person in the classroom, the status of Raoul himself improves in the eyes of his peers.

By having a group of students tackle a project, after they receive training in time management, organization, and research skills, the teacher may be able – subsequently – to give a student with behavioral difficulties an opportunity to "belong". The teacher may want to ensure that the important characteristics of groups[6] are put into place in order to maximize the individual's sense of belonging. Because this type of student may have difficulties interacting with others, training – of both the group members and the individual – before the new student is introduced into the group, should be completed by the teacher in order to avert potential difficulties. In one instance, Mahta, the student being placed in the group, lacks polished language skills but is an expert on the experiences of newcomers; within the group, students are willing to overlook Mahta's nervous stumbling speech in order to benefit from her immigrant background as they prepare their project on multiculturalism.

Empowerment

In any field, the concept of empowerment relates to feelings of control; in an educational context, consequently, the individualized plan must provide opportunity for as many choices as the student can handle. In one situation, Monique has the choice of completing either the Math questions or the Language Arts independent activity. Later, as she is given a greater range of time slots, she will choose from a larger number of options. For the purpose of training students, during the early days of the term the school day is very structured; then, as individuals demonstrate their mastery of classroom procedures, more flexibility is introduced. Gradually, as a parallel approach is applied to individual students while they become acclimatized, the goal should be made clear to the students so that they may to participate in reaching it.

Not only may students now be given fewer directives, they must also have somewhat independent opportunities to complete contracts. In addition, as often as possible, each student should be trained to take more initiative by being involved in decision-making. When Moh refuses to write a poem, Ms. Kujak asks him what other options he has in mind. As soon as Moh explains that he wants to complete his drawing, the teacher checks his timetable, and together they choose another time-slot for his poem writing. She also suggests that, prior to starting the poem, he might meet briefly with his "buddy" to discuss the assignment. If these arrangements are made discreetly, most class members will not be affected by the divergent options.

In the classroom, another form of empowerment is achieved when the teacher is willing to discuss and even to share aspects of power. In the web-based module entitled "Share the Power: Applying Democracy in the Classroom"[7] , the point is made – about power – that students must be taught how to use it rather than abuse it:

- to take responsibility for the actions they choose

- to explore various models of power in order to find a substitute for the traditional one, that is based on force and aggression

The affective needs – safety, prizing, and empowerment – are often not addressed as vigorously as the concern for classroom management, outlined in the next section. A point which cannot be emphasized enough is that focus on management efforts without recognition of affective needs will always undermine the positive classroom environment.

Classroom Management

Because many teachers perceive student behavior as related to management issues, the plan that is prepared for the student may pinpoint the making of additional rules as well as defining consequences for rule violation. Situations which appropriately identify a need for classroom management, however, are those that students are often unaware of, have forgotten, and/or do not clearly understand as they relate to classroom expectations. In many cases, these may involve behavior that should actually be ignored by the teacher. On the other hand, inappropriate behavior in such a classroom may be neither accepted nor encouraged. When Michaela is working quietly on her assignment, Mr. Duchniky is busy correcting papers at his desk, and only when she leaves her seat to wander aimlessly around the classroom does he stand, move towards her, and suggest she go back to work. If Mr. Duchniky is concerned about Michaela's out-of-seat behavior, an evaluation of how such activity is generally handled will suggest that a management issue is involved. Mr. Duchniky will first ensure that Michaela has a good understanding of classroom expectation regarding in-seat behavior. He will test the depth of her understanding by describing potential school situations and asking her to judge whether in-seat behavior is expected. In the next phase, he will plan to go to Michaela's desk, when she is working on her assignment, at which time he will be sure to comment on and encourage her in-seat behavior. Meanwhile, he will ignore her out-of-seat behavior unless the safety needs of the people in the class are an issue. Although different from the usual identification of the "crime", that is, rule-breaking followed by a punishment, the recommended procedure here focuses on "catching a kid being good"[8].

Expectations

Classroom and language behavior

Although the major classroom expectations should be posted and referred to on a regular basis – particularly at the beginning of a semester – some tacit expectations must be highlighted when a student appears to be unaware of them. Boris might be chatting with Maury about the outcome of the baseball game because he is unaware – or has forgotten that, just then, each student is supposed to be engaged in independent study. At this moment, as a reminder, it may be appropriate for his teacher to give him a non-verbal signal, but if Boris persists, what is the next step? Perhaps he does not de-code the non-verbal signal. If this is the case, and a brief explanation is warranted, what is the result if Boris feels compelled to share his news anyway? A young child will often become so excited that delaying an impulse is impossible. Mrs. Marchand says, "Boris, I realize you're excited about your news. Share it with Maury once you finish the question you're working on." Depending on her assessment of Boris' limitations, the teacher may request that he wait a longer period of time – until the end of class. When Boris, awhile later, completes his tasks and returns to share his news, Mrs. Marchand not only congratulates him for his willingness to comply, but walks over to the two boys to chat about the baseball game.

It is important to recognize that Mrs. Marchand does not shout, "Keep quiet!! Don't you realize that there is no talking during independent study? You are disturbing everyone!" Such an interruptive and punitive action to control Boris' behavior would have been a short-term solution in addition to teaching Boris unanticipated notions about the classroom and his teacher. To summarize, a management issue often reflects a lack of knowledge – on the student's part – about what is expected or even about the way things are done in the classroom. In order to address the inappropriate behavior, Mrs. Marchand will find ways to provide the necessary information and then to encourage the desired behavior.

Assignments

Teachers often place emphasis on student behavior associated with assignments left incomplete or submitted irregularly, an approach which may also be directed to work of poor quality. Planning for such behavior requires that expectations about completion, submission, quality, and other criteria be defined on the basis of the student's current level of functioning. It is also necessary for a teacher to ascertain the amount of monitoring required to accomplish these objectives. For example, Marla has to show each question, as she completes it, to her "buddy", whereas Jared is expected to check in with his teacher every five minutes during an independent study period. While Ms. Marchetti prefers to see Jared's work in order to monitor its quality, at the same time she hopes to encourage him by means of extra attention.

Attendance and punctuality

Students – for a variety of reasons – fail to attend classes regularly and/or repeatedly arrive late. Some examples are suggested in Figure 6-1; typical instances would include:

- Parker, generally five minutes late, because he tries to avoid a certain group of students who tease and chase him

- Marika, arriving late to make a grand entrance

- Moesha, coming to school when she chooses

- Luigi, usually a little bit disorganized, not ready to make punctuality a priority

- Amina , experiencing academic problems and thus finding the work difficult and frustrating

- Diana, an anxious student, reluctant to initiate activities involving other people

Planning to deal with attendance and punctuality as a classroom management issue requires a focus on expectations – defining, identifying, teaching, and devising procedures for encouraging such behavior[9], whereas a focus on other issues involves rather different interventions.

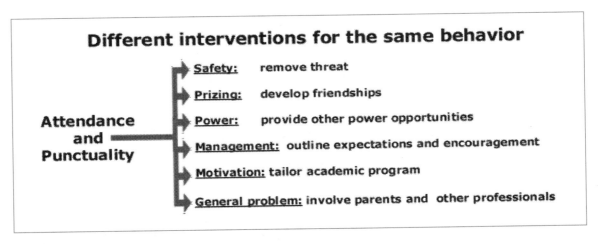

Figure 6-1. Distinct interventions result from various starting points: attendance problems and punctuality difficulties.

Interacting with others

Because of their unfamiliarity with acceptable interactive procedures, some students may require descriptions of acceptable ways of interacting with teachers as well as with other students. When specific attention needs to be given by the teacher to such activities as communicating thoughts, stating intentions, and asserting needs, often such students will receive feedback that is puzzling to them. When Raphael helps himself to Armand's pen in order to scribble the homework assignment in his notebook, he is surprised to have Armand grab it out of his hand. Clearly, Raphael is unaware that a polite verbal request will clarify his intentions. By observing student interaction, the teacher is able to pinpoint the type of instances that will warrant special attention. When the teacher incorporates into the existing curriculum a few relevant mini-lessons about interaction breakdowns, many of the problems in student communication can be redressed. In situations in which an uncooperative student is confrontational, similar procedures may be implemented. Usually, however, the plan must also include classroom management strategies to handle typical situations. Adequately outlined descriptions of such strategies should be shared with all teachers – in a rotary program, for example – as well as with the students themselves, the key being to clarify expectations.

Pattern of Ignoring

An individualized plan might identify a list of behaviors to be ignored, especially if such a pattern of passivity will involve a considerable effort on the part of the teacher and/or students. Stefan, a student with a "short fuse," has a temper tantrum each time others in his grade one class are unwilling to give him what he wants – a toy, a pencil, a cookie. To appease him, habitually, the teacher and the students, ultimately, give in to his demands. In Stefan's individualized plan, the outline by Ms. Ariel identifies the behavior, focusing on the circumstance in which it will be ignored. Finally, alternative ways to behave, not only for the teacher, but for all students, are outlined as they will apply prior to, during, and after the tantrum. At the outset, everyone should be reminded that behaviors dealing with safety – of both students and teachers – must never be ignored.

In the classroom, behaviors that violate school policies should not receive a great deal of attention; rather, these should be reported to and dealt with at the Office level. Usually, the principal, vice-principal, or guidance department will be responsible for handling violent, aggressive, and hurtful behavior. In the individualized plan, either a supervisory person or the teacher will outline the policy and procedure – to the student and even to the parents – in careful detail. When no policy has been established, for example, regarding inappropriate language, the school's administration, in conjunction with the staff, should move to have one developed.

Praise and Encouragement

Praise and encouragement represent the most effective means to ensure that a positive form of behavior will recur. Implemented frequently, for reinforcement, encomiums not only contribute to a positive climate, but become indicators of classroom expectations.

When planning a program for a particular student, the teacher may encourage specific target behaviors, for example, good attendance and punctuality, consistent task completion, cooperative actions, noticeable effort, and skills improvement. Some of the ways in which students may be encouraged include:

- increasing the frequency of praise, compliments, and/or feedback to a student for accomplishing the target behavior

- providing positive teacher and/or class attention when the student engages in the target behavior

- charting the frequency of the target behavior so that the student will be able to visualize improvement

- awarding "honorable mentions" to recognize student improvement – certificates, bulletin board notices, chalkboard citations, greeting cards

- bestowing privileges – extra computer time, washing the boards, free reading period, running errands to the office, etc.

Because the attention of everyone in the classroom is normally drawn in the direction of disruptive situations, it is recommended that the teachers and the students consider ways to rehearse planned ignoring, and, in addition, to develop ways to recognize and acknowledge both pro-social and cooperative behavior.

Motivation

When it is evident that inappropriate behavior is prompted by the student's negative response to low academic achievement, the individualized plan should address motivational factors by altering the structure and/or content of classroom tasks and activities.

Meaningfulness

The content of academic tasks should be scrutinized for personal meaningfulness, especially when the student disengagement results from the academic work seeming to be "boring" or irrelevant. "Why do we have to learn this anyway?" is a familiar chorus. The individualized plan might consider presenting academic skills in the context of the student's own interests, and, therefore, the initial entry might describe ways to discover these interests if they are unknown. When Mrs. Archambeault discovers that nine-year-old Ivan is contemplating a career as a professional hockey player, she first of all includes library books on the subject of hockey in his language arts program. Then, she plans to dedicate parts of several classes to methods of searching the newspaper for news of various students' favorite sports events and their scores. Another way to help students find meaningfulness in the curriculum is to show that knowledge learned at school may relate to real-life situations. For example, activities might include writing:

- an effective shopping list

- a "refrigerator" message to a family member

- a telephone message taken for someone else

- an e-mail message

- a request to a company for nutritional information about its products

- an order for classroom supplies

- a letter to Miss Manners or Abby Landers

- a note to the Humane Society

- a proposal to the principal requesting a new purchase for the school

- a request inquiry for information about sunscreen

- an inquiry regarding a Saturday clean-up activity at the conservation area

- a complaint to a manufacturer describing a defective product

- a question to the editor of a newspaper

- a request to a radio or TV program

- a follow-up reminder to a government representative

- a note to congratulate a sports figure

- a résumé for the purpose of obtaining part-time employment

When working with adolescent students, the teacher, in discussion with the class, is able to identify the knowledge domain relevant to this age group. For example, classroom discussions regarding Shakespeare's *Romeo and Juliet* can compare and contrast teenage interactions and parental expectations then and now.

Difficulty

In some classrooms, it is not unusual for certain students to act inappropriately if faced with assignments that are too difficult. For many students with weak skills, to avoid the task altogether is sometimes more expedient than asking for help. When students are asked to state the worst label they can be given by someone else, a large majority want to avert any chance of being called "stupid." Such an attitude may typically be evident in older students who want the class to believe that they are challenging the teacher's authority instead of admitting an inability to do the assigned work. Such class members quickly discover that defiance can sometimes earn them popularity points with the peer group, particularly in those classrooms lacking a positive climate. When such situations are evident, the teacher's plan must begin by including strategies that provide a range of difficulties so that all students will find appropriate levels of challenge.

In the same classroom, but on other occasions, some students will behave inappropriately if the level of the assignments is not sufficiently challenging. This problem is most apparent in younger students who may have well-developed literacy skills of which the teacher is unaware. Boredom resulting from being asked to complete low-level activities will inspire certain students to engage in other – often inappropriate – activities. For example, Hiro is always playing at the computer terminal and refuses to join in other classroom procedures.

While many different strategies exist that will help reduce the difficulty level of classroom tasks, the efficiency of each of these depends on the pattern of strengths and weaknesses of the individual student as well as on the nature of the task itself. For example, Melanie, when faced with questions, finds it easier to write answers than to respond orally, although, from a typical developmental perspective, speaking is less difficult than writing. In some cases, motivation is achieved by making tasks more challenging through adjustment of the depth and the breadth of a particular activity. Because Hamide has developed a passion for astronomy, he is encouraged to consult the books in the local university library to complete his science project about nebulae.

When a teacher hopes to alter projects, planning considerations for varying the difficulty level of a given task may include:

- *Increasing or reducing the amount of spoken versus written language:*

    - "talking books"[10] will help a student acquire more information from text

    - instructions on tape allow the student to replay them as needed

    - discussion of a topic in a structured group setting permits the student to explore it before beginning to write about it

    - providing a range of references and text materials gives the students choices

- *Increasing or reducing the amount of written work, by allowing:*

    - a student to dictate information to a peer or the teacher

    - the student's ideas which have been read into the tape recorder to be transcribed by a peer or a teacher

    - the student to employ a word processor, including both spell check and grammar check, to improve writing quality

    - the student to utilize voice-activated software to compose written text

    - the student to film a creative story, by Camcorder, using student "actors"

- *A modification in methods of evaluation, by giving:*

    - more time for the student to complete the assignment

    - an allowed period of time with a hand-held electronic dictionary

    - permission to use a calculator in checking answers to math questions

    - an assignment to create a personal spelling dictionary, including words most often used

- *A system for providing access to other students' notes and assignments, by using:*

    - a carbon copy or photocopy of another student's notes to upgrade and pattern

    - a comparison to show the way one student's assignment differs from each of the ones done by others to demonstrate that there is not a norm and that there need not be

Novelty

Novelty – when introduced in classroom procedures and activities – can serve two potential outcomes: it can either motivate or confuse students. Familiarity, the polar opposite of novelty, is an important factor when teaching a new concept or procedure, or whenever a high degree of predictability is warranted, because students feel safer in known situations, within identifiable surroundings, and with familiar people. For example, Mr. Crozinsky must question Odel when she complains that each task seems so different from the previous one that she can never be sure what she should be doing. In response, Mr. Crozinsky's plan for Odel underlines the importance of utilizing a familiar task format when a new concept is introduced. To avoid confusion, he changes the appearance and the demands of the task only when Odel is comfortable with the new idea. Mr. Crozinsky will also undertake to bring Odel's attention to the structure of particular tasks, outlining the way they differ from each other, as well as the ways such differences impact what she is required to do.

Once a student develops a sense of the way the classroom operates, a feeling of safety vicariously follows. In addition, the introduction of unexpected activities and methods into this comfortable environment can create a level of excitement and enthusiasm. By breaking the pattern of familiarity, such novel events as field trips, guest speakers, and chances to work under a tree on a warm June day serve to motivate learning. For example, when Brayden refuses to complete his work, complaining that it is boring, Mr. Markarian not only gives Brayden more challenging tasks but also modifies certain activities so that they involve different, less stressful, modes of presentation and expression[11].

To modify the level of novelty, a plan might consider:

- *reducing or increasing the variety of assignments, by*

  - teaching students how to approach a range of questions: multiple choice, fill in the blanks, and true/false; how to respond to essays or to write them; how to manage task variables associated with assignments; e.g., reviews, poetry, précis, résumés and reports; how to learn note-taking and other written forms such as summarizing

  - varying the way information is acquired; e.g., interview a witness, watch a documentary, make a comparison chart of information contained in several textbooks, elicit suggestions

- *narrowing or expanding the range of multi-media presentations; identify*

  - the student's preferred modality; e.g., visual, visual-auditory, verbal, aural, and/or visual-motor, then use it to present new information

  - any distractors in the classroom that interfere with task completion; e.g., noise level, sitting by a window, open doorway, or other problem item

  cont'd

> - *providing different locations, so that students may choose to do work individually or in a group setting; for example, access to:*
>   - reference books for notemaking
>   - computers for word processing, reviewing important concepts; games that provide drill; other pastimes
>   - personal areas for independent work
>   - tables where cooperative work with other students is positively encouraged

Many other ways exist in which to create a positive learning environment. By finding the level of novelty that suits a student in a particular context, the teacher can increase that student's learning capacity. In the gymnasium, Arianna requires a very structured presentation in order to grasp the required movements on a piece of gymnastic apparatus. When engaged in a mathematics activity, however, she enjoys a variety of tasks to reinforce the skills she is acquiring. Across a broad range, the level of novelty applied to a situation depends on many factors, including age, competence, mood, difficulty, personal interest, and many others. On any given day, depending on the activity in question, the student who was motivated yesterday in a certain way may react differently this morning.

Personal Goals and Objectives

Within a school career, each student should be encouraged to develop sets of personal goals and objectives which might include elements related to future careers, personal growth, and ways of learning. By developing the ability to formulate goals and objectives, a student is empowered to shape a personal future and to take responsibility for individual behavior. Initially, a student's plan might include learning to differentiate a goal from an objective; later these skills may be utilized in learning to deal with personal concerns.

It is interesting to note that the majority of self-help books[12], as well as programs that claim to provide the secrets to success, invariably describe the importance of formulating a plan to visualize personal goals and objectives. Devising such a plan allows the student to consider and itemize personal goals in priority order and then to establish, also in a list, a range of means for reaching them. Even if goals are modified weekly, a student equipped with a plan is one with a sense of direction and purposefulness.

Career Goals

Why is it important for a student to consider career goals? For students in the Intermediate Division, as well as for those in secondary school, thinking about career options impacts on course and program selection; but what is even more important, such a pattern of thought provides a sense of direction.

Because students come into personal contact with a relatively small number of occupations – mostly those of their parents, relatives, and friends – when a student plans to explore career options, the procedures should include a range of opportunities to interact with people in various fields. This can be facilitated by inviting guest speakers, by visiting and/or shadowing a person within the work environment, and also by discussing aspects of the professional lives of characters in books, videos, and film.

When a more structured study is required, the student should be encouraged to acquire the following information about each career possibility:

- the educational training associated with a job can be discovered by identifying the course requirements of a program; such information can be accessed by:

    - contacting staff in Guidance Department

    - consulting university and college calendars

    - researching the chosen vocation on the Internet

    - talking with someone in that position or profession

- the skill requirements for the job in question, for example, that of a dentist, include fine manual dexterity. Insight into the application of those skills can be acquired by:

    - shadowing a person working in a job

    - speaking to different people in a field to find out about a typical day

    - visiting a school or college where people receive training for the respective job

    - interviewing a knowledgeable person about the position

    - reading job catalogues

    - looking at job descriptions in advertising supplements

cont'd

- the behavioral or social requirements for the person wanting the job; for example, salespeople must enjoy interacting with shoppers in order to persuade them to buy the product; similarly, anyone working in a service industry must relate to customers in a polite and cheerful manner; to find out more, students must try :

  - speaking to different people in a field to find out about language and behavior codes associated with the job

  - visiting a person to observe verbal interaction – how does the individual speak with and relate to other workers? support staff? consumers? telephone callers?

By encouraging students to observe, examine, and reflect about various occupations, teachers can help them to be sensitive to the requirements of the work world, which means that they are more likely to make informed choices about career goals. Once a career goal is adopted, the student is readily able to connect what is learned in school to the chosen occupation.

Personal Growth

When still in the process of gaining an education, a student must learn to recognize that personal growth is a lifelong process whose goal is *self-actualization:* becoming the person one needs, wants, or ought to be. Part of that process involves discovering strengths and weaknesses; developing talents and creativity; understanding personal actions as well as the behavior of others; and discovering the ways in which society works. A plan hoping to address such goals might identify helpful and relevant literature, movies, videos; might lead to the organization of discussions and drama, as well as group and individual presentations; and might focus on assigning personal projects to address the individual need. Topics that students find relevant include:

- Making friends
- Working at part-time jobs: baby-sitting; counter clerking
- Dating
- Volunteering
- Getting along with family
- Forming groups with shared interests
- Dealing with peer pressure
- Becoming one's own boss
- Self-employment strategies
- Handling money
- and other varied but related topics

Learner Goals

Like personal growth, learning must be perceived by students as a life-long process. Consequently, as they begin to equip themselves with skills that augment learning, they must recognize the value of:

- Acquiring time management and organizational skills:
  - focusing on getting to class before it begins
  - scheduling homework and study time
  - timetabling recreational opportunities
- Defining and acquiring instructional objectives:
  - learning how to identify the purpose of an assignment
  - beginning to understand procedures outlined
  - determining the amount of effort to apply to a task
- Relating school knowledge to personal knowledge:
  - learning to introspect – thinking about personal behavior and evaluating whether it should be modified, maintained, or altered
  - looking at the way school work relates to other activities – what has the student learned at school that will be useful both in personal life and in the work world ?
  - realizing that planning is productive; the student will learn that the more detail a plan includes, the more useful it becomes

In the preceding sections, some considerations are outlined for designing a plan for a student. Using the structure of the model for creating a positive learning environment, first introduced in Chapter Four, the suggestions lead to the formation of a social curriculum. Once outlined, this plan, employing a variety of media, is easily integrated into a language arts program. It is evident that the individual education plan addressing social and behavioral needs will promote the development, among other useful data, of transferable language skills.

What follows is an actual case study, accompanied by a plan.

Case Study

In the process of planning for a student with socio-emotional needs, the educators involved should first examine a relevant and up-to-date case study. When asked to submit such a case study in the form of a report, Ms. Papadopoulos offered these remarks about the classroom behavior of Scotty Freeman, a student in her class:

> *Scotty, an 11 year old Grade Six student is being referred for a second IPRC this year to determine whether, in September, he should be placed in a self-contained Behavioral class. Although Mrs. Freeman, Scotty's mother, has expressed her opposition to any changes in Scotty's identification – from Learning Disabled to Behavioral/Learning Disabled – she would like him to have access to the services available to both groups.*

> *Scotty almost always begins his day by saying "Good Morning" to me, giving me a smile, or volunteering a hug. Usually, he is the first student to offer to deliver the attendance sheet to the office, to clean up a work area, or to run an errand. On the other hand, he seldom makes it through a class, let alone a day, without getting into some sort of trouble. For example, in response to finding a scrunchie – a decorative hair elastic – on his desk one Monday morning, Scotty began screaming "What's this f...ing thing on my desk?" When becoming bored with it, he threw it on the floor adding, "Yeah, you stupid idiot!"*

> *Later in the period, Scotty began repeatedly calling out my name. At first, I thought he was trying to get my attention, but he did not stop when I answered him. Before the 10:30 a.m. break, Scotty and I had a conference to explore alternatives to the choices he had made. Immediately after what I had thought was a very productive conference, Scotty, at dismissal, climbed into the closet instead of leaving the classroom. When I asked him to come out of the closet, he did, and yet, at some point, he must have slipped past me and found a place to hide, as I found him in the locked classroom when I returned from break.*

> *Upon re-entering the classroom after break, Kayhan, with whom Scotty had had a conflict earlier in the morning, found his major project in shreds. Immediately, Kayhan accused Scotty of being involved, but when I asked him to tell his side of the story, Scotty ran out of the building and off school property. As soon as he returned, the principal decided to send him home for the remainder of the day. Such a series of experiences as this one is definitely the norm rather than the exception.*

When he is spoken to, I have noticed often that Scotty holds his head down and doesn't make eye contact. In a conversation about this habit, Scotty's mother said that there are no cultural reasons why he should do this. When he does speak to another student, Scotty will often sit on that person's desk and lean forward while speaking, until the other student backs away. While, at other times, he wanders off mid-conversation, he will frequently interrupt other people's chatting or lesson periods.

Now and then, I have observed Scotty reacting rather strongly to what appears to be a benign facial expression in someone with whom he is interacting. In a recent incident, when asked why he jumped on a student and began punching him, he replied, "He was looking at me. I've always hated people looking at me. I hate it when people look at me. I hate it!"

In my experience, Scotty rarely completes an academic task. Lacking adequate writing skills, Scotty prints very slowly, often refusing to attempt cursive writing. Instead, he says, "I don't do that!" although when he actually does attempt it, his cursive writing is more legible than his printing. In the area of task completion, still in the context of writing, Scotty sometimes completes a single sentence in his journal. He even manages two or three computation questions in one sitting, provided I maintain close proximity to his desk. This academic year, the only two activities assigned that were not disguised as games – and yet held his attention for more than 20 minutes – involved, in the first case, making symmetrical designs using pattern blocks, and, in the second, reading a poem in two voices. Although Scotty did not actually read the poem aloud to the class, he demonstrated an amazing skill when he was able to recite the entire two-page poem after rehearsing it only a few times.

Occasionally, Scotty responds to positive reinforcement; for example, towards the end of school year, he was sometimes willing to complete a small academic task such as writing five words that begin with a given letter; before doing this, he made the condition that he have some free time and a chance to telephone his mother.

Looking at the entire picture, I have a clear impression that the severity and frequency of his inappropriate behaviors has decreased since we instituted the daily, early-morning trouble-shooting conference.

Ms. Papadopoulos also contributed this background information about Scotty Freeman:

According to his student records, Scotty, who immigrated to Canada from Jamaica at the age of 6 months, has attended an urban school since Kindergarten. In Grade One, he was involved in a program of remedial reading and writing. In Grade Two, after Scotty was identified as Learning Disabled, he was placed in a Home School Comprehensive Program. In Grade Five, when it was decided that Scotty should receive the support of an LD-Core program, he was transferred to his present school in order to receive such service.

In the words of Mrs. Freeman, his mother, at this point Scotty's behavior "changed for the worse". One of his special education teachers reported that, during the first months of the year, Scotty and his friend could not be permitted to travel, unescorted, between special education classes because they would "terrorize" Ari, another LD-Core student. When Ari's parents eventually withdrew him from the school, they stated mistreatment as a reason for the move.

Shortly thereafter, both Special Education Resource teachers went on Long-term Disability leave, with the result that Special Education was taught by a succession of occasional teachers. According to the principal, the first teacher was asked to leave as a result of the way he handled an incident involving Scotty who was reported to have punched the teacher in the face. When this happened, the teacher is alleged to have grabbed Scotty, pushed him against a desk, wagged his finger at the boy, and warned him not ever to do that again. At this juncture, Scotty was sent to the Alternative-to-Suspension program; incidentally, according to his Child and Youth Care Worker, during his time there, Scotty was suspended twice from the program.

Scotty is the youngest of three children. According to Mrs. Freeman, his 13-year-old brother has been identified as Behavioral/Gifted, and his 16-year-old sister has recently left home. Because her husband is currently in prison for a drug-related offense, Scotty's mother calls herself a single parent. Mrs. Freeman has also wondered aloud if Scotty's problems in school could be related to a history of poor nutrition and high stress levels which she experienced while pregnant with Scotty.

Given this information about Scotty, a teacher must ask what needs are expressed by his behavior. Ms. Papadopoulos has decided to focus on three major areas which she has listed in priority order: empowerment and prizing are the first two and an individualized program is the third. The last one of these will target both learning about cause-effect relationships and about addressing his retaliation responses.

In dealing with Scotty's empowerment issue, Ms. Papadopoulos recognizes that, in classroom situations at least, Scotty's behavior may perhaps be motivated by his need to be in charge. In Table 6-1, by describing her unsuccessful attempts to encourage Scotty to do his work, especially when she altered levels of meaningfulness and difficulty, Ms. Papadopoulos provides a reason for her focus on empowerment. If she had not previously tested his response to a tuning of motivational factors, it is possible that she would have targeted motivational elements rather than empowerment in her plan.

Once the need is chosen, Ms. Papadopoulos, basing the decision on her knowledge of Scotty's previous classroom experience, identifies strategies that she will implement over the following month. Notably, a short time frame will allow her to re-evaluate her plan as well as to make the necessary changes based on Scotty's responses to her interventions.

Table 6-1. Planning for Scotty's need for empowerment.

Scottie Freeman   Age: 11 years   Grade 6   Ms. Papadopoulos

Student Needs	Programming Strategies
Empowerment: Scotty often goes through an entire day refusing to do any of his work. He is unresponsive to efforts which have been devised to adjust the level of difficulty and/or make the work more meaningful. Unless a lesson is disguised as a game, Scotty either refuses to begin the activity or acts out to avoid it	• give Scotty some choices about the order of work, location, materials, and in some circumstances, group members; always involve him in the decision making • let him set some objectives about skills that need developing • establish a contract that clarifies what will happen if he refuses to do his work or if he engages in a power struggle that cannot be defused by humor • follow the contract to the letter; for example, ask Scotty to leave; inform the office that he needs time away from the group; if he refuses, notify the office again so that the principal can come to get him; his mother will be called; he will be sent home • praise Scotty when he attempts an assignment, and, especially, when he completes work • give him the choice of a fun activity to follow his task completion

In Table 6-2, Ms. Papadopoulos substantiates her evaluation that only by developing a sense of belonging will Scotty begin to feel himself to be part of the class. Because of Scotty's evident desire to have friends, the teacher recognizes that part of the trouble is his lack of skill in making friends. In addition, a range of implicit behaviors involves factors that undermine his success. Moreover, on the basis of Scotty's family circumstance, she decides that by helping him to explore various aspects of families, she might provide him with some comfort.

Because Ms. Papadopoulos recognizes that focusing on personal and sensitive issues like a student's family may create stress and anxiety, she therefore wisely chooses bibliotherapy as the vehicle for the introduction of such topics. By examining the thoughts and feelings of a character in a story, Scotty will have the opportunity to learn safely, as well as impersonally, about families.

In order to maximize the plan's effectiveness, other significant people in Scotty's life – the principal, his former French teacher, an older buddy – are incorporated in the plan. Also, Ms. Papadopoulos is specific about the language she will use to showcase his strengths. By providing this level of detail, she ensures that the plan will be useful to other teachers who interact with Scotty.

Ms. Papadopoulos recognizes that the prizing aspect of Scotty's plan involves a long-term goal. In fact, although she does not expect Scotty to demonstrate success in the new plan within a month, she will nonetheless review it to update the data and to include new resources.

Table 6-2. **Planning for Scottie's need for prizing.**

Scottie Freeman Age: 11 years Grade 6 Ms. Papadopoulos	
Student Needs	**Programming Strategies**
Prizing:	
Although Scotty seems to need and to want very much the friendship of his peers, he lacks the skills for making friendships succeed; in addition, he does not maintain an appropriate distance when conversing. Either he leans too close, forcing the other person to back up, or he wanders off	• determine whether Scotty is sufficiently comfortable with a family topic to discuss it • comfort Scotty when he is upset; give him the option to converse in private, to go to the quiet area, or to speak to the guidance counselor
	cont'd

Student Needs	Programming Strategies
Prizing: Scotty constantly holds his head down when asked a direct question, failing to make eye contact, shuffling his feet, and mumbling his answers. Perhaps Scotty suffers from being compared with his older brother, a gifted and very verbal young person. Moreover, it is obvious that Scotty suffers greatly not only from his father's incarceration but also from his sister's departure. Scotty cries whenever mention is made of family issues	• assure that Scotty has access to biblio-therapy in order to expose him to the concept of "different family structures". Such exposure, which may help him deal with the notion of a "parent who takes drugs," might include, among many titles: Jenesse, Aylette (1990). *Families, a Celebration of Diversity,* Boston: Houghton Mifflin Simon, Norma (1976). *All Kinds of Families.* Chicago: Albert Whitman & Company. Seixas, Judith (1989). *Living with a Parent Who Takes Drugs.* New York: Greenwillow Books. • arrange for companionship with an older buddy • demonstrate caring by asking about his interests and experiences outside the classroom; for example, go to watch him playing basketball or participating at a track meet • incorporate in Scotty's lessons a range of varied materials related to his sports' interests, in hopes of increasing his motivation • spend a few minutes before class, apparently spontaneously, chatting about the sports scores of the previous day • choose Scotty for special errands that are proof of his trustworthiness – he is dependable when he knows someone is counting on him • incorporate comments about his strengths whenever speaking to him and the class; for example, "I need someone trustworthy to deliver this message. Scotty, you deliver it". • arrange for Scotty to show his work to the principal and also to his former French teacher whom he loves

On the basis of Scotty's classroom behavior, described in great detail in Table 6-3, Ms. Papadopoulos believes that Scotty is unaware of the cause-effect relationships that exist between his behavior and the manner in which people react to it. Again, she relies on bibliotherapy to broach the subject, in order, first, to teach him to identify the cause-effect relationships in other people's behavior. By targeting other media, such as TV programs that Scotty already watches, the teacher is promoting the analysis of a broad range of behaviors. When providing specifics about the "What if" game, Ms. Papadopoulos' plan is very clear in that it focuses on the way Scotty will begin to learn to identify cause-effect relationships:

Table 6-3. **Planning for Scotty's need for an individualized program dealing with identifying cause-effect relationships**

Scottie Freeman Age: 11 years Grade 6 Ms. Papadopoulos	
Student Needs	**Programming Strategies**
Individualized Program: identifying cause and effect Scotty is prone to temper flare-ups which involve swearing, smashing whatever is in reach, and resorting to physical violence. Scotty tends to overreact to people's facial expressions, body language, and verbal statements by responding with a temper outburst. When punished for demonstrating such a reaction, he says that he is not being treated fairly because the other student started the fracas When Scotty regularly makes comments that are put-downs of his classmates, they respond angrily, yet he fails to see why Scotty often hides in the classroom at dismissal time, begs to stay, or disrupts so that he will be asked to remain behind. This is probably related to the fact that he constantly annoys older children as they walk by the classroom door, running into the classroom to seek refuge. At recess, it is difficult for him to escape the students he has antagonized	• Bibliotherapy focused on problem solving and class discussion about applying Pooh's suggestions to one's own life Allen and Allen (1995 *Winnie-the-Pooh on Problem Solving:). In which Pooh, Piglet and friends explore how to solve problems so you can too.* New York: Dutton • provide direct instruction about cause/effect relationships in social situations • have Scotty observe situations in TV programs; he should be instructed that as he watches, he should note and record one or more examples of cause/effect situations; repeat the same process using literature, scripts, drama presentations, poems, and other media • employ examples of realistic situations to role play; these should be offered by Scotty and others – the class will role-play different scenarios, having been encouraged to discuss varying possibilities • ask Scotty to identify the cause and effect of his actions when he is being given positive reinforcement for appropriate behavior *cont'd*

Student Needs	Programming Strategies

Individualized Program: identifying cause and effect	• repeat the same process when he is asked to sit out as a consequence for inappropriate behavior
	
	• teach and play the "What if ...." game to have the students consider choices and consequences; for example, "What if someone walks past the open classroom door and looks in?"
	
	   – identify various responses and their consequences; write a dialogue
	
	   – construct a flow chart as a visual reminder
	
	   – compose a short story about a typical event

In the final section of the plan described in Table 6-4, Ms. Papadopoulos has incorporated an aspect to deal with Scotty's need to retaliate against his peers. Although she feels that his behavior is probably related to both the empowerment and the prizing need addressed respectively in Table 6-1 and Table 6-2, an extra effort to deal with the issue in an individualized program might accelerate the process of integrating Scotty into the classroom community:

Table 6-4. **Planning for an individualized program that Scotty needs in order to deal with his retaliation response**

Scottie Freeman   Age: 11 years   Grade 6   Ms. Papadopoulos

Student Needs	Programming Strategies
Individualized Program: Retaliation Always, Scotty is very protective of his conference time, perhaps because it addresses his need to be prized. Thus, when Kayhan interrupted us, although Scotty was able to hold back his anger until recess, at that juncture, he shredded Kayhan's project. Scotty often retaliates by concealing or even damaging either his classmates' schoolwork or their belongings	• explore through discussion the purpose and the "pay offs" of retaliation • establish reasons why people choose to retaliate anonymously • list methods of avoiding or replacing retaliation and revenge • introduce and rehearse language that will allow Scotty to express his feelings when he is displeased; for example, "Kayhan, please wait until my conference with Ms. P. is over!" or "Kayhan, this is my time!" • praise and encourage Scotty when he uses appropriate language to communicate his feelings

Ms. Papadopoulos' outline for Scotty incorporates features of an effective plan. In her overview, she:

- identifies relevant episodes of Scotty's behavior that have been previously observed

- generates a hypothesis that responds to the needs implied by his behavior

- describes specific interventions to meet the relevant outlined needs

By sharing her plan with various members of a multi-disciplinary team, Ms. Papadopoulos creates an opportunity for individuals to offer insights from their different perspectives. For example, while it is evident that Mrs. P's plan for Scotty Freeman targets his immediate needs, an aspect that receives no mention – although it surfaces several times in the case study – is Scotty's apprehension about being abandoned. Throughout the story of Scotty's case, evidence emerges:

- The prison sentence of Scotty's father seems to have caused him to abandon the boy .

- his sister abandons him when she leaves home

- his sense of abandonment is typical of some children who, after emigrating, feel a subsequent sense of rootlessness and/or alienation

- his fear of abandonment is ameliorated somewhat because of the privilege that Ms. P. has found effective: Scotty is allowed, from time to time, to telephone his mother

- his sensitivity to family topics is chronic: Scotty cries when the subject of his family comes up

Although, in her outline, Ms. P. has not emphasized this "abandonment" aspect of Scotty's feelings, she has nonetheless addressed his prizing and empowerment needs. This emphasis means that her planned interventions have a chance of meeting most of his affective needs.

Because each teacher demonstrates a different style in preparing plans, within the following pages several more actual plans that might be appropriate are outlined. After looking over these, the reader may find it useful to evaluate their effectiveness by referring to the criteria established for Ms. Papadopoulos' plan.

In Table 6-5, Mr. MacIntosh's individual plan for eleven-year old Juan is shown. Here, management need as the primary focus is isolated. In formulating this plan, Mr. MacIntosh first establishes that Juan's behavior results from the boy's lack of knowledge about acceptable class routines. From the start, Mr. MacIntosh creates opportunities that will teach Juan the expectations associated, for example, with attempting an assignment before requesting help. In addition, Juan will be given other procedures: ways to access help, methods involving taking turns, processes for working with a peer tutor, and other related options. As part of the overall picture, Juan's academic program has already been modified to ensure his capability in completing assignments.

Table 6-5. Planning for Juan's management issues.

Planning for Students with Socio-emotional Needs	
Juan DeLuca Age: 11 years	Grade 6 Mr. MacIntosh
Student Needs	**Programming Strategies**
Management: Juan yells out such statements as "It's too hard!" or "I can't do this!" when given seatwork he perceives to be too difficult Often, although it has been modified at his insistence, Juan will not even try the assignment Usually, Juan becomes very frustrated when he must wait for assistance from the teacher	• ask Juan to attempt to start the assignment before he requests help; inform him that the appropriate way to receive help is first to raise his hand and then to wait quietly • remind Juan to wait his turn while indicating that other students also require assistance • assign him a peer-tutor who will address his preliminary questions and help to formulate more probing ones • ignore Juan when he yells out • respond readily with help when he raises his hand; praise his effort; e.g., "You raised your hand and you are being quiet; very good!" • continue to monitor the difficulty of Juan's assignments, modifying them so that he is able to work independently

Initially, because of the underlying assumption that Juan is untutored in the matter of classroom expectations, Mr. MacIntosh has dealt with Juan's inappropriate remarks by establishing guidelines, encouraging adherence, and ignoring his "calling out". Inherent in Juan's remarks – "It's too hard!" and "I can't do this". or "I need help". – is the possibility that his assignments really are too difficult. Basing his diagnosis on this scenario, Mr. MacIntosh has already ruled out a "difficulty" factor and may want to look at another possibility: could it be that Juan is using this approach to elicit fatherly attention? If the teacher finds evidence to support this hypothesis, contingent upon Juan's behavior, he might consider spending a few minutes in conversation with him after school. If no male figure exists in Juan's life, Mrs. De Luca, Juan's mother, could be encouraged to contact such an organization as Big Brothers.

With reference to a different case, Richard's Grade Two plan, prepared by Mr. Westermann, shows that the priorities for the student include meeting certain affective needs: safety (Table 6-6), prizing, (Table 6-7), and empowerment (Table 6-8). By observing Richard's behavior after a Saturday and Sunday spent with his Father, Mr. Westermann concludes that some of the weekend's activities may destabilize Richard, especially when he is exposed to adult themes that may frighten him. In formulating the plan, had Mr. Westermann provided more detailed observations of Richard's classroom behavior, possibly, the other members of the multi-disciplinary team would have offered additional suggestions for dealing with Richard's issues.

Table 6-6. **Planning for Richard's safety issues.**

Planning for Students with Socio-emotional Needs	
Richard Lionheart Age: 7 years Grade 2 Mr. Westermann	
Student Needs	**Programming Strategies**
During the weekends, when Richard is with his father, he watches videos some of the time; for example, *"Freddy's Dead"* and *"Hell Raiser."* On Mondays, he invariably acts out the models presented in the films; for example, after seeing the infamous Michael Jackson video, he indicated by his actions that the video had had a profound effect on him; Richard's behavior suggests he is exposed to some negative role models	• present literature such as C. S. Lewis' *"The Lion, the Witch and the Wardrobe"* in which the roles of good and evil are clearly defined • meet with Mr. Lionheart for the purpose of outlining the benefits of a parenting-skills workshop to be presented by the principal and the school psychologist • have the students role-play situations involving the classic theme of good vs. evil; follow the presentations with a class discussion

Because Mr. Westermann observes the negative feedback Richard receives from his peers, in addition to being aware of the boy's clear inability to engage in positive interactions, he targets meeting Richard's prizing needs. Showcasing his achievement and providing opportunities for Richard to shine help to achieve this objective. By scheduling – for the whole class – a unit dealing with friends and feelings, Mr. Westermann is careful not to single out Richard, allowing him to participate with everyone else.

Table 6-7. Planning for Richard's prizing issues.

Planning for Students with Socio-emotional Needs	
Richard Lionheart Age: 7 years Grade 2 Mr. Westermann	
Student Needs	**Programming Strategies**
Prizing: Although Richard is a bright and capable student, his peers cringe at the thought of including him in their work group because he always "bugs" or hurts them. Being often left to work alone, Richard rarely receives any positive feedback from peers	• create opportunities to showcase Richard's individual achievements • assign him leadership roles in which he can be proud, such as "recorder" on the field trip • involve the whole class in the Dellcrest[13] Outreach Program, *"Friends and Feelings";* pair him with a buddy, preferably an older student who shares Richard's interest in the visual arts

To deal with Richard's insolence, Mr. Westermann hopes to make him responsible for his behavior by focusing on altering his need to do as he pleases. Such a goal is achieved by providing a range of choices regarding academic task completion. Because Mr. Westermann also recognizes that one-on-one social skills training program cannot be managed because of budgetary limitations, he, therefore, searches for and finds a suitable counselor in the community.

Table 6-8. **Planning for Richard's empowerment issues.**

Planning for Students with Socio-emotional Needs	
Richard Lionheart Age: 7 years Grade 2 Mr. Westermann	
Student Needs	**Programming Strategies**
Empowerment: Not only does Richard seldom admit to wrongdoing, but he often blurts out inappropriate remarks. For example, when I asked, "What's the first thing we do when we enter the gym?" Richard, in the midst of his own laughter, answered, "Kiss my ass". Usually, Richard chooses to speak and behave inappropriately	• avoid asking him rhetorical questions or queries that leave openings for his inappropriate comments • allow him to choose one of only two activities: "You may either complete your math assignment or work on your geography project" • speak to his parents about enrolling him in the one-on-one *"Social Skills and Decision-Making"* program at Dellcrest[13] at the cost of $15.00 per week • speak to the principal and/or social worker about contacting a service organization that might sponsor Richard in the event that his parents cannot afford the fee • role play *"The Joker and the Nerd"*, to demonstrate ideas related to the way power is achieved

Turning to focus on the situation of another student, Ms. Van Huyen has prepared, for Jack Alltrada, a plan targeting both his prizing and his empowerment needs. In Table 6-9, the teacher identifies Jack's overwhelming need to belong as the basis for the boy's inappropriate classroom behavior. If Ms. Van Huyen can pin down more details about the kinds of assignments that cause him to interrupt – especially when he wants to know whether he is on the right track – she may reveal further aspects of Jack's difficulty. Ms. Van Huyen must ask herself questions: "Is this a general problem or one limited to a specific subject area, a limited context?" Another query might be, "Does this behavior occur in the gym or even at recess?" Further focus yields a realization that a clear description of his behavior with peers is needed. More questions come up: "What provokes the other students to laugh at him?" "Does he make weak jokes?" "Is his wardrobe too uncool?" Such additional information would allow Ms. Van Huyen to generate more plausible hypotheses that could be tested in the context of her plan.

Table 6-9. Planning for Jack's prizing issues.

Planning for Students with Socio-emotional Needs	
Jack Alltrada Age: 10 years Grade 5 Ms. Van Huyen	
Student Needs	**Programming Strategies**
Prizing: Jack, who has a strong need to feel accepted and worthwhile, will often interrupt a quiet work time to ensure that the project he is engaged in meets the expectations of the assignment. While usually demonstrating a lack of social skills, he desperately tries to belong to the group. Not only are his attempts at interacting inappropriate and immature, often his efforts cause his peers to laugh at him instead of with him	• provide activities that offer Jack a self-correcting format; e.g., computer games for math and language • create a personal chart on which he can record, in confidential consultation with his teacher, how well he has done in each class, both in completing his work and in coping socially • create a "friendship" centre containing books, filmstrips, videos, comic strips,and other media where the ideas of making friends and being a friend are outlined and dramatized • organize a daily work-group situation in which the score is based on points assigned for each group's work habits, their ability to stay on task, and their record of cooperation. Over a period of months, a weekly prize is awarded to each winning group

Ms. Van Huyen recognizes Jack's empowerment need in her planning (see Table 6-10). When delineating his situation, she mentions his large stature as a factor in his power-seeking behavior. As his teacher, she asks herself whether his size is the brunt of his peers' ridiculing behavior mentioned in the prizing section of the plan. Although it is true that he may experience a sense of helplessness, expected to be addressed by this plan, Ms. Van Huyen should also consider teaching Jack the language of self-defence.

Table 6-10. Planning for Jack's empowerment issues.

Planning for Students with Socio-emotional Needs	
Jack Alltrada Age: 10 years Grade 5 Ms. Van Huyen	
Student Needs	**Programming Strategies**
Empowerment: Often, in the school, Jack enters into a rather fierce power struggle with teachers. He will refuse to cooperate, notably when he: is embarrassed in front of peers; is openly challenged; and/or is given no options. His power-seeking behavior has been enhanced by his large stature as well as by the responses he's received. His expressed attitude is, first, that he never gets to choose what he wants; and second, that his teachers automatically assume he will be disruptive	• give Jack choices: which project will he work on first? review privately the class expectations • praise him in front of his peers both for being cooperative and for showing leadership • shift the focus of responsibility – in any power struggle with Jack – by asking, "What do you expect me to do about this?" • involve Jack in decision making • allow him to chair classroom meetings • grant Jack permission – when his assigned work is completed – to choose from several "fun" activities: reading a book of his choice, completing a crossword puzzle, playing a number game, or starting another activity

In general, Ms. Van Huyen's description of Jack's behavior is not sufficiently detailed to allow for supplementary interpretations; in short, she customarily uses such abstract terms as "social skills" or "power struggle", and even "cooperate", without providing examples of actual observations that have led her to make such conclusions. In spite of these weaknesses in the case outline, many of the interventions she has planned will undoubtedly impact on Jack's behavior.

Turning to the story of Sam – a student in Grade Nine who is exhibiting truancy problems – his teacher, Ms. Cristensen , reports that she believes these may relate to safety, prizing, and motivational needs. In Table 6-11, her plan to meet his safety needs suggests that some students in the class are in the habit of harassing Sam. Significantly, he complains of illness, a pattern that is supported by his parents. Ms. Cristensen's first intervention, the one guaranteeing that Sam will receive a thorough medical examination, is imperative.

Table 6-11. **Planning for Sam's safety issues**

Planning for Students with Socio-emotional Needs	
Sam Yosemity Age: 14 years Grade 9 Ms. Cristensen	
Student Needs	**Programming Strategies**
Safety: Sam avoids going to classes, especially those in which he doesn't feel emotionally safe or in which he has a record of performing poorly. Over a period of time, Sam's habit of absenteeism has been involving him in a pattern of frequently complaining about illness and habitually signing out of school – with his parents' permission – just before his afternoon English class. In a discussion with the guidance counselor, Ms.Cristensen learns not only that Sam is afraid of certain "tough" students in the class but also that he is failing the course	• refer Sam to the school nurse or a physician to ensure that there is no medical basis for his absences • set clear procedures and expectations; for example, Sam is responsible for handing in all missed assignments; if the teacher states that these will be due when he returns, Sam may find it more convenient to come to class • assign Sam a seat in front of the teacher's desk, not simply away from the "tough" students but close enough for eye contact with the teacher • give Sam opportunities to work with a partner, not only to teach cooperative skills but also to establish a friendship • initiate a class discussion about people's expectations in the realm of safety in both its physical and emotional aspects

The more Sam feels part of the group, the more probable it is that he will come to class. In Table 6-12, Ms. Cristensen develops strategies that will allow Sam first to become part of and then to receive the support of the classroom community. By first establishing a caring relationship between Sam and herself, she is able to initiate the process, but, in so doing, she should be careful how this unfolding process is interpreted by the rest of the class – Sam must become part of the group rather than be seen as an outsider, or worse, as Ms. Cristensen's "pet".

Table 6-12. **Planning for Sam's prizing issues**

Planning for Students with Socio-emotional Needs	
Sam Yosemity. Age: 14 years Grade 9 Ms. Cristensen	
Student Needs	**Programming Strategies**
Prizing: Sam needs compliments and recognition	• ensure that there is a personal greeting to Sam from each teacher to help establish a caring relationship • organize a program for Sam to make journal entries; teacher-writing responses will follow these in order to allow personal but confidential interaction • give Sam small quizzes and daily assignments which are marked and returned immediately; through these, he will become aware of receiving feedback and experiencing "instant" success

To motivate students, the teacher should ensure that the curriculum be as personally relevant as possible. In Table 6-13, Ms. Cristensen recognizes that Sam is more likely to come to class when the topic is one that interests him. This means that the reading of a warlike scene from *The Iliad* will more readily draw him to class after lunch on Friday than the recitation of a poem from the English Romantic period.

Table 6-13. **Planning for Sam's motivational issues**

Planning for Students with Socio-emotional Needs	
Sam Yosemity Age: 14 years Grade 9 Ms. Cristensen	
Student Needs	**Programming Strategies**
Motivation – Meaningfulness: If the classes include material of personal interest to Sam, he may be more likely to attend those sessions	• make sure that Sam's interest in computers is enriched by allowing him to word process assignments in class • speak to Sam about his interests, career goals, and other personal predilections in order to incorporate elements from these wherever applicable; e.g., Ms. Cristensen's awareness of his rock collection and his desire to become a geologist will provide topics for videos, reading, and drawing

In attempting to improve Sam's attendance, the teacher recognizes one potential limitation: it may not improve noticeably because the boy's negative feelings, associated with other classes, will outweigh his positive feelings about Ms. Cristensen's class. Another possibility, of course, is that Sam will find a new way to limit his attendance to this particular class. At first, it may be useful to involve his other teachers and then to provide an inducement to have him participate in school-wide activities – camera club, intramural sport, students' council. By learning about Sam's personal interests, the teachers may be able to provide more momentum.

In summary, Ms. Cristensen's proposal is that because Sam's truancy is associated with characteristic feelings of fear, anxiety, and malaise, the plan will, at the outset, rule inapplicable any medical basis for the chronic absenteeism. Moreover, she recognizes that her plan must include ways to alter these feelings, by creating opportunities that will allow Sam to experience and associate positive emotions with classroom activities.

Commentary

No such magical document exists as a foolproof plan! Different hypotheses regarding each student's behavior will yield different plans. When a strategy undergoes revision, the teacher has usually become aware of changes that are implied by the student's reaction to the interventions involved in the initial outline. Initially, the chief importance lies in having a plan in place. From the moment of its inception, the plan is regularly modified on the basis of feedback resulting from its implementation. Importantly, a plan is not a promissory note; rather, it simply describes a course of action indicated by the available information. Without it, parents and administrators may hold a teacher responsible for attempting to teach effectively without one.

At no time does the purpose of a plan include a hope of perfection. After all, the course of action is always based on hypotheses and on the teacher's informed priorities at the moment. For example, a student who is violent – for whatever reason – has first to be made to comply with the non-violent expectations of the classroom. Interventions related to individual need would take a secondary position in any plan, especially one directed, for example, to group safety needs. Ultimately, the teacher is probably the best judge of the appropriateness of a given intervention.

Sharing the plan with the student

As previously emphasized in Chapter Three, the role of the student in the structuring and execution of classroom intervention is extremely important to the ultimate success of the program. Regardless of the young person's age, the teacher must find a way to involve the student – at a developmentally appropriate level – in both the organizging and the selection of interventions. Without the approval of the student, a plan may be doomed from the beginning. Conversely, the student who is involved in the process and is consulted has a vested interest in maximizing the success of a new approach. A student who has had no voice in creating a plan cannot be held responsible for its outcome. In the positive classroom environment, mutual respect and cooperation between teacher and students must be a fundamental tenet.

Summary

In two earlier stages, Chapters Four and Five, a behavioral model is outlined, demonstrating the application of recommended approaches to assist the teacher in creating a positive classroom environment. In this present chapter – Six – the process is delineated by which an individual plan may be created to address individual needs. In the course of the chapter, several examples of actual plans are shown, in order not only to highlight the process of planning itself, but also to demonstrate how classroom observations are recorded and evaluated for the purpose of focusing on implicit student needs which have been isolated. Also illustrated are the ways in which each teacher covers the gamut of information: from observations to identification of needs and then to outlining potential interventions. In addition, the chapter underscores the necessary coherence that exists among these essential stages. During the course of the detailed case study and plan for Scotty Freeman, contributed by Ms. Papadopoulos, and in the details of the other interventions, included as examples, commentaries related to the various contributing teachers' reflections are offered for the reader's evaluation and assistance.

To grasp fully the planning process described here in Chapter Six, teachers might consider examining each strategy – focusing on both format and structure – in order to compare and contrast them. By considering the possible answers to typical questions, some of which are given below, teachers who hope to become involved in planning similar courses of action may find clarification of procedures and priorities:

- How effectively does each plan reveal the nature of the problem's details through its presentation of the relevant behavior?

- Is the need that has been isolated by each reporting teacher supported in the observations of student behavior and in the examples of classroom contexts?

- Are the interventions described in adequate detail for another teacher to be able both to comprehend their intention and to implement them?

- Is each of the plans clearly enough outlined to serve – in a new situation – as a blueprint for both the teacher and the student?

- Can parts of any of the case studies and/or plans be taken out of context and applied to the building of new plans in different circumstances?

Endnotes

[1]   Counselors at the Children's Aid Society can advise teachers – in advance of taking any steps – on how to proceed in hypothetical situations.

[2]   Stated in an essay by Carol Tavris (2002) in the *Chronicle Review*.

[3]   See Johnson & Johnson (1997).

[4]   See Wiseman (2002).

[5]   See page 141: the example of Tony.

[6]   See the group characteristics outlined on page 176.

[7]   This interactive web-based module is available at the following URL: http://www.learncanada.org/e-showcase.html#cabd

[8]   This phrase was a favorite of Special Educator Peter Lorimer who taught courses on Applied Behavior Analysis in the City of Toronto.

[9]   Some common procedures, such as shaping and charting, are outlined and described in Chapter Seven.

[10]   Talking books, as a learning device, are described in Chapter Seven.

[11]   See the model of a task illustrated on page 121.

[12]   Napoleon Hill has written many books that demonstrate ways of finding "the keys to success".

[13]   Dellcrest is a Mental Health centre that specializes in treating children with behavioral disorders. As part of its mandate, it offers after-school programs to students with behavioral problems.

C H A P T E R   7

Behavioral Interventions
Used in the Classroom

In this chapter – Seven – a variety of classroom interventions regularly used by teachers will be described, reviewed, and compared. In some instances, sections of the Chapter might serve as a glossary of common interventions, ready to be examined in some detail as a reference base. Because both the Behavioral and Humanistic paradigms place emphasis on the value of consequences – also known as the teacher's best weapon – the two approaches are investigated with the intention of revealing and explaining underlying mechanisms. To allow teachers to accommodate individual differences found in students, schedules of reinforcement are outlined, as are special reinforcement systems, in an exploration of relevant procedures. Here, also, attention is given to solving problems associated with the Criticism Trap in addition to techniques of modeling. Investigative procedures that promote wanted behaviors – and those that discourage unwanted ones – are followed by an overview of ways for teachers to promote feelings of safety, prizing, and empowerment. Following these are suggestions regarding class management along with recommendations for adapting the academic curriculum, for promoting language development, and, finally, for applying cognitive interventions. Towards the close of Chapter Seven, a short allusion to the role of suggestion highlights the importance of monitoring subtle messages in the classroom while, at the same time, educating students to recognize the many indirect factors that impact on their behavior.

Consequences

Many behavioral strategies regularly used in classrooms are useful to examine in terms of the intention and effectiveness. While the application of consequences to student behavior is often mentioned as an appropriate intervention, an examination of the assumptions underlying this strategy will:

- define the nature of a contingency

- describe what occurs when contingency rules are not used to link behavior to consequences

- examine the nature, as well as the similarities and differences, between *time-out* and *extinction* interventions, each of which is used to reduce the frequency of unwanted behavior

- understand why a consequence must follow the behavior, instead of the reverse process; recognize the way preferred and less-preferred activities can double as consequences (The Premack principle)

- explore the nature and usefulness of various types of consequences

What is a contingency?

A *contingency* is a rule that governs the delivery of a consequence. When going to the gym is **contingent** upon finishing an arithmetic exercise, each student will be expected to hand in a completed assignment before dismissal to the gym. A contingency describes the delivery not only of *reinforcers* but also of *punishers*. If a phone call to parents is **contingent** on a student's speaking impolitely to the teacher, each class member should be certain that parents will be contacted when inappropriate language is used.

A contingency is easily accommodated by an **if-then** statement: "If behavior A occurs, then expect *reinforcer* or *punisher* B". By employing this format, the teacher easily converts the earlier examples:

- If the assignment is completed then students are allowed to go to the gym

- If someone speaks impolitely to the teacher then the relevant parents will be contacted

If-then statements are indicators of cause-effect relationship; in these instances, going to the gym is caused by completing the assignment, while having the teacher contact parents is the result of speaking impolitely. For this reason, making students aware of the contingencies associated with a given individual's or group's behavior gives the teacher a clear opportunity to highlight the cause-effect relationship that exists between behavior and the consequences that follow.

Unaware of the contingency between inappropriate classroom behavior and the consequence that follows it, does Jamie feel that he has control over the situation? Will he be willing to accept responsibility for the behavior? Or will he conclude that Mr. Zjan just doesn't like him? Empowerment involves the ability to identify such contingencies with the intention of changing the behavior, especially if the consequence is unwanted.

What is non-contingent reinforcement?

In some cases, events and people furnish *reinforcers* that, because they are not linked to a behavior are consequently non-contingent, meaning that no contingency rule is in place. While Marcia, in Grade 1, is chattering with her neighbor, a high-school assistant distributes stickers to the whole class. Although the sticker is not meant to encourage Marcia's behavior, it inevitably does so because the student interprets the event as an unintended contingency. In a similar situation, when Tristram, in Grade 12, is not well prepared for his Math test in period two, an impromptu assembly, scheduled during the same time frame, supersedes the test. Because there may be inferred contingency between not studying and the reward of a test cancellation, what is the likelihood that, after such a coincidence, Tristram will plan to study for the next test?

Because rules of contingency outline the cause-effect relationship existing between events, people generally, but students most certainly, learn to apply such rules, particularly to events occurring within a single time frame. As a result of confusion, however, a tendency to create causal links may sometimes be responsible for connecting unrelated events. As evident in the examples provided in the paragraph above, a *reinforcer* occurs independently, when a non-contingent *reinforcer* is mistakenly connected with proximal events. An additional example of this phenomenon is observable in the ritualistic behavior of certain athletes. The great baseball player, Reggie Jackson, wore a brand-new pair of socks every time he played, a behavior which may have stemmed from a victory achieved on a day when he was wearing new socks. Although the victory and the new socks were unrelated elements, their temporal proximity produced a contingency in Jackson's mind. Subsequently, the two conditions were treated as rule-governed: "If I wear new socks, then I will win the game."

In the Grade 2 classroom, a further example of this process occurs. Here, a non-contingent consequence causes a student to connect unrelated events when Farley places his art materials in the appropriate bin just before Ms. Ramoli asks him to go to the Nurse's office for his immunization. Because of the memory of that painful needle administered immediately after art class, Farley may interpret the two as contingent, with the result that, in the following days, Farley is reluctant to go to the storage bin[1].

Interesting and also important is the realization that people are generally unaware of creating contingencies between events that are non-contingent. A good example of such a process may be seen in superstitious behavior; superstitious persons may not recall the initiating events, probably followed by non-contingent consequences, that lead them not to walk on the left side of the street. Everyone knows, however, that not walking under ladders will mean not having paint cans fall on one's head: a universal example of cause-and-effect contingency.

Time-out and extinction

Time-out and *extinction* are two techniques which may be used to reduce a target behavior or discourage a behavior pattern. Sharing some similarities and frequently confused with one another, they can often lead a teacher to misunderstand new emerging behavior.

To clarify the concepts of *time-out* and *extinction*, each is outlined by means of a definition, a description, and a set of examples. In addition, the critical difference between the two is identified, and, finally, the idea known as *resistance to extinction* is explained.

Time-out

In the *time-out* procedure, the plan must include certain necessary conditions:

> - withdrawal of all reinforcers takes place during a fixed period of time
>
> - suspension of reinforcers following inappropriate behavior will always occur
>
> - inappropriate behavior, as a result of such an intervention, will occur less often; *i.e.*, it decreases in frequency

By watching Mr. Rapaport teaching a small group lesson, a teacher would see an interesting example of *time out*. When Arnel, a member of the group, begins pushing and shoving the student next to him, Mr. Rapaport attempts to ignore him and to praise Michelle for being so attentive. Meanwhile Arnel continues his inappropriate behavior. After a few minutes, when Mr. Rapaport matter-of-factly states "Arnel, stay still", the shoving subsides. Within a few minutes, however, Arnel starts his inappropriate actions anew. Mr. Rapaport, who has decided that his next step will be to place Arnel in *time-out,* signals, "Arnel, time-out", with the understanding that Arnel is expected – immediately – to travel to the *time-out* area. There he will remain for a pre-arranged interval. As soon as Arnel is in the *time-out* area, located within hearing and visual distance, Mr. Rapaport recognizes the importance of investing all his energy in ensuring that the classroom activity is so interesting and so much fun that Arnel will be kicking himself for being excluded. When Arnel returns, after the prescribed time, no mention is made of his earlier disruptive behavior, and Mr. Rapaport makes every attempt to recognize as well as to comment on Arnel's positive behavior – no matter how small – in order to establish immediately a positive mode of interaction with him.

In a school, a *time-out* area can be located within the classroom, while, generally, a treatment center is equipped with a special *time-out* area in a padded room. Included will be a two-way mirror for observing and ensuring the safety of the student. If the *time-out* area is located inside the classroom, while a barrier is recommended preventing the student from watching the rest of the class, at the same time, the student is clearly in the field of vision of the teacher or the child care worker. In any *time-out* arrangement, the physical safety of the child must be the chief priority.

In order to deal with the needs of particular students, several *time-out* schedules are available. In this type of intervention a teacher might say:

- "Stay in **time-out;** think about how you are expected to behave; and come back when you are committed to behaving appropriately".

- "Stay in **time-out** for one minute – to a maximum of five minutes – timed from the moment you are quiet".

- "Because you took seven minutes to settle down before serving your one-minute time-out, you will have to make-up those seven-minutes after school or at lunch time or during library period".

The teacher will know which timeslot will be most disadvantageous to the student.

It is advisable to limit the *time-out* interval to a maximum of five minutes, depending on the age of the student. Almost certainly, because the student will become bored, an interval of longer duration will encourage further inappropriate behavior. When a child is given the option of determining the length of the punitive interval, the decided time must be long enough to accommodate a reflection on the offending behavior and a consideration of an alternative future course of action.

Extinction

According to behavioral definition, the time-out procedure serves as a mild *punisher. Extinction,* though the process also involves the idea of discouraging a behavior, achieves this goal differently – by removing the reinforcing event that encourages the behavior in the first place.

Interestingly, without being aware, a teacher may encourage a particular inappropriate behavior. Each time a teacher gives attention or another "pay-off" to a student's behavior, that activity is not only encouraged but the teacher should expect that its frequency will increase. In such instances, the student has learned from observation: "If I want X, then I should do Y". For example, when Justin wants to avoid working on his assignment, he slaps Filomina, predicting rightly that Ms. Alcock will ask him to leave the classroom. In another instance, when Justin wants his teacher's attention, on the basis of past experience, he expects to obtain it by shouting, "Ms. Alcock, this is boring!"

When it is evident that a particular teacher reaction always reinforces a predictable inappropriate behavior, the permanent withdrawal of the response, *i.e.*, the process of *extinction* is an effective  option. The teacher may expect, then, that once it is no longer encouraged, the offending student action will be extinguished. There is little doubt, however, that the student will test this new contingency: Justin will, for a time, believe that if he shouts louder or calls and waves, Ms. Alcock will respond as she has done in the past. Only when Justin recognizes that his teacher is no longer responding will he discontinue his inappropriate actions.

The process of *extinction* involves these stages:

> - identifying the reinforcing event that encourages the inappropriate behavior
>
> - omitting the reinforcing event that usually follows the student's unruly behavior
>
> - expecting the unsuitable activity to increase in frequency and quality while the student tests the new contingency
>
> - observing a reduction in the frequency and quality of the inappropriate behavior

A generic explanation may be used to trace the pattern: the student exhibiting X is responded to by the teacher who demonstrates Y. Because the frequency of X is increasing, it is apparent that Y is encouraging X. By implementing the process of *extinction*, the teacher shows that Y is no longer occurring after X. The corollary is the expectation that X will extinguish. In applying this process of weakening a behavior, the teacher must be certain that X is indeed reinforced by Y. If this critical factor cannot be assured, a different diagnosis may be necessary.

As a response to tantrum behavior, *extinction* is a process often applied, because a child resorts to tantrums, expecting the adult to accede to demands – "I want the chocolate bar!" Usually, such a prediction arises from the child's past experience with this adult. It becomes evident that if the child resorts to tantrums, the adult gives in. When the process of *extinction* is applied, therefore, the child thinks, "Surely, if I scream louder and bang my fists on the floor, I will get my chocolate bar." If, however, the adult fails to give in, the tantrum behavior will soon cease because the child sees it is no longer of any value.

Extinction is a very difficult procedure to carry to a satisfactory conclusion because the teacher, initially, must be prepared for increases in the unwanted behavior, as the student attempts to re-establish the formerly reliable contingency. A possible consequence of misapplying the process of *extinction* is that the child, by persisting with the tantrum behavior, will eventually succeed in having the adult give in. When the adult is thwarted and unable to complete the process of *extinction*, the attempt to weaken or eliminate the tantrum behavior is unsuccessful. Most detrimental is the realization that an incomplete *extinction* process serves usually to further strengthen the tantrum or other behavior with the result that subsequent *extinction* attempts are more difficult to carry out.

To augment the chances of successful *extinction*, the teacher should consider possible methods for tolerating the expected increase in tantrum behavior. For example, when Mr. Riddle and his class are planning to go on a field trip, how does he anticipate dealing with Gregory's tantrum behavior? Maybe, Gregory should be excused from the trip, or, perhaps, he must be accompanied by one of his parents. If the school is the location for dealing with *extinction,* Mr. Riddle can encourage the class to disregard Greg's tantrum, or, if this is not an option, at the onset of Greg's tantrum, the Office is asked to send a monitor to ensure Greg's safety needs, while Mr. Riddle and the class play games in the school yard. This solution not only ensures *extinction* – those who previously rewarded Greg's tantrum behavior are not there to do so – but also includes the mild punisher of *time-out*: Greg cannot participate in the impromptu schoolyard games.

A final insurance policy for maximizing the success of extinction is to use language to explain both the old and the new contingencies, that is, the plan, and to help the student find other ways to satisfy personal need. For example, Mr. Riddle might say to Greg,

> "In thinking about your tantrums, Greg, I now realize that by giving in to you I was doing you a great disservice. Because I like you and I care about you, I have vowed that I will longer do that. I expect, however, that when I don't any longer pay attention to you, you will test whether I really mean what I am saying to you right now. I would prefer it if we could both agree that having a tantrum is the not the best way for a lad your age to get what he wants. Can we discuss more grownup ways of achieving what it is you want? We will begin to chart the reduction of your tantrums so that we can have a record of our success".

The critical difference between time-out and extinction

There are at least two factors that distinguish time-out from extinction:

- In *time-out*, during a specific period, all reinforcers present in the context of the situation are withdrawn, whereas, in the process of *extinction*, the only reinforcer removed is the one associated with the particular behavior to be weakened. In the meantime, all other appropriate responses continue to be encouraged

- The *time-out* situation fashions a new contingency between inappropriate behavior and a mild punisher – withdrawing all reinforcers available in the situation – for the purpose of reducing the frequency of the specific behavior. In contrast, *extinction* attempts to nullify a past contingency which serves to maintain or even to increase an undesired behavior

The major reason for making the distinction between these two strategies lies in the way each unfolds. By correctly identifying the technique in question, the teacher is able first to interpret feedback available in the situation, then to manipulate, and finally to tweak the process to ensure a satisfactory conclusion.

Resistance to extinction

Some behaviors are so effectively overlearned that when it comes time to dissolve the contingency by applying the process of *extinction*, the behavior is still exhibited although no longer reinforced. When asked the question, "How long would a person who is no longer paid continue to work?", an obvious response is, "It depends!" It depends on:

- the length of time the person has previously worked while being paid

- the type of work, whether self- fulfilling or important to the community

- the character and the perception of the person

- the present financial situation of the person

- a range of other such considerations

Because it is evident that many variables contribute to resistance to *extinction*, the amount of anticipated resistance should be contemplated when deciding on the feasibility of eradicating a behavior by this strategy. In the case of tantrum behavior, the resistance to extinction interval relates to the length of time during which the child continues to resort to tantrums, that is, when the adult no longer "gives-in". Often, because of the tendency of the offending behavior to initially increase – in frequency and sometimes in quality – before it is extinguished, teachers are reluctant to use the process of *extinction*. The more important consideration, however, is the level of resistance to *extinction*.

Usually, because resistance to *extinction* is dependent on the degree to which the behavior is entrenched in the repertoire of the student, *duration* is an important factor. The longer the student has behaved in this manner – the *duration* of the behavior – the more often it has been encouraged, and, consequently, the more resistant to *extinction* it becomes.

An additional characteristic associated with *extinction*, one that exacerbates the process further, is the behavioral phenomenon called *spontaneous reaction*[2]. Once a behavior has been extinguished, when it is reinforced anew even only a few times, the frequency of the behavior returns to its previous levels. When it is again reinforced, that is, an extinguished behavior with a long learning history reappears in full force – in both quality and frequency – it becomes almost impossible to extinguish. Awareness of such a phenomenon implies that teachers, unless they are aiming to encourage the recovery of old behaviors, should avoid the danger of reinforcing extinguished behavior.

To summarize, the use of the *extinction* strategy involves:

- the attempt to extinguish a contingency denoting a cause-effect relationship between an unwanted behavior and the consequence that strengthens it

- the frequency of the undesired behavior slowly decreasing once it is no longer followed by the reinforcer that previously maintained it

- the repetitiveness of the undesired behavior initially increasing while the student tests whether the contingency still exists

- the knowledge that some behaviors take a longer time to eradicate than others; that is, some behaviors are more resistant to extinction, depending on several factors, the most important being the number of times the particular behavior has been previously reinforced

- the realization that the longer a behavior is part of a student's repertoire, the more resistant it is to extinction

- the awareness that once a behavior has been extinguished, that is, when it appears that the contingency is dismantled, only a few new reinforcing events will return the behavior to previous high levels – *spontaneous recovery*

Resistance to extinction is a central factor in the recovery of addicted persons. Extinguishing the behavior takes an inordinate amount of time and energy, but, substance abusers who "fall off the wagon", by, for example, consuming a single drink, continue to be prone to abuse, often throughout their entire lives.

The Premack Principle

Because students typically prefer to engage in certain activities rather than in others, Premack demonstrated that activities – not just objects or praise – may be used to encourage appropriate behavior. For example, for a student who prefers playing volleyball to writing a creative story, an opportunity to play the game may be used to reinforce appropriate behavior. *The Premack Principle* proposes that if playing volleyball is made contingent on writing the story – if Mordecai writes the story, then he may play volleyball – story writing will be encouraged. This means that many students will subsequently ask to write creative stories knowing they may play volleyball afterwards. Most important to teachers, however, is the corollary – this process of pairing activities will ultimately make creative writing a preferred activity in its own right. To summarize, the *Premack Principle* states that any preferred activity made contingent on a less preferred activity will strengthen the perceived value of the "inferior" one. Ms. Raventos notices that Carmencita, who loves to read mystery novels, is reluctant to invest any effort into completing her Math assignments. Recognizing that reading is the preferred activity, and that Math work is the less-preferred, Ms. Roventos schedules Carmencita's morning activities by time-tabling a Math period followed by independent reading. It is expected that Carmencita will eagerly complete her Math assignments in order to read mystery novels. The success of the Premack Principle rests on an assurance that the preferred activity is indeed very rewarding to the student.

Ms. Roventos is well aware of Carmencita's passion for reading, but in situations in which the student's preferred activities are not evident, implementing the *Premack Principle* involves the following stages:

> - determine the preference level of various activities for an individual student by observing, interviewing, or asking the student to complete a questionnaire (see Appendix A)
>
> - require the student to complete a classroom activity that is less preferred
>
> - schedule a more preferred activity immediately following
>
> - observe changes in the completion time of the less-preferred activity

Why does the Premack Principle work? Several possible reasons exist. Although it is evident that the preferred activity, which follows the less-preferred one, serves to reinforce it as would be the case in any operant conditioning situation, such an explanation does not account for the change of status of the less-preferred activity. In Carmencita's case, why would completing the Math assignment become a more preferred activity? By avoiding such assignments in the past, she connected the Math experience with threats, expectations of failure, and other negative internal states. Now that Carmencita is anticipating reading her novels as soon as her Math assignments are completed, new associations that are forged include positive internal states. Some of these result when Ms. Raventos does not have to nag Carmencita; some are connected with her passion for reading[3]. By actually completing her Math assignments, and doing so in non-threatening conditions, Carmencita now has the opportunity to experience the positive consequences associated with task completion. Not only the good grades but also the compliments she is receiving serve to make Math a more preferred academic subject.

What is a natural consequence?

While the Behaviorist paradigm is willing, first, to create special environments, and then to include planned consequences for the purpose of promoting particular behaviors, the Humanistic paradigm's view – in contrast – is to interfere as little as possible in the growth of an individual. For Humanists, because growth is perceived as a natural unfolding, consequences are not planned but are identified as the direct effect of behavior. According to Dreikurs, a natural outcome of not doing chores around the house is that no clean dishes or laundry will be available, a situation that gives family members several options: eating on dirty plates, washing plates, buying paper plates; wearing soiled clothes, buying new clothes, and other possible actions. The natural consequences of people's behavior ultimately shape the decisions they make.

Without any doubt, natural consequences are effective as learning tools. In the classroom, however, teachers feel compelled to intervene, especially when safety issues are involved. A typical example is going hungry as a natural consequence of forgetting one's lunch at home; being hit by a car is a predictable crisis, a result of not looking both ways; but, in each of these cases, the outcome, although very instructive or even lethal, seems too harsh. Traditionally, adults have made it their responsibility to shield children from extreme natural consequences.

Using reinforcers as a consequence

Preceding or following a course of action, a *reinforcer* is an event which increases the probability that a behavior will be repeated. Typically, because *reinforcers* are expected to strengthen behavior, basic physical needs like thirst, hunger, sleep, warmth, and several others ensure that, for instance, water and food will act as *primary reinforcers* to a person who is thirsty or hungry. While primary reinforcers do not need to be taught or learned, many other reinforcers, especially those involving some type of learning, are called *secondary reinforcers*. While it is foreseeable that Abul will complete his homework on the promise of receiving a chocolate bar – his favorite snack – it is not self-evident why Uri will do unpleasant chores around the house for the privilege of being given an hour to read. Because he loves reading so much, for Uri, reading is a *secondary reinforcer*. At first, Uri must learn that reading is a pleasurable experience; then it becomes a reinforcing event. Clearly, *secondary reinforcers*[4] play a major role in encouraging behavior.

What is a social reinforcer?

When an individual recognizes the actions and words of significant people as desirable, this *social reinforcer,* a special type of *secondary reinforcer,* may serve to strengthen the person's behavior. How does this happen? In a process similar to generating *secondary reinforcers, a social reinforcer* is created by a process of classical conditioning. Occurring in one of two ways, a primary reinforcer is presented in close temporal proximity with a social event – one involving the actions or words of people. After many such pairings, the social element begins to behave like the *primary reinforcer.* The soothing effect of Mother's voice is believed to be derived from early associations between the infant feeding while hearing her voice. Another option involves the pairing of a social event with an established *secondary reinforcer;* for example, because Uri is given the opportunity to read aloud to a group of six-year olds, eventually, working with the first-graders becomes a reinforcing event in its own right. Enabling a social event to become a *social reinforcer* warrants the following steps:

- identifying an event based on the behavior of a person who until this moment has no reinforcement value

- presenting this social event and following it with a known *reinforcer*

- observing that the social event begins to function as a *reinforcer*. In the classroom, many teachers rely on "praise" to perform as a social reinforcer, because children have frequently learned to be encouraged by pleasant comments directed to themselves or to their performances. Although this is a workable arrangement in the majority of cases, the teacher always keeps in mind the realization that for some students the praise will have no effect. In such uncommon cases, weaning the unresponsive students from reacting mostly to primary reinforcers, the plan should include enabling *secondary* and *social reinforcers* to be tried, using the procedure described above

What is a token reinforcer?

Another type of *secondary reinforcer* is the *token reinforcer,* which includes money systems, stamps to exchange for prizes, points, and other forms of positive reinforcement. Usually, these tokens, earned by and given to students, will subsequently serve as barter for desired items, preferred activities, and social time. This system has been found to be effective with younger or low-functioning students, as well as with any individual child who does not yet value social reinforcers. Token reinforcers are helpful, too, in teaching students to "delay gratification". Through experience with such devices, they

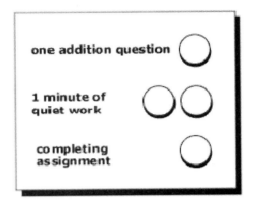

learn to wait for reinforcement over increasingly longer periods of time. On the other hand, depending on the student's individual needs, the time interval between receiving a token and redeeming it can be as short as 15 seconds or as long as a week. A process known as *shaping*[5] is used in lengthening this interval.

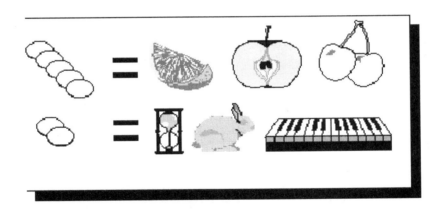

Figure 7-1. A menu of *reinforcers* indicating that five tokens can be exchanged for a piece of fruit, while two tokens may buy one minute of play with the class pet or the same minute at the piano.

Tokens are as reinforcing as the items for which they are to be exchanged. Usually, to permit individual students to choose personally significant tokens, the teacher will have a variety of reinforcers available. In addition, by issuing verbal praise and encouragement every time a token is awarded, the teacher ensures that these phrases will in themselves become *social reinforcers,* eventually to replace tokens. The use of token reinforcers involves:

- identifying a series of items and/or activities known as *reinforcers*

- developing a system of points or tokens that will focus on, first, the barter value of each *reinforcer*; then, the number of tokens awarded for desirable behaviors; and finally, the procedure for earning and exchanging tokens

- awarding and redeeming tokens in keeping with the stated procedures

- changing the menu of reinforcers as they begin to lose their strength

- modifying the token system – increasing the token value of reinforcers, including more wanted behaviors; delaying exchange periods

- pairing praise and encouragement with the award of each token

- modifying the token system so that it eventually becomes obsolete as social reinforcers evolve to replace it

Token reinforcers are sometimes necessary when the teacher hopes to strengthen the positive behavior of students who require concrete *primary* and *secondary reinforcers*. Such a program should be implemented only for students who require it; this means that instead of a class-wide arrangement, a reduced token system is structured in as simple as possible a manner for the purposes of management. In some circumstances, token systems will become so elaborate that a huge portion of the school day is spent awarding and exchanging tokens.

Ways in which reinforcers will appear to lose their effectiveness

Earlier in these pages, a reinforcer is defined as an event whose association with a behavior – one which precedes or follows it – increases the likelihood that in the future the same behavior will be repeated. Also mentioned is the idea that reinforcers are unique to each individual; for example, in the adult world, one person will reward hard work by drinking a cup of coffee and eating a chocolate, while a second individual prefers a doughnut or a brisk walk. The corollary is that teachers have to invest effort in creating reinforcers appropriate to the whims of each class member. As might be expected, some reinforcers have broad appeal: doing classroom work under the shade of a tree on a hot summer's day, while others are less appealing to children: eating such exotic foods as snails, known, in their gourmet context, as *escargot*.

Once reinforcers have been identified and are used to encourage behavior, in certain cases, they begin to lose their ability to strengthen positive responses. Several reasons exist which explain this outcome:

- Competing *reinforcers* that are present are more appealing. For example, while Mr. Brophy is using praise to motivate Darwin to stay on-task, Alfred is handing out chocolate bars on the other side of the room. Who could blame Darwin for preferring chocolate bars? In this situation, Mr. Brophy might intervene by saying, "Alfred, it is good of you to share these chocolate bars with your classmates. Please continue to do that when everyone has finished the assignment"

- A favorite reinforcer is used or over-used until it loses all strength. For example, for the completion of a task, Ms. Slamecka is awarding 15 minutes of playtime with the pet mice. The problem, in this case, is that students are stimulated by playing with the pet mice for only a limited time. By keeping the interval brief – one minute, perhaps – the teacher may assure that an activity remains appealing over a longer period of time

- The student may be unaware that a reinforcer will follow the encouraged behavior. Such a situation may occur when new tasks are introduced, especially if students are unsure of expectations and procedures. As a result, during periods of predictable confusion, a form of desirable behavior may appear to decrease. To circumvent this possibility, the teacher will recognize that attention to student work habits, along with feedback on student performance, often provides the same outcome as a reinforcer. Of course, it is important for students to expect such types of encouragement and to grow with them

With the intention of emphasizing the contingency that is implied when a behavior is followed by an event designed to encourage or discourage it, this section has been exploring the concept of consequences – those associated with various types of reinforcers, as well as with time-out and extinction. In the subsequent section, both timing and application of consequences will be outlined in relation to schedules of reinforcement.

Schedules of reinforcement

While the concepts that underlie various types of consequences are outlined in the foregoing pages, here, different procedures are presented as means of administering reinforcement to achieve specific outcomes. Although these schedules are usually described in relation to reinforcement, it is interesting to note that similar formats may be applied to punishment. Well known to teachers, however, is the realization that reinforcing a desired behavior is much more instructive than punishing an undesired one. For this reason, comments here are limited to schedules of reinforcement.

Whether the teacher reinforces every desirable behavior or only some of them, and whether the reinforcement is carried out in a predictable manner or in an unforeseen fashion, each of these possible conditions will produce a different result. Equipped with this knowledge, Mr. Fine applies a schedule to Marcus' behavior in order to encourage it. A description of the reinforcement schedules reveals the nature of each:

- Continuous Reinforcement: **every** appropriate response is reinforced; for example, every time Marcus asks to **borrow** an item instead of **grabbing** one from a class member, Mr. Fine will award him a token

- Intermittent Reinforcement: only **some**, not all, appropriate responses are reinforced; for example, Marcus will earn a token on some occasions when he asks to borrow an item. Intermittent Reinforcement can be made available under predictable and unpredictable circumstances

  ° Predictable Intermittent Reinforcement: a response occurring either within a fixed time period or within a fixed series of responses is reinforced; for example, one appropriate response every two minutes, or only the third or the fifth appropriate response. Schedules with a fixed ratio, or a fixed interval are also included in this category. Marcus is aware that Mr. Fine will award him a token after every three instances of politely borrowing an item. In another scenario, he is aware that a token-earning opportunity will arise only once at the end of every thirty minutes

    * Fixed-ratio: a requisite number of appropriate responses is required before the last one is reinforced; for example, Marcus will be given a token once he has asked politely to borrow an item five times. The ratio of 5:1 – 5 appropriate responses for one reinforcer becomes part of the contingency rule

    * Fixed-interval: for desirable responses like time on task, reinforcing a fixed time interval is more appropriate. Under this condition, the contingency rule spells out at what point during the interval reinforcement is forthcoming. Marcus, for example, receives a token after two minutes of on-task behavior

  ° Unpredictable Intermittent Reinforcement: a response may be occurring within a fixed-time interval or a series of appropriate responses may be reinforced variably. Schedules with a variable ratio and variable interval are included in this category; for example, Marcus is unable to predict when during a 30-minute time frame, Mr. Fine will observe his behavior

    * Variable-ratio: a requisite number of appropriate responses is required before one is reinforced, but the student is unaware which will be reinforced. In the case of Marcus who is receiving a reinforcer based on a ratio of 5:1, unlike the fixed ratio condition in which Marcus

cont'd

234

could count on a token after five appropriate responses, in the variable ratio condition, the ratio is on the average 5:1. This means that Marcus might receive a token after the first, second, third, fourth, or fifth response, but overall, an average of 5:1.

* Variable-interval: instead of reinforcing a desirable response at the end of interval, reinforcement can arrive at any point during the interval based on an average time interval. In Marcus's case, the token may be awarded on an average of one token for two minutes of on-task behavior which means Marcus does not know during the prescribed time interval when he will receive the token.

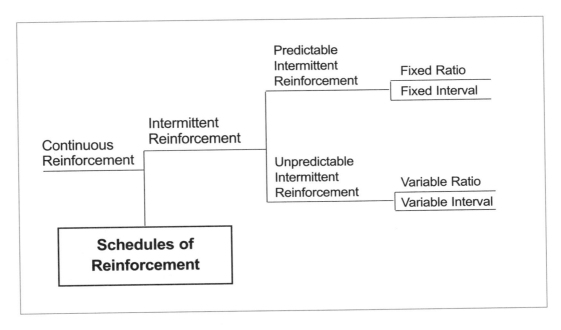

Figure 7-2. Schedules of reinforcement

What schedule to use?

Given so many options of schedules of reinforcement, when is one used in favor of another? A *continuous* schedule is most important when teaching a **new** task because **unfamiliar** responses are acquired more rapidly when each correct response is encouraged. In this process of one-to-one correspondence, the student is able to recognize the contingency between the two events. Obviously, any delay in feedback may promote incorrect responses without the student's being aware that such wrong answers are inappropriate.

An *intermittent* schedule is most important, especially **after** a pattern of responding has been established. By moving from a continuous to an intermittent schedule, the teacher, by reinforcing only some of the desired responses, ensures that they will become more resistant to *extinction*. Within the context of intermittent schedules, when does the teacher elect for a predictable rather an unpredictable schedule? If reinforcement is predictable, the student learns that responding is essential only when likelihood exists that reinforcement will occur. Therefore, in the course of introducing a new concept, the teacher is advised to begin with a continuous schedule, then to move to an intermittent predictable schedule, to ensure that desired responses are learned quickly.

Interestingly, once a consistent pattern of the wanted behavior is well established, an *unpredictable* schedule is warranted, especially when the teacher decides that established behaviors can be maintained by reinforcement that is presented once in a while. This schedule – which further bolsters resistance to *extinction* – is one often associated with gambling behavior, where, although the odds of receiving a "pay off" are remote, people continue to gamble. In circumstances existing when the teacher is trying to introduce behaviors that require the student to persist, a *predictable* schedule should also be avoided. Such conditions might include: paying attention, working on-task, continuing to work when initial attempts are not successful, to name only a few.

As a final comment about schedules of reinforcement, it is useful to note the importance of reinforcing **improvement** in performance. If a teacher reinforces only an absolute level of performance, students who are more proficient at the stage when the task is first introduced will receive more reinforcement than will those students who start slowly and need much more improvement. By making reinforcement contingent on demonstrable **improvement**, the teacher assures that each student has an equal opportunity to access *reinforcers* and therefore to learn and to feel prized.

In order to modify behavior, when introducing an intervention that focuses on establishing contingency rules with consequences, the teacher relies heavily on the skillful application of the appropriate schedule of reinforcement. Also involved is a pattern of teaching students to respond to social and other intrinsic reinforcers. When teachers fail to move from predictable to unpredictable schedules, continuing to rely on primary or concrete secondary reinforcers, it may become obvious that students will respond positively, with dedicated hard work, only when concrete pay-offs are offered. Such an unwanted situation is easily remedied by shifting to unpredictable schedules of social and intrinsic reinforcement.

The Criticism Trap

Up to this stage, positive reinforcers and punishers are outlined and described in terms of their value as consequences. In addition to these, negative reinforcers should also be mentioned because they are able to alter behavior. When the presentation of an annoying stimulus persists until a wanted behavior is attained, negative reinforcers may become essential. A particularly salient example of this phenomenon is experienced in the "Criticism Trap."

Interestingly, the "Criticism Trap" refers to situations in which adverse comment and/or nagging behavior will be employed by the teacher to induce students either to behave appropriately or to comply with a request. Often used by parents and teachers, critical comments serving as **negative reinforcement,** may cause an increase in compliant behavior, at least momentarily, with the result that authority figures are encouraged to use this approach again. When it was Manfred's turn to wash the dinner dishes, his mother reminded him every few minutes as he watched the basketball game on television. Finally, in order to stop her nagging behavior, Manfred complied, but in doing so, he demonstrated to his mother that her nagging procedure was effective. When Manfred's next chore – tidying the television room – needed to be done, a larger amount of nagging was necessary before he roused himself to do it.

Why is it a trap? Because nagging produces compliance, parents and teachers consider its use to be an effective means to encourage wanted behavior. What is overlooked is that the strength of this negative reinforcer inevitably wanes – as is the case when any reinforcer is over used – so that, increasingly, more nagging will be required to maintain the earlier level of compliance. Moreover, nagging itself, although effective in the short term, encourages people – especially young ones – to avoid naggers, because being around them involves an unpleasant state of affairs. Finally, the trap creates a situation in which a student will not be encouraged to take responsibility for the desired action, and, as a result, when the nagger is not present, the expected behavior is not executed. Manfred is not likely to wash the dishes when his Mother is visiting the school on Parent-Teacher Night.

Another unexpected consequence of the trap involves a situation in which the criticism not only forces compliant behavior but also functions to encourage the unwanted behavior, even as the parental or teacher attention serves to reward it. The trap is complete when the desired behavior not only fails to occur after the nagging but it elicits a longer session of nagging as a result of each occurrence. Meanwhile, the unwanted behavior increases and the nagger is avoided whenever possible. As anyone knows who has experienced this syndrome – either as nagger or as recalcitrant adolescent – the more the mother or teacher nags, the more the nagging will have to be increased at each new stage.

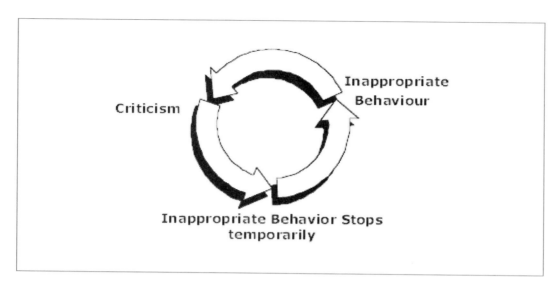

Figure 7-3. The Criticism Trap

Getting out of the Trap

To escape the trap, Manfred's mother changes the dynamics of the situation by replacing the consequence – instead of using negative reinforcement, she switches to positive reinforcement. Rather than nagging Manfred, which means focusing her attention on the fact that he has so far failed to complete his chore, his mother should offer praise and attention only when the dishes have been washed, dried, and put away.

Criticism is more spontaneous than praise. Especially common in response to violations of expected behavior, which are quick to catch the attention of the teacher, criticism seems the most expedient way to instruct the student to comply: "Sit down!", "Turn around!", "Get to work!" However useful such reactions may appear, teachers must train themselves to avoid noticing, commenting about, and investing attention on inappropriate behavior. Obviously, because such a reversal of response will create difficulty and will warrant an investment of strength and patience on the part of classroom teachers, it is worth looking at a list of methods collated to assist them in meeting this goal:

- inappropriate behavior of one student can become a cue to encouraging improvement in another student's action. In noticing that Geoff is out of his seat, Ms. Lacaille directs her attention to Freda and Habib, who are in their seats, when she says, "Freda and Habib are sitting and doing their assignment. They will be the first to work with the computers"!

- tokens or other concrete reminders can be employed to prompt the use of encouraging remarks. Attention is paid by the teacher to the idea of increasing the number of encouraging gestures. To facilitate the process, the teacher may carry ten stickers to be awarded within a 15-minute period, thereby ensuring that, along with the awards, 10 encouraging remarks are made for a total of 40 per hour. As the teacher becomes more accustomed to making encouraging remarks, the tokens will be eliminated, their obvious usefulness established but no longer required

- signs posted around the classroom serve to remind the teacher – as well as the students – to praise and encourage

- variable verbal remarks can be stockpiled. Teachers who are reluctant to use praise because they feel awkward saying "Good!" or "Great idea!" or "Excellent!", several dozen times a day, will find that encouragement can take many forms, each of which may be explored and practiced. Usually, a positive verbal remark should include:

  - the student's name and a smile

  - a description of the behavior being encouraged

When Ms.Telfer says, with a pleasant but not obvious grin, "Felicity, this is a very creative solution to this puzzle", she incorporates these criteria. In the event that nothing complimentary comes to Ms. Telfer 's mind, she might approach Gisella to make "small talk", by inquiring about hobbies or pets and by asking whether the homework instructions are clear. Such an approach is both effective and positive in recognizing the individual. A useful procedure for recording change, *charting*, on a daily basis, involves graphing results, along with elements of praise and/or critical comments, on a daily basis. With such a chart, the teacher tracks personal improvement in each student with the aim of motivating further change. The objective in noting these data is to increase significantly the frequency of positive teacher remarks as they are shown to affect behaviors

Getting out of the "Criticism Trap" can reduce the teacher's stress level, while, at the same time, contributing to the positive climate of the classroom.

Special reinforcement systems

On occasion, special reinforcement systems are necessary to promote student learning when the application of contingency rules and schedules of reinforcement is not, alone, sufficient to obtain desired outcomes. Sometimes, procedures involving a more involved and/or systematic means of encouraging behavior are warranted in cases in which:

- no instances of the desired behavior emerge for reinforcement. When Ms. Vallis plans to encourage Melissa's on-task behavior during the independent activity portion of the class, Melissa either leaves class or is unexpectedly absent. In another situation, Colby, an autistic student, does not respond when asked to state his name

- the student is unable to model the wanted behavior in order to establish a contingency. By reinforcing Joscelyn's and Jamil's in-seat behavior in a positive manner, Mr. Pietre expects that other students will be encouraged to model them. Unfortunately, Marin, a student with attentional problems, is unaware of the interaction and, as a result, shows no change in his inappropriate behavior. A similar situation is evident with Michel, a student who has pervasive development disorder

- the student's language and/or attentional skills do not permit an understanding of contingency rules. Ms. Lopez has noticed Pier and Larry are unable to respond to her description of the following contingency: "By completing the assignment, the class will be allowed to play baseball." Pier, as a result of his language disability, is not skilled enough to detect the meaning of the contingency, while Larry, an impulsive student, is unaware of the cause-effect relationship. Not only does he miss the cues, but he will certainly believe that Ms. Lopez does not like him if he is not allowed to play baseball

- the desired behavior is sufficiently complex that it must be simplified into a less elaborate series of responses, each to be established individually. Ms. Pyne who is planning an individualized program for Jennifer, realizes that empathy is an abstract notion that must be sub-divided into component actions. It is likely that Ms. Pyne will reflect about the various behaviors that demonstrate empathy, by asking herself, "How do empathic persons behave?" Once a list of appropriate actions is compiled, she will choose to address each one individually and in combination: 'Can you place yourself in the person's shoes?'; 'How is the person feeling?'; 'What is the person thinking?'; 'Have you ever been in a similar situation?'; 'How did you feel in a similar situation?'

Special reinforcement systems share the following principles:

- reinforcers are always administered rapidly and easily

- consequent events function as reinforcers

- schedules of reinforcement – continuous or intermittent – are administered on the basis of student progress

- strategies planned to reduce the future need for special reinforcement systems are incorporated into the plan

Shaping

Shaping, a special reinforcement system, is employed with low-functioning or challenged students who require activities to be subdivided into manageable parts. In this process, not only are reinforcers more readily applicable but students can now learn complex tasks. Clearly, good pedagogy warrants a procedure for subdividing learning into simple components: for example, this underlying reasoning forms the basis for introducing separately each of the four basic operations in arithmetic. To present them all at once would overload and confuse the student. For some children, curriculum items that are accessible to many other students must be subdivided further to accommodate unusual learning needs. For example, because Kellaway, an autistic student, is learning to interact socially, Ms. Kampf has subdivided the domain of social interaction. As the first priority, she has determined that Kellaway must learn to establish eye contact with any person who is speaking with him. As such interventions require slow and careful focus, both teacher and student will work, from time to time, over a period of weeks, on mastering the task. A key aspect of the *shaping* procedure, then, involves reinforcing successive approximations of the desired performance. Although a quick shift in eye gaze is initially reinforced, Ms. Kampf will subsequently require that Kellaway maintain eye contact for progressively longer intervals until he is able to reach the final target, looking at her, in the eye, for the length of time she is speaking to him.

Used in tandem, the shaping procedure, then, consists of two approaches:

- Differential reinforcement

- Shifting criterion for reinforcement

Differential reinforcement

A systematic pattern of strengthening, the element of the shaping procedure called *differential reinforcement*, encourages responses only when they meet a certain criterion, while all others are immediately extinguished or ignored. In any contact with Kellaway, Ms. Kampf will signal him to look at her eyes – she may even use a "prop" to attract his attention – and he will be rewarded the moment eye contact is made. At this juncture, he may for 15 seconds hold the toy which he likes so much, while Ms. Kampf praises him and smiles directly at him. If he does anything other than make eye contact, the teacher will look away from him, saying nothing. As he eventually learns, the only behaviors to be reinforced are those associated with eye contact.

Shifting criterion for reinforcement

Because the shaping procedure moves toward the student's mastery of the component parts in a pattern of behavior, a system which establishes rules to guide the student should involve the following steps:

- Initially, the criterion for reinforcement is set to provide the student access to reinforcement for behavior that resembles the target. In Kellaway's case, after many unsuccessful attempts, during which he remains unable to look at her eyes, Ms. Kampf begins to emphasize looking at the "prop", placed in his viewing field, as a means of establishing the road to eye contact

- As the student's responses move closer to the target behavior, the criterion is again shifted. Since Kellaway is soon able to focus on the "prop" placed in his viewing field, Ms. Kampf then shifts the criterion by expecting him to turn his head to look at the "prop", now that it is presented adjacent to his viewing field

- Each time the criterion is shifted, the changed criterion is a little closer to the desired behavior. As Kellaway, on command, learns to look at the "prop", it is moved closer to Ms. Kampf's face until, finally, it is in front of her eyes. Ultimately, a shift is made involving removal of the prop, along with reinforcement of successively longer periods of eye contact

Steps involved in building a shaping program

While building a shaping program may initially involve some trial and error, the following steps are usually helpful:

- define the behavior to be learned by the student. Ms. Kampf chooses eye contact as the target behavior because it is a procedure fundamental to establishing social interaction

- establish the student's present functioning level to modify the difficulty range of the potential behavior. Ms. Kampf notes that the boy does not establish eye contact with her. Because Kellaway will look at the toy when it is placed in his line of vision, Ms. Kampf uses that behavior as her starting point

- identify reinforcers by observing the objects, and, in addition, praise forms or activities that are known to be encouraging to the student. After observing Kellaway playing with his favorite toy, Ms. Kampf chooses it as a reinforcer. She is also aware that playing with the toy has increased Kellaway's willingness to become engaged in the target behavior

- outline the program steps required to move from the present behavior to the target or to-be-learned behavior. Ms. Kampf begins the sequence by having Kellaway focus on the toy, which is later moved closer and then placed in front of her face. Removing the toy, she ensures that gazing at her face for longer intervals is reinforced. Finally, having him looking at her as she speaks to him is the final target

- establish the criterion for reinforcement to be used for training the first step in the planned sequence. Ms. Kampf determines how long Kellaway needs to look at each of the targets before reinforcement follows

- shift to the next step when the student has mastered each current step. As long as Kellaway shows progress, Ms. Kampf shifts to the next step of the sequence of behaviors she has previously defined for herself

- vary the program if the student demonstrates difficulty in getting to the next step; in this case, either return briefly to an earlier step or add a new stage between two others. When Kellaway fails to look at Ms. Kampf's face as the toy is removed, she places the toy back near her eyes and reinforces the pattern each time his eyes catch hers; she continue to shift the criterion as the student progresses toward the target behavior. Ms. Kampf and Kellaway are able to complete the pre-set sequence to the final step – establishing eye contact whenever she speaks to him

If a teacher feels interested in using shaping procedures, these will be found helpful, but not just when established on paper. As plans, they are interesting, but when employed to record the stages of the student's improvement, they become more relevant. For instance, it can happen that once a student has mastered the entire shaping sequence, the earlier behavior which initiated the process is forgotten, and, consequently, a true awareness of the improvement, from the original problem through the stages of change, is lost. To document progress, beginning at the earliest stage, the teacher may consider videotaping the student's behavior at each step of the shaping sequence in order to preserve – for the child and the parents, as well as for the teacher – an accurate perspective of the often remarkable behavioral change that has been mastered.

Modeling

In addition to learning directly from the consequences of personal actions, students also acquire information about appropriate ways to act by observing the behavior of others and its end result. This procedure, known as modeling, is a learning process proposed by Bandura and Walters to explain *social learning*, acts of imitation both consciously imitative and intentional. By watching the activities of people and noting how others respond to those ways of acting, each person learns what is acceptable in a series of situations. In examining the phenomenon of modeling, teachers will find that asking and answering the following questions may help to predict imitated behavior.

- **Who is modeled?**

  - *parents* Parents are often the first people whom children imitate. For example, upon watching her Mother scold Michael for not keeping his room clean, three-year old Emma will not only mimic Mother's actions, but will be rewarded because everyone finds her imitative habits so cute

  - *significant others* Whether the idol is a member of a peer group or a person who is a best friend, children will not only mimic the characteristic actions but will also want to dress similarly to the individual or to the styles common to more than one person

  - *authority figures* A teacher need only suggest that a student take over the class to observe the degree of modeling

  - *entertainment and athletic heroes* The media exposure and the adulation received by such persons make them primary targets of modeling. In the 1940s, most young girls wanted to dress and look like Shirley Temple, while, in 2002, young boys like Spiderman. Fashion, body posturing, language, and other behaviors are adopted, particularly by adolescents

  cont'd

- **What is modeled?**

  - behavior observed to be socially reinforced and encouraged. When Mr. Bouma encourages Gila's arguing by debating with her rather than ignoring her behavior, in effect, he encourages all class members to argue with him

  - activity seen as either unpunished or at least not discouraged. When Mira's homework is not done, but she receives no adverse consequence for this situation, some class members may deduce that doing homework is optional

  - neutral action or state identified as neither encouraged nor punished. As long as Mr. Santorini makes no comment about appropriate dress, Mischa and Sascha will wear track suits and backward-turned baseball caps to class

- **Why are many social behaviors learned by modeling?**

  - If high social costs are likely to result from trial and error, many students will select forms of behavior to be learned by modeling. In a classroom, for example, Clarissa, a new student, will readily observe and model the behavior of classmates – especially in her response to Mr. Cabot's incomprehensible questions – rather than risk inappropriate queries that would lead to laughter as a form of ridicule

  - Used in a given social situation, modeling is a strategy that evaluates the appropriateness of particular behavior. In Chapter Four, the idea is introduced that the acceptability of a given social behavior is context dependent – what is appropriate in one situation is not suitable in another. In consequence, for young persons, as for adults, observing the behavior of others is a safe and commonly used strategy

  - In many social contexts, students learn that imitating group behavior is a means to gain acceptance. Regularly, such modeling may include showing a preference for currently popular types of dress, language, music, and values. This imitative element is evident in the extent to which some adolescents will go to adapt their own preferences in order to belong to a peer group. Not only the young, but some adults, too, will repress certain views or avoid mentioning some topics if their acceptance into a social club or a loose in-group structure is in jeopardy

For the reasons already stated, modeling can be a very effective learning strategy. Students should not only be alerted to its usefulness in social situations as well as to its appropriateness, but should also be made aware of its limitations.

Techniques which promote a wanted behavior

In this section, choices other than reinforcement are identified as helpful to teachers who plan to encourage specific student behaviors. In addition, some strategies not previously outlined are here given detailed description.

When Mr. Perlitz is about to create a plan to improve Danny's social skills, he will identify specific target behaviors: Danny needs to smile more often, wait his turn, share the materials, and generally behave as a social being. Once a desirable behavior is selected, Mr. Perlitz will include all or some of the following strategies to promote learning: feedback, shaping, prompt and fade, modeling, planned attention, and charting.

Feedback

When maladaptive behavior is noted, a student deserves planned feedback from the teacher. In this case, Mr. Perlitz has chosen to focus on social skills in Danny's plan because, in situations involving other class members, he has observed Danny's being shunned when he does not, for instance, share materials, or even wait his turn, nor does he present pleasant facial expressions. By sharing his observations with Danny, Mr. Perlitz communicates that group membership is within his grasp if he alters the way he interacts. At the moment when Danny agrees to participate in a plan to help him become more socially appropriate, Mr. Perlitz feels positive about the success of the venture.

Shaping

If the target behavior is difficult to encourage because it rarely occurs spontaneously, then merit is acknowledged for successive close approximations. When, for instance, Danny is having trouble learning to smile, and therefore his teacher has difficulty observing him on those rare, successful occasions, Mr. Perlitz may encourage Danny to start by trying facial expressions of a neutral or less serious kind, gently shifting the criterion until he smiles frequently. Because the importance of Danny's effort must not be overlooked, Mr. Perlitz can maintain his motivation with such comments as, "Danny, you are doing your best." or "Danny, you are really trying hard."

Prompt and Fade

This strategy recognizes that at the onset of an intervention a student might require a prompt in order to exhibit a desired behavior. If Mr. Perlitz feels that a cue, such as pointing to his own mouth, will be sufficient to remind him to smile, he may use this technique with Danny. As Danny begins to smile on a consistent basis, slowly the prompt is removed. In the *Prompt-and-Fade* pattern, the teacher

- uses cues and prompts to help the student engage in the desired behavior; – an example of a verbal prompt is, "When you've finished, what should you do next?"

- Gradually removes the prompts, without sacrificing attention to the performance level, once the student establishes a consistent pattern of responding

Modeling

Modeling can occur when the student is encouraged to observe the targeted behavior in the context of a film, novel, play, or television program, and then to comment on various aspects of the observation, possibly in a discussion mode. By asking such questions as

- how did the character behave in the situation?

- what happened as a result of the behavior?

- in what other ways could the character have acted? why did the character decide to act in the way you observed?

- what was the character thinking, not only before but during and after the observed behavior?

- other similar questions can be devised by the students and teacher

Another modeling procedure which addresses the target behavior directly is implemented when the teacher becomes the model. In this process, students imitate the teacher's action by progressing through a three-step process:

- "Watch me do it". Mr. Perlitz asks Danny to observe his facial expression and mannerism as he models attentive listening

- "Do it with me". Mr. Perlitz asks Danny to mimic facial and body language as he is performing the activity

- "You do it by yourself". Danny is expected to engage in the appropriate behavior on his own by first observing, next imitating – while the model is in view – and then responding independently, students modify behavior according to the shifting criterion

This sequence of steps is helpful in teaching a variety of behaviors.

Planned Attention

Because, for many students, attention from an adult and/or from peers is a powerful reinforcer, taking notice of a student can be used by a teacher to promote a desirable behavior. Of the many different forms of attention, three useful types are:

- recognizing the effort of an individual class member by scheduling time with that student. When Danny has worked hard to fulfill the requirements of his contract, Mr. Perlitz takes him to lunch

- moving closer to the student when the wanted behavior is being demonstrated, an especially effective ploy with younger students who enjoy spatial proximity[6] to the teacher

- establishing eye contact with the student, at first, and then adding an approving smile or a nod

Charting

In almost every case, a student will benefit from concrete indicators of improvement. By learning to chart their skills in daily records that show improvement, students can be mentored by teachers in ways of monitoring progress; thereby, they will be able to motivate their own further success. Record-keeping can be accomplished through the use of simple teachable graphs, a few of which are illustrated here:

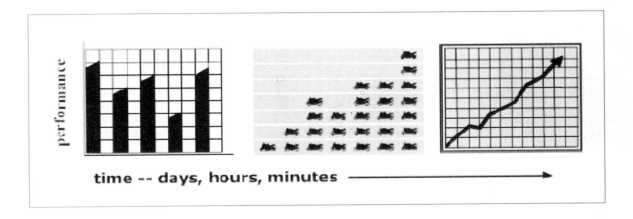

Figure 7-4. **Examples of simple graphs used to record desirable behaviors**

In the context of promoting desirable behavior, above, the techniques known as feedback, shaping, prompt and fade, modeling, planned attention, and charting are outlined. An ongoing evaluation of the student's particular circumstances may lead to the use of one or several of these techniques to achieve the selected objective.

Techniques to discourage unwanted behavior

Although teachers are usually encouraged to focus on promoting wanted behaviors, from time to time they must simultaneously target unwanted ones. Reducing the frequency of an unwanted behaviors involves the application of *punishers* which emphasize – in the student's mind – only what is unacceptable. To counter this impression, an effective plan, first and foremost, must teach new and acceptable expectations. As a corollary, such a plan will include interventions in hopes of discouraging a few target behaviors. In setting up such a program, the teacher might consider the series of procedures outlined here:

Reinforcement and Encouragement

On occasion, a student can be induced to engage in an activity incompatible with an unwanted behavior. Each time Ricco calls out an answer, Ms. Colinette makes a point of standing next to a quiet student who is then asked to respond. If Ricco learns to recognize that teacher attention reinforces desirable actions, his "calling out" behavior will begin to decrease as he is aware of gaining access to the attention he prefers. In this case, as Ricco learns to raise his hand to offer an answer, Ms. Colinette will show friendly approval.

Extinction

The plan warrants that the teacher identify a reinforcer which continues to maintain the frequency of the unwanted behavior. Once that is accomplished, the teacher will remove the reinforcer, hoping that the frequency of such behavior will decrease. Whenever Marshall sits in the desk by the door, he always fails to complete his assignments. By observing his behavior, Mr. Desjardin is able to postulate that the "goings-on" in the hallway are encouraging his lack of task completion. As soon as Marshall moves to a desk away from the door, he is able to finish his work on time.

Time Out

While many have complained that *time-out* is not an effective strategy for reducing unwanted behavior, they have also realized that the fundamental assumption associated with this procedure is not always met. For the time-out penalty to succeed, the student must find the classroom environment inviting and reinforcing. This means that unless motivated to want to be in class, the student will not perceive as punisher the idea of being removed to a neutral area. *Time-out* works very effectively with Norris, however, who really enjoys classroom activities. When Ms. Rampersand asks him to go to the *time-out* area, because of his habit of squeaking his pencil case, he becomes so angry with himself that he is willing to promise good behavior in order to return as quickly as possible.

Included, along with the strategy of *time-out* as a penalty, is some cautionary advice. The teacher should be in the habit of:

- increasing the entertainment value of the lesson or task when a student has been sent to the time-out area

- ensuring that the time-out area neither becomes a reinforcing environment nor affords the student a way to escape the situation in the classroom

- assuring that the time-out intervention is not used to penalize students who are already withdrawn or depressed, thereby allowing them to escape interactive situations

250

By keeping track of the number of occasions when a student requires the penalty, the teacher should observe a decreasing pattern in the undesirable behavior. This charted outcome will determine whether time-out is appropriate, in the context, for dealing with this particular behavior on the part of this specific student. The question may also be asked, "Has the time-out penalty been applied correctly?"

Response Cost

At times, the price of behaving in a certain manner can be too costly: engaging in an unwanted behavior may result in the withdrawal of privileges. When Angelo, who has a truancy problem, wants to go on the Science Center field trip, planned for next week, Mr. Romanov will warn him that if he skips a class for any reason he will be excluded from the trip. Angelo's behavior will depend on the personal worth he assigns to the trip.

Pattern of ignoring

When teachers ignore behaviors, hoping to discourage them by failing to give undue (or any) attention, the process shares some similarities with the intervention called *extinction*. The two should not, however, be confused. Whereas extinction involves identifying the *reinforcer* responsible for encouraging an unwanted behavior and then removing it, ignoring, as a pattern, simply entails discouraging undesirable behavior by ensuring that it receives no teacher notice. The corollary is that ignored behaviors have no prior learning histories.

- When applying patterns of ignoring, the teacher may find the following suggestions useful:
  - when ignoring an unwanted event, the teacher should use the moment as a cue to encourage a different student, one who meets classroom expectations
  - as with extinction, when behavior is ignored, a teacher should expect an initial increase of the inappropriate behavior as long as the student continues trying to attract attention
  - within the classroom or other area, a teacher should **never** ignore behavior that will threaten the safety needs of any person

Corporal Punishment

- Corporal punishment is included in this list because some parents believe it to be an effective punisher. It is, however, important to argue that such activity is unacceptable because:

  - it generates more negative outcomes than benefits

  - it is ethically questionable in the context of a humane, democratic society

  - it is outside the mandate of teachers

  - it is now illegal in some jurisdictions

Corporal punishment teaches students to comply only with powerful people – either those who are taller and stronger or those in positions of undisputed authority. Compatible with this objection is the danger that the habit of inflicting harm may be passed on in the form of physical damage to younger students, pets, and wildlife. An unforeseen outcome, too, is the possibility that the student will avoid or dislike any people who administer corporal punishment, an adverse result in a learning environment. Finally, and very sadly, some children learn to seek out this kind of punishment because it represents a form of human contact when no other sources of attention are available.

Charting

If the teacher is in the habit of recording improvements in the reduction of unwanted behavior, while, at the same time, noting all data that indicate increases in desirable behavior, student progress will usually be encouraged and positive activity motivated. A useful enforcer of this process would take the form of a series of discussions held in discreet teacher-student conferences. In an approach of this kind, the entire process is strengthened when the student is empowered to take personal responsibility for behavior.

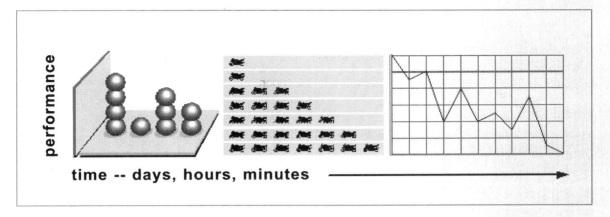

Figure 7-5. **Examples of simple graphs used to record decreases in undesirable behaviors**

The techniques known as reinforcement and encouragement, response cost, patterns of ignoring, corporal punishment, and charting are outlined above as they relate to the discouraging of undesirable behavior. With the exclusion of corporal punishment, one or several of these techniques may be found useful to a teacher evaluating an individual student's circumstance. If the teacher's purpose is to establish a plan for change, some or all of the ideas presented here may assist in achieving the selected objective.

Ways to Promote Positive Feelings in the Classroom

Promoting Feelings of Safety

In the context of the classroom, where the safety needs of students are of primary importance, many possibilities exist for meeting them, some of which include these frequently tried ideas. Teachers may experiment with such suggestions as:

> • developing policies and procedures that address specific ways of handling violence or the threat of violence
>
> • focusing class attention on pro-social behaviors by asking students to bring, discuss, and display pictures or articles about people helping others
>
> • describing the idea known as "Random Acts of Kindness" and encouraging such behavior in the classroom, in the school, and at home
>
> *cont'd*

- providing acceptable ways for venting anger, a process which may be accomplished by teaching students the necessary language. In special cases, a particular area may be designated – preferably an office or seminar room, rather than in the classroom – in which a student, in the company of teacher or child care worker, will not be penalized for genuine expressions of anger

- refusing to allow any student to be "scape-goated" even in a situation which indicates or suggests that the individual's behavior seems to encourage such a response

- forbidding any racial, ethnic ,or religious slurs, even harmless "jokes" or clichés; e.g., "too many chiefs; not enough Indians"; "Some of my best friends are Lithuanian"; "low man on the totem pole"; "It's all Greek to me"

- planning, occasionally, a special treat for the class for no reason other than enjoyment

- asking each student in turn to make a positive statement about a classmate whose name is pulled out of a hat. Students should be pre-briefed, through suitable examples, so that appropriate effort and tone will be invested in such a task

- allowing students to personalize their own work area with pictures of pets and family members; posters; souvenirs; calendars; postcards; and other memorabilia

- choosing to let the teacher's voice be raised only in important negative situations which warrant such action – when it counts

- letting students discuss ideas about temper, relating to valid and invalid expressions of anger

- keeping classroom noise to a "comfortable" level, instead of demanding silence or allowing pandemonium

In the following case study, feelings of safety are an issue. Ms. Ferreira is faced with the predicament of making her student more anxious by tending to her academic needs: Charmaine is one of many children in a single-parent household in which there is alleged drug abuse by the mother. The teacher, Ms. Ferreira, who is concerned about Charmaine's behavior in class, has observed that the young girl is very protective of information about her home life. Among other aspects of secretiveness, lying seems to be fairly common, possibly the result of her haunting memories of the time when, a few years ago, the Children's Aid Society disrupted her family's life. At that time, because Charmaine and her siblings were placed in foster care, she still fears to lose the little familiar home life she still has.

Within the classroom, while Charmaine has developed elaborate strategies to avoid completing assignments, she will go to great lengths, in a friendly way, to help her teacher – washing blackboards, stapling papers, running errands, and doing other useful duties. In short, Ms. Ferreira finds Charmaine a very likeable student who needs her help. What courses of action are open to her?

Before identifying actual options, Ms. Ferreira lists several particulars worth reviewing:

- first: Charmaine's academic work continues to be left incomplete

- second: the strategies Charmaine employs to avoid work are numerous

- third: the girl's co-operative manner during non-academic activities is notable

- finally: her distrust of school personnel when they are discussing family issues cannot be misconstrued or ignored

Up to the present, Ms. Ferreira has made many unsuccessful attempts to discuss her concerns with Charmaine's mother – telephone calls and notes have not ever been responded to. As a result, Ms. Ferreira meets with the in-school support committee[7]. When this group makes general recommendations to modify Charmaine's program, their ideas include: reducing the amount of schoolwork assigned at any one moment; allowing Charmaine to work with a "buddy"; and giving special attention to her when possible. Although Ms. Ferreira implements these revisions, she does not, subsequently, observe a significant change in Charmaine's behavior.

Now, Ms. Ferreira is considering a referral to the special services team[8] in order to initiate an assessment of Charmaine's capabilities and achievement. It is the role of this group to ascertain whether she is able to do age-appropriate work and/or whether she has learning difficulties. Regardless of their findings, because parental permission is required for a psycho-educational assessment, the board social worker will attempt to establish contact with Charmaine's mother, while, at the same time, hoping to offer support services. On the other hand, Ms. Ferreira faces a dilemma: this course of action will create overwhelming anxiety for Charmaine as she sees the school infringing on her home turf. In spite of this realization and her own obvious concerns, Ms. Ferreira will, at the outset, refer Charmaine's case to the special services team, and then, when that group is prepared, will seek recommendations for dealing with the young student's affective needs.

In the meantime, Ms. Ferreira will continue to establish rapport with Charmaine, by allowing her to stay after school. A contract might be devised, as well, requiring Charmaine to complete a single small piece of schoolwork to be shown to Ms. Ferreira for her approval. Perhaps, around this same time, Ms. Ferreira will be able to identify just the "right" classmate to be Charmaine's buddy. All these steps will begin to establish, for Charmaine, an increasing feeling of safety in the classroom. During these early stages, however, it is important to ascertain that when Charmaine learns about the school's contact with her mother, the child does not feel her teacher is practicing subterfuge by being so pleasant in the classroom while negotiating with authorities behind the scenes. How much should Charmaine know in advance about the inquiries that are necessary to the overall success of the plan?

Promoting Feelings of Prizing

When it is obvious that a student longs to feel prized and valued, teachers may be able to increase a sense of belonging by a variety of approaches:

- making an effort to spend five minutes of personal time, separately, each day with three or four designated but different students – talking about non-academic issues

- ensuring that each member of the class – from time to time – has a chance to be selected for a high-status activity

- encouraging students to discover innovative, sensitive ways of picking teams and groups

- describing and discussing with students notions of equality and fairness that incorporate equity

- attending after-school intramural sports activities, from time to time, to cheer on particular students and school teams

- reinforcing the application of *The Golden Rule*

In the following case study of 12-year-old Chandler, a teacher would identify a student with significant prizing needs. Mr. Belmundo recognizes that Chandler's feelings of isolation exacerbate his learning difficulties:

> Both Chandler and his younger brother have the same type of learning disability. Generally, Chandler has difficulty reading social cues; for example, he annoys classmates when they have made it clear they do not want to be disturbed; in addition, he has no concept of the classroom pecking order and, as a result, will challenge the "head gorilla". Because of such social *faux pas* as well as a lack of awareness of the expectations implicit in the classroom context, Chandler is not accepted by his classmates. Perceived as an outsider, he is fair game for teasing and ridicule when he cries in frustration at assignments perceived too difficult.

When this reaction occurs, Chandler "loses it" by retaliating physically, with no apparent control over his anger. On other occasions, when class members simply ignore him, he responds, often, by sitting alone, away from the group, and, at other times, by engaging in solitary games at recess; one option is to play with his brother Colby in a group of younger friends.

Although Chandler's temper and lashing out are the main concerns of several parents as well as of the teacher's, Mr. Belmundo is convinced that sensitive and likeable Chandler must first develop a feeling of belonging and of being prized in the context of the classroom before other issues can be directly addressed. With his entrance into high school a year or so away, Chandler must be reached by people willing to teach him the skills of getting along with others. Slowly, he may also obtain an invitation into the peer group.

Because Mr. Belmundo realizes the importance of making Chandler feel that he belongs, the teacher will begin to create a positive climate through which his attempts to teach social and academic skills will be rewarded. By attempting a variety of methods, he might achieve this goal. First, Mr. Belmundo must find or create opportunities in which Chandler will be able to shine, perhaps by showcasing his achievements outside the class. If this is difficult to do, the teacher might consider assigning the boy a high-status peer buddy to help with classroom assignments. By choosing Gabriel, one of the more popular boys in the class, the teacher will enable Chandler to be perceived differently by the rest of the students. This assumes, of course, that Gabriel is willing to take him under his wing and gradually impart to him the various social expectations implicit in group inclusion. Furthermore, some ground rules have to be set about how Chandler is expected to react to Gabriel's suggestions. As the other students observe Gabe's gentle teaching style, Mr. Belmundo will watch to see whether they will model his behavior. Chandler's tentative approaches to more appropriate responses will induce the class, over a period of time, to adopt him.

By coaching Gabriel, the peer buddy, Mr. Belmundo is able to ensure Chandler of the opportunity to learn and model adaptive group behavior. When he reaches high-school, it is this knowledge and his memory of many successful experiences that will allow him to be valued by classmates as well as to take part in the larger patterns of student life.

Ways to Promote Empowerment

Because feelings of empowerment are closely tied to a sense of personal control, each student should be given adequate opportunity to direct the activities of the group. Here, in the classroom, individuals will be exposed to a concept of "leadership", the teacher serving as the chief model. For this reason, in any classroom, a discussion is warranted on the topic of leadership; topics are directed in the form of questions: "What is a leader?" or "What are important qualities of a leader?" or "Can a person provide leadership without others knowing it?" and other similar questions that the students may provide. Such empowering activities include things that these same students can learn to do:

- leading opening exercises

- recording class attendance and taking results to the office

- setting up equipment in the school yards – basketball nets, hurdles, field hockey nets

- monitoring younger children

- correcting student assignments, with the use of an answer key

- acting as a peer-tutor in academic contexts

- informing the teacher when checked work or homework is incomplete

- role-playing a mentor in social situations

In addition to learning to identify issues of control, students begin to recognize that empowerment also involves taking responsibility for personal actions. When they admit to making mistakes or to reacting impulsively, teachers demonstrate leadership in an informative way. Equally important – in strengthening the notion of empowerment – is the accomplishment of personal goals. Interestingly, a teacher can offer students the *backward technique* to help them not only to identify the objectives involved in reaching a goal but also to discover a means of analyzing behavior. In the *backward technique,* students begin at the end point, cautiously working backward to the beginning by asking, "What do I need to do, know, think, say, learn, or remember to get to a given point?" Alternatively, they may ask, "How did I get to this point?"

In taking responsibility for yet another element, the appearance of the environment, both teacher and students are charged with:

- making the classroom a comfortable area

- picking up litter

- removing graffiti

- cleaning up the school property

- donating pictures and books

- arranging the classroom materials attractively

- volunteering to help keep the conservation area clean

- planting flowers and trees

Empowerment is achievable in a classroom atmosphere that both encourages student initiative and provides, through the role of the teacher, a democratic model of leadership. At the same time, such empowerment strives to verify personal responsibility while elevating pride of accomplishment.

Power struggles

When behavior management is based on compliance, some students will be indirectly encouraged to become confrontational or manipulative. In such instances, the actions usually affirm student desire for control as well as signaling a need for change in classroom management.

Table 7-1. **Examples of moderating or friendly teacher responses to confrontational or manipulative student statements.**

Student Statement	Teacher Response
"I'm not doing this!"	"What would you rather do instead?"
"I'm leaving!"	"You are expected to stay on school property."
	"Let's discuss this privately."
"I hate you!"	"You have reason to be upset."
	"I'm sorry you feel that way because I like you."
"I didn't do it!"	"Assigning blame isn't important right now, please clean it up."
"Carrie did it!"	"I am not accusing you, please pick it up."

On the other hand, in a management style based on a demand for compliance, the teacher appears to be making the following statements:

- "Do what I ask because I am asking it"! "Do what I ask, but only in the manner in which I direct"!

- "Do what the rules say, without exception, because I set them down"!

Given classroom conditions of this kind, many students will bow to authority; others, unafraid of the consequences, will confront the teacher; meanwhile, the rest of the group, unwilling to bend or be punished, will find sly ways to assert themselves.

Not unlike the compliance-seeking manager, the non-compliant ones – students who resort to confrontational and manipulative actions – convey the following:

- "I will do whatever I feel like doing"!

- "I will do it, but only in my own way"!

- "I know rules are made to be broken, especially by me"!

The case study of Micaela

Because Micaela is an only child living with a divorced parent, the immediate family and the mother's boyfriends have treated her as an adult. Within the school, her teachers of both the French Immersion and the gifted programs in which she is enrolled have concerns about her manipulative behavior with classmates. Not only does Micaela use her extensive vocabulary and excellent general knowledge to force herself into peer conversations, she also interacts with the teacher as if with an equal, seeming to feel superior to her peers.

Whereas her teachers see Micaela as a precocious student, her peers perceive her as a know-it-all who should be avoided because they are intimidated by her verbal put downs. Left unchecked, the problem is becoming more serious as Micaela continues to scheme to get her own way.

From Micaela's behavior, the teacher sees it is evident that any attempt to usurp her authority leads to inappropriate means on her part to maintain her power position: she insists on being the "Queen Bee". If, for the moment, the teacher assumes that Micaela knows no other way of behaving, then the corollary must be that she needs to learn new ways of interacting with her peers. Having deduced this, Ms. Zuchowski may decide to target the acquisition of empathic skills. Perhaps Michaela can be prompted to ask herself questions like: "How does Joellen feel when I say this?" or "How will I feel if Joellen treats me the way I treat her?" But first, Micaela must be made to recognize and identify with the pushy behavior of a TV character or to see herself as a person in a novel; as well, she must perceive the effect of such behavior on others. Then, she may be asked to compare the offending behavior with her own, the intention being to create a plan for change.

Another line of intervention might involve Micaela in a role in which she is helpful to other students in the class. In preparation for this, the teacher will provide appropriate guidelines for her to become familiar with and role models with whom she may identify. When some of these ideas have been implemented, it will be time, finally, but importantly, to recognize Micaela's strengths and to place her in leadership roles.

In a classroom environment which assures that students will have feelings of safety, of being prized, and of empowerment, it is possible to reduce examples of confrontational and manipulative behavior. In some instances, however, forms of inappropriate behavior will emerge in students whose lives, outside the particular classroom, are experienced in oppressive environments – at home, in the social peer group, in another class, or when visiting relatives. When the situation can be seen in its full range, many forms of teacher response are both able to diffuse the power struggle and to let the student choose cooperative behavior. In Table 7-1, p. 259 a number of such interventions are outlined.

Promoting Classroom Management

To create a classroom infrastructure strong enough to enable the day-to-day routines to emerge and run smoothly in a predictable environment, the teacher must adopt a management system that allows the attainment of academic and social goals and objectives. In the section below, guidelines are offered, first, for the development of classroom expectations, then, for the teaching and learning of these, and, finally, for ways of focusing on classroom procedures which require attention.

What Should Classroom Expectations Include?

Teachers are able to follow simple guidelines in developing classroom expectations by:

> • first, outlining with the students, in a discussion forum, the notion of rules, expectations, and conventions in society. In an interactive symposium, such ideas should focus not only on the way these processes are present in everyday activities, but also on their manner of benefiting people who must live and work together
>
> • second, still in co-operation with the students, making a list of expectations they believe useful and/or necessary in human interaction. In such an interchange, students can be prompted with such questions as "How do we want people in this class to feel, act, and inter-relate?" and "What expectations and even procedures would allow us, as a group, to accomplish this?"
>
> *cont'd*

- When expectations are being formulated, they should be worded in a positive manner, stating, for example, "Only polite behavior is acceptable". rather than "No swearing allowed"! Once the list is generated, the group may decide to omit any items that are either redundant or not relevant

- In deliberating, the students will want to reduce the list to four or five items, by combining as many as possible

• Teachers working on a rotary system may consider having each class select one expectation. Ultimately, all will be combined in an agenda that, in turn, several groups may focus on, debate, discuss, and evaluate

• The assumption underlying this process is that individual commitment to the fulfillment of these expectations relies on each student's actual involvement in discussing:

- whether each is acceptable

- whether modifications are necessary

- whether there is a consensus in adopting them. Usually, it is inadvisable to put the items to a vote which might alienate students who do not support the majority sentiment. In addition, where there is a power element in the class, a consensus allows the milder students to receive an impression of having the final word instead of having to agree with the bossy ones

Teaching classroom expectations

Once expectations are adopted by the class, the teacher faces the task of ensuring that all students can not only recite them, but will readily recognize a violation. This goal may be accomplished by the teacher in a number of ways:

• engaging in role playing both types of behavior – appropriate and inappropriate; in this process, each student raises a hand when observing an infringement

• reviewing expectations over a period of several weeks

• displaying expectations visually, in both graphic and text form, on chalkboards and bulletin areas.

cont'd

- giving a quiz – this is especially useful for older children – requiring each student to:

  - list every expectation and write its description

  - rate personal success and consistency in meeting each expectation

  - write a story using one of the expectations as a main theme

  - create a chart with columns and a system for checking

- recapping, after the first month, and then fortnightly, the appropriateness of each expectation because once it is consistently adopted in any student's repertoire, a different expectation may be substituted

In addition to its outlined classroom application, the same process can be extended to school-wide expectations. Because each school has a set of both stated and tacit expectations, students may need to be familiarized with both so each one's profile in the school is positive from the outset.

Although there may be a great deal of social pressure to meet expectations, some students may have ongoing difficulties. In such situations, the teacher may:

- outline them and discuss the consequences of not meeting some or all

- implement these consequences, following an action sequence set down in advance

- notice tacitly but fail to focus on disruptive behavior

Teaching Classroom Procedures

Coming to terms with classroom management entails teaching students about procedures in a manner similar to the one described in the section about learning to meet expectations (p. 112). Evertson and Emmer (1982) isolate five general areas, each of which has procedures that warrant outlining, discussion, and teaching:

- use of the classroom space and facilities by students

- behavior that is acceptable outside the classroom – washroom, lunchroom, drinking fountain, playground, and other relevant locations

- activity to be engaged in within the class as a whole – raise hand to speak; submit work as requested; learn ways to access help during seatwork; understand rules for communicating with and signalling others; become aware of all appropriate procedures for work that is carried out in small-groups[9]

- routines to be followed at the beginning and end of the day

- response/actions which are suitable when visitors arrive

In schools with rotary programs, certain priorities should be established across the entire system so that students are familiar with and follow procedures for:

- class beginning

- late arrival; early leaving

- group work; meeting in pairs

- special departure: library, nurse's office

- whole-class activities

- assignments/homework

- class closing, interruptions, fire drills

- absenteeism, exams

Developing an infrastructure in the classroom, one that will provide a predictable basis for behaving, is a requisite condition for creating the desired positive climate. Clear expectations serve to minimize both student guesswork and teacher annoyance, as well as to encourage appropriate and pleasant conduct.

Adapting Curricula for
Students with Behavioral Difficulties

Teachers whose classrooms involve only "behavioral" students are able, almost always, to set academic objectives for them in the same manner as all other teachers set their goals. Contrary to popular folklore, self-contained behavioral classrooms do not provide traditional forms of *treatment*, unless the educational component is situated in a mental health center with such a mandate; for example, at Dellcrest, Thistletown, and Sacred Heart, as well as some other locations, treatment may accompany educational elements in the program.

Like other young people, students with behavioral difficulties are entitled not only to a curriculum that targets academic skills, but also to forms of socialization as the school's contribution to their well-being. Always included in such a curriculum will be literacy and numeracy skills as well as social skills training, in addition to procedures geared to promoting the social/emotional development of each student.

Earlier, reference was made (p. 117) to the ways in which an academic curriculum may sometimes actually encourage student misbehavior, especially when motivational factors are not regulated. Once curricula are made personally relevant, however, as well as sufficiently difficult and unexpectedly novel, – all of these, clearly, from the point of view of the students – the teacher will be ready to introduce social issues in some of the ways outlined here.

Personal Growth

It is very helpful to most students if the teacher leads discussions which present and examine typical situations. These would be activities that not only encourage the examination of "personal" growth processes but also include such possible themes as:

> • *thinking before acting* Students can propose examples of situations in which such a process encourages the desired outcomes. Suggestions are elicited by the teacher or the student-chairperson of the group about how to prompt oneself to reflect on the subject of personal behavior: "What will you say to yourself, Angelica, the next time Josee calls you a rude name?"
>
> *cont'd*

- *making fun of others* In discussion, students learn to realize that sometimes they will engage in debasing others in order to feel better about themselves. By exploring the reasons that explain such behavior, students can begin to invent alternative means to feel worthy

- *being the scapegoat in the class* Why does a group direct negative emotion toward a particular individual? What can any student – even the scapegoated person – do to break the cycle?

- Other equally valid themes will be suggested by the students themselves

Literature

One of the safest ways to approach sensitive issues is to examine them in the context of literature. Sometimes known as Bibliotherapy, this idea involves open-ended stories about children or adolescents that are read with the expectation that by observing characters from afar, evaluating their behavior, and proposing alternatives to the actions of the players, students learn something about their own struggles. Readers of stories are also able to take a long-term perspective by providing other endings to the various tales that the students as a group subsequently compare and evaluate. (see Appendix for examples)

Interviewing

By interviewing classmates, peers, and adults, students can be encouraged to learn from the experience of others and to explore ways that lead to successful outcomes. By interviewing parents – or friends or relatives – with a set of pre-written questions, students are able to discover the skills that contribute to accomplishment. When structured with care, such an activity can also serve to bolster the parent-child relationship or to build contacts within the larger group.

Script Writing

In situations in which a student runs into difficulty because of an inability to use the appropriate language for communicating intentions, a chance to formulate writing and to practice pre-set scripts will allow pre-planning. When scripts are created for real-life situations, they empower the student who may begin to feel confident about handling a situation that was previously unpleasant. Because, in this method, it is possible to take time to consider the situation, to determine in advance how best to handle it, and most important, to establish carefully what is to be said, the student can make self-assured decisions.

Easily integrated in the Language Arts program, script writing promotes an in-depth examination of a particular problem situation while being addressed in a group context. Students, who are formed into fives or sixes, are then asked to identify an awkward conflict or problem, perhaps one experienced by a character in a story. As the students gather various points of view and evaluate many described suggestions, they will generate a script for the character. If time is taken to perform the script, the context and realism of the situation will indicate changes and refinements that are warranted. At a later time, in a discussion regarding the problems and solutions depicted in the groups' skits, the various ideas can be compared and evaluated.

- If students are willing, a more personal example may be used, involving an event described by a student who volunteers to present a familiar problem; e.g., a student who is a "loner" in the school yard identifies and perhaps even dramatizes the problem; then the class or group will give assistance by making recommendations. A possible procedure is to:

  - allow the group to ask questions about the problem

  - encourage a discussion and evaluation of potential solutions

  - ask the student who is proposing the problem to choose the most appealing solution

  - give an opportunity to the group and the student – or the teacher and student – to generate a script that will outline a workable as well as believable procedure for dealing with the unpleasant incident

  - organize contexts in which the student may practice the dialogue in the script

  - present the play as realistically as possible, with the student playing his or her own role, for example, as the "loner"

  - schedule an opportunity after the strategy is implemented for the student to report on its effectiveness. If the results seem to lack practical solutions, the group will then debate the possibility of further modifications

Journal or Diary Writing

In some instances, it may be fitting to require students to keep their own personal diaries or journals that will chronicle social development. Personal writing is a means of objectifying feelings and problems: once on paper, this record can be re-examined by its writer, now with different intentions. If the contents are shared with the teacher or with an appropriate child-care worker, diaries not only help students to obtain feedback, but allow an emotional closeness to be forged between the parties.

For this activity – the writing of the diary or journal – students may be given 15-20 minutes daily which may be banked and used later as needed. Providing time on a Monday morning – to reflect or distance oneself from activities of the weekend – may be a good way for both the teacher and the students to start the week.

Because journals and diaries contain private thoughts and feelings, students should be provided with a secure place to store them, thus being assured of confidentiality. Without such a guarantee, the activity simply becomes a writing exercise with little value to the student because few serious thoughts will be revealed.

Film and Video

Popular films and videos, as well as those created for the educational market, can be used in the promotion of appropriate social behavior. In the process of encouraging the examination of film-generated social situations, evaluating them, predicting consequences, and proposing alternative courses of action, a teacher will find a variety of techniques that are helpful, especially by choosing sections of films and videos that suggest interesting conflicts. The teacher may intensify the usefulness of such excerpts by:

- showing a cut that reveals a social situation

- stopping the tape at a critical point in the narrative

- having students – individually or in groups – generate subsequent dialogue

- restarting the tape

- noting and evaluating variations: this is carried out in discussion mode, perhaps in groups

Dramatization

An essential aspect of acquiring and promoting the importance of empathy, Drama allows students to experience the feelings, thoughts, and actions of another person or of more than one person. For this reason, it is recommended that teachers of students with behavior difficulties augment their pedagogical skills by taking courses and workshops in drama education. A pertinent example of a project with middle-school students is offered by Gollobin & Gruhn (1991) who present their use of the medium in outlining the experience, the dilemmas, and choices of immigration to America.

Whereas creating dramatic presentations written and performed by students is a major project, the role playing of social conflicts is a more manageable application easily used on a daily basis. By employing the same technique as the one described for examining videos and films, the teacher can help the whole class to participate in the experience.

Bibliotherapy

Literature, an essential platform for learning about the human condition, succeeds as a means of helping students to role-play because it unfolds explicitly in many different situations. Given literature's constant usefulness, the classroom can be organized to include a display of fiction and non-fiction materials related to student-picked themes. The existence of a Book Corner encourages students to share their personal books, exchanging them for others borrowed from both the school and public libraries. Of course, students must be taught to differentiate between books on loan and books that are owned. A system of small fines can help to teach the idea of returning library books. Once such a "lending library" center is established, a variety of activities can be launched:

- reading aloud several pages of a book, daily, to the entire class; either the teacher or a literate student does this

- dramatizing parts of a book for presentation

- organizing a debate on points of view taken by opposing characters or by different books

- playing the roles of various characters to emphasize certain decisions and actions

- discussing the pros and cons of a character's decision

- composing a sequel to the events of a book

269

To augment the titles in Table 7-2, students will gladly offer suggestions for the Book Corner.

Table 7-2. **Example themes and resource materials included in a Book Corner**

Theme	Suggested Materials
Making Friends at School	Kellogg, Steven (1986). *Best Friends*. New York: Dial Books Mathews, John (Dir.) (1987). *Frog and Toad are Friends/Frog and Toad Together*. Los Angeles, Calif.: Churchill Media (video)
Death and Dying	Buscaglia, L. (1982). *The Fall of Freddie the Leaf: A Story of All Ages*. New Jersey: Charles S. Black. Mellonie, B & Ingpen, R. (1983). *Lifetimes, The Beautiful Way to Explain Death to Children*. Toronto: Bantam Books.
Tolerance and Diversity	Andersen, Hans Christian (1955). *The Ugly Duckling*. Walt Disney Productions (video) Munsch R. & Askar, S. (1996). *From Far Away*. Toronto: Annick Press Ltd.
Dealing with Anger	Amos, Janine (1993). *Angry*. Bath, Avon: Cherrytree Press Ltd. Dube, Pierre (1995). *Sticks and Stones*. Richmond Hill, On: Scholastic Canada Kulling, Monica (1992). *I Hate You, Marmalade*. Toronto: Penguin Books

Methods that promote language development

In human interaction and especially in social behavior, language plays a major role, often displacing many types of action deemed less than acceptable. When Sharona is displeased because she is not picked to play, she tells the other children "f— off!" Previously, when annoyed, she chased and hit the others, but eventually, just as Sharona has learned to replace violence with language, after some appropriate coaching, she will learn to choose more acceptable language to convey the pain she feels as a result of their exclusion of her. In addition, language patterns prove their usefulness when they start to establish personal control over behavior. As they begin labeling, describing, and evaluating feelings or events, students are able to reflect on what has happened, with the option of changing outcomes. In summary, language forms serve both to soften the effects of aggressiveness and to scrutinize the acceptability of one's own or others' actions.

Active Listening

Some students are unable to communicate effectively with their teachers and peers when they are only partly paying attention to, half listening to, or vaguely thinking about what is being said to them. Because active listening is a procedure involving both listening and responding, its intent, in verbal interactions, is to foster mutual understanding. By directing the student's attention to the relevant aspects of the encounter, the teacher is able to ensure that effective communication becomes possible. Students can also learn to teach one another this valuable skill, especially when they work in mentoring groups or role-playing contexts.

At least four of the strategies associated with active listening can be itemized:

> - *encouraging* When someone is speaking, the listener has the task not only of demonstrating interest but also of behaving in a manner that invites the speaker to continue. This is accomplished by remaining objective – refraining from agreeing or disagreeing – and, instead, making positive comments, such as, "I see or "That's interesting". By interpolating such responses, the listener's responsiveness demonstrates to the speaker both an interest in the interaction and a willingness to continue participating
>
> *cont'd*

- *restating* To monitor comprehension, all the while demonstrating commitment to the words of the speaker, a restatement of the main ideas and relevant facts of what is being heard is an effective strategy. Statements such as: "In other words, this is what you plan to do...." and "If I understand, you think that..."

- *reflecting* Although similar to the restating strategy, this one focuses on the feelings conveyed by the speaker. Often overlooked yet so important, the speaker's feelings are acknowledged. Empathic reactions of this intent can be conveyed through statements such as, "So, you feel that ...." and "I can see that you find this upsetting..."

- *summarizing* A final wrap-up of the important ideas, as well as a précis of the feelings conveyed by the speaker may be advisable if the listener wishes to engage in further discussion, perhaps at a later time. This is also useful if the purpose of the interaction is to solve a problem or accomplish a task. Some possible approaches would be: "These are the ideas I heard you express...." and "If I understand your ideas correctly, you feel this way about the situation:..." Not only should students incorporate these strategies in verbal interactions, but they can also practice by placing themselves in the context of a story where they can review the words of a character, offering more appropriate utterances than were in the original text. For example, Murphy runs into the house and describes to Josh the altercation he has just witnessed outside. Josh responds by saying, "Can't you see I'm watching TV? "Students are asked to create a speech that Josh might utter if he were an active listener and to continue the dialogue between the two boys in the form of a script

Vocabulary Building

In the course of learning to label and to describe behavior, students must acquire the relevant vocabulary. Often, the words used in social interaction – such as "honesty," "deceit," "fair," and others that are common to adults – describe complex concepts that may be incomprehensible to some children. Also, language that depicts different shades of emotion is important to consider: will all students understand the distinctions? – "anger," "disgust," "outrage," "shame," and similar subtle words, for instance. By being conscious of words worth exploring, the teacher can ensure that time spent in clarifying them is effectively used.

Script Writing

Because, in schools, so much emphasis is placed on using words that convey intention, many students make socially inappropriate statements – gaffes – when they are unable to communicate what they intend. When Millicent wants to get a drink and just walks out of the room, fearing a crisis scenario, Mr. Kravitz becomes very upset upon realizing she is missing. The truth is that Millicent's self-consciousness about having to speak to the teacher means she often becomes "tongue-tied". With the help of Mr. Kravitz, Millicent is able to write a series of requests on a card to carry with her. As soon as she runs into verbalizing difficulty, she simply reads aloud from the card or uses it as a speech cue. As may be obvious, writing scripts helps not only chronically anxious students but also those learning to use new language patterns.

Language for Self-Defense

Interestingly, one of the critical functions of language is its use as a form of self-defense. This important role must be explored with children because, only by knowing what to say will they become empowered; for example, Mr. Lam asks, "What could Madeleine have said to feel better about the situation?" In another situation, he queries, "What was the appropriate thing to say when the group laughed at Marcie?" In conflict that emerges in the classroom, he gently mediates: "If you were Felix, how would you answer Eugene's insult?"

The Discussion Group Format

In order to encourage the development of cognitive and speaking processes, teachers will find language to be a powerful medium. Among the many procedures that benefit the learners, a few are: analyzing a concept, outlining an issue, evaluating an idea, and appraising a course of action. Because discussion, which is an exchange of ideas, involves personal language as the primary mode of expression, its use is particularly important. The reason is that, traditionally, classrooms present limited opportunities to use this form of exploration. Unfortunately, it is more usual for students either to listen – receptive language – or to write their ideas – written language.

Often, in classrooms, the size of the group discourages the use of discussion. When too many students are involved, only a few are able to be effectively engaged at one time in oral presentation or in conversation. What often happens is that while a single student is speaking and another responding, many more are uninvolved or are striking up their own conversations. Because the process can quickly deteriorate, teachers validly question the usefulness of the discussion medium for accomplishing instructional objectives.

Although dividing the large group into smaller ones is one means of addressing the lack of individual involvement, the teacher usually is at a disadvantage. While attempting to ensure that all students have met the instructional objectives by standard means – moving around – Mr. Martello, in running from one group to the other, in directing the discussion, and in trying to evaluate the contribution of each student, loses the original purpose of encouraging each contributor. Meanwhile, the students miss the coherence and strength that would emerge if the small-group method were employed.

To make greater use of the discussion medium, teachers may prepare themselves to present traditional procedures for running effective discussions, ensuring that each group is aware of:

- the purpose of the discussion
- the role of each person in the group
- the rules by which each member is required to participate

By standardizing the format of discussions, the teacher ensures that all participants practice and learn the set phases. Once an adequate level of mastery is achieved, all class members are able to focus exclusively on the topic being discussed. Sometimes, it may be useful to outline instructional objectives which include the need not only for critical evaluation of information but also for problem solving. Many other higher-level processes, which may be identified by the teacher in such handbooks as *Robert's Rules of Order*, easily lend themselves to the discussion medium as long as students are familiar with the format; *i.e.*, they are not only clear about the duties of each person in the group but also fairly definite about any goals that, as individuals, they are expected to achieve.

Although a well-developed format for the exchange of information, opinions, and ideas is generic, with minor revisions, it can be applied to different contexts. Based on a structure like that used to run efficient professional meetings, it is the procedure assumed in any discussion. By learning to employ such a process, students develop a sense of the expectations implicit when the discussion mode is used. As an additional positive outcome, their new ability to show serious attention to detail and result will be observable.

The Procedure

In preparing for discussion, the teacher usually outlines several stages:

- *Selection of group participants:* In a heterogeneous grouping of four to six students, chosen because of their varying abilities and histories of achievement, each one is likely to learn well from the others

- *Assignment of roles and duties:* In no more than three minutes, each group will designate a *chair, secretary,* and *timer.* Each *secretary* will immediately note this information at the top of the minutes, along with the date. Each of the other members will be designated *participant*

- *Discussion:* The discussion is expected to have a duration of 10 to 25 minutes. Short time frames provide students with a sense that no time is available except for the task at hand

- *Reporting:* This part takes place in a full forum, all the students having moved into a circle or other appropriate grouping. Each group's *secretary* will present a summary of the main points made during the discussion:

  - The teacher may choose to highlight certain issues

  - Further class discussion, which occurs if necessary, will take five to ten minutes, usually to clarify or rationalize opposing points

  - A complete summary of findings may be completed, although this is optional, as it requires amalgamating all the findings in a manner that avoids duplication. Sometimes a gifted student enjoys such a challenge

Roles and Duties

- *Chair:* the person holding this role:

  - states at the outset the purpose of the discussion, outlining what is to be accomplished

  - regulates the discussion by: allowing only one person to speak at a time; preventing students from "hogging" the interchange; and soliciting comments from quiet individuals

  - re-directs the discussion – tactfully – when it is off-topic or whenever irrelevant remarks are made

  - instructs the *secretary* to write down an important idea, re-phrasing or dictating it as necessary

  - clarifies a confusing point by asking the *participant* to re-state or to try different phrasing

  - requests that the *secretary* read back the notes to the group in order to obtain approval and/or corrections

cont'd

- **_Secretary:_** this member:

  - brings paper and pen

  - records issues prompted by the _Chair_

  - reads back the notes to obtain group approval for a given point or a series of elements

  - reports, as appropriate, the findings of the group to the whole class

- **Timer:** this member:

  - keeps track of time limits agreed upon for each phase of the discussion

  - informs the _Chair_ if a limit is exceeded

  - grants additional time when it is available

- **_Participants:_** these members:

  - contribute arguments, thoughts, and ideas about the topic

  - actively listen to arguments made by other members and subsequently formulate appropriate responses

  - record personal notes for use in making points when speaking

As students are in the process of learning their roles and procedures, the experience will at first be tedious. Commonly, in this early stage, a relatively simple topic is focused on, in order for participation to become easy and confident. This helps all participants to see that the goal of initial discussions is "learning the process". To maintain a high level of motivation, however, this activity should be fast paced, and, for this reason, suggested time lines are provided. Such controls will maximize the potential participation of all students. Eventually, when the format becomes transparent, students will recognize the need to focus complete attention on the content of the discussion. The topics, by now, are more demanding and require the concentration for which the students have been training.

Cognitive Interventions

Cognitive approaches promote the idea that a reciprocal relationship exists among perception, emotions, goals, and behavior. As a result,

- a change in perception will alter emotions, goals, and behavior
- a change in one's goal is especially influential in altering behavior
- new activities and novel kinds of behavior alter perceptions

Factors such as becoming aware of one's actions, developing intrinsic motivation, applying knowledge acquired in one's own situation to a new circumstance, using language to mediate difficult tasks, and learning problem-solving skills – all of these varied processes are included among the interventions that rely primarily on thinking processes.

Self-evaluation/Self-instruction

Simply requiring the student to record and count occasions when a particular undesirable behavior occurs can significantly change a target behavior. In such a procedure, the change occurs independently from any external reinforcement. Importantly, though, the effectiveness of this strategy depends on maintaining the student's interest about and attention to the behavior for an extended period of time – at least three to four weeks. Without this long period of concentration and attentiveness, it is likely that frequency of the negative behavior will return to previous levels because the student is no longer paying attention to examples of it.

Self-regulation versus External Regulation

The procedure for self-regulation consists of highlighting situations in which the student is personally responsible for observing and reinforcing target behaviors. In contrast, external regulation places the teacher – or any person separate from the student – in the role of observing phenomena and dispensing encouragement. To circumvent problems of dishonesty or clarity of expectation, when personal behavior data are being reported, the student is initially expected to match the teacher's count.

Eventually, as the two totals consistently match each other, the teacher may decide to withdraw from maintaining an active role in the procedure. Of course, continuing interest must still be shown so that the student believes the self-regulation to be important.

Although both techniques have been found to be equally effective, because a shift from external to self-regulation at an appropriate moment will help to promote the personal growth of the student, such a change is highly recommended.

Maintenance and Transfer of Skills

Transferring skills learned in one situation to the circumstances of another is not only a difficult proposition for students acquiring social skills but is also a challenge in all branches of learning. When the desire for such an outcome is being incorporated in the planning of programs, the teacher at first presents a series of situations that differ slightly and then asks the student to make the necessary adaptation in order to implement the skill. Teaching the student to seek the answer to the following questions, when a new task is encountered, encourages the transfer of knowledge:

- Does this situation resemble one that I previously encountered?
- How is it similar and how is it different?
- How did I handle those past situations?
- How can I handle the present situation?

Verbal Mediation

As exemplified in the foregoing section, language is a powerful method for exercising self-evaluation and self-control.

In dealing with the problems of some students, however, mediation essays can be more effective as consequences for inappropriate behavior. In this procedure, the student is expected to write an essay that provides answers to the following questions:

- What did I do wrong?

- Why shouldn't I do this?

- What should I have done instead?

- Why is that a better option?

First, by re-examining past behavior, with the intention of evaluating it, and then by proposing a more appropriate course of action, a student will be encouraged simply to reflect, a process that, clearly, is incompatible with impulsivity. Most important is that such re-examination is very likely to lead to behavioral change: this happens because perceptions and beliefs are altered.

Problem-Solving Training Programs

Although a variety of problem-solving programs exists, most incorporate the following stages:

- *Problem definition:* the student describes the problem in order to arrive at an understanding of the existing conditions

- *Goal statement:* the student describes the desired outcome

- *Impulse delay:* the student considers ways of reflecting about the problem – **stops and thinks before acting**

- *Generation of alternatives:* the student lists as many potential solutions as possible

- *Consideration of consequences:* the student systematically evaluates each of the alternatives – **thinks about the respective situation that may follow each solution**

- *Implementation:* the student chooses and implements an appropriate course of action

- *Recycling:* the student evaluates personal behavior in order to consider outcomes that were not projected – **reflects on self-evaluation and error-correcting options**

Traditional methods of problem-solving encourage success by teaching students to apply a set of steps, similar to the ones described above. But how successful are students in applying these strategies to new and personal situations?

Perhaps, the steps involved in problem-solving are best learned though a process of discovery. In the unit **Small Challenges: Solving Everyday Problems**[10], a group is asked to choose a problem of personal relevance and then to propose as many different solutions as possible. After these responses are mounted on a chart and considered by the group, participants are asked to record the anticipated consequences (positive and negative) of each action. Once this early process is complete, each group of students is next asked to contemplate the steps that allowed them to arrive at the solutions on their respective record charts. It is not unusual for several groups to generate models that are slightly different from one another, even when they are addressing the same problem. Such variety is welcomed, and the social implications of such variability – in a democracy – should be discussed and debated.

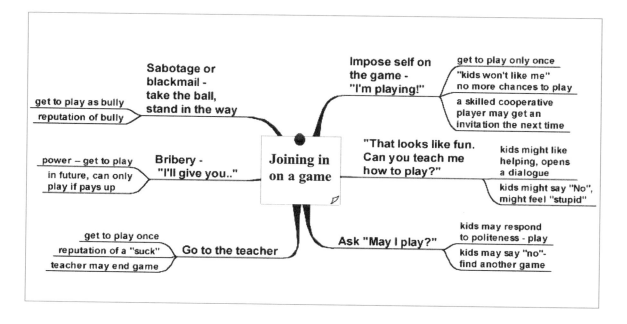

Figure 7-6. **An example of a solution chart**

At first, this method of discovering the process of problem solving puts emphasis on the "doing". Only then does it switch to a meta-cognitive analysis.

The Role Of Suggestion

In North America, suggestion or auto-suggestion processes associated with learning are not as readily studied as they are either in Russia or in other Eastern European nations. Written in the 1970s by Lozanov, an interesting work, entitled *Suggestopedia*, proposes that environmental events may facilitate imitation not only of behavior and attitudes, but also , perhaps, of beliefs through the action of an unconscious mechanism. Many of the Lozanov's techniques – some of them using rhythm and music in promoting language learning – are applied in a process called *Super Learning*. Possibly, one can explain the *Super Learning* phenomenon as resulting from an unconscious association of two events not commonly related. For example, the advertising industry which traditionally is very much interested in changing the attitudes, beliefs, and behaviors of consumers, especially regarding particular products, will attempt to alter purchasing habits by connecting, to state a few examples, sex to cars, medications to motherhood, and liquor to desirable lifestyles, as well as employing many other interesting juxtapositions. The more a potential consumer is "off guard", that is, unconscious of the "real" intent of the message, the more prone that individual will be to suggestion. Because this subconscious process is always in play, at school as well as in the marketplace, the teacher is encouraged to attend to subtle messages present in the classroom, many of which may shape ideas and beliefs. These are present, of course, in student commentary as well as in books, newspapers, and television programs, and also in many other sources of information. A typical example of student thinking in some schools is the notion that, to be properly dressed, a student must have new designer clothing, according to the latest fad. That this custom is totally impractical in a neighborhood of low-income homes could be made part of a discussion topic. In some regions, students take it as a matter of pride that their clothes are found in Goodwill and Salvation Army sources. These elements and other similar ones will form strong bases for discussion possibilities among students.

Summary

In this chapter, various strategies for introducing learning approaches, especially in the behavioral classroom, have been outlined and presented in overview. Arising out of a range of reports, books, and discussions with school personnel, the forms of intervention, both defined here and described in some detail, are presented with the purpose of helping teachers to create positive classroom climates while integrating behavioral elements into existing curricula. Interested teachers are encouraged to seek additional information about these techniques from library sources and also from the Internet. Another source of good ideas is the pool of experienced colleagues within the school or board.

Endnotes

[1] In this example, because the requested behavior, putting art work in the bin, is associated with an unpleasant internal state, fear associated with getting an injection, it is apparent that classical conditioning procedures are also at play.

[2] Both resistance to *extinction* and also *spontaneous recovery* are phenomena important to the learning of adaptive behavior. For example, resistance to *extinction* is a measure of the strength of learning, while *spontaneous recovery* is a process by which old, seemingly forgotten, behavior can inadvertently be encouraged to re-surface with relatively small effort.

[3] The reader is reminded that associations between events and internal states are acquired by classical conditioning.

[4] Secondary reinforcers acquire their strength to encourage behavior as a result of their association with positive and pleasurable internal states, in the process known as classical conditioning.

[5] Shaping is described in detail, later in Chapter Seven.

[6] The spatial distance between teacher and student should never exceed what is appropriate in the social context or comfortable in the environment. A teacher should never invade the personal space of a student.

[7] A committee comprising regular classroom teachers, special education teachers, and principal or vice principal.

[8] This team usually includes one each of: psycho-educational consultant, psychologist and/or psychiatrist, social worker, special education teacher, principal or vice-principal, school-area superintendent.

[9] See the discussion-group format described later in this chapter.

[10] This interactive web-based module is available at the following URL: http://www.learncanada.org/e-showcase.html#cabd.

CHAPTER 8

Common Behavior Problems and Selected Disorders

Unlike the previous chapter, which focused on curricular issues, the present one addresses some of the common behavior problems and disorders found in children and adolescents, in addition to the interventions usually employed to respond to them. Outlined first are problems commonly encountered by school-aged children and adolescents: bedwetting, temper tantrums, lying, stealing, aggressive behavior, social withdrawal, and self-stimulatory behaviors. The next topic focuses on childhood fears, which, although common in the behavioral repertoire of children, are chiefly developmental, disappearing apparently without anyone's effort being expended. Then, issues that relate to anxiety are examined, followed by an evaluation of the effects of the stress reaction. Finally, a series of selected disorders prevalent in children and adolescents is presented.

Before a close examination of behavior problems can be undertaken, it is important to note that two major types of information – research and clinical evidence – are available to the teacher interested in acquiring knowledge about various treatment interventions. For example, Christophersen and Mortsweet (2001) report that the Canadian Task Force on Periodic Health Examination identifies a need for better "quality of evidence" in fields concerned with treatment practices. Typically, because treatment interventions arise as the result of clinical practice, they are not sufficiently scrutinized for effectiveness with larger audiences.

Empirically supported treatments must incorporate the following criteria. In such therapies, the intervention:

- is carried out in more than one setting; an intervention that works in one setting may be ineffective in another

- is evaluated by using random assignment to multiple treatments. By randomly placing participants in several treatment groups, the therapist will know whether the specific treatment – rather than the attention and/or other factors associated with an intervention – may be responsible for any improvement in the participant

- is undertaken by using multiple measures; as many measures as are reasonably possible should be collected because a single measure may not be sufficiently sensitive[1] to pick up treatment differences between groups

- is studied by focusing on participants who are carefully selected and well-defined. By having a good grasp of the type of participants who respond positively to a treatment intervention and by comparing the similarity between participants and the classroom recipient of the interventions, the teacher is able to predict whether the intervention is likely to work

In the case of a particular student, when the teacher is trying to determine whether an intervention is warranted, several elements may be considered. In examining the treatment literature, the teacher should be cautious. Unless an empirical study meets the criteria previously described, relying exclusively on such evidence reflects only general tendencies. It should be expected that clinical evidence based on relatively small groups of individuals will also include biases. By studying the essential findings collected by both approaches – empirical and clinical – foresighted teachers can decide to consult not only with the parents and the principal but also with the special services team.

Teachers should be aware of an additional factor: the incidence of common behavioral problems is affected by developmental and gender factors, and, for this reason, by the time the children reach age fourteen, most of the difficulties have vanished without direct intervention. If many of these common behaviors usually disappear as the child matures and becomes more self-assured, what signs should prompt teachers to decide that there is cause for concern? Consider the following conditions in which the behavior:

- appears so frequently that it interferes with the overall development of the child. Philippe is absent seven to ten days each month, and, as a result, he is, first of all, experiencing difficulty sustaining friendships, and, in addition, doing poorly in assigned academic tasks

- is inappropriate for the cognitive level of the child; twelve-year old Sheena spends most of her social time playing schoolyard games with eight and nine-year-old students in Ms. Farsi's class

- is unsuited to the child's age group. Ten-year old Aline continues to suck her thumb

- has persisted, in duration, from weeks to months with no apparent reduction in frequency. Despite Mr. Rivera's attempts to reduce the number of fist fights during recess, Jarod continues to argue with peers, inevitably resorting to physical altercation

- interferes, because of its frequency, with the social development of the child. As a result of Pier's persistent and hurtful sarcastic remarks to his classmates, he is shunned and has no friends

- promotes, in the teacher, a "gut feeling" that intervention is the appropriate course of action. Although seven-year old Tara's reluctance to submit an assignment – unless it is perfect – is responsible for her meticulous classroom work, Ms. Gudofsky has a feeling that leaving this behavior unchecked might, in later years, lead Tara to experience difficulty. A few or many of these factors may prompt the teacher to initiate an intervention plan

Common Behavior Problems

Several common behaviors, typically associated with childhood and adolescence, are witnessed and reported on by teachers and parents. Among these are: bedwetting, soiling, temper tantrums, aggressive behavior, lying, stealing, social withdrawal, and self-stimulatory behaviors. All are examined in the sections that follow, not only in term of incidence and causes, but also in connection with the various interventions used to lessen symptoms.

Bedwetting (Enuresis)

Although bedwetting is a problem that occurs most commonly among younger children, a relatively high incidence of enuresis is found in boys in their early teens. For boys at that age, this problem is particularly devastating as a result of the social ramifications, especially the secrecy and shame associated with the problem. Ruling out physiological causes is the first sound course of action to be taken.

Prevalent subtypes of *enuresis* are identifiable, each one based on the locus of occurrence:

- nocturnal only – at night

- diurnal only – during the day

- nocturnal and diurnal – day and night

Of the three, the first subtype, bedwetting occurring during sleep, is the most common, while wetting during waking hours is far less common. Here, the young person is often likely to be a girl, under the age of nine years, who is reluctant to use the toilet because of shyness or distracting involvement in tasks. The last subtype, the one involving wetting during both day and night can be the most extreme. The diagnostic criteria for *enuresis* are listed in Table 8-1.

Table 8-1. DSM-IV-TR Diagnostic Criteria of Enuresis

A. Repeated voiding of urine into bed or clothes (whether involuntary or intentional)

B. The behavior is clinically significant as manifested by either a frequency of twice a week for at least three consecutive months or the presence of clinically significant distress or impairment in social, academic (occupational), or other important areas of functioning

C. Chronological age is at least five years (or equivalent developmental age) The behavior is not due exclusively to the direct physiological effect of a substance (diuretic) or a general medical condition (e.g., diabetes, spina bifida, a seizure disorder)

Reprinted with permission from the Diagnostic and Statistical Manual of Mental Disorders, Fourth Edition, Text Revision, Washington, DC, American Psychiatric Association, 2000.

Causes

Depending on the paradigm consulted, several possible causes of *enuresis* are documented and/or postulated. The *Psychodynamic* view, for example, perceives the condition as symptomatic of basic emotional disturbance at a profound level in the psyche, while a *Physiological* and *Behavioral* perspective proposes several varying possibilities:

- an absence of development in central and sub-cortical mechanisms (maturation of neurological factors) – the brain is not sending appropriate messages

- a failure to develop conditioned reflex – the child should first be able to recognize a sensation indicating a full bladder and then to act on it

- an insufficient level of neural maturation along with a poor learning history – the child has not developed adequate bladder control

- a pattern of weak over-learning; perhaps, in addition, the process is associated with punishment; the child, as a result, develops bladder control and then loses it

Other typical causes include, on the one hand, a hereditary component prominent in 40 to 55% of enuresis cases, and, on the other, a sleep-pattern factor. Certain children with nocturnal enuresis, who reach a deep level of sleep very quickly, may find it difficult to respond to physiological cues indicating a full bladder.

Interventions

A variety of ineffective interventions, commonly used to treat enuresis, includes special diets, injections, bladder and rectal irrigations, supine sleeping arrangements, and hard mattresses. In contrast, some methods that have shown more positive results include drug, behavioral, and psychotherapy procedures.

Although some medications such as Desmopressin and Imipramine have been helpful to certain individuals, parents are often concerned about the side effects common to such interventions, including the possibility that when medication is no longer given, the bedwetting re-appears. To date, a most useful way of combating enuresis has involved variations of the *Bell and Pad procedure* developed by Mower and Mower in 1938 – also known as bedwetting alarms. In this intervention an apparatus worn by the child is capable of detecting minute levels of moisture. At the first indication of wetness, a circuit that closes in the electrical process causes a bell to ring. When the sound is heard, the child usually awakens and goes to the toilet. From a behavioral perspective, the sound of the bell acts as a negative reinforcer – like the nagging ring of an alarm clock. Traditionally, negative reinforcers train avoidance responses: in the same way as a person learns to awaken just before the alarm clock rings, the child becomes able to wake moments before the bell is triggered.

Also used with moderate success is a range of operant conditioning, modeling, and shaping techniques. In such cases, the child can be given positive reinforcement at the same time as the bedwetting is inhibited; sometimes, that same child is directed to observe other children and to realize they do not wet the bed. Such interventions have been found to be successful when used in conjunction with the *Bell and Pad* method.

In some cases, a "shaping" strategy can also be devised to treat the problem. At first, the child is awakened to go to the toilet every half hour; then, the intervention occurs at progressively longer intervals, with the aim of having the child eventually – without bedwetting – sleep throughout the night.

While the *Bell and Pad* method has been found effective in 85-95% of cases, encouragement methods such as "star charts"[2] show 20% success, and psychotherapy is deemed to have helped in 18% of cases. On the other hand, with no treatment at all, 11% of cases resolve themselves. When enuresis is evident, teachers should encourage parents to seek professional help as well as to join relevant parent-support groups that will give them access to the latest available information, including age-appropriate books for the child[3].

Soiling (Encopresis)

In contrast to enuresis, soiling or *encopresis*, a behavioral condition that is rare in children after they reach age five, is more likely to be present in developmentally delayed students. When it occurs in isolation, however, a teacher might suspect such physiological triggers as intestinal problems, seizures, poisoning, etc. Because of potentially serious health concerns, any such incident should immediately be reported to parents. In cases of this kind, parents and guardians should be advised to seek medical advice.

In developmentally delayed children, soiling may be a consequence of inadequate toilet-training, a procedure which requires the mastery of the following milestones:

> • the student becomes trained to recognize physiological cues
>
> • the student is able to carry out the behavioral routine that follows the response to such cues

Toilet Training

Several steps are established before the actual training begins:

> • the teacher establishes a baseline that demonstrates when bowel movements occur by recording time of occurrence over a week-long period
>
> • the teacher records the temporal relationship between meals and snacks and bowel movements
>
> • the teacher observes the child's reaction to the experience of using washrooms and toilet

Equipped with information about average daily time of bowel-movement occurrence, predictability of the event after meals, and the child's level of comfort with toileting, the teacher is free to decide when the toileting routine will be initiated. If the child is likely to have a bowel movement one hour after eating, then the toileting routine begins 45 minutes following meals. At the pre-arranged time, the child is placed on the toilet and made comfortable. If, at this juncture, the child shows signs of distress, the teacher or worker may decide to interrupt the training. If a *desensitization* procedure is instigated to relieve fear and anxiety, the child is entertained and diverted until the bowel movement response is made. The teacher or worker follows the success with a reinforcing event – preferably not food. When such a process is maintained consistently, it becomes predictable to the child.

A program of this kind, both requiring such attention to and proving so labor intensive, teaches an important life skill which will increase the child's social and educational opportunities. Of some concern is the realization that the length of time required for toilet training will vary according to the learning ability of the student. Some encouraging observations may be made:

- over a period of time, a decrease will be evident in the clocked interval between the child's being placed on the toilet and the onset of a bowel movement

- the child begins to predict the onset of the toileting routine, just **prior** to the set time, not only by moving in the direction of the toilet but also by communicating intent in some other way recognizable to the teacher

It is important to remember that a soiling response in a student – one who is toilet trained – should be taken as a serious marker. Parents should be immediately contacted and encouraged to involve the family physician.

Temper Tantrums

Tantrums are a cluster of behaviors that include crying, screaming, pounding the floor, throwing objects, and demonstrating other forms of loud attention getting. When a person's goal is blocked, the frustration felt is often the cause of a violent emotional reaction – a tantrum. When examined, the consequences that follow such behavior are believed by many theorists to maintain and strengthen the habit. Temper tantrums are seen as a way for children to exercise their will – the outburst is about *power*. When told to get ready for bed, a youngster throws a tantrum, after which the relenting parents allow the child to stay up for another half hour. The learning process demonstrates that throwing tantrums is an effective means of achieving something previously denied.

Children in classrooms also learn to use the tantrum device by modeling the behavior of others; that this imitative response is reinforced is evident as soon as the maladaptive behavior of one student becomes contagious. In both the operant and modeling explanations, the tantrum's usefulness lies in its ability to achieve or elicit the desired gratification.

Why do parents and teachers give in to tantrum behavior? On the basis of experiences with adults, many children learn that persistence "pays off", especially if behavior that is initially ignored is followed by the achievement of the desired item or procedure. After this initial surrender, each subsequent attempt to extinguish the adverse behavior becomes more difficult for the adult, during which time the child holds out for longer periods. When the situation becomes public, usually the adult finds it easier to buy the child the ice cream: anyone observing knows that the adult will be the first to "blink".

Interventions

In such diverse situations, usually the most effective strategy is to apply learning principles consistently and predictably. The procedures include:

> • *Extinction.* Tantrums are no longer reinforced as they usually are when the child's demand is granted. If the adult feels that an audience – as might exist in a public place or in the classroom – will sabotage the process, evade these competing reinforcers by removing the child, or, in the case of the classroom, by having the class go to the library. With these new conditions in place, the teacher (or the parent) should expect the tantrum behavior to initially increase before the undesired behavior responds and begins to decrease. For a more extensive explanation, consult the section on Extinction in Chapter Seven.
>
> • *Ignoring.* Tantrum behaviors are ignored, but praise and encouragement are accessible only for actions incompatible with the tantrum; for example, cooperative behavior.
>
> • *Time out.* If the tantrum occurs in a situation with other children, the disruptive child is placed in social isolation for a given period of time. Of course, if the social situation is a positive one, the child is eager to return to it. Again, for a more developed review of this procedure, teachers may consider reading the section on Time-out in Chapter Seven.

Aggressive Behavior

Classified as aggressive are such behaviors as: hitting, shoving, biting, scratching, kicking, taking objects from others, and other similar ones. Clarizio and McCoy (1976) suggest that learning to handle personal aggression is an important aspect of being socialized. Because the show of aggression contains a cultural component, families in a heterogeneous society may have individual preferences; often these will be divided along gender, age, or group-membership lines. For example, while it may be acceptable for boys of the same stature to hit each other, such activity will not be appropriate for girls; in some groups, a younger child may hit an older one, but not *vice versa*; within some cultures, punching strangers is not discouraged, but members of one's own family or gang may not be hit.

From the Psychodynamic perspective, aggression is viewed as an instinctual drive manifested by the *Id* portion of the personality. In contrast, Dollard *et al.* (1939) consider aggression to be the outcome of a feeling of frustration when goal-directed behavior is blocked. If Ari wants to play basketball and Tim runs off with the ball, it is likely that Ari will first chase him and then use force to pry the ball from his grip. If Tim persists, Ari may resort to violence.

An alternative explanation proposed by *Social Learning Theory* attributes aggressive behavior to the modeling procedure – the imitation of aggressive ideal models. When the negative activity of aggressive individuals is perceived to be successful in achieving its goals, children are prompted to adopt such behavior in their repertoire. Although the theory accepts the role of feelings of frustration in aggressive behavior, the relationship is thought to be facilitative rather than necessary, which means that aggressive behavior may be present even in the absence of frustration.

In their investigation of physical, verbal, and indirect aggression, Osterman *et al.* (1999) discovered – in the case of boys but not girls – a high correlation between aggression and external locus of control. This suggests that boys who are aggressive are also likely to blame external factors for their behavior – "He made me hit him!" Together with the ability to sympathize and empathize with victims, however, the act of owning one's actions is a major factor in minimizing aggressiveness.

Well into the twenty-first century, parents and educators continue to be concerned about the negative effects on children who view a great deal of violence in television programs. In an analysis of television programs aimed at children, on 23 channels, including specialty cable channels dedicated to children's programming, daily from 6 a.m. to 11 p.m., Wilson, *et al.* (2002) report that viewers under the age of 13 years witness a violent incident every four minutes, in contrast to the level of one incident every 12 minutes, the norm in programming which is not targeting children.

In observing significant factors relating to violence in television programs, several writers have commented (Wilson , *et al.*, 2002; Wilson, Colvin & Stacy, 2002; Smith, Nathanson, & Wilson, 2002). Analyses about music videos include those by Smith & Boyson (2002). Among the findings, some of the following points are instructive:

- Characteristics of the perpetrator:
  - *physical attractiveness.* 40% of perpetrators are attractive characters who will easily serve as role models
  - *age.* Almost half the perpetrators depicted demonstrate violence against characters their own age
  - *gender.* The large majority of perpetrators in television programming are male
  - *ethnicity and race.* Rap and R&B – Rhythm and Blues – music videos are likely to feature black characters, whereas Rock and adult contemporary music involve white characters   *cont'd*

- Characteristics of the situation:

  - *blood and gore.* Only 1% of scenes in children's programs contain this emphasis, while 20% is characteristic in shows that do not target children

  - *violent acts appear justified.* In programs aimed at children, a third of the violent incidents are depicted as justified; for example, when a super hero is defending a victim, the implication seems to be that this is a just use of violence

  - *violent acts are rewarded or not punished.* In 32% of the scenes in programs aimed at children, violent perpetrators receive desirable rewards and/or praise

  - *realism of the portrayal:* Perpetrators often take non-human forms; for example, cartoon animals. For younger children, who do not distinguish fantasy from reality, this discrepancy may be problematic

  - *humor.* Although slapstick incidents are accompanied by deadly violence in 60% of the cases, humor minimizes the consequences. Whereas older children are able to distinguish the incongruencies in the situation, younger children are not

- Types of weapon:

  - *use of guns.* In the television units observed, less gun use appears in children's programs but more use of guns is depicted by teen perpetrators

  - *use of own body as in kicking and punching.* Because the violent depiction uses a weapon (the body) that is readily available to the child

Bandura (1986) has identified four sub-processes implicated in observational learning which are outlined in the context of violence in television programs:

- *Attention.* The observer identifies various salient features of the situation. When watching violent characters in television programs, the young person is aware of features such as the attractiveness, sex, age, ethnicity of the perpetrator, the use of guns, and the realism of the situation. During the viewing, all these elements are attention-getters and therefore encoded

- *Retention.* How much of the observed information is retained? The effect of watching repeated instances of violent television programming increases the probability that such information is integrated in the viewer's knowledge base. Two-thirds of teens depicted were shown engaged in repeated violent acts against the same victim

- *Behavioral Reproduction.* Is the viewer able to translate what is observed into a course of action? The observer can imagine her- or himself performing the witnessed actions and may actually practice them
  cont'd

- *Motivation.* Which observations are more likely to be mimicked? Observed behavior that is rewarded – rather than actions not rewarded but punished – is most likely to be modeled. In violent stories on television, seventy percent of children depicted and fewer than half of teens shown are likely to go unpunished in contrast to what happens to adult characters

From an affective perspective, television is unrealistic because victims are depicted as not likely to suffer the consequences of violence. As a pair of corollary effects, victims appear not to be hurt while perpetrators are not shown to experience regret.

Interventions

Several effective methods of reducing instances of aggressive behavior – not only in the classroom but also in other areas of the school – include:

- outlining non-aggressive behavioral expectations – classroom and school expectations should preclude the use of aggressive actions

- exposing students to non-aggressive models – such models can be found in literature, actions of sports heroes, current events, films and stories, among other places

- observing aggressive behavior that is punished or disapproved of – school policies on violence are implemented swiftly each time an inappropriate event occurs

- ignoring overt negative and aggressive activity while rewarding cooperative or non-aggressive behavior – available energy and attention in the class should flow toward students who are helpful and accommodating

- isolating – temporarily – aggressive students from the social context, through the use of *time out*

- avoiding the use of corporal punishment entirely; practices that rely on repression through physical pain are known to increase rather than decrease aggressive behavior; "fire" should, therefore, "not be fought with fire" when teaching self-control techniques (see Chapter Seven) and strategies for accepting responsibility for one's actions

- restricting television watching to programs that portray the consequence of violence in a consistently effective manner

- discussing the incongruence of violence depicted in television programming in comparison with real-life violence, the intention being to minimize its attractiveness. This approach also requires that the student learn to consider the feelings of the victim, in the form of sympathy, as well as being given the opportunity, through role play or other safe methods, to empathize with the victim

Because the issue of violence in the schools has become such an important one, it can be seen to warrant a coordinated effort among teachers, students, and their parents. An overview of the subject of violence at the school level is outlined in Chapter Eleven.

Lying

The highest incidence of lying is found in children about the age of five years, because they use it as an expedient means to escape punishment. When a large sample of ten to twelve-year-olds were asked the question: "Why do you think a person lies or does not tell the truth?" they provided answers that focused on escape from punishment as the overwhelming reason to lie. In smaller categories, answers also suggested that lying:

> • involves exaggeration or fabrication in order to improve social status and gain acceptance
>
> • may exhibit a feeling of power on the part of the liar
>
> • is a contagious behavior
>
> • can be used for self-defense
>
> • is associated with personal fantasies
>
> • is a means to avoid shame
>
> • is a form of creativity, like writing an imaginary diary
>
> • in *Figure 8-1,* the real-life student responses to the question about the social concept called "lying" indicate the richness of student conceptualization. These replies also demonstrate that because the same behavior may be motivated by a variety of personal causes, such justifications must influence the effectiveness of an intervention

Lying is one of a series of typical transient behaviors that serve a particular purpose; in fact children are more likely to lie when they find themselves in a punitive environment. If the lying persists, possibly personal needs are being served. Another possibility is that lying is an over-learned response. Finally, it is also possible for a person to make a conscious decision to stop lying when the realization comes that it is a childish habit that can be set aside, like nail biting.

Stealing

In normal situations, stealing is observed in children between the ages of three and five years, before they have formulated any concept of "ownership". Later, however, during the teen years, the desire to steal may resurface as a means of testing social expectations, as an experience in "thrill-seeking", or as a component in an "initiation" ritual of a gang or group. Here again, children appear to be including behaviors in their repertoire which they identify as serving a social purpose.

A person lies because they want attention and they want to act like they are cool when they are not.

A person does not tell the truth because they don't want to get in trouble.

They do not tell the truth because they're scared or they might get into trouble. Also if somebody tells a lie and the other person listens to them that person could or might tell a lie also.

Someone might lie to hide something such as if their parents are divorced. Other people might lie in such a way that they use it as a weapon, "My father will come and arrest you, he's a policeman".

Most people lie because they want to be someone else, someone that is better than they are or to fit in a group.

I think a person lies or does not tell the truth because they want attention so more people notice them. Also if they want to get out of trouble they tell a lie to cover up what they did.

They do not tell the truth because they do not want to get in trouble or they do not want to be hurt. Also because they try to act big and get lots of attention. Example "I've got a big house, nine dogs and ninety dollars in my pocket."

I think a person lies because he or she wants attention or they want to be popular and have more friends.

Because they're too embarrassed to admit what they did.

I think they lie because they want to be a show off in front of their friends.

They probably lie to stay out of trouble or to make themselves a different person.

I think someone lies because they might want to defend their friend from getting in trouble. They also might want people to like themselves, for example someone might say that they are rich and that they've traveled all the way around the world when they really haven't. They would do that to be popular. They might also do it to protect themselves from shame and trouble.

Figure 8-1. **Sample of student-responses to the question: "Why do you think a person lies or does not tell the truth?"**

As a way of introducing the idea of stealing and possession, a teacher should give students a chance to explore the concepts in discussion groups where the relevant social values will be aired and debated. Both issues – lying and stealing – can be introduced to students in the context of literature, where analysis of moral dilemmas becomes part of a series of general discussions.

Social Withdrawal

Social Withdrawal represents a class of behaviors observed in individuals who are resistant to interaction with others – this form of reaction may manifest itself as shyness or introversion. Typically, forms of social withdrawal seem to escalate during the adolescent years, becoming of serious concern to researchers who report that as many as 25% of high school students show the unmistakable signs.

While many explanations of *social withdrawal* are offered, a few stand out; for example, some students:

- inherit an introversion/extroversion genetic factor. Both of Lucien's parents are quite reserved, and his teacher describes him as a shy person

- become anxious in social situations as a result of experiences in previous social contexts which have left them with negative internal states; as an instance, children were either made fun of or bullied in front of others. Melina, who is not athletic, regularly skips her Grade 11 Physical Education class as a means to avoid being ridiculed by her classmates

- fail to acquire appropriate social skills; that is, children are unaware of or uncertain of the social response appropriate to a particular setting; While Chinua is not confident about making new friends in the class because he is a new immigrant to Canada, Marcello has not acquired the necessary social skills because he has had few opportunities to be with children of his age

- are both anxious as a general rule and lacking in social skills; because Isador has always felt anxious when outside the house, he declines all opportunities to interact with his peers

- perceive themselves as having body images which are atypical and therefore wish to escape the ridicule of others; in this form of withdrawal, many contributing factors are associated with the development of anxiety: disproportion of physical development, acne, skinny legs, and other details that could cause jocularity. Because Marek is always at least a foot taller than his peers and his teachers, he has become sensitive to the ridicule of his peers. Over the years, he has tried to make himself invisible

- experience a period of social isolation that undermines their confidence; this may be the case, for example, when children are hospitalized, are placed in segregated classrooms, are separated from their families/siblings, or in some other way are displaced

Interventions

When students are socially withdrawn, they can often be encouraged to become more outgoing if the teacher uses some of these approaches:

- Modeling. By inviting students to observe and examine the social behavior of others, teachers or mentors are able to help them acquire social skills in an indirect way. Attention should be given to prominent people who share the undesired characteristic that causes the student to suffer. In Marek's case, he can learn to realize that the majority of basketball stars are extremely tall. Teaching the student to "make lemonade" is helpful in minimizing distress.

- Encouragement. Although not actually manipulating opportunities to establish social contact, the teacher can reinforce all spontaneous occurrences as they emerge in the classroom.

- Direct instruction of social skills. By creating learning opportunities that incorporate role playing, stories, discussions, and forms of acting, the teacher establishes a social-skills curriculum readily integrated with other classroom curricula. In such an environment, an effective procedure is to choose a social situation – maintaining a conversation during lunch, for example, – and then to identify appropriate conversation topics. From agreed-upon scenarios, students may develop roles and generate scripts to be memorized, rehearsed, and performed.

- Acceptance of individual differences. By recognizing that people are different from one another, the student is encouraged to embrace uniqueness, all the while observing, acquiring, and, finally, possessing the social skills necessary to actualize personal goals.

Sleep disturbances

Problems with sleeping are frequently encountered in families with children, especially when younger siblings become aware that they may be "missing something" if separate family members – the older ones – retire at different times. Another sleep inhibitor sometimes emerges because preschool children are prone to developmental fears: a reluctance to go to sleep sometimes turns to fear when strange and unfamiliar noises are heard; part of the problem may be a simple fear of the dark, a state easily remedied with a night light.

Of course, children awaken during the night for a variety of reasons – nightmare, illness, unusual location, and other causes, but a pattern of awakening is easily established as a generalized response readily aggravated when additionally reinforced by parental attention. After insuring that the child is comfortable, parents might utilize one of two divergent patterns, the first ignoring and the second reinforcing elements in the range of bedtime behavior. Children's reaction to each of these approaches may indicate the next move.

Many children, – both boys and girls, between the ages of three and ten – complain of having disturbing dreams, but, around age ten, the frequency of these dreams peaks and then decreases. Usually stress-related, nightmares become a problem if their frequency escalates, but more frightening to parents are *night terrors*. These phenomena comprise recurring episodes of sudden awakening, initiated by a scream; following the opening cry is a stage of intense agitation of the "fight-or-flight"[4] variety. Although, the following morning, the child often does not remember these traumatic events, each of the episodes, when it happens, may last as long as ten minutes. While this condition is more common in males, it seems to occur either when the young person is tired, perhaps stressed, or in response to a certain medication, an antidepressant, for example.

Although parents are certainly troubled by a range of sleep disturbances in their children, more importantly, such problems have an impact on classroom behavior. If the student's pattern of learning and deportment in the classroom is affected, apparently by a lack of sleep, the teacher should inform parents. In such a case, the school will perhaps recommend seeking the advice of a professional – a physician specializing in sleep disorders will be most helpful.

Self-Stimulatory Behaviors

Self-stimulatory behaviors represent a class of intrinsically rewarding responses whose performance alone serves to reinforce them because they not only soothe the individual but they often also reduce stress. These actions include such common behaviors as nail biting and thumb sucking as well as less socially acceptable responses: masturbating, hair pulling, nose picking, sore scratching, biting, sucking, and chewing sections of clothing or other objects. The list will be extended if students are asked for suggestions.

While common in infancy, thumb sucking usually declines with age, in sharp contrast to nail biting which increases during the pre-adolescent and teenage years. The Psychodynamic paradigm views both thumb-sucking and nail-biting as demonstrating underlying conflict, usually associating them with Freud's psycho-sexual *oral* stage. In contrast, the behavioral paradigm defines all self-stimulatory behaviors as intrinsically self-reinforcing, considering that they are, perhaps, modeled behavior.

Interventions

Depending on the individual and the specific nature of the problem, certain strategies are quite effective:

- *Punishment.* Whenever possible, making the activity a punitive rather than a reinforcing event is an adequate deterrent. For example, applying a commercially available bitter-tasting substance to the thumb or the finger tips nullifies the stress-reducing power of the activity; eventually, the behavior declines and disappears. Not all self-stimulatory behaviors lend themselves, however, to such an approach.

- *Contingencies.* When a sample group of five-year-olds had to choose between thumb-sucking and watching cartoons, thumb-sucking was eliminated. In the procedure employed, a child watched favorite cartoon characters in the presence of an adult. Each time the child's thumb was observed entering the mouth, a watchful adult automatically touched the remote control to end the cartoon. Only when the thumb was withdrawn, did the cartoon resume.

- *Cooperative Pact.* When two or more children are thumb suckers or nail biters, they can decide among themselves to stop for whatever reasons seem appropriate: it is babyish, there will be a reward, or perhaps they've been promised a trip to the zoo. Their mutual reinforcement of the pact makes possible its success; no adult intervention is needed.

- *Self-monitoring procedures.* When ten-year-olds were trained to identify and record the incidence of an inappropriate behavior, the attention given to what was, for each individual, a somewhat automatic action was sufficient to reduce its frequency.

- *Changing the context.* Interestingly, the level of social appropriateness can be modified by insisting that self-stimulatory behaviors occur only in private settings; for example, a twelve-year-old, with a thumb-sucking habit, who risks being ostracized by peers, therefore limits the behavior to home or another private setting.

- *Intrusive procedures.* In thumb-sucking incidents, sometimes an instrument called a palatal-crib is worn as a deterrent. Made of wire and covering the roof of the mouth, this device not only serves to eliminate the stimulation from the suction, but has been found 100% effective. Because this is an expensive and drastic procedure, the use of the palatal crib should be reserved for only the most serious of cases.

Childhood Fears

Typically, children of different ages exhibit fears associated with particular situations. For example, it is not uncommon for very young infants to fear loud noises or to be frightened of falling. By six to nine months, these same babies have grown fearful of strangers. A little older, school-age children too can be apprehensive of things they encounter at kindergarten or elsewhere: injury, natural events, and social situations. Connected with such elemental problems, gender differences are closely tied to maturational distinctions evident in the varying development of boys and girls. Although girls more commonly report fears that continue to be present in older children, predictable social or cultural reasons may figure prominently in this outcome. When three-year old Sherry and Matthew began to cry, frightened by the large dog coming towards them, Mrs. Dogherty comforted the pair. In a similar situation, nine-year old Marcelle and Peter were treated differently. While Marcelle was reassured, Peter was told to "grow up." While such upsets may be socially accepted in girls, they are often punished severely in boys. General agreement determines, however, that many fears are often related to learning experiences; as a corollary, developmental fears disappear as quickly as they originally surfaced when children reach new milestones.

In a limited range of situations, fears persist and worsen, especially if children acquire them as a consequence of particularly upsetting or traumatic events (see the section on Anxiety and Anxiety Disorders). Orlando has become so fearful of cars, noise, dogs, and strangers, that most of his attention is directed towards ways to avoid going to school or leaving the house. When such crippling effects on development are apparent, professional attention is necessary.

Anxiety

While the existence of high levels of anxiety in a student will interfere with performance, this circumstance is usually limited either to new situations and experiences or to the fear of being evaluated. Therefore, it can be anticipated that all children and adolescents will at times experience elevated levels of anxiety, as measured by ranges of arousal, some which will motivate, others which will cripple performance (see Figure 8-2).

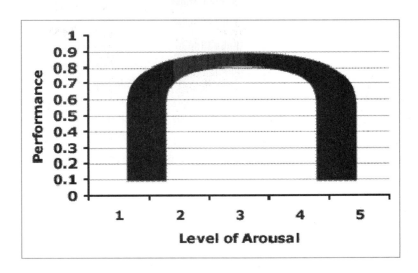

Figure 8-2. The relationship between levels of arousal and performance.

What is anxiety? Whereas the Psychodynamic paradigm identifies anxiety as the consequence of feuding components in the personality, other, more compelling, explanations are of greater interest:

- from a physiological perspective, because individual differences exist between people, some who are more prone to anxiety than others are therefore more vulnerable

- from a behavioral point of view, a person's accidental pairing of a life event with anxious feelings, the result of classical conditioning, can initiate anxiety responses when that person again encounters an echo of the original event or a similar element

- from an environmental standpoint, when parents and teachers push children prematurely into situations that demand greater levels of coping skill than are available, an anxiety response is inevitable

Traditionally, feelings of anxiety are closely associated with responses leading to avoidance and fleeing. In a school, as the anxiety rises past a particular threshold, the student looks for ways to escape the environment that produces such feelings. Without teacher or other intervention, the situation worsens as the threshold level alters, while the anxiety becomes less tolerable.

In contrast, Anxiety Disorders consist of various conditions identified in the DSM-IV-TR Manual. The National Institute of Mental Health in the United States considers anxiety disorders to be the most common of all mental health conditions, afflicting some 19 million adults (13%). Manassis (2000) indicates that research studies pinpoint the incidence of anxiety disorders in children in the range of

10 to 20% – with a slightly higher proportion of girls after puberty – and an expectation that anxious children are likely to develop further disorders. In the section below, a series of conditions will be outlined: General Anxiety Disorder (GAD), Obsessive Compulsive Disorder (OCD), Panic Disorder, Post-traumatic Stress Disorder, Separation Anxiety, and Social Phobia.

Although diagnosed by psychologists and psychiatrists, these conditions are included here in order to provide a more detailed examination of them. This is because the teacher has an important role to play – being vigilant of the warning signs; sharing observations; encouraging parents to seek professional help; and creating a positive learning -environment which will consider and minimize the student's discomfort.

Generalized Anxiety Disorder (GAD)

Previously called Overanxious Disorder, this condition means that students with GAD not only satisfy the criteria outlined below, (see Table 8-2) but usually require a great amount of reassurance from the people around them. When children experience GAD, they worry excessively about most things – school performance, personal safety, the safety of family, natural disasters, and any upcoming event such as a school concert, a family vacation, or any forthcoming activity. When compared with the anxiety of other children, not only is the intensity and frequency of worrying greater but there is also an inability to control or block it. As a result, much like students with OCD, these young people are consumed by worry to the point that their attention to classroom work will suffer. Further exacerbating the problem is the perfectionism often observed in these students. In general, children with GAD are also likely to experience separation anxiety in addition to depression during the adolescent years.

Wagner (2000) presents an interesting case study of a 6-year old boy who worries about everything. Moreover, the child's school functioning is affected not only by actions to circumvent anxiety but also by fatigue, a consequence of fretting instead of sleeping at night.

Table 8-2. **DSM-IV-TR Diagnostic Criteria of Generalized Anxiety Disorder.**

A. Excessive anxiety and worry (apprehensive expectation), occurring more days than not for at least six months, about a number of events or activities (such as work or school performance)

B. The person finds it difficult to control the worry

C. The anxiety and worry are associated with three (or more) of the following six symptoms (with at least some symptoms present for more days than not for the past six months)

    Note: Only one item is required in children:

    1. restlessness or feeling keyed up or on edge, fatigue, easily induced difficulty concentrating, or mind going blank

    2. irritability

    3. muscle tension

    4. sleep disturbance (difficulty falling or staying asleep and/ or restless unsatisfying sleep)

D. The focus of the anxiety and worry is not confined to features of an Axis I disorder, e.g., the anxiety or worry is not about having a Panic Attack (as in Panic Disorder), being embarrassed in public (as in Social Phobia), being contaminated (as in Obsessive-Compulsive Disorder), being away from home or close relatives (as in Separation Anxiety Disorder), gaining weight (as in Anorexia Nervosa), having multiple physical complaints (as in Somatization Disorder), or having a serious illness (as in Hypochondriasis), and the anxiety and worry do not occur exclusively during Post-traumatic Stress Disorder

E. The anxiety, worry, or physical symptoms cause clinically significant distress or impairment in social, occupational, or other important areas of functioning

F. The disturbance is not due to the direct physiological effects of a substance (e.g., a drug of abuse, a medication) or a general medical condition (e.g., hyperthyroidism) and does not occur exclusively during a Mood Disorder, a Psychotic Disorder, or a Pervasive Developmental Disorder

Reprinted with permission from the Diagnostic and Statistical Manual of Mental Disorders, Fourth Edition, Text Revision, Washington, DC, American Psychiatric Association, 2000.

How can the classroom teacher support students with anxiety disorders? In the classroom, the observable compelling behavior focuses on a series of avoidance and escape maneuvers. Usually, these are the central focus of the student experiencing a high distress level. In determining ways to respond to such phenomena, an individual plan for the student should consider the following:

- *Identifying the level of distress associated with various classroom activities.* By making a list of various activities that are common to each day, the teacher can encourage the student to rate each on the basis of the associated emotions. A rating of 1 is assigned to activities during which the student feels very comfortable while a rating of 10 will reflect those that provoke great distress. Such an exercise will provide valuable information that can be taken into account by the teacher as well as helping the student to place on a continuum the activities that are more and less stressful

- *Teaching techniques associated with the relaxation response.* Is the student able to practice self-calming techniques when anxiety levels rise? Relaxation training sessions, in addition to Yoga and Meditation activities, are usually available in local hospitals as well as in mental health and community facilities. Parents should be encouraged to enroll the student in such a program after consulting their child's psychologist or psychiatrist[5]

- *Allowing the student to signal when the situation becomes unbearable.* Variables existing in certain classroom situations have negative effects on the anxiety level of the student. Such distress can be minimized quickly if a signal known only to the student and the teacher is exchanged, instantly establishing a plan to allow the student to leave the class for a short period of time

- *Putting an action plan in place, especially for situations in which the student has signaled a distress.* The plan must not only provide the student relief from anxiety but must also work to reduce the number of times the distress signal is used. For example, the teacher will ask the student to take an envelope to the office with the understanding that the student will seek out the school counselor and will return after a consultation. Teacher and student must collect data that will serve to modify a plan which does not simply enhance the anxious element in the situation

Treatment of GAD

In the treatment of GAD, the types of intervention most recommended include: relaxation training (see section on Systematic Desensitization, p.p. 318-320), cognitive therapy (see section on Cognitive Behavior Therapy, p. 307), regular exercise, avoidance of caffeine and alcohol, and a variety of prescribed medications. Sleep disturbances, outlined in a previous section of this chapter (p.p. 8-14), may also accompany symptoms of GAD.

Obsessive Compulsive Disorder (OCD)

Whereas obsessions involve recurrent and persistent ideas, usually intrusive in a person's thought processes, compulsions are repetitive and purposive behaviors. For example, if persistent thoughts of the house burning down prevent a student from completing a classroom task, such thoughts are labeled obsessions. In contrast, compulsions would refer to a student's uncontrollable desire to pull the hair of the student sitting in the desk just ahead. Interestingly, not only do both obsessions and compulsions worsen with stress, in only approximately 10% of the cases are the two transient in nature.

While it is true that some individuals with head injuries are known to have acquired OCD, such cases are rare, while a more probable explanation is that OCD has a genetic origin. Found in children as young as two years of age, with most reaching the age of seven before their cases are actually diagnosed, a strong overlap between Tourette's and OCD is present – the individual with OCD may acquire Tourette's and *vice versa*. In fact, OCD is often present with other psychiatric disorders.

Teens who are diagnosed with OCD (see Table 8-3) find the condition particularly difficult because the symptoms are embarrassing. While hoping to fit in with their peer group, they may try to hide their conditions and feel guilty about doing so. The feelings that a teen may experience when obsessions and compulsions present themselves are disturbing to them – particularly the feeling of powerlessness when these cannot be controlled.

When a student with OCD is part of a group, classroom interventions should be similar to those described for Tourette's – the other students should have access to pertinent information in order to develop empathy for the student. A book particularly recommended for this purpose is Judith Rapaport's (1989) book, *The Boy Who Couldn't Stop Washing,* and the video recording written by Medley and Russel (1996): *Twitch and Shout: a Documentary about Tourette's Syndrome.* Regarding both conditions, it is important to recognize that obsessions, compulsions, and various twitches occur with little control of the student – no person can control or be responsible for such behavior.

Treatment of OCD

Cognitive-Behavior Therapy (CBT), described in the next subsection, is a commonly used intervention for OCD. Another helpful strategy involves symptom substitution, a procedure that trains the student to switch to another ritual, one that is either less self-injurious or more socially appropriate.

Because the functioning of the seratonin system is implicated in OCD, treatment often includes medication. At the outset, medication is prescribed for a six-month period, after which dosages may be decreased. In medication programs of such long duration, physicians may prefer to initiate treatment during the summer months.

Table 8-3. DSM-IV-TR Diagnostic Criteria of Obsessive-Compulsive Disorder

A. Either obsessions or compulsions:

Obsessions as defined by (1), (2), (3), and (4):

    1. recurrent and persistent thoughts, impulses, or images that are experienced, at some time during the disturbance, as intrusive and inappropriate and that cause marked anxiety or distress

    2. the thoughts, impulses, or images are not simply excessive worries about real-life problems

    3. the person attempts to ignore or suppress such thoughts, impulses, or images, or to neutralize them with some other thought or action

    4. the person recognizes that the obsessional thoughts, impulses, or images are a product of his or her own mind (not imposed from without as in thought insertion)

Compulsions as defined by (1) and (2):

    5. repetitive behaviors (e.g., hand washing, ordering, checking) or mental acts (e.g., praying, counting, repeating words silently) that the person feels driven to perform in response to an obsession or according to rules that must be applied rigidly

    6. the behaviors or mental acts are aimed at preventing or reducing distress or preventing some dreaded event or situation; however, these behaviors or mental acts either are not connected in a realistic way with what they are designed to neutralize or prevent or are clearly excessive

B. At some point during the course of the disorder, the person has recognized that the obsessions or compulsions are excessive or unreasonable.
Note: This does not apply to children

C. The obsessions or compulsions cause marked distress, are time-consuming (take more than 1 hour a day), or significantly interfere with the person's normal routine, occupational (or academic) functioning, or usual social activities or relationships

D. If another Axis I disorder is present, the content of the obsessions or compulsions is not restricted to it (e.g., preoccupation with food in the presence of an Eating Disorder; hair pulling in the presence of Trichotillomania; concern with appearance in the presence of Body Dysmorphic Disorder; preoccupation with drugs in the presence of a Substance Use Disorder; preoccupation with having a serious illness in the presence of Hypochondriasis; preoccupation with sexual urges or fantasies in the presence of a Paraphilia; or guilty ruminations in the presence of Major Depressive Disorder)

E. The disturbance is not due to the direct physiological effects of a substance (e.g., a drug of abuse, a medication) or a general medical condition

Reprinted with permission from the Diagnostic and Statistical Manual of Mental Disorders, Fourth Edition, Text Revision, Washington, DC, American Psychiatric Association, 2000.

Cognitive Behavior Therapy (CBT)

Cognitive behavior therapy utilizes concepts and ideas associated with both the cognitive and behavioral models. From the cognitive standpoint, thinking patterns associated with symptoms are examined in terms of three criteria: how well they reflect the circumstance; how they relate to feelings of anxiety, depression, and anger; as well as how they provoke maladaptive behavior. The behavior therapy component focuses on the mind-and-body connection established by classical conditioning, with the intention of weakening past associations. This is achieved through a process of "Exposure" – which involves placing the person in contact with the feared stimulus – and "Response Prevention", a process preventing the person from engaging in ritualistic behavior. Relaxation responses are taught as a means of establishing control between internal states and actions.

Unlike other types of psychotherapy, CBT requires that both the therapist and the individual be actively involved in solving personal problems. This aspect makes the intervention similar to the educational context in which the teacher acts as a tutor or a coach. Likewise, by modifying ways of thinking as well as teaching the necessary skills to control physiological responses, the instructor is able to design a structured plan to effect behavioral change.

Usually selected as the primary intervention, CBT is sometimes used in conjunction with medication in cases with severe symptoms. Although extensive research demonstrates its effectiveness in the treatment of both anxiety and depression, CBT is also the preferred treatment for shyness, headaches, panic attacks, phobias, post-traumatic stress, eating disorders, loneliness, and procrastination.

Panic Disorder

What is a panic attack? The criteria included in the DSM IV-TR description of Panic Disorder Without Agoraphobia are presented in Table 8-4. The intense fear associated with these attacks causes the individual to become even more fearful as anticipatory anxiety builds. The ideation associated with the loss of control, the physical consequences – it may feel as if the person is having a heart attack – and the feeling of going crazy cause the individual further concern.

Although anxiety symptoms are first noticed in childhood, panic disorders, which run in families, are likely to express themselves fully during the adolescent years. Separately from panic attacks, both children and teens may feel anxious most of the time. In the case of children, such a form of anxiety may present itself as school phobia or separation anxiety. In many cases, teens either may avoid situations that have previously led to panic attacks or may have such expectancies that leave them homebound. In many of these situations, the isolation created by the anxiety may lead to depression and suicidal behavior. Attempts on the part of the sufferers to relieve their anguishing symptoms may lead them to alcohol and/or drug abuse.

Table 8-4. **DSM-IV-TR Diagnostic Criteria of Panic Disorder Without Agoraphobia**

A. Recurrent unexpected Panic Attacks

   Criteria for Panic Attack: A discrete period of intense fear or discomfort, in which four (or more) of the following symptoms may develop abruptly and may reach a peak within 10 minutes:

   1. palpitations, pounding heart, or accelerated heart rate

   2. sweating

   3. trembling or shaking

   4. sensations of shortness of breath or smothering

   5. feeling of choking

   6. chest pain or discomfort

   7. nausea or abdominal distress

   8. feeling dizzy, unsteady, lightheaded, or faint

   9. de-realization (feelings of unreality) or depersonalization (being detached from oneself)

   10. fear of losing control or going crazy

   11. fear of dying

   12. paresthesias (numbness or tingling sensations)

   13. chills or hot flushes

B. Absence of Agoraphobia

C. The Panic Attacks are not due to the direct physiological effects of a substance (e.g., a drug of abuse, a medication) or a general medical condition (e.g., hyperthyroidism)

D. The Panic Attacks are not better accounted for by another mental disorder, such as Social Phobia (e.g., occurring on exposure to feared social situations), Specific Phobia (e.g., happening on exposure to a specific phobic situation), Obsessive-Compulsive Disorder (e.g., beginning because of exposure to dirt, in someone with an obsession about contamination), Post-traumatic Stress Disorder (e.g., responding to stimuli associated with a severe stressor), or Separation Anxiety Disorder (e.g., reacting to being away from home or close relatives)

Reprinted with permission from the Diagnostic and Statistical Manual of Mental Disorders, Fourth Edition, Text Revision, Washington, DC, American Psychiatric Association, 2000.

Treatment of Panic Disorder

For this disorder, early intervention is necessary in order to avert the additional complications of depression, phobias, and substance abuse. Depending on the severity of symptoms, a combination of medication and psychotherapy is usually recommended. Cognitive-Behavior Therapy – with a focus on controlling both anxiety and panic attacks – is the therapy of choice.

For the student with a panic disorder, the classroom interventions outlined for GAD would also be appropriate.

Post-traumatic Stress Disorder (PTSD)

As a result of being exposed to traumatic events, the person may respond to new situations with intense fear and other symptoms of distress (see Table 8-5). Very probably, a student is likely to experience a traumatic event in a variety of ways. First, for example, students can be victims of violence in their communities or in their homes. In addition, students who are recent immigrants may have experienced and/or witnessed many types of horror in their countries of origin and, as a result of the violence of a civil war or a totalitarian government, the family has been prompted to leave. To ensure that the appropriate professional sees the student, the teacher is instrumental in supporting the family and in securing the help of people in the family's ethnic community.

Gender differences in PTSD include a higher incidence of occurrence in women whose symptoms are likely to persist throughout their lives. Whereas rape and physical assault trigger PTSD in women, parallel symptoms in men are likely to arise from being victimized in physical assault or from witnessing the serious maiming or killing of someone. This disorder also affects individuals with a history of depression, children, and teens with conduct disorders, (see Chapter 9) and substance abusers of cocaine and cannabis.

Lipschitz *et al.* (2000) studied adolescent girls in the inner-city, 24% of whom developed partial or full PTSD as a result of witnessing both community and family violence. Although depression and substance abuse resulted in some victims, others became aggressive, in an attempt to exercise control over their lives, with the outcome that their actions were penalized with school suspension and arrests.

School violence

Almost always, common reports of school violence in the media affect not only those students who are the recipients and the ones who witness it first-hand but also those parents, teachers, and students who subsequently develop the belief that schools are no longer safe and that, very soon, such an incident will be repeated in their local schools. When the act is committed in the school, every individual is affected in some manner. The ones chiefly at risk are those most closely involved in the event – people who are injured, those who observe the injury or death, and persons who witness any of the violence. Individuals who are friends with either the victims or the perpetrators, – or even of both – and any other person in the school – student, parent, or teacher – is also impacted.

As the grim event is broadcast many times by the media, people who are involved, as well as students who are either prone to anxiety or who have previously experienced violence, are forced many times to relive the incident.

Table 8-5. DSM-IV-TR Diagnostic Criteria of Post-traumatic Stress Disorder

A. The person has been exposed to a traumatic event in which both of the following were present:

 1. the person experienced, witnessed, or was confronted with an event or events that involved actual or threatened death or serious injury or a threat to the physical integrity of self or others

 2. the person's response involved intense fear, helplessness, or horror. Note: In children, this may be expressed instead by disorganized or agitated behavior

B. The traumatic event is persistently re-experienced in one (or more) of the following ways:

 1. recurrent and intrusive distressing recollections of the event, including images, thoughts, or perceptions
 Note: In young children, repetitive play may occur in which themes or aspects of the trauma are expressed

 2. recurrent distressing dreams of the event
 Note: In children, there may be frightening dreams without recognizable content

 3. acting or feeling as if the traumatic event were recurring (involves a sense of reliving the experience, illusions, hallucinations, and dissociative flashback episodes, including those that occur on awakening or when intoxicated)
 Note: In young children, trauma-specific re-enactment may occur

 4. intense psychological distress at exposure to internal or external cues that symbolize or resemble an aspect of the traumatic event; or physiological reactivity on exposure to internal or external cues that symbolize or resemble an aspect of the traumatic event   *cont'd*

C. Persistent avoidance of stimuli associated with the trauma and numbing of general responsiveness (not present before the trauma), as indicated by three (or more) of the following:

1. efforts to avoid thoughts, feelings, or conversations associated with the trauma

2. efforts to avoid activities, places, or people that arouse recollections of the trauma

3. inability to recall an important aspect of the trauma

4. markedly diminished interest or participation in significant activities

5. feeling of detachment or estrangement from others

6. restricted range of affect (e.g., unable to have loving feelings)

7. sense of a foreshortened future (e.g., the individual does not expect to have a career, marriage, children, or a normal life span)

D. Persistent symptoms of increased arousal (not present before the trauma), as indicated by two (or more) of the following:

1. difficulty falling or staying asleep

2. irritability or outbursts of anger

3. difficulty concentrating

4. hyper-vigilance

5. exaggerated startle response

E. Duration of the disturbance (symptoms in Criteria B, C, and D) is more than one month

F. The disturbance causes clinically significant distress or impairment in social, occupational, or any other important area of functioning

Specify if:

- **Acute:** if duration of symptoms is less than three months

- **Chronic:** if duration of symptoms is three months or more

Specify if:

- **With Delayed Onset**: if onset of symptoms is at least six months after the stressor

Reprinted with permission from the Diagnostic and Statistical Manual of Mental Disorders, Fourth Edition, Text Revision, Washington, DC, American Psychiatric Association, 2000.

Treatment of PTSD

When medication is prescribed to minimize symptoms of PTSD, as it often is, the psychotherapies considered to be effective include Exposure Therapy – part of Cognitive-Behavior Therapy – and, more recently, Eye-Movement Desensitizing and Reprocessing (EMDR) Therapy, described below.

Eye-Movement Desensitization and Reprocessing (EMDR)

EMDR is an intervention, introduced by Francine Shapiro in 1989, specifically for the treatment of PTSD. Based on information-processing theory, the model recognizes that associations in memory are made among sensations, feelings, images, and thoughts. In turn, connections between earlier and later memories are also expected. When a person experiences a traumatic event, the memory network created by the event contains distorted thoughts and perceptions which, in turn, produce the symptoms of PTSD because these events intrude on everyday experience.

Unique to EMDR is the notion that the vividness and the salience of memories can be reduced with the use of dual-attention stimuli, in particular eye movements. By reducing the intensity of disturbing memories, Shapiro (2002) anticipates that clients will be more likely to confront them and work through them.

In the classroom described here, it becomes evident that re-directing attention can reduce the distress associated with a topic. In a class of high school students with severe behavioral problems, the teacher and childcare worker schedule a class meeting each Friday afternoon. Attempting to encourage the students to take a more active part in management of the classroom, the teacher and worker explained that the purpose of the meeting was to discuss aspects of the daily round that should be improved, discarded, or retained. At the outset, the leaders had an expectation that students would become responsible for their actions when they were given the power to fashion the environment. In order to reduce apprehension, students were forewarned that strict guidelines would be imposed both to prohibit personal attacks and to avert scape-goating. Nevertheless, class meetings were less than successful. Students developed elaborate strategies to insure that such meetings would not take place; for example, they violated rules that called for time-out consequences, they skipped class, etc. After several weeks, it became obvious that students were against the idea of the class meetings. When considering the reasons that might explain the failure of this undertaking, the teacher and worker replaced the weekly classroom meetings with Friday periods of Arts and Crafts. In the process of fashioning leather wallets, students freely discussed ways to improve the classroom environment, much to the surprise of the teacher and the worker. By focusing their attention on arts and crafts, the students demonstrated that such an environment more readily encouraged a discussion of classroom issues.

Although a similar notion is found in EMDR therapy, its process is accomplished in eight phases, each with a specific objective:

1. *Identifying the targets.* By taking a full history, the therapist evaluates the required changes necessary to make the individual adaptive. Targets such as affect management (regulation of emotions), disturbing memories, historical incidents that pertain to the problem, present situations that the client finds difficult to handle, as well as efficacy and outcome expectations required for future positive actions: all of these are incorporated in a plan.

2. *Preparation for therapy.* Because traumatic memories are so painful, techniques to equip the client for treatment are introduced. First, the client-therapist relationship[6] is established. Then, self-calming interventions, including "safe place" visualizations, are taught and practiced.

3. *Processing the traumatic event.* A baseline of the sensory (visual images), affective (feelings and emotions), and cognitive (irrational beliefs) components is established. The client is asked to rate and label the feelings that occur when the visual images and the negative beliefs are presented together and then to identify and locate body sensations that are elicited.

4. *Introduction of eye movements to reduce intensity of traumatic experience.* The client is asked to focus on three targets: images, beliefs, and body sensations, while moving eyes from side to side for 15 or more seconds. Because the process is intended to reduce the intensity of the targets, client feedback about them is sought after each eye-movement episode; the exercise may be repeated many times. In this pattern, the therapist is guided by standardized procedures.

5. *Promotion of cognitive insights.* This phase begins only when the individual is capable of accessing the disturbing memories without experiencing emotional distress. Usually, at this point, creating an association between memories and positive internal states encourages self-acceptance and a positive attitude.

6. *Reducing tension and negative body sensations.* The focus of this stage is to eradicate tension associated both with the images and with the thoughts to complete the EMDR process. Generally, this aspect of the treatment is accomplished by using the various techniques that promote relaxation.

7. *Processing of memories.* To ensure that memories have been reprocessed, each client is asked to maintain a journal outside the sessions, to insure that new learning is transferred to everyday situations. It is very probable that the client will experience a sense of accomplishment when this objective is met.

8. *Re-evaluation client success.* Although clients are encouraged to evaluate success at the onset of every stage, at this point, they reflect on the entire process, noting all the milestones along the way. During this period, therapists may test the old triggers and attempt to assess the level of change or improvement by administering post-tests of measures initially collected.

Although an attempt has been made to dismiss EMDR – by unduly focusing on the eye-movement aspect – an evaluation of its eight phases demonstrates the richness of the intervention. In Shapiro (2002), a practical and positive description involves a case study of Lynne, a woman severely affected by earthquakes. Mounting empirical evidence collected on both civilians and combat veterans supports the effectiveness of EMDR in treating individuals suffering from PTSD.

Separation Anxiety

In the past, it was commonly noted that young students starting school were reluctant to leave caregivers with whom they had spent most of their early childhood. In contrast, today, most urban children are almost blasé about attending kindergarten or junior kindergarten, seasoned nursery-school pupils that they are. Nonetheless, when it occurs, separation anxiety represents a condition involving more than slight distress for the young person taken from a caregiver. The DSM-IV manual identifies the following diagnostic criteria:

Table 8-6. **DSM-IV Diagnostic Criteria of Separation Anxiety Disorder**

A. Developmentally inappropriate and excessive anxiety concerning separation from home or from those to whom the individual is attached, as evidenced by three (or more) of the following:

1 recurrent excessive distress when separation from home or major attachment figures occurs or is anticipated

2 persistent and excessive worry about losing, or about possible harm befalling, major attachment figures

3 persistent and excessive worry that an untoward event will lead to separation from a major attachment figure (e.g., getting lost or being kidnapped)

4 persistent reluctance or refusal to go to school or elsewhere because of fear of separation

5 persistent or excessive fearfulness or reluctance to be alone or without major attachment figures at home or without significant adults in other settings

6 persistent reluctance or refusal to go to sleep without being near a major attachment figure or to sleep away from home

7 repeated nightmares involving the theme of separation

8 repeated complaints of physical symptoms (such as headaches, stomach aches, nausea, or vomiting) when separation from major attachment figures is anticipated   *cont'd*

B. The duration of the disturbance is at least 4 weeks

C. The onset is before age 18 years

D. The disturbance causes clinically significant distress or impairment in social, academic (occupational), or other important areas of functioning

E. The disturbance does not occur exclusively during the course of a Pervasive Developmental Disorder, Schizophrenia, or other Psychotic Disorder and, in adolescents and adults, is not better accounted for by Panic Disorder with Agoraphobia.

Specify if:

Early Onset: if onset occurs before age 6 years

Reprinted with permission from the Diagnostic and Statistical Manual of Mental Disorders, Fourth Edition, Text Revision, Washington, DC, American Psychiatric Association, 2000.

When Alafair first attended her Junior Kindergarten class, she seemed excited: after all, her parents had worked very hard in preparing her for the experience. On that very first day, although reluctant to allow her mother to leave, a despondent Alafair eventually settled in a corner of the classroom. Ms. Fairfax, her teacher, was so touched by the little girl's sadness that she decided to intervene. First, the teacher gave permission for Alafair to bring to school some family photos, which she could consult at her discretion. In addition, an arrangement was made with her parents: contingent on her class participation, Alafair was allowed to telephone her mother at work. Initially, the calls were made on an hourly basis, then every second hour; soon it was twice a day and gradually they diminished to none. Very important in this intervention was the agreement by the parents to pick up Alafair daily at the designated time.

Parents can play an important role in encouraging the adaptiveness of a reticent child by recognizing the value of the company of other children and adults, away from the watchful eye of parents. Such opportunities prepare the child for the first day at school.

Some clinicians regard Separation Anxiety as the expression of GAD in younger children. When parents and teachers are insensitive to the feelings of students with the disorder, their attitude may further exacerbate the consequences of anxiety. Such a syndrome, during the teen years may manifest itself as depression.

Social Phobia

Social anxiety can be a crippling condition with high risks of depression. At the same time, individuals who are born anxious often fear not being socially accepted, and have negative expectations of social situations (see Bandura's self-efficacy model in Chapter Two, pp. 40-41).

Table 8-7. DSM-IV-TR Diagnostic Criteria of Social Phobia

A. A marked and persistent fear of one or more social or performance situations in which the person is exposed to unfamiliar people or to possible scrutiny by others. The individual fears that he or she will act in a way (or show anxiety symptoms) that will be humiliating or embarrassing.

Note: In children, there must be evidence of the capacity for age-appropriate social relationships with familiar people and the anxiety must occur in peer settings, not just in interactions with adults.

B. Exposure to the feared social situation almost invariably provokes anxiety, which may take the form of a situationally bound or situationally predisposed Panic Attack.

Note: In children, the anxiety may be expressed by crying, tantrums, freezing, or shrinking from social situations with unfamiliar people.

C. The person recognizes that the fear is excessive or unreasonable.

Note: In children, this feature may be absent.

D. The feared social or performance situations are avoided or else are endured with intense anxiety or distress.

E. The avoidance, anxious anticipation, or distress in the feared social or performance situation(s) interferes significantly with the person's normal routine, occupational (academic) functioning, or social activities and relationships, or there is marked distress about having the phobia.

F. In individuals under 18 years, the duration is at least six months.

G. The fear or avoidance is not due to the direct physiological effects of a substance (e.g., a drug of abuse, a medication) or a general medical condition and is not better accounted for by another mental disorder (e.g., Panic Disorder with or without Agoraphobia, Separation Anxiety Disorder, Body Dysmorphic Disorder, Pervasive Developmental Disorder, or Schizoid Personality Disorder).

H. If a general medical condition or another mental disorder is present, the fear in Criterion A is unrelated to it; e.g., the fear is not of Stuttering, trembling in Parkinson's Disease, or exhibiting abnormal eating behavior in Anorexia Nervosa or Bulimia Nervosa.

Specify if:

Generalized: if the fears include most social situations (also consider the additional diagnosis of Avoidant Personality Disorder).

Reprinted with permission from the Diagnostic and Statistical Manual of Mental Disorders, Fourth Edition, Text Revision, Washington, DC, American Psychiatric Association, 2000.

Social Phobia in children (see Table 8-7) is also seen in the conditions of School Phobia and Selective Mutism.

Selective Mutism

What compels children with normal language skills to elect to stop speaking in a designated environment? In order to qualify for the disorder, the student must meet the selection criteria outlined in Table 8-8.

Table 8-8. **DSM-IV Diagnostic Criteria of Selective Mutism**

A. Consistent failure to speak in specific social situations (in which there is an expectation for speaking, e.g., at school) despite speaking in other situations

B. The disturbance interferes with educational or occupational achievement or with social communication

C. The duration of the disturbance is at least one month (not limited to the first month of school)

D. The failure to speak is not due to a lack of knowledge of, or comfort with, the spoken language required in the social situation

E. The disturbance is not better accounted for by a communication disorder (e.g., stuttering) and does not occur exclusively during the course of a Pervasive Developmental Disorder, Schizophrenia, or other Psychotic Disorder

Reprinted with permission from the Diagnostic and Statistical Manual of Mental Disorders, Fourth Edition, Text Revision, Washington, DC, American Psychiatric Association, 2000.

To the present, psychodynamic interventions have not been successful in treating *selective (or elective) mutism*. While it is true that some small positive achievement is reported in behavioral procedures consisting of a combination of a planned ignoring of the mutism and a structured reinforcement of "speaking" events, these benefits have been discouraging. Predictably, the setting of the intervention limits its usefulness because students find it difficult to transfer the acquired skill to new situations. When elective mutes are compared with children who have speech disorders, along with a control group, they are discovered to be more immature in development and excessively shy, as well as demonstrating higher rates of familial psychiatric problems (Kolvin and Fundudis, 1981).

In an interesting case, Kaarina, a grade two student in Ms. Chan's class, did not speak in the classroom. When Ms. Chan spoke to her mother, Mrs. Mateo – while describing Kaarina as a very shy but sufficiently talkative child at home – conceded that the same problem had been evident in the previous year when Kaarina had attended a different school. Furthermore, her grade two classmates reported that Kaarina spoke with them, but only in the school yard. By first ensuring a positive climate in the classroom, Ms. Chan intervened, initially setting up small-group sessions centered on non-academic activities and then creating an individual session. In the small-group session, four students, one of them Kaarina, learned to play the card game "Go fish". For this activity, Kaarina and her group were given a set of gestures by which they could identify cards and suits. If the desired card did not appear to be part of a player's "hand," a knock on the table would indicate "Go fish." After several weeks of playing, the group was given, each week, one new spoken phrase in exchange for each gesture.

In Kaarina's ten-minute individual session, Ms. Chan concentrated on academic tasks and, at first, questions to Kaarina were in a phrased manner requiring, in reply, either a yes or a no. At this stage, however, Kaarina was expected to respond by gesture. Then, Ms. Chan introduced a cardboard barrier which allowed Kaarina to hear but not to see her teacher. Using a plastic telephone, Kaarina, at first, was first expected to answer "yes/no" questions orally. Systematically, however, as the length of her responses was increased, the visual barrier was decreased. During the entire procedure, of course, praise and encouragement were extended regularly to the young girl.

School Phobia

Statistically, an estimated 17 children in a group numbering one thousand suffer from school phobia. In this group, an equal number of boys and girls will be represented, their age of onset peaking around eleven-to-twelve years; a smaller peak is evident in the five-to-six year range. Because these children avoid attending school – in order to circumvent the heightened sense of anxiety and the "flight" response they experience – they accumulate histories of very poor attendance. Although the prognosis for older children is poorer, interventions offer a good short-term outlook. In fewer than half the cases, medication is prescribed to create a climate supportive of other less-intrusive approaches.

Among the interventions recommended for the treatment of school phobia, several are: Cognitive Behavior Therapy outlined in a previous section (p. 8-22). Systematic Desensitization and Modeling which are described in detail below.

Systematic Desensitization

Originally, Wolpe and his colleagues (1969, 1990) developed a treatment called *Behavior Therapy* or *Systematic Desensitization*, a procedure that has become a most successful way to treat fears and phobias. In this intervention, the main assumption is that fears and phobias arise as a result of *Classical Conditioning*. When a physiological and/or cognitive response – especially one aroused by fear or anxiety – is associated with a specific stimulus event, the bond created insures that a similar emotional reaction will be present each time the event is encountered again.

As is apparent in the Little Albert case outlined in Chapter One, response generalization is an unfortunate outcome of the association between an object and a fear reaction. Eventually, objects or events that share similar characteristics with the initial trigger initiate the fear reaction; for example, a fear of spiders will often escalate to a fear of crawling insects, all insects, and, finally, all crawling creatures. Similarly, students who are afraid or anxious in the schoolyard may generalize their fear to every area in the school. Two major aspects of learning are elicited when a teacher structures this form of intervention: first, the individual begins to learn – consciously – to generate physiological and cognitive responses incompatible with the one experienced originally in the fear reaction. Usually, such a procedure entails relaxing muscles, breathing slowly and deeply, and other such behaviors. Once the individual masters relaxation techniques, new associations must be forged between a relaxed internal state and the feared object or event. In this *counter conditioning* process, the two phases are known, first, as "relaxation" and, second, as "counter conditioning" itself.

Relaxation Phase

At the outset, the teacher or worker, using strategies such as progressive muscle relation, creative imagery, and breathing exercises, teaches relaxation skills[7]. A person involved in such instruction, whether as teacher or as learner, must be able to master the relaxation response so that it can be invoked on request. In a typical case, the student might need a minimum of ten formal sessions as well as daily practice.

Counter Conditioning Phase

In the opening step of this phase, the learner identifies the events that trigger the fear reaction, taking care to list them in order of their occurrence, from greatest to least. For example, for the person, thinking about snakes invokes a smaller reaction than being in the same room with a boa constrictor. It is interesting that spatial proximity to the feared event – the closer or further away from the stimulus – affects the strength of the emotional reaction even in a state of imagination; for example, a person imagining a visit to the zoo and pretending to be *50 feet* from a live snake exhibit is less fearful than when simulating being present in a room, *two feet* away from a snake.

As soon as the relaxation response has been mastered, the method proceeds to an *imagery* phase in which the person is asked to create mental images of different situations involving the trigger while maintaining a physiological state of relaxation. Of course, the process begins with creative mental representation of the least threatening triggers, those furthest away. As soon as imagined stimuli no longer provoke the fear reaction, even at the closest proximity, this *shaping* process will begin to include *in vivo* conditions.

In vivo conditions involve the "real life" introduction of the feared object in a process that mimics the *imagery* condition. Again, physical proximity of the stimulus is manipulated while the person maintains a state of relaxation – yet knowing that the snake is in a box 20 feet away, then 10 feet, and then closer. If, at any time during the process, the individual suffers discomfort that cannot be controlled, the process immediately reverts to the previous steps, specifically to the one at which a state of relaxation was able to be maintained. In order to displace an earlier association, *Systematic Desensitization is employed*, a shaping procedure which is able to teach a new association between a stimulus and an internal state. When Barik, an autistic boy, is fearful of getting a haircut, his teacher introduces an informal pseudo-desensitization program. Barik's level of functioning precludes a relaxation training phase, but information from his parents identifies the occurrence of the most violent reactions as taking place either just outside or actually inside the Barber Shop; when he sees the scissors the response is also very strong. It becomes the aim of the intervention to expose Barik to a series of haircut scenarios that do not provoke a reaction, at the same time inching slowly towards the *in vivo* phase. First, Ms. Armitage compiles a Book Corner stocked with barber shop and haircut books. Over a four-week period, as she reads each of the books to the class, Barik's reaction is being monitored. During that same time frame, a part of Barik's Language Arts program involves the hair-cutting theme, and, whenever it arises, a student with a new haircut is asked to give to the class a full account of the experience.

Once Barik appears comfortable with the in-class activities, the *in vivo* phase is initiated with a walk to the park. On the way, the class strolls on the side of the street opposite to the barbershop, and, after several outings to the park, Ms. Armitage points out the barbershop to everyone, again watching Barik's response. Another four-week period passes, and now, on its way to the park, the class walks on the same side of the street as the barbershop. When no negative response is evident, the class stops briefly in front of the shop, and, eventually, Barik and other students enter the shop to watch a person getting a haircut; at this juncture, Barik actually sits in the barber's chair and even has a haircut. Although the entire process has taken more than six months, his ability to get a haircut – which is important to his family as well as to him – demonstrates the triumph of the painstaking process, so helpful to phobic individuals.

Modeling

According to Bandura and Walters, classical conditioning is not the only explanation for the way fears are acquired. By simply observing the fear reaction of people in their environments children can learn such behaviors. Offered as evidence by these researchers is the fact that not every person afraid of dogs has been bitten by a dog. Some individuals may have witnessed other people being injured, while others may have had parents tell them to stay away from dogs because they bite and hurt children. Because of similar home conditioning, members of the same family may share a distaste or a fear regarding the same focus, although a case can also be made that such a group perhaps shares a genetic connection.

When modeling is the medium for learning to counter a fear response, the teacher may consider reading stories, watching movies, and encouraging role playing, activities that involve positive experiences with dogs – *Lassie Come Home* or *Babe*, for example. As part of the process, the teacher might introduce a study of dogs or provide a chance to watch owners playing with their dogs and having fun. An *in vivo* phase – a situation where the feared object is present – might require the fearful child to pat a small furry dog. In this instance, the key is that, first, the child associates no negative emotions with the experience; and, second, the child is aware of this condition. In a unique case, the child may be exposed to potentially fearful – although safe – situations in order to experience, first hand, the absence of expected negative outcomes.

While operant conditioning and psychotherapy also offer treatment measures, they are relatively ineffective in comparison to Systematic Desensitization and Cognitive Behavior Therapy. Operant methods are inappropriate because the learned associations, especially in cases involving fear and anxiety, refer to internal states. Using reinforcers – for example, feedback, – serves an important role when the teacher promotes the child's progress through the *systematic desensitization* stages.

Summary

In this foregoing section, behaviors that are fear- and anxiety-based must be emphasized because the teacher, upon observing such symptoms, can advise parents to consult medical practitioners. Teachers are also able to support anxious and fearful students by applying the following procedures:

- making the classroom environment a positive one by meeting the affective needs of students (safety, prizing, power). In addition, implementing management procedures that are clear and predictable also serves to bolster these needs

- presenting the student with a series of achievable tasks based on an evaluation of what the student is able to manage comfortably

- encouraging appropriate responses, such as self-calming ones

- modeling opportunities spontaneously provided by the child's peer group

- encouraging parents to seek professional help for the child as well as support from a relevant parents' group

Conditions associated with the stress reaction

At one time, medical and other practitioners defined physical ailments – those not traced or understood – as psychosomatic, which meant they were believed to originate in the mind. Because such problems were often attributed to conflicts arising in one of the psychosexual stages, for many years, such labeling was an easy way to explain any disorder whose physical origins were not yet understood. Recently, however, advances in the field of medicine have isolated physical conditions, some of them aggravated or worsened by psychological components, especially when complicated by elements of stress.

Basic research implicating the role of stress in psychophysiological disorders – most of them physical ailments with psychological origins – was originally undertaken by Hans Selye (1978). As a result of his research, Dr. Selye demonstrated that activities demanding high output levels and/or intense levels of concentration were stressful. A corollary of this finding showed that excessive levels of anxiety can make the human body prone to physical illness, often focused on its weakest element.

Selye's Diathesis Stress Model

In the Diathesis Stress Model, the research proposes that not only *stress* but also *biological predisposition* may provide requisite conditions to produce a psychophysiological disorder. Interestingly, evidence explaining the development of stomach ulcers is a good instance of this process. Selye demonstrates, in animal research, at least three stress conditions that elicit ulcers: (1) wrapping rats in towels or tying their legs to immobilize them will produce lesions in their stomachs; (2) placing animals in a situation in which electric shock is administered, whenever they approach food or always causes them either to develop ulcers or to die as a result of a prolonged period – two weeks – of *approach-avoidance* conflict; (3) treating animals with unpredictable shock is more likely to produce ulcers than is the application of shock following a warning signal; hence, the opportunity to control a stressor reduces the severity of the ulcers.

Further studies, these conducted on humans – airplane pilots and air traffic controllers – indicate that ulcers are twice as frequent among the latter, perhaps because pilots are under less stress, in that they have more control over their planes, while air traffic controllers have – or believe they have – a greater responsibility for the safety of large numbers of passengers.

In recent years, new evidence in stomach ulcer research indicates that, in some cases, such ulcers are the consequence of an infection; such data proves again that, with time, new physiological, rather than psychological, causes of diseases thought to be psychosomatic are discovered.

Anorexia Nervosa

Anorexia Nervosa, one of several conditions categorized as an *Eating Disorder* in the DSM IV-TR manual, is associated with the stress reaction that results from feeling too little control over events in one's life. Considering that the average size and weight of people has increased over time, it is difficult to understand how individuals might starve themselves. Yet, in spite of greater availability of food potentially able to cause weight gain, starvation occurs – a paradox. *Anorexia Nervosa*, well known in cultural groups where stringent expectations are placed on adolescents, had a high incidence during the Victorian era, and, both then and now, its devastating physiological consequences may include loss of menses – menstrual periods – and even death. Recent evidence indicates that depression experienced in during early adolescence is often a pre-cursor to the development of eating disorders during middle adolescence or early adulthood. Symptoms of Anorexia Nervosa are described in Table 8-9.

What causes a person to refuse to eat? Obviously, the provocation must be complex, but, as might be expected, the data conform to the *Diathesis Stress* model. First is a predisposition to be thin, which is coupled with the values of the culture – what is reinforced – and, of course, conditions of stress. Interestingly, young women involved in classical dance and/or strenuous exercise programs are more vulnerable than those in other groups; for example, whereas the average weight for a female gymnast in 1970 was 105 pounds, or slightly more than 47 kilograms, at present the average female gymnast it is 88 pounds or 40 kilograms. In addition, while advertisements in the media continue to employ increasingly thinner female models, especially since the 1960s, news reports have given eating disorders so much attention that *Anorexia* may have become an "in" or "cool" condition to acquire. Moreover, practitioners agree that, psychologically, the Anorexic habit is rooted in the family system where the manipulative child often uses it as a weapon.

Some stress conditions that may trigger *Anorexia* include:

- adolescence high crisis periods or divorce – the child may see such an extreme action as a way to reunite parents. The growing rate of divorce equates with the rise in numbers of anorexic adolescents

- reluctance to accept an adult role

- fear of pregnancy

- conflict about sex

Table 8-9. DSM-IV-TR Diagnostic Criteria of Anorexia Nervosa Disorder

A. Refusal to maintain body weight at or above a minimally normal weight for age and height (e.g., weight loss leading to maintenance of body weight less than 85% of that expected; or failure to make expected weight gain during period of growth, leading to body weight less than 85% of that expected)

B. Intense fear of gaining weight or becoming fat, even though under-weight

C. Disturbance in the way in which one's body weight or shape is experienced, undue influence of body weight or shape on self-evaluation, or denial of the seriousness of the current low body image

D. In postmenarcheal females, amenorrhea, i.e, the absence of at least three consecutive menstrual cycles. (A woman is considered to have amenorrhea if her periods occur only following hormone, e.g., estrogen, administration)

Reprinted with permission from the Diagnostic and Statistical Manual of Mental Disorders, Fourth Edition, Text Revision, Washington, DC, American Psychiatric Association, 2000.

Bulimia Nervosa

Some individuals manifest signs of the disorder known as *Anorexia Nervosa* when they engage in binge eating and purging rather than in forms of starvation. In the condition called *Bulimia Nervosa,* two subgroups are identified: first, a *Purging* and second, a *Nonpurging* Type, depending on whether self-induced vomiting and other probably cathartic purging measures are present. The criteria associated with Bulimia are described in Table 8-10.

Table 8-10. DSM-IV-TR Diagnostic Criteria of Bulimia Nervosa Disorder

A. Recurrent episodes of binge eating. An episode of binge eating is characterized by both of the following:

  1. eating, in a discrete period of time (e.g., within any two-hour period), an amount of food that is definitely larger than most people would eat during a similar period of time and in similar circumstances

  2. a sense of lack of control over eating during the episode (e.g., a feeling that one cannot stop eating or control what or how much one is eating)

B. Recurrent inappropriate compensatory behavior in order to prevent weight gain, such as self-induced vomiting; misuse of laxatives, diuretics, enemas, or other medications; fasting; or excessive exercise

C. The binge eating and inappropriate compensatory behaviors both occur, on average, at least twice a week for three months

cont'd

D. Self-evaluation is unduly influenced by body shape and weight

E. The disturbance does not occur exclusively during episodes of Anorexia Nervosa

Specify if:

Purging Type: during the current episode of Bulimia Nervosa, the person has regularly engaged in self-induced vomiting or the misuse of laxatives, diuretics, or enemas

Nonpurging Type: during the current episode of Bulimia Nervosa, the person has used other inappropriate compensatory behaviors, such as fasting or excessive exercise, but has not regularly engaged in self-induced vomiting or the misuse of laxatives, diuretics, or enemas

Reprinted with permission from the Diagnostic and Statistical Manual of Mental Disorders, Fourth Edition, Text Revision, Washington, DC, American Psychiatric Association, 2000.

In cases of *Anorexia* or *Bulimia Nervosa* interventions are necessarily outside the scope of the classroom. In serious cases, the young person may have to be admitted to hospital and accept a regimen of tube feeding, all the while being reinforced for eating and weight gain. Although such measures have produced only short-term gains, a systems approach referred to as *family therapy* has produced good results. Unlike other types of family therapies – those which focus on the young person as "ill" – the systems approach considers that, although all the members of the family, as individuals, may be "OK", when brought together they create a totality which is a "sick" family. In such a procedure, no one family member is perceived as causing problems. Within the stereotypical family, the Anorexic or Bulimic individual – playing out the family pathology – confronts parents and their high expectations. For remediation, each family member is given a prescription to alter his or her contribution.

What can be done in the classroom? When issues of body image crop up in curricular materials or in the social context of the classroom, the teacher will recognize the importance of encouraging frank and open discussion. Initially, for all students, a balanced lifestyle that promotes healthy eating habits, in conjunction with daily exercise, should be encouraged. Subsequently, students should be helped to challenge and examine typical media standards. Why is *Anorexia Nervosa* so prevalent now? Why is it commonly found in affluent societies?

Asthma

Although it may appear unusual to discuss Asthma as a psychophysiological disorder, the condition nevertheless conforms to the diathesis model. Interestingly, asthma has a tendency to run in families: a ratio exists of one in two boys who experience attacks. Although, in some cases, reduced or spontaneous remission occurs after the onset of puberty, asthma that not only begins but also persists may be triggered by two root causes:

- psychological factors

- physiological factors – allergies, infections, and other physical causes

In older adolescents and young adults, Hommel *et al.* (2002) found that both anxiety and depression exacerbate asthma symptoms.

Left undiagnosed or poorly controlled, the asthmatic student is frequently absent from school and/or physical education classes, and, in addition is restricted in terms of exercise. Therefore, the student may be reluctant to participate at recess in physically strenuous games. In addition, loss of sleep due to asthma symptoms will result in fatigue as well as, frequently, academic underachievement. On-going medical supervision, identification of triggers, and knowledge of self-calming techniques should improve the quality of life of the student who suffers from asthma.

Relief of the Stress Reaction

Available to students looking to relieve the stress reaction is a variety of individual techniques. Although it is beyond the scope of this book to provide a detailed description of all of these, generic categories are listed here. In the list, each procedure has been derived from the myriad of programs now on the market. During their compilation of this range of anxiety reducers, researchers hoped to counter the effects of stress by generating new responses incompatible with it.

Progressive Muscle Relaxation

Programs emphasizing this process are available in the community, often through private practitioners, but sometimes at hospitals. Such procedures might involve group training in 10-12 weekly sessions. Usually accompanied by relaxing music in the background, the practitioner will instruct the group to:

- constrict muscle groups and relax them, because *for every action there is an equal and opposite reaction*

- use *imagery*, in order to visualize parts of the body with the goal of making each feel lighter or heavier

The rational of this technique lies in the realization that constricted muscles are present when the individual is experiencing stress. By implementing muscle relaxation, the individual is able to learn to establish a reaction incompatible with stress.

Breathing Exercises

In the practice of Yoga, some processes deal exclusively with breathing. Generally, slowing down the rate of inhalation as well as taking deeper breaths will increase levels of relaxation. In some cases, the individual is further required to count breaths as a means of providing a focus.

Vigorous Exercise

Vigorous exercises, especially those involved in running, jogging, skipping, and swimming, as well as some others, are commonly used for recreation and relaxation.

Imagery

By teaching students the skills of creative imagination, an instructor can transport those individuals instantly to relaxing contexts. Often, the trainer asks the participants to imagine a scene or to create a personal quiet spot. Also very useful is the creating of a pattern of imagery to reshape self-perception; for example, people may be able to see themselves succeeding, especially when previous self-images have concentrated on defeat. Many instructors teach their students to experience the strength of positive personal statements, often referred to as *mantras*: "I will be able to complete this…I will be able to complete this…I will be able to…" The repetition is wholesome and positive, helping the student to overcome the effects of negative habits of thought.

Music

Certain types of music have a calming and relaxing effect – even on laboratory rats and milk cows. Some possibilities include:

- music with a tempo of 60 beats per minute; this practice is based on the belief that the simulation of a heart rate has a calming influence

- Baroque music or similar types of classical music; typical examples would be *Sheep May Safely Graze*, by Bach and *The Dance of the Blessed Spirits*, by Gluck

- music that incorporates natural sounds – a babbling brook, birds chirping, waterfall, ocean waves, or other sounds of landscape. A good example here is the *Sixth Symphony* of Beethoven or a range of music by Grieg or Vaughan Williams

Meditation

As a society, people in the Western Hemisphere were introduced to meditation in the 1960s, the result of the *East-Meets-West* movement. Around the same time, TM – Transcendental Meditation – became a very popular way for people to "get in touch" with themselves; several types of meditation have emerged, especially those involving:

- Mantras, which depend on the repetition, over and over, of one statement, perhaps "OM", as is common in TM

- the heightening of sensory impressions

- aromatherapy

- stoppage of thoughts – more realistically, the person may be experiencing the space between thoughts

- prayer

Biofeedback

Some attempt has been made to use technology in the quest for relieving the stress reaction: equipment is now available which provides feedback about an individual's internal state; the intent is to teach relaxation. Generally,

- the person is connected with a machine which will provide feedback – in the form of a tone which varies in pitch or light – about levels of relaxation

- the individual, on the basis of such response, learns to generate a consistent pattern of positive feedback

Through Biofeedback, the participants learn to be able to will Beta brain waves or to alter their galvanic skin response. Although biofeedback is an expensive procedure, in comparison with other relaxation training processes, it is preferred by some people.

Summary

Each of these techniques outlined above has attracted its share of controversy, especially when proponents have made claims that go beyond the goal of relaxation training value to improve health, fight cancer, and offer special cures. In addition, extreme theories that have subsequently become associated with many of these techniques have often turned out to be esoteric, while some are proved to be unscientific. Regardless of the various publicized attitudes, both pro and con, many people show individual preferences for one or more of these procedures. For some of these individuals, stress may be reduced, whether because of or in spite of the chosen process. It is reasonable to conclude, however, that knowing ways to relieve the stress reaction is today a much-sought-after *life skill.*

Movement Disorders

Tics and Mannerisms

Tics and Mannerisms consist of sudden, stereotypic motor or verbal responses whose frequency occurs in "bursts". In fact, transient eye blinks and facial tics seem to appear and persist for several months. Interestingly, 12 to 24% of school-aged children can be afflicted, in a ratio of three boys for every girl. Tics, which do not occur during sleep, can be willingly suppressed in some people for varying periods of time.

Although such tics have been in existence in humans for thousands of years, the reasons for their existence or the causes – which might be able to explain this type of condition – are not yet known to medical or psychiatric researchers. Although, in most cases, symptoms disappear within a year, a procedure of *massed practice* has been used to reduce the frequency of their occurrence. In this - very successful – if unusual – process, the individual is made, purposefully, to repeat the tic over and over, by enforcing the movement, until the muscle group involved is exhausted.

Tourette's Syndrome

Tourette's Syndrome, a tic disorder whose onset seems to be between the ages of two and thirteen years, shows increasing evidence of being the product of genetic factors: in support of this view, researchers have, in several cases, isolated the existence of the tic in many generations of the same family.

Students with Tourette's can be very disruptive in class, usually because motor and verbal tics not only interrupt lessons but also slow the bustle of work activities. Outlined here are a few strategies that teachers can implement to minimize disruption:

- *Information.* In order to reduce sensationalism, the teacher, with the permission of the student, may create opportunities for the class to acquire knowledge about Tourette's – reinforcing the idea that the individual has very little control over the tics

- *Empathy.* As a means of developing empathy for the student, the teacher may give the class opportunities to think about and to feel what it is like to have this condition; for example:

  ° "How would you feel if you were at a baseball game and **the person next to you** started to bark uncontrollably?"

  ° "How would you feel if you were at a baseball game and **you** started to bark uncontrollably?"

  ° "How would you feel if, when you were in a church, temple, or mosque, **the person next to you** started cursing uncontrollably?"

  ° "How would you feel if you were in church, temple, or mosque and **you** started cursing uncontrollably?"

- *Tic suppression.* Because a tic can be controlled for a period of time, the teacher may design a *shaping* procedure to help the student increase the time-span of such an interval – smaller intervals at first, followed by a series, each one of increasing duration. Immediately after the tic-free interval, the student will require some privacy to express the inevitable, perhaps embarrassing, outburst

- *Massed practice.* To exhaust the muscles involved in the tic behavior and therefore suppress the tic temporarily, the student is given an opportunity – in a private setting – to engage in exaggerated rehearsal of the tic behavior

In extreme cases, to suppress tics, a physician may be willing to prescribe anti-psychotic medications, but while tic reduction will occur, side effects include a drastic reduction in alertness and in beneficial physical action and reaction.

Excessive Activity

Although levels of excessive activity – that is, activity beyond the usual range found in children – are equivalent at age three, reports of "normal" children indicate that boys remain more active than girls. Whereas activity in boys peaks around age five and then begins to decline, levels in girls do not show marked increases, but they then sharply decline by age ten. It is possible that this behavior reflects gender differences in patterns of maturation and physiological temperament.

On the basis of Simner's (1985) analysis of factors in Kindergarten that predict future academic achievement, it is interesting to observe that ability to sit still while doing paper and pencil tasks is an important predictor. For this reason, young school children unable to remain in their seats should be given opportunities to learn slowly to increase their capacity do so. Also indicated in these cases are programs of daily physical education. For students who are unable to concentrate or to remain seated, strong physical play is warranted, especially in the primary division.

Mood Disorders

Although mood disorders in childhood and adolescence are more prevalent than previously suspected, in those cases in which diagnosis and treatment are introduced early in the course of the disorder, encouragingly positive outcomes may be experienced in adulthood.

Within the past several decades, when moodiness has been perceived as a characteristic of adolescence, mood swings in teenagers have usually been considered a "normal" expectation of this developmental milestone. New evidence suggests, however, that because the incidence of these personality-altering conditions should generally remain constant, adolescents experiencing a greater frequency in such swings should be referred to a psychiatrist for evaluation.

As researchers have come to accept that mood disorders can also be related to certain medical conditions – Multiple Sclerosis, brain tumors, and other illnesses, as well as to substance abuse, medical practitioners should be involved early in the process of diagnosis and treatment when students appear to experience serious mood swings.

Manic Depression – Juvenile

Manic Depression is a bipolar condition in which an individual can experience one of three phases: a phase of *mania*, a phase of *depression*, or a cycle involving the two extremes. While five to fifteen percent of young persons afflicted will experience only a single episode, for the remaining members of the group the episodes will recur. An individual subject to multiple episodes will probably experience the cyclical form, involving the two opposed elements.

In the 1850s, medical researchers believed that puberty was the stress instigating *Manic Depression*, but today, juvenile onset of the condition – occurring between the ages of 12 and 18 years and especially when showing classical symptoms – is thought to be linked to genetic factors. In addition, early onset seems to affect the duration and acuteness of symptoms: when they persist longer and are more acute. If this is the case, their recurrence and cycles seem to mirror the extreme aspect of the condition, leading to longer cycles of greater frequency.

In order to support the students' psychosocial development and to help them acquire coping resources, it is important that teachers refer these young persons for psychiatric evaluation that will lead to their being diagnosed and given treatment. As might be expected, primary intervention by medical practitioners involves the prescription and monitoring of drugs, some of which, while efficacious in treating the symptoms, have side effects that influence each individual's general abilities and/or social skills.

Depression

Today, many mental disorders previously associated with aberrations of the mind are not only being explained physiologically but are being treated medically. Although medical interventions are not new, in the past they consisted mainly of symptom reduction. Today, on the other hand, biogenetic explanations aim to describe the brain processes that cause a specific mental disorder and then to intervene to *normalize* physical states.

Of course, additional explanations for depression exist outside a medical perspective. In each of the three models of depression examined – Seligman's *learned-helplessness model*; Lewisohn's *reduced-reinforcement model;* and Beck's *cognitive* a different focus is highlighted. Worth noting is that the three innovators initiated their differing programs of research about depression from varying starting points, Seligman using animal research with dogs and Lewisohn employing the reinforcement history of his clients; Beck, the third researcher, who had initially trained as a psychoanalyst, began his work by evaluating the content of his patients' dreams. Regardless of their different origins, each of these three models attempts to delineate causes of the same phenomenon: the depressed state that many humans experience.

Seligman's learned-helplessness model

The first of the three types of experiment is that of Seligman, dealing with dogs that received painful electric shock in two different sets of conditions. Prior to the main experiment, Seligman trained two groups of dogs to react when their cage floors were electrified. In the first group, after each dog was placed in a box with electric grids in the flooring, it then experienced shock, while having no means of escape. Meanwhile, each dog in the second group, although subjected to the same shock condition, could leap over the partition to a "safe" compartment when a warning buzzer sounded.

After training both groups of dogs and then introducing a control group[8] with no prior history, Seligman tested all three groups in an apparatus structured to permit all the dogs to avoid the shock. In this stage, the three groups of animals responded differently: dogs that had learned earlier to avoid the shock – along with the control group – quickly learned to escape being shocked. The third group of dogs, those with the learning history of being unable to escape the shock condition, made no attempt to escape. In fact, soon after receiving the first shocks, they stopped running around in a distressed manner, appearing to "give up". Passively, they accepted the painful stimulation, nor did they ultimately learn the avoidance response in the "escape condition" as efficiently as the untrained control animals or as readily as those programmed with a history of escape. Seligman was able to conclude that an individual confronted with aversive stimulation, especially when it is not under the personal control of the individual, readily acquires a sense of helplessness.

Lewisohn's reduced-reinforcement model

In the second model, – Lewisohn's – the researcher attributes depression to a reduction in activity when the situation lacks reinforcement. On the basis of Learning Theory, it is generally assumed that that while the frequency of a response increases when it is followed by reinforcement, that same frequency decreases when followed by a punisher. Finally, in the absence of a consequence, it is extinguished. In a wide-ranging survey, Lewisohn collected data on self-report questionnaires that focused on 320 pleasurable events. Interestingly, the results indicated that the more depressed the subject seemed to be, the fewer pleasant events were reported.

Beck's cognitive theory

Comparing the dreams of his depressed patients with the dreams of patients who were non-depressed, Beck noted that depressed patients more frequently made self-critical statements, reflecting low self-esteem. In addition, these same persons expressed emotions about being unwanted and alone. As a corollary, their dreams reflected similar themes, often depicting these dreamers as either victims or losers. Whether the dream emphasized victim or loser, something of value would be lost, especially because most dream actions would lead to negative outcomes. Given the pattern of these experiments, Beck's observations led him to focus attention on the self-critical attitudes and negative-thinking styles of clients.

Assumptions made by the three models

As a result of his findings, Seligman's model proposed that depression comes about through *learned helplessness*. This fairly logical notion is based on the assumption that anxiety, the initial response to a stressful situation, gives way to depression, especially when the individual comes to hold the view that no personal control can be exerted over the situation.

In contrast, Lewisohn perceives the symptoms of depression as the result of having few reinforcing events. When a cycle is established that exhibits a sparse schedule of positive reinforcement, the pattern steadily reduces activity, with the result that ever fewer opportunities emerge to provide reinforcement. Access to positive reinforcement is a function of three aspects: the individual's personal characteristics, the factors in the environment, and the repertoire of behaviors that gain reinforcement. Therefore, people who either do not experience success or do not have encouragement from family and peers will further isolate themselves, increasingly reducing the possibility of social approval. Because some of these people are naturally reticent, as a result they reduce their chances of receiving feedback from others; in addition, certain individuals are physically isolated; still a third group lacks the skills to interact socially, thereby potentially obtaining reinforcement.

At the heart of Beck's central thesis is the idea that depressed individuals feel as they do because of committing errors in logical thinking. As if repeating patterns, these people distort whatever happens to them, skewing it in the direction of self-blame and catastrophe. As a corollary, depressives draw illogical conclusions, not only in the evaluation of themselves, but also in the appraisal of their immediate world and of their understanding of the behavior of peers and family members. Moreover, their perception of the future is skewed, especially as it appears in the way they view their chances of success. Extending this notion, Beck describes several types of logical errors:

- *Arbitrary Inference.* An influential conclusion is drawn in the absence of evidence or of sufficient evidence

- *Selective Arbitration.* A far-reaching conclusion focuses on only one of many elements in a situation

- *Over-generalization.* An overall sweeping conclusion is drawn on the basis of a single, perhaps trivial event

- *Magnification or Minimization.* A faulty conclusion arises out of gross errors which, when they evaluate performance, tend to overrate or berate its value

Although appearing distinct, the treatment interventions suggested by all three models are, unexpectedly, more similar to one another than they seem at first glance. The first of these, the treatment measures of Beck, include confronting – with gentle but probing and consistent questions

– the patient's faulty assumptions and errors in reasoning. Obviously, such an approach represents, initially, an attempt to clarify erroneous thought patterns and, subsequently, to suggest alternative ways of thinking about events. Here, the depressed patient is encouraged to self-monitor dysfunctional thought by keeping records of feelings, thoughts, events, interpretations, and potential alternatives. During the therapy, records of homework assignments and, often, personal experiments, undertaken by the client, are subsequently shared with the therapist who makes certain that the focus of the intervention is the specific skill(s) involved in performing the task.

Coming from another direction, Lewisohn emphasizes the need for the depressed person to develop social skills in pursuit of social rewards. In the therapy procedures, treatment is directed towards circumventing the depressed pattern. By training the individual to develop skills that will allow more access to reinforcement from the environment, the therapist hopes to relieve the depression. In one mode, recording devices are used to teach depressives to observe that good moods are often the corollary of pleasant experiences, and that, conversely, bad moods are associated with unpleasant events or actions. In every case, the individuals being assisted are taught how to increase the likelihood of positive experiences, while lowering the potential for unpleasant ones. In a program of this kind, the person is taught, among other procedures, the planning of daily schedules that will maximize the chances of experiencing rewarding events. Because family conflict is often a source of unpleasant events, the therapist will help the client develop appropriate skills for learning to avert as well as skillfully to respond to such situations.

Of the three approaches, the findings of Beck seem to hold the most promise, probably because his treatment is thorough and comprehensive. At present, when they are used in tandem, cognitive therapies and drug therapies seem to offer the most optimistic prognosis.

In overview, an integration or synthesis of these models provides a picture that shows depressives to be individuals who have faulty perceptions, who make logical errors, and who are likely to alienate themselves from the very persons who could serve as sources of reinforcement. Their inability to attribute the loss of reinforcement to their own actions – actions always mediated by their faulty perceptions – results in a sense of personal helplessness. When the loss of a significant other occurs, as in the death or separation from a loved one, the likely result will be a lessening of reinforcement opportunities. Moreover, a logical error, perhaps in the form of *over generalization,* may lead the depressed person to generalize, and thus to conclude that no control over this event was possible, and, therefore, control over all subsequent events will not be possible.

> How does divorce affect children of different ages?

In examining the criteria for Major Depressive Disorder, in Table 8-11, the teacher will be able to get a sense of the devastating consequence of the disorder. By becoming familiar with the symptoms listed in Table 8-11, the supervising teacher should be in a position of recognizing problem behaviors and communicating observations with the all interested parties. By encouraging parents to seek professional help, teachers, in these cases, can hope that early intervention will minimize the long-term impact of the condition.

Table 8-11. **DSM-IV-TR Diagnostic Criteria of Major Depressive Disorder**

A. At least one of the following three abnormal moods which significantly interfere with the student's life:

  1. Abnormal depressed mood most of the day, nearly every day, for at least two weeks

  2. Abnormal loss of all interest and pleasure most of the day, nearly every day, for at least two weeks

  3. Abnormal irritable mood most of the day, nearly every day, for at least two weeks in persons who are 18 years or younger

B. At least five of the following symptoms have been present during the same two-week period of depression:

  1. Abnormal depressed mood (or irritable mood if a child or adolescent) [as defined in criterion A]

  2. Abnormal level of loss of all interest and pleasure [as defined in criterion A2]

  3. Appetite or weight disturbance, either:

   • Abnormal weight loss (when not dieting) or decrease in appetite

   • Abnormal weight gain or increase in appetite

  4. Sleep disturbance: either abnormal insomnia or abnormal hypersomnia

  5. Activity disturbance: either abnormal agitation or abnormal slowing (observable by others)

  6. Abnormal level of fatigue or loss of energy

  7. Abnormal amount of self-reproach or inappropriate guilt

  8. Abnormal level of poor concentration or indecisiveness

  9. Abnormal pattern of morbid thoughts of death (not just fear of dying) or suicide

C. The symptoms are not the result of a mood-incongruent psychosis

D. There has never been a Manic Episode, a Mixed Episode, or a Hypomanic Episode

E. The symptoms are not caused by physical illness, alcohol, medication, or street drugs

F. The symptoms are not connected with normal bereavement

Reprinted with permission from the Diagnostic and Statistical Manual of Mental Disorders, Fourth Edition, Text Revision, Washington, DC, American Psychiatric Association, 2000.

Summary

Although some common conditions such as childhood fears, aggression, and withdrawal behavior are developmental, and are sometimes transient in nature, other conditions, especially those which are more serious, warrant referral to professional personnel. Strongly emphasized in this section is an additional element: the maturational and physiological basis of many of these behaviors. Important to note, too, is the realization that, for certain conditions, the causes of the onset are not yet understood either by medical or by psychiatric professionals and researchers.

Some of these conditions, moreover, have the potential of overlapping each other; for example, correlations may exist among depression, separation anxiety, and Tourette's Syndrome. Whereas young children are more likely to present a range of generalized fears, separation anxiety, and school phobias, older children and adolescents manifest GAD, panic attacks, and OCD. In both groups, affective needs – as outlined in the model in Chapter Four – must be considered of foremost concern in any classroom intervention.

When considering the possible presence of these serious childhood and adolescent conditions, teachers and parents must remain vigilant in order to be able to identify the warning signs, because both early medical evaluation and prompt classroom intervention will have a good chance of improving the student prognosis in students.

Endnotes

[1] Ceiling and floor effects are extreme examples of this lack of sensitivity within a measure. When ceiling effects are encountered, all participants score very high, receiving almost perfect marks on the measure. In the case of floor effects, the opposite occurs with participants scoring very low, almost zero, on the measure. In both cases, the lack of variability in the participants' scores renders the measure ineffective in discerning the presence of treatment differences.

[2] Star charts combined with restriction of the child's fluid are sometimes used to treat nighttime wetting. A reward system is set up by the parents with the contingency that for every night that the child stays dry, a gold star is awarded for staying dry through the night and a silver star for waking after a small amount of wetting. The chart serves as a reminder of the child's success.

[3] For children four to eight years old, a book called *Accidental Lily* is recommended. Written by S. Warner and J. Rogers, (1999) it is published in New York, by Knopf.

[4] The "fight-or-flight" response, an autonomic physiological reaction to a real or perceived threat, is characterized by noticeable muscular tension, increased heart rate, stronger breathing, and accelerated adrenaline flow, as well as decreased sensitivity to pain. This response can also be induced by stress.

[5] In some situations, relaxation training can invoke a dissociative episode -- the student loses touch with reality; when this happens, parents should first consult the supervising psychologist or psychiatrist.

[6] The client-therapist, or the student-teacher relationship, is found to account for a large part of the success of interventions.

[7] A more detailed explanation of these strategies appears in a following section (pp. 319-320)

[8] A control group, when used as a comparison group in an experimental situation, is made up of participants who are neither involved in nor are they affected by any of the experimental conditions; they receive no stimuli, drugs, or other control elements and are free of all programming influences. Thus they form a contrast, representative of uninfluenced, natural units.

CHAPTER 9

Behavioral Problems in Special Populations

In this chapter, the focus is on the various special populations of children and adolescents who attend schools – in either regular or special education classes – and who exhibit behaviors that warrant discussion. Although these students may not, at the outset, be categorized as having behavioral problems, they, nevertheless, bring their own unique challenges to the teacher whose job is – among other elements – the managing of behavior.

Relevant in this chapter is the review of primary and secondary behavior problems, those already detailed in Chapter One. This backward look is necessary because the groups of students that will be examined, those with Learning Disabilities, Attention Deficit Disorder (ADD), Autism, and Asperger's, as well as those called Young Offenders, are for the most part in the category called secondary behavior problems. Whereas it is evident that the source of behavioral problems in the first three groups lies in the way they process information, in their flawed level of attention, or in their having a communication disorder, by contrast, Young Offenders present problems associated with socio-economic, cultural, psychological, learning, or social factors.

Learning Disability

When students are diagnosed as having learning disabilities (LD), they manifest a variety of maladaptive behaviors, including avoidance of classroom procedures, frustration with the work of the classroom, feelings of helplessness, perceptions of themselves as unable to learn, difficulty getting along with peers as a result of poor social skills, and communication difficulties. To exacerbate difficulty further, such students may present more than one problem, for example, they may have Attention Deficit Disorder (ADD), Tourette's, Conduct Disorders, and other combinations of conditions.

Although, on the surface, students with LD are no more depressed than their non-LD counterparts, they may feel ineffective. In comparing these two groups, Heath & Ross (2000) identify some interesting gender differences:

- girls in both groups experience more difficulties related to negative mood but have fewer interpersonal problems than boys

- whereas girls with LD report more depressive symptoms than do girls without LD, no such differences are found between the two groups of boys

- while such a pattern is not present in boys, LD girls report more instances not only of loss of pleasure, but also of low self-esteem. In comparison to non-LD girls, they exhibit a larger range of interpersonal problems

Adolescents with learning disabilities demonstrate higher rates of depression, which, together with factors such as impulsivity and poor social skills, predispose them to higher rates of suicide (Bender *et al.,* 1999). Specifically, students with nonverbal learning disabilities and those with severe academic problems are more prone to end their lives than are other groups in the entire student group.

There are other compelling reasons for providing early behavioral intervention to LD students. For example, having a learning disability in childhood increases the risk of developing psychiatric problems in adulthood. When Klein & Mannuzza (2000) followed 104 children with reading disorders – a group who, at the time, demonstrated no evidence of psychiatric problems – they also used an age-matched control group. When they retested sixteen years later, the LD group, now consisting of adults, not only retested with lower IQ scores as well as poorer educational and occupational attainment, but they also had more psychiatric diagnoses.

In summary, as they get older and reach adolescence and adulthood, students with learning disabilities portray more serious behavioral problems. At school, some adolescent behavior is sufficiently severe to warrant targeting it as the primary locus of intervention, as exemplified in the case of Luciano.

The Case of Luciano

A twelve-year old boy in a Grade 6 class, Luciano is placed in a Resource Withdrawal program, for 45 minutes each day. Assessed as having "average" intelligence, Luciano nevertheless exhibits severe reading and spelling difficulties. On the basis of teacher comments in his report cards and other student-file records, the following developmental profile of his school performance emerges; his teachers' comments point to four major areas related to Luciano's:

- *poor memory for information which he finds non-meaningful*

- *limited time given to on-task behavior*

- *poor organizational skills*

- *lack of achievement in many aspects of the language arts curriculum*

At the end of Kindergarten, the first indication of learning problems was detected when his teacher reported that Luciano could count to "59" by rote but was still unable to associate all the colors with their names and could not recall the alphabet in its entirety. In addition, his attention span was somewhat shorter than those of his peers. In Grade One, when Luciano was frustrated and confused by oral and written work, he began to demonstrate an impulsive style even in his artwork.

In Grade Two, when the school's psychologist assessed him, Luciano's reading and spelling skills were about a year below his peer group's although his work in arithmetic was age appropriate. Through a psychological test, the WISC-R, Luciano's performance was shown to be within the average range on both the Verbal and Performance sections, although his record was better on the former. When he was found to be uncertain of letter shapes, especially those which shared similar features, the examiner concluded that Luciano had problems in the visual-spatial realm. While he scored in the superior range on the Arithmetic subtest, Luciano's results were very low on the Digit Span subtest. Interestingly, the weak performance on this test, primarily about working memory, was attributed to lack of interest, notably because Luciano was seen to yawn frequently throughout the testing period. Meanwhile, in the classroom, Luciano was easily upset when asked to do things other than what he preferred. At this juncture, it was suggested that his teacher keep praising him.

In Grade Three, Luciano began participating in extra-curricular hockey. Concurrently, a modified reading program seemed to yield better results than his report cards had shown in Grade Two, although his poor work habits, disorderly printing, and low achievement in speaking were discussed with the parents. Arising from this meeting, recommendations included a series of suggestions: that Luciano start to listen more attentively; that he begin to take pride in his written work; that his teachers praise him for participating more readily in class discussions; and that he be sent home for forgotten books.

In his Grade Four year, Luciano continued to experience difficulty in all language arts areas, although there was an exception in his speaking. Moreover, Luciano's teacher stated that when his temper was under control, the boy was hardworking. At this time, he began to receive resource withdrawal help from a special education teacher. In conference reports for this period, some academic progress was reported, but Luciano's "stubbornness" and his negative and angry attitude began to warrant consideration of a special class placement. In April of Luciano's Grade Four year, an IPRC[1] was held. In Grade Five, although Luciano's performance was noticeably below grade level, his special class teacher commented that he was making very good progress in Reading and Mathematics, although it was emphasized that reading fluency was in need of an increase. In Grade Six, a conference report described progress in Luciano's attitude towards his academic subjects, although a concern was expressed that his behavior seemed erratic. At times, Luciano could be courteous, while, at other stages, he would be loud, rude, and disruptive. Even though he continued to require close supervision to complete his work, his special education teacher commented that Luciano always experienced a significant range of difficulties.

In an overview, Luciano's teachers can agree that he has had learning difficulties throughout his academic career. Moreover, his academic progress has continued to be slow in spite of the program modifications implemented by the school.

Assessment

A subsequent assessment supports the idea that Luciano – over a long period of time – has been experiencing difficulties with visual memory and/or visual-motor functioning. Also, it is especially notable that Luciano has consistently demonstrated difficulties with tasks containing a visual memory component or more than one of these.

Sufficient evidence continues to indicate that Luciano has difficulty remembering visual clues as well as information that he finds non-meaningful: of course, this is a possible explanation for his lack of reading skill development and spelling acquisition.

Although Luciano's language functions appear intact, his performance on two particular subtests – one that requires him to produce the names of symbols such as red circle and yellow triangle and another that emphasizes speech sounds – Luciano made a considerable number of errors because he confused either the name of the color or the recognition of the geometric form. Because these words are so familiar to him, this test is an evaluation of how quickly and accurately even well-known words are retrieved from memory. Moreover, a similar difficulty is evident in his reading, for example, when he is identifying short words as well as words which he actually knows. Although he often "blurts out" an incorrect response when reading words in isolation or in context, a few seconds later, Luciano will correct himself.

In a particular evaluation, Luciano was also required to listen to a sentence and then to provide a missing word. Although he is quite able to acquire information by listening to spoken language, he encounters specific difficulties when particular words are to be retrieved. This weakness may contribute to problems he has when associating the written with the spoken word.

Although Luciano is twelve years old, his reading achievement – especially of words in isolation – is still at the mid-Grade Two level, the result obtained two years previously. When spelling achievement was assessed at the end of Grade Two, Luciano showed a one-year-in-two improvement.

In Arithmetic, Luciano demonstrates an understanding of the concepts required to solve the four basic operations and their algorithms. He has not, however, acquired an automatic knowledge of number facts, an omission that has led him to invent ingenious methods for generating solutions. Unfortunately, because these strategies are very elaborate, incorrect responses are inevitable. When verbally coached through the steps, however, Luciano will find the solution. By means of an over-learning technique, teachers tried remedial methods to strengthen knowledge of number facts. In this case, precision teaching was used, but, over time, Luciano did not demonstrate significant improvement. Possibly, his retrieval difficulties were also indicated by this task.

When looking at the deficits that explain Luciano's inadequate academic achievement, a teacher would see not only that they that they date back to his Kindergarten year, but that they include his short attention span; his poor memory for what he regards as non-meaningful information; his weak visual memory; and his ineffective word retrieval. Moreover, Luciano's overall pattern of low achievement is also attributed to his lack of organizational skills, his impulsivity – which involves an absence of reflection in company with think-aloud incidents. Finally, taken into account are Luciano's behavioral manifestations of anger, frustration, and learned helplessness.

At this point, it appears that Luciano's classroom behavior and attitude readily overshadow his academic problems. For this reason, the focus should be switched from improving academic achievement to developing age-appropriate behavior and social skills. Such a change is supported by Luciano's reaction to remedial activities, those he complains of as "boring". Characteristically, he exerts little mental effort during instruction, probably because, over the years, his experience of failure has taught him that effort does not "pay off". Consequently, Luciano finds it easier to respond, "I don't know".

Recommendations

Foremost for the future will be the concern for Luciano's affective needs because, by experiencing successes, he may be able to re-gain control over his performance. At the same time, he must be given opportunities to develop social skills that will allow him to achieve group acceptance.

- *Because Luciano continues to like play, it is possible that lessons including a "game" format might motivate him. In addition, many language arts activities could be undertaken on the computer – a medium that fascinates him.*

- *Likely, Luciano would thrive in small-group instruction settings rather than in one-on-one contexts. In the individual setting, when the spotlight is on him, he responds by relinquishing responsibility, investing no effort. In a group setting, Luciano would be able to model the behavior of other students who, despite their respective difficulties, are involved in the remediation. When the opportunity arises for the teacher to ask him, initially, to repeat an answer, he will begin to access reinforcement. Because the stages of the process are clearly delineated, this format is also conducive to demonstrating the way a student might "think" through an activity.*

- *Luciano finds discussions and oral language situations more motivating than other forms of learning. For this reason, knowledge acquisition in content subjects such as Science and Social Studies[2] should be undertaken in a verbal Context. When Luciano was involved in a project about the Olympics, he showed himself quite pleased. Advantageously, such group and thematic work provided him with an increasing exposure to written language. In Luciano's case, then, indirect methods of acquiring reading and spelling skills are recommended.*

- *Luciano must begin to take greater responsibility for learning, a goal which he may start to attain by scheduling and doing 15 to 30 minutes of homework assigned on a daily basis. Projects may include listening, copying, drawing, cutting out an article from the newspaper, or other activities. While, it is evident that Luciano has a hectic after-school schedule – including hockey practices and a paper route – his parents must be encouraged to support and value the need for personal learning time. If possible, a specific work area and a time each evening should be designated for homework activities, instead of the teacher's requiring a set amount of work with quick completion as the aim. Somehow, Luciano must come to realize that persistence will eventually "pay off", especially if he recognizes the outcomes as desirable. A referral to an after-school counseling group at a local Mental Health Center or to a psychologist/psychiatrist may help both Luciano and his parents to deal with learned helplessness and, perhaps, depression.*

- *A review of Luciano's case should be undertaken in a year with the intention of planning for his secondary school placement.*

At this point, it is evident that the major obstacle facing Luciano is his inability to invest effort in academic activities. Because he has received so much encouragement from his parents and coaches, Luciano believes that he will pursue a career in professional sport. When parents are asked about this possibility, they confess that his hockey achievement is, at best, mediocre. As he approaches adolescence, if he is pushed too hard, Luciano may begin to act-out his anger and frustration. On the other hand, because he craves the social milieu of the regular class, he resists attempts for "special" placement. Assigning him a peer-tutor – a student with high social standing in the class – may spark his achievement.

Commonly, students in the LD grouping find themselves outside the peer group because membership often requires a deciphering of the group's covert signals and vocabulary. For example, Luciano will not grasp the in-jokes nor be able to comprehend the tacit requirements of group membership.

In summary, in a secondary school, students like Luciano are easily overlooked because they try so hard to become invisible. Often, they will have illusions about untenable career goals, eventually "dropping out" in order to escape the anxiety and frustration of academic demands. If planning can be directed towards teacher support, these students may be kept in school, both away from the criminal element and in positive learning situations.

Attention Deficit Disorder (ADHD)

Known as Attention Deficit Disorder (ADHD), this syndrome pertains to a condition that was once referred to as *hyperactivity* – when the focus was exclusively on the child's high levels of kinetic activity. At present, the central factors associated with ADHD relate to processes of inattention, hyperactivity, and impulsivity. (see Table 9-2)

While it is not clear whether the incidence of this disorder is on the rise, estimates are that around 7.5% of school-aged children are affected. Consequently, a teacher of a class of 30 might expect to have only one or as many as three students in the ADHD category. Usually, students diagnosed with ADHD are expected to have other accompanying problems, some of which might be conduct, mood, anxiety, and learning disorders.

Concurrently, those students with psychiatric disorders demonstrate high rates of social disability. When a conduct disorder is present, it points to potential substance abuse. Also evident is the realization that a student with ADHD – along with an anxiety disorder – can expect to experience more severe symptoms as time goes by. Other risk factors associated with ADHD may include: low socio-economic level; high rates of crime in the adjacent neighborhood; large family size, along with crowding and lack of privacy; a deviant peer group; an antisocial personality, especially in the father; mental disorders, often found in the mother; as well family conflict (Biederman, Faraone, & Monuteaux, 2002).

While children diagnosed with ADHD eventually become adults with ADHD – and although both are influenced by similar factors and treatment interventions – what is most compelling is that, subsequently, children of adults with ADHD are most at risk for the disorder. In the process of planning an intervention, therefore, the teacher should remain aware of these factors.

More boys than girls have ADHD – three to six boys for every girl, and some major differences exist along gender lines. Although a girl will be more likely to be inattentive, a boy may be more prone not only to have a learning disability but also to manifest problems at school and in the community. Boys with ADHD more often have accompanying disorders such as depression, disruptive conduct, and oppositional defiant disorders; they are also potential substance abusers (Biederman *et al.,* 2002.) Unlike those with LD, adolescents with ADHD, especially those with higher IQs and more successful educational achievement, are most likely, at an early age, to have their first cigarette and initial illegal drink. (Molina, & Pelham, 2001).

Although ADHD students generally experience school problems associated with their impulsive actions and lack of on-task behaviors, a subset of these students is likely to be diagnosed with one or another learning disability. Whereas such a dual diagnosis has severe educational consequences, it does not appear to impact social or psychiatric factors (Faraone, *et al.* 2002). Teachers are encouraged, however, to request an LD assessment, in addition, when referring students suspected of ADHD.

What does attention have to do with it?

Although the same word "attention" is used in a variety of contexts, it does not always refer to identical mental activities. As this syndrome is primary in ADHD, it is important that all its facets be examined. Not only Posner and Boies (1971) but also Krupski (1981) describes the range of aspects implied in the idea of attention.

Posner and Boies (1971) determine that attention may involve as many as three possible factors: it could refer to

- *Alertness.* This aspect of attention has to do with an individual's arousal level as well as with accompanying internal factors; for example, when a student is tired, it is a problem to focus attention. Similarly, depressed individuals who often lack sufficient arousal find it difficult to initiate a task.

- *Selection.* This meaning of attention has to do with the ability to select certain elements in the environment for special attention. When having lunch in a noisy cafeteria, a student will necessarily have to attend to the discussion at the table, in spite of background noise, if there is a hope of carrying on a conversation. This situation is often referred to as a *figure-ground process.*

- *Effort.* The concept of attention may also refer to its deployment toward a certain place or a certain type of content. Ordinarily, the less familiar an activity, the more attention is required for its completion. Of course, the inverse is also true: the more familiar – or the more practiced – the less attention will be required. Given this assumption, when involved in an editing exercise, the student purposefully decides to direct personal attention towards both the spelling of words and the coherence of phrases. In cognitive circles, this procedure is described as *levels of processing.*

Krupski (1981) identifies three distinct types of attentional processes, each closely related to classroom environments:

- *Selective Attention.* The student is able to attend to only one stimulus while disregarding all other forms of distraction and irrelevant stimuli. As with Posner's concept of *selection*, certain students may have problems trying to work in moderately noisy environments. Even the productive "hum" of a class at work or the "buzz" of a fluorescent light will be sufficient to distract a student diagnosed with attentional problems. In such cases, because of the need, simultaneously, to push all other sounds to the background, a difficult order, the student is unable to focus on the task at hand.

- *Sustained Attention.* The student is able to maintain attention for an extended period of time. Initially, younger children sustain attention for shorter periods, and, as they mature, are able to engage in an activity for a longer interval. Teachers often refer to this factor as the "ability to stay on task".

- *Voluntary Attention.* Once distracted, the student is able to pull attention back to the task at hand. Although able to stay on-task for an age-appropriate interval of time, certain students, the minute they are distracted, cannot re-direct their attention to their respective activities.

In an overview of all these aspects of attention, it is apparent that ability to focus – and its opposite – may play different roles in the behavior of children with ADHD. Because each attentional factor will be addressed differently, this perspective is especially important for the teacher who is planning an intervention; Table 9-1 shows specific elements to be taken into consideration.

Other Conditions with Attentional Components

Who has ADHD? Often, individual symptoms associated with children who have been diagnosed as experiencing ADHD are also found in "normal" children as well as in those with other special needs. Attentional difficulties are found in children who:

- are depressed – this is especially noticeable if they have low levels of mental or emotional arousal
- are pre-occupied – they appear to have problems showing voluntary attention
- are developmentally challenged – they regularly demonstrate difficulty in sustaining attention
- are younger – they show maturational differences when expected to engage in sustained and voluntary attention
- have educational histories with few or no opportunities to develop adequate attention spans and so have difficulty sustaining attention

Hyperactivity and impulsivity, two additional criteria of ADHD, are observed in other exceptional children. Those:

- with autism appear driven and very active
- with developmental challenges tend to be in constant motion
- with high levels of anxiety frequently engage in activity intended to reduce anxiety
- with poor nutritional habits – especially when their diets lack sufficient protein – seem listless
- with higher intelligence, especially in primary grades, are bored because the program is not sufficiently challenging
- with parents who may mistake activity for hyperactivity; when they themselves were raised in quiet environments, some parents have low tolerance for this behavior

Table 9-1. **Interventions associated with components of attention that are deficient.**

Alertness:	physical exercise, improved nutrition, adequate sleep
	breathing exercises
	referral to professional personnel
Selection or Selective Attention:	work in quiet environments and systematically increase noise level slowly -- *shaping*
	use a study carrel to provide a visual as well as a partial sound barrier
	place earphones over ears to supply mild pressure
	play games to train vigilance, e.g., say the words "Clap your hands when you hear the word *George*"; and then follow this with "Michael, Sam, Clap, Whistle, *George*."
Effort:	identify the low-level skills whose lack of proficiency causes the learner's attention to be deflected
	examine the student's level of proficiency in these skills
	re-teach these poorly developed skills to a level of overlearning
Sustained Attention:	establish the duration of on-task behavior easily sustained by the student
	assign tasks that set length and reinforce completion
	systematically increase the length of the assigned work as well as the time allotted for the on-task interval -- *shaping*
Voluntary Attention:	ask each class member to volunteer methods used to re-focus after being distracted
	ask each student to choose a personal method that seems to afford the best fit
	create mock situations in which the student who is distracted has to implement a relevant strategy to get back on-task -- implement this to the point of overlearning
	give friendly reinforcement to the student each time a relatively successful attempt is made to implement re-focusing strategies

Reported Symptoms of ADHD

On the basis of classroom observation, students with ADHD are likely to present many characteristic symptoms which demonstrate:

- an *impulsive* style – the student will respond quickly but inaccurately because insufficient time is taken to consider, weigh, and ponder the appropriateness of an action or response

- difficulty in investing sufficient attention in an activity – the learner is likely to start but not finish

- poor self-concept because of being continuously reprimanded – the student does not want to consider the need for making contributions to situations

- aggressiveness, although such behavior is perceived as unintentional – "It wasn't my fault!" or "I didn't do it on purpose!" are typical responses

- fickleness, influenced by distraction – this learner will move from one task to another with poor goal direction

- rapid patterns of frustration – the student becomes annoyed when events do not unfold effortlessly

- poor interaction with peers – this student will not only have few friends, because of a lack of social skill normally acquired tacitly, but may play exclusively with younger children

When a student displays some or many of these symptoms – to a degree that interferes with academic and social development – a referral for psychological assessment is warranted. Before being labeled *ADHD*, the student must meet the criteria outlined in the DSM manual (see Table 9-2).

Table 9-2. DSM-IV-TR Diagnostic Criteria of Attention Deficit Disorder.

A. Either (1) or (2):

    1. six (or more) of the following symptoms of inattention have persisted for at least 6 months to a degree that is maladaptive and inconsistent with developmental level:

        a. often fails to give close attention to details or makes careless mistakes in schoolwork, work, or other activities

        b. often has difficulty sustaining attention in tasks or play activities

        c. often does not seem to listen when spoken to directly

        d. often does not follow through on instructions and fails to finish schoolwork, chores, or duties in the workplace (not due to oppositional behavior or failure to understand instructions)   *cont'd*

     e.   often has difficulty organizing tasks and activities

     f.   often avoids, dislikes, or is reluctant to engage in tasks that require sustained mental effort (such as schoolwork or homework)

     g.   often loses things necessary for tasks or activities (e.g., toys, school assignments, pencils, books, or tools)

     h.   is often easily distracted by extraneous stimuli

     i.   is often forgetful in daily activities

2.   six (or more) of the following symptoms of **hyperactivity-impulsivity** have persisted for at least 6 months to a degree that is maladaptive and inconsistent with developmental level:

Hyperactivity

     a.   often fidgets with hands or feet or squirms in seat

     b.   often leaves seat in classroom or in other situations in which remaining seated is expected

     c.   often runs about or climbs excessively in situations in which it is inappropriate (in adolescents or adults, may be limited to subjective feelings of restlessness)

     d.   often has difficulty playing or engaging in leisure activities quietly

     e.   is often "on the go" or often acts as if "driven by a motor"

     f.   often talks excessively

Impulsivity

     g.   often blurts out answers before questions have been completed

     h.   often has difficulty awaiting turn

     i.   often interrupts or intrudes on others (e.g., butts into conversations or games)

B.   Some hyperactive-impulsive or inattentive symptoms that caused impairment were present before age 7 years.

C.   Some impairment from the symptoms is present in two or more settings (e.g., at school [or work] and at home).

D.   There must be clear evidence of clinically significant impairment in social, academic, or occupational functioning.

E.   The symptoms do not occur exclusively during the course of a Pervasive Developmental Disorder, Schizophrenia , or other Psychotic Disorder and are not better accounted for by another mental disorder (e.g., Mood Disorder, Anxiety Disorder, Dissociative Disorder, or a Personality Disorder).

Reprinted with permission from the Diagnostic and Statistical Manual of Mental Disorders, Fourth Edition, Text Revision, Washington, DC, American Psychiatric Association, 2000.

Previously a general label of ADHD was considered sufficient: DSM-IV-TR calls the entire group ADHD with the following subtypes:

- **ADHD — Combined Type:** criteria of inattention and hyperactivity-impulsivity are met for at least six months
- **ADHD — Predominantly Inattentive Type:** the inattention criteria are met primarily
- **ADHD — Predominantly Hyperactive-Impulsive Type**: if the reverse occurs, hyperactivity-impulsivity criteria are met
- **ADHD — Not Otherwise Specified:** some prominent symptoms of inattention or hyperactivity-impulsivity are present but some stated criteria for ADHD are not met

Conduct disorders[3] are associated with a small proportion of ADHD students who, because they are very difficult to work with, therefore warrant all the resources available.

What Causes ADHD?

Several potential causes of ADHD may be outlined even though explanations of the ways ADHD is acquired take into account all the information available; to a large extent, the evidence points to biological rather than environmental factors. On the basis of three major lines of investigation, the likelihood is that ADHD is caused by biological rather than by any of environmental factors, neurological abnormalities, or arousal defects; each of these has produced unique lines of evidence.

- Biological *versus* Environmental Factors:
  - Epidemiological data
  - Twin studies
  - Adoption studies
  - Allergies and dietary sensitivities
- Neurological Abnormalities
  - Brain damage
  - Neurotransmitter deficiency
- Arousal Defect

Theoretical Framework

ADHD has been conceptualized in many different ways; as expected, practitioners of each theory provide their own ideas about procedures for treatment.

A Deficit Model

When Strauss & Lethinen were investigating the relationship between behavior and damage of the brain, they found a correlation between brain damage and hyperactivity – at the time, it was considered the central symptom. In their investigation, they discovered a group of children who, although hyperactive, presented no hard signs of brain damage, yet these children behaved like individuals who were brain damaged. Given this observation, the two researchers arrived at an erroneous conclusion: hyperactivity is caused by brain damage. With no evidence, both concluded that the new group of children suffered from MBD - minimal brain damage.

This model speculates that children with ADHD, because they have deficits caused by minimal brain dysfunction, are therefore lacking in some ways. To substantiate this position, the following arguments are proposed in conjunction with the implied interventions:

> - Children with ADHD are perceived as qualitatively different from "normal" children, an idea compatible with the MBD hypothesis
> - Children who have such deficits respond paradoxically to medication – it produces a reaction opposite to the accustomed one. The following evidence is offered:
>   - Stimulants such as caffeine and Rytalin slow the subjects down
>   - Stimulants allow them to focus their attention
> - Children are helped when the stimulation in the environment is reduced – the new milieu is called *Bland Environment*

In reality, many children, "normal" or otherwise, obtain paradoxical effects from medication. In fact, when stimulants are used to slow down the individual, the process causes an activation or normalization of the brain responsible for inhibiting responses.

In chemical interventions, the side effects of medication are important elements; for example, Rytalin is known to slow down growth. Another danger is related to *state-dependent* learning because such learning is associated with the learner's internal environments; as a result, information is retrievable only when subsequent conditions are similar – in the "drugged" state, originally attained.

Finally, this perspective opens the door to abuse – one way to test for and diagnose ADHD is to examine the child's reaction to stimulant medication. Many individuals who respond to such chemicals have no ADHD symptoms; for example, students are notorious for drinking pots of coffee while cramming for exams.

Signs of Brain Damage?

When referring to people with impaired performance, neurologists talk about "hard" and "soft" signs of brain damage. If evidence of "hard" signs of brain damage is present, objective measures, such as EEG or other brain-scanning technology, have clearly identified brain injury. Typically, brain injuries resulting from trauma – in the cases of car and diving accidents, tumors, aneurysms, etc. – produce "hard" signs. In other situations when there is no hard evidence of brain injury, neurologists use a set of clinical measures including balance, eye movement, grip strength, etc., to determine whether these persons behave as if they were brain injured. In such cases, positive clinical symptoms if present are referred to as "soft" signs of brain damage.

Delay Theory

Delay theorists who take a developmental perspective, propose that persons with ADHD display forms of maturational lag rather than deficits illustrated by "soft" neurological signs. Such individuals are perceived, therefore, as immature but otherwise normal. It is expected that if left alone they will grow out of their delayed states.

Consonant with this view is the notion that children with ADHD are *quantitatively* rather than *qualitatively* different, implying that their behavior is just an exaggerated form of what is called "normal". In taking a developmental stance, however, this view relinquishes the potential for introducing appropriate interventions, by suggesting that only "time" is needed.

Difference Theory

In this theory the existence of *qualitative* differences in persons with ADHD is also negated. Rather, a statistical perspective is adopted, proposing that such children represent the extremes of temperament distribution. Marcel Kinsbourne's view suggests that – on a temperament continuum consisting of reactions and attentiveness to stimuli – everyone varies. In *Figure 9-1*, individuals with ADHD represent extremes along these two dimensions.

Because of the probability that such differences are normally distributed[4], researchers obtain evidence to support their view by observing noticeable differences in the way neonates – new born babies – react to stimuli. If children with ADHD are rated on the extreme ends of the distribution, such placement would assure their impulsive behavior. Unfortunately for them, society does not reward quick but inaccurate responses.

On further examination, the mismatch between temperament and environment seems the culprit responsible for ADHD. Because, for some children, certain environments may be too stimulating, interventions should focus on matching temperament and environment. The student easily distracted by noise may prefer to work in a quiet area, while the energetic student may do better with short tasks interspersed with breaks that allow for physical activity.

Figure 9-1. **Four extreme positions on a temperament continuum.**

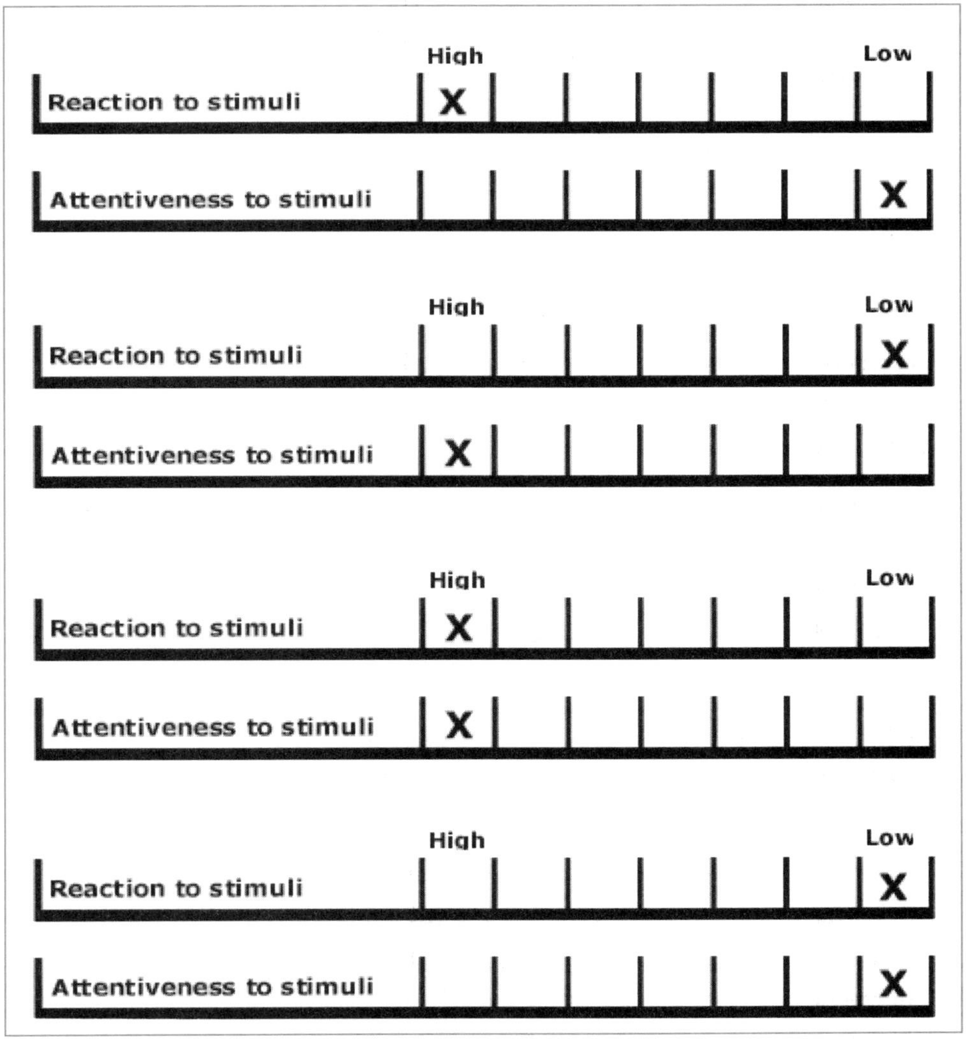

Optimal Stimulation Model

First proposed by Zentall (1977), this model suggests that children with ADHD lack the necessary stimulation. Zentall's argument supports the theory by suggesting that:

- children with ADHD are given stimulant forms of medication
- children with ADHD are indistinguishable from their "normal" counterparts when observed in the playground where there are no limitations on activity level
- children who are tested reveal that each individual has a personal level of sufficient stimulation

Recent evidence from Tannock and Schachar (personal communication, 1994) indicates that a child with ADHD will continue to respond impulsively even when engaged in playing a video game, an activity not only stimulating but known to provide immediate feedback. Interestingly, Pope and Bogart (1996) developed a video game to train an extended attention span.

When interventions are proposed in relation to this model, they contradict the recommendations of other views, especially because they suggest increasing stimulation by

- heightening task difficulty
- providing more stimulation in the classroom
- adding greater novelty to situations

Latest Views of ADHD

Biological: This theory sees ADHD as a physical consequence of problems relating to arousal mechanisms in the brain, warranting, therefore, both chemical interventions and cognitive mediation.

Motivational: This view, closely related to the learning history of the individual, proposes that by manipulating the environment – making contingencies more evident – the mediator can achieve behavioral change.

Treatment Approaches

While a range of major treatment approaches exists for modifying the behavior of ADHD students, the approach used in any situation is, typically, closely linked with the view of ADHD adopted by the respective special education team.

Medication

In the current treatment environment, the most common medication utilized is methylphenidate – Rytalin, a stimulant. This intervention is effective in controlling the behavior of ADHD children with severe symptoms. Several concerns exist, however, about using a prolonged chemical intervention, including such notions as:

- once a drug is effective, it is often treated as a cure; such an attitude may lead to abuse

- drug dosage is increased until desired effects are obtained, with the result that many children are over-medicated

- drug use traditionally has yielded differential effects throughout the day because the medication leaves the system in four to five hours, but long-acting forms of the drug which exist now are able to counter this problem

- drug therapy has side effects which, although reversible, include loss of weight – because the medication suppresses appetite – and height

- in a drug-based program a loss of incidental learning is probable because weekends and vacations are used as opportunities to relieve the system of medication

Drug interventions are most successful as an adjunct to behavioral approaches, especially those focusing on both a reduction of impulsive behavior and an increase of attentional skills.

Dietary Intervention

Not only the Feingold (1976) diet but also other elimination diets have been successful with particular individuals. Because this form of intervention has not, however, survived experimental scrutiny, it is perhaps true that food allergies are not a necessary condition in ADHD. If, for any reason, food allergies are suspected, it is recommended that a pediatric allergist sees the child.

Behavioral Modification

The main thrust of this type of behavioral approach is to ensure the clarity of cause-effect relationships – the contingencies – present in the child's environment. Such an attempt may be accomplished by:

- providing concrete rewards immediately
- shaping towards more abstract rewards – social reinforcers
- moving in a way that increases the interval between action and reinforcement – delaying gratification
- moving from concrete reinforcers to social reinforcers

The problem inherent in this approach is that children may have severe problems attending to contingencies. When this is the case, behavior modification approaches in conjunction with medication may be more effective because the drug therapy creates within the student an internal environment conducive to attending to contingencies highlighted by the teacher. Once learning starts occurring consistently, the hope is strong that medication can be systematically decreased and eventually eliminated.

If it is true that behavioral approaches are so fundamental that they apply to even the simplest living organism, why do some students with ADHD fail to respond to *operant*[5] methods? In general, it would seem that nature favors creatures who recognize cause-effect relationships existing between behavior and its consequences. Usually, those creatures unable to grasp the gist of this relationship pay the ultimate consequence – they are eaten.

In contrast to the harsh conditions in the natural world, humans and certain other creatures have caregivers – parents, teachers, etc., who shelter children during years of learning required by the species. If the ADHD child is unable to perceive the causal relationship between action and consequences, it is the responsibility of that young person's caregiver to mediate. When the child is amenable, language can be used to flag and direct the student's attention to critical aspects of the action-consequence relationship.

If this mediation is not central to the child's program, the ADHD student may interpret the consequences of behavior as arbitrary and independent. By not recognizing that consequences follow a form of action or behavior, the student may erroneously conclude that any punishment and/or encouragement which follows actions is a result of whether people like or do not like the perpetrator. Of course, such misconceptions have the ultimate effect of producing a negative impact on the self-concept and the self-esteem of the student, especially because the behavior of ADHD students is usually followed by punishment.

Teachers may highlight contingencies in various ways, some of which include:

- adjusting the time interval occurring between behavior and consequence so that, at first, consequences immediately follow student actions

- supplementing the program with language mediation to direct the student's attention toward the causal relationship not only *before* the behavior occurs but also *as* the behavior is occurring and finally *after* the behavior occurs (see Table 9-2). For example,

    - "Mario, what will happen if your assignment is not completed by dismissal time?"

    - "Mario, you did not complete the assignment and it is now dismissal time. What will happen next?"

    - "Mario, you have had to stay and complete your assignment after school! Why did that happen?"

- identifying the contingencies evident in the behavior of other students using Socratic – simplified – techniques

Cognitive Behavior Modification[6]

Meichenbaum and Burland (1979) describe the Matching Familiar Figures test (MFF), an index of impulsivity, to evaluate ADHD according to this dimension. For this test, each student must match pictures varying slightly in detail with a standard picture. Because the student has to find the one matching perfectly, time must be taken to examine each picture carefully.

Generally speaking, results on this test indicate that impulsive students although they had fast reaction time made many errors. Luria hypothesized that when individuals mature – around the age of seven years – they acquire the ability to control their actions in rhythm with their overt verbal behavior. The corollary is that the child is now ready to undertake such activities as pointing to an object and saying "one", pointing to the next object while saying "two", and so on. On the other hand, apparently, impulsive students are not able to parallel actions with verbal commands.

Table 9-3. Language mediation for the purpose of highlighting the contingency between two events.

Teacher Question	Student Response
Arthur, what will happen if you rip the notebook?	*If I rip the notebook, I will have to tape the pages.*
Arthur, what is the expectation about notebooks?	*They should not be ripped. We should look after them.*
Why are you expected to tape the notebook?	*Because I ripped it.*
Would you be expected to tape the notebook if you had not ripped it?	*No! Whoever did it would tape the pages.*
What happened when Sam ripped his notebook?	*Sam had to tape the pages.*

The central aim of the Cognitive Behavior Modification intervention is teach the student to slow down and become more reflective. By using overt verbal commands to control motor behavior, the student has more time and so more attention can be given to considering a course of action.

The *cognitive behavior modification* involves four phases:

- overt modeling – "Watch me do it! I touch the pencil. Let's do it and say it together".

- whispering to self – "Let's do it and whisper it".

- covert modeling – "Let's do it and say it in our minds.".

- no modeling but covertly carrying out the task – "You do it and say it in your mind".

Additional activities, which are nested within each stage, include teaching the student to:

- define the problem by asking, "What should I do in this situation?"

- attend to the important requirements of the task by asking, "What's important? What must I be sure to do?"

- find ways to correct errors by stating, "This didn't work. What should I do instead? How do I improve this?"

- use self-encouraging techniques; for example, "If I slow down, I can do this!" or "I finished it!" or "I'm proud of my work on this task".

The use of language to direct and control behavior is a tool that not only develops a more reflective style in students with ADHD but also provides them with an increased feeling that they can exercise control over their actions and environment.

Parent Training

Students with ADHD, like other types of *exceptional* learners, do not transfer easily what is learned in one setting to another. To promote transfer of learning, the teacher will find it necessary to provide consistency across settings for example, by arranging for an application of a set of contingencies in the classroom and at home. To accomplish this task, parents and teachers must be cooperatively involved in the intervention program to contribute and coordinate the plan across the two settings.

The parents of ADHD children may require specific training to implement *shaping* techniques so that both parent and child can experience success. Because an ADHD child demands such a high level of effort from caregivers, social agencies may be contacted to inquire about providing specialized baby-sitting simply to allow parents some time off. By minimizing parental frustration, an intervention of this kind may maximize the success of behavioral interventions in the home.

Classroom Intervention

Students with ADHD, depending on the severity of the condition, require a lot of teacher attention, particularly if they are placed in the regular class. To begin the process of creating an education plan for an ADHD student, the teacher might first consider answering to the following questions:

> - Does the student understand the instructions? To assume that attention is the not only factor responsible for disregarding instructions does not rule out the possibility that language comprehension is a problem.
>
> - Is the student initiating a power struggle – oppositional, defiant? When such behavior is evident it must be a primary source of concern and will require a team intervention (administrators, parents, psychologist, special education teacher, and other interested parties.)
>
> - Does the student know how to manage time and how to organize? Basic life skills such as time management and organization skill training may be helpful to the older student.   *cont'd*

- Is the schoolwork too difficult or too easy? When academic work is too difficult, the student often becomes frustrated, whereas when it is not sufficiently challenging, may be bored. Both conditions are expected to lead to behavior repercussions.

- Are medical or nutritional factors able to explain the student's restlessness? If the student is under the care of a physician and/or allergist, the teacher must be aware of the medical intervention in place.

Typically, in working with students with ADHD, classroom interventions focus on the following presenting behaviors: impulsivity, attention span, self concept, language mediation, aggression, distractibility, frustration, and peer relations. These issues are examined in the sections that follow.

Impulsivity

When a student responds (R) immediately after hearing the question (S), without processing the information, but blurting out the first thing that comes to mind, such behavior is considered impulsive. Training involves helping the individual to engage in self-talk during the interval between S and R (see Figure 9-2). In this mock-dialogue, the talk incorporates questions that will direct the student to undertake the necessary mental activity to answer the question. Systematically, the program plans to lengthen the interval between the question and the answer, thereby increasing the skills needed for reflective behavior.

Further attention is given to reinforcing attribution – the student's ownership of personal behavior. By asking questions about cause-effect relationships that exist within events, the teacher increases the number of opportunities to direct the student's attention to such details. It is also important to take the time to consider the consequence of personal action as well as the actions of others. In order to highlight contingencies, the teacher takes every opportunity to ask the student to state the reasons associated with administering a consequence (see Table 9-3).

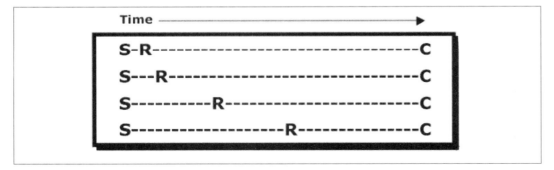

Figure 9-2. **Increasing the time interval between stimulus and response.**

Attention Span

Unless the student is able to focus attention on completing the demands of the task at hand, learning can be severely compromised. For this reason, teachers of students with ADHD (and younger or less mature students), create plans to increase attention span. This is accomplished with the following procedure:

- Ascertain the average time interval – even as brief as a minute – during which the student is able to stay on task
- Shape[7] the attending behavior from one up to 50 minutes
- Begin with an egg timer
- Use a tape recorder as an independent time keeper

Equipped with a bell, a blank tape, a tape recorder, and a stopwatch, the teacher can make tapes of one-minute, two-minute intervals, subsequently extending them. Making a one-minute tape involves recording one-minute intervals beginning with the instructions, "Begin working". This order is followed by one minute of silence, in real time on the tape, a ring of the bell, and a message saying, "Pause". The same sequence is repeated 15 to 30 times. Similarly, with the same procedure, tapes reflecting a variety of prepared intervals can be made.

An advantage of the "tape" procedure lies in the student's ability to be trained independently. Once the procedure has been practiced and the format is apparent, the student is able to direct the training and be involved in the decision to switch to a tape with a longer interval. Equipped with earphones, the student is able to improve attention span in the context of independent activities in the classroom. In some cases, the student may require a longer period of monitoring which can be accomplished by recruiting the help of a peer-tutor.

Students are motivated by this strategy because they are able to observe improvement that is easily recorded on a chart. By working with small tasks and slowly increasing their length, the student becomes more skillful and experiences success almost immediately. After all, the starting point was an interval of time that the student found manageable. Motivation is also affected by the student's participation in the decision-making process which provides opportunities to establish realistic goals.

Self-concept

When students are constantly reprimanded and are rarely praised for a job well done, self-concept issues may present themselves. "Don't touch this you will break it!" "Larry get back to work!" "Let

Marcia, Kamal, and Kisha finish!" In the classroom and at home, such is the situation experienced by a student with ADHD. Leading them to the conclusions that they are not liked are the negative feedback and the lack of personal control over behavior experienced by such students. To strengthen self-concept, the teacher creates programs that will develop academic competencies in order to foster feelings of being capable of completing school work and of belonging to the group. This can be accomplished in various ways, but the most significant include the following:

- School task and activities are constructed and modified to insure student success

- Improvement and successes are generally depicted in a visual manner, easily understood by the student, and placed in a strategic place for the student to see

- Positive encounters between the teacher and student are increased, sometimes by introducing "goodies" and/or "warm fuzzies" for no obvious reason – the opposite of the student's normal expectation

- With the use of language, the student is trained to make positive self-statements – to others, too

Language Mediation

By being able to use covert language to monitor and direct personal behavior, the student with ADHD will establish more control over personal actions. In doing so, assuming responsibility for both the behavior and its consequences becomes the next step in the teaching sequence. The earlier section on Cognitive Behavior Modification (p. 359) illustrates the strategies to be implemented by teachers.

Bibliotherapy

Reading books on a subject relevant to the student's situation promotes an objective method to address personal behavior. For example, a primary-aged student would appreciate the book entitled *Shelley, the Hyperactive Turtle,* by Moss (1989) because symptoms of ADHD can be discussed in relation to the turtle's behavior. Similarly, books for teens and young adults are available for the purpose of acquiring more information and dismissing misconception, but also to examine, discuss, and problem-solve. The book entitled *I Would If I Could: A Teenagers's Guide to ADHD/Hyperactivity* by Michael Gordon (1993) is appropriate for this age group. The teacher can enlist the help of the school librarian in identifying children's and teens' literature that incorporates characters with various special needs.

Aggression

Although the aggressive subgroup of students with ADHD represents only a small percentage, the teacher and students are encouraged to remember that meeting **safety needs is primary** which means it is of paramount importance. Breaches of the safety norm should be treated like all other safety violations.

If a general policy about procedures for aggressive behavior in the school is not available, the teacher should inquire about it by approaching administrative personnel; if it exists, it should be followed exactly.

Distractibility

Distractibility, often defined as the inability to maintain attention, also incorporates inappropriate change from one focus to the next. For example, in the course of a discussion with a peer, Farley's mindset is triggered by isolated words that will direct him to a complete change of topic. As a result, his responses are not relevant to the discussion at hand and those who speak to him may conclude that he is not listening.

The first step in tackling this problem is to increase the student's awareness of the phenomenon. Is Farley aware of the topic change? To accomplish this objective, the teacher might require Farley to discuss a topic with a peer who would be instructed to raise a card every time that Farley's responses were outside the subject.

Organizational Skills

A variety of strategies and procedures exists that can facilitate the orderly sequencing of events. Acquiring such organizational procedures is helpful to most students but particularly to teens with ADHD. The student is taught to direct personal activities by setting personal goals and objectives, not only immediate aims but also long-term goals.

- By acquiring time management skills, the student can learn to use time more productively
- In learning organizational skills, the student is able to establish control over actions and tasks

Tolerance to frustration

Students with ADHD are easily frustrated when goals are not immediately achievable. Increasing levels of frustration lead to an outburst when a threshold level is surpassed. Ordinarily, students who recognize mounting frustration seek means to defuse it with socially appropriate and adaptive methods. An awareness of internal states and feelings and the ability to label these feelings correctly, for example, differentiating between frustration and anger, represents the first step. Applying relaxation and other calming techniques as well as using language to evaluate the situation and to determine ways to improve it, is the next move. The teacher can facilitate the process by utilizing the following recommendations:

- The teacher, by demonstrating relaxation techniques and showing the student how to practice them when frustrated, may help the young person become more tolerant of such personal and universally annoying feelings

- The teacher may schedule activities in an accessible range, enabling the student to begin with easy tasks and then to conquer more difficult ones

- The teacher ensures that the student is given a new or novel presentation of a task only when mastery has been achieved in previous work

- The teacher provides the student with the vocabulary to convey feelings and internal states, and then supports this language usage in situations

As the student is able to reduce frustration levels, feelings of control and mastery of challenging situations will develop.

Peer Relations

Like other students with special needs, students with attentional problems have difficulty in both making friends and participating with peer groups. Often ostracized, they can be observed in the schoolyard, playing with younger children, or in the cafeteria, eating alone.

Because the affective need to belong and feel prized is so fundamental, it must be addressed in the educational plan of ADHD students. When they add *social skills training* to the student's classroom program, teachers may devise a remedial curriculum that addresses issues of "making friends", "reading faces", and attending to other nonverbal cues". Another focus will develop the language of social interaction and self-defense so that the student learns to communicate intentions to teachers and peers. Being able to respond verbally to taunts is likely to help the student reduce the temptation to risk physical aggression. These and other such approaches can be incorporated in the student's educational plan (see Pelligrini & Horvat, 1995).

Learned Helplessness

Learned helplessness, a concept introduced by Seligman, who demonstrated that dogs, first subjected to punishment while being given no chance to avoid it, subsequently did not attempt to escape punishment when the opportunity was present. By generalizing this idea to human behavior, teachers and workers will understand why some students resign themselves to failure.

In experiments, Diener and Dweck (1980) compared students who demonstrated *helplessness* with others who were successful in their activities. In Table 9-4, group differences are shown as they relate thinking processes to behavior when the student is confronted with either failure or success, and, most important, to situations designed to ensure success or failure.

Table 9-4. Comparison of groups with either Learned Helplessness or Mastery Orientation on the basis of belief and behavior.

	Helplessness	**Mastery Orientation**
Thoughts	• failure is believed to be inevitable and overwhelming	• success can be repeated
When failure occurs:	• individuals dwell on the present	• individuals look towards the future
	• individuals dwell on the negatives	• individuals emphasize the positives
	• individuals seek to escape the situation	• individuals invest energy in generating strategies
When success occurs:	• prior success is forgotten and considered irrelevant to future success	• prior success remains salient and is linked with the ability to achieve success again
	• success is attributed to luck rather than skill	• successes are accurately recalled
	• individuals discount their successes and over-estimate their failures	
When the "dweck" is stacked!	• individuals do not define themselves as succeeding even when success is inevitable as in "grasping failure from the jaws of success"	• individuals do not define themselves as failing, even when failure is programmed

It is evident that student belief about the ability to succeed is an important variable (Dweck, 2002) to be addressed in the education plan of students with ADHD. These students are particularly vulnerable to attribution errors because, as was previously discussed, they are often unable to recognize contingencies between personal behavior and the consequences that follow.

Autism

In the 1940s, Autism was first defined as a disorder. Prior to that, autistic children were thought to be either retarded or psychotic, sometimes both. Because media attention, in films such as "Rain Man", often focuses on individuals with limited but unique abilities, many people have the impression that most autistic individuals are *"idiots savants"*. The truth is that the idiot savant category represents much less than one percent of the autistic population, while the other 90%, unfortunately, demonstrate various degrees of mental retardation.

Found in the classification Pervasive Developmental Disorder, Autism is included with Rett's Disorder, Asperger Syndrome, Childhood Disintegrative Disorder, and PDD not otherwise specified. In Rett's Disorder, the normal development present in the first five months after birth is followed by a deceleration of head (cranial) growth during the period from five to forty-eight months. At this time, previously acquired hand skills disappear, to be replaced by such movements as hand wringing and hand washing. Besides the onset of severely impaired language and psychomotor functions, as well as poor motor coordination, a loss of social engagement occurs, although this element returns later. Another condition mentioned earlier — Asperger Syndrome — is outlined and described in detail in the major section following, because those students diagnosed with Asperger Syndrome are frequently found in the regular classroom.

In students diagnosed with Childhood Disintegrative Disorder, normal development is characteristically present in the first two years of life, but, before the age of ten, a loss of either language or of social, motor, or play skills occurs, sometimes in addition to bowel and bladder control. In these students, social and language skills demonstrate characteristics similar to those found in autistic individuals.

When some atypical individuals appear – ones who do not meet all criteria for Autism, and are excluded from other diagnoses – they will probably be found listed in the PDD – "not otherwise specified" – category.

Table 9-5. DSM-IV-TR Diagnostic Criteria of Autistic Disorder

A. A total of six (or more) items from (1), (2), and (3), with at least two from (1), and one each from (2) and (3):

   1. qualitative impairment in social interaction, as manifested by at least two of the following:

      a. marked impairment in the use of multiple nonverbal behaviors such as eye-to-eye gaze, facial expression, body postures, and gestures to regulate social interaction

      b. failure to develop peer relationships appropriate to developmental level

      c. a lack of spontaneous seeking to share enjoyment, interests, or achievements with other people (e.g., by a lack of showing, bringing, or pointing out objects of interest)

      d. lack of social or emotional reciprocity

   2. qualitative impairments in communication as manifested by at least one of the following:

      a. delay in, or total lack of, the development of spoken language (not accompanied by an attempt to compensate through alternative modes of communication such as gesture or mime)

      b. in individuals with adequate speech, marked impairment in the ability to initiate or sustain a conversation with others

      c. stereotyped and repetitive use of language or idiosyncratic language

      d. lack of varied, spontaneous make-believe play or social imitative play appropriate to developmental level

   3. restricted repetitive and stereotyped patterns of behavior, interests, and activities, as manifested by at least one of the following:

      a. encompassing preoccupation with one or more stereotyped and restricted patterns of interest that is abnormal either in intensity or focus

      b. apparently inflexible adherence to specific, nonfunctional routines or rituals

      c. stereotyped and repetitive motor mannerisms (e.g., hand or finger flapping or twisting, or complex whole-body movements)

      d. persistent preoccupation with parts of objects

B. Delays or abnormal functioning in at least one of the following areas, with onset prior to age 3 years: (1) social interaction, (2) language as used in social communication, or (3) symbolic or imaginative play.

C. The disturbance is not better accounted for by Rett's Disorder or Childhood Disintegrative Disorder.

Reprinted with permission from the Diagnostic and Statistical Manual of Mental Disorders, Fourth Edition, Text Revision, Washington, DC, American Psychiatric Association, 2000.

Relationship of Autism and Developmental Language Disorders

Although some debate continues about which symptom of autism is foremost, little doubt exists about the realization that Autistic children present a unique set of language difficulties. In their difference from other children with developmental language disorders – aside from a skill deficit – they often lack the motivation to communicate. Like other children with language disorders, when they may fail to respond to sounds, sometimes they are perceived as hearing impaired. Similarly, they appear not to comprehend the bias of a sound – chirping of a bird, the siren of an ambulance, or the tone of instructions given by a voice.

Autistic young people also differ from children with other language disorders along several dimensions. For example, these children are recognized by their echolalia – the parrot-like shadowing and repetition of sounds and verbal commands – and also by their misuse of pronouns; for example, instead of saying, "I eat lunch", an Autistic child is more likely to say, "You eat lunch". Finally, whereas other children with language problems may be motivated to communicate by using gestures, Autistic children rarely show any such willingness.

Theoretical Approaches

Traditionally, the Psychodynamic model has perceived Autism as caused by adverse parental involvement, with the result that development is somewhat blocked. Unfortunately, in this view, parents shoulder the entire responsibility, whereas behaviorists take the focus away from them to pinpoint the cause of Autism as relating to distorted perceptual processes. More radical behaviorists, such as Lovaas, propose that causes are rooted either in inappropriate contingencies or in speech deficits. Yet another view, the biophysical perspective of neuropsychology, indicates that physiological anomalies in the brain and sensory apparatus explain the distorted perception and motor processes found in Autistic individuals.

While it is evident that the causes of this disorder are still unclear, interventions used in a school are likely to reflect the salient features of the respective view adopted by the local special-education team. Often, behavioral objectives such as those listed below are treated independently of one another:

- *Reducing the incidence of self-injuring behavior.* Sometimes, this process is attempted through punishment. Such a controversial intervention, which may employ water squirted in the student's face or application of mild electric shock, succeeds only in the rare cases where self-injurious behavior is so extreme as not to respond to other interventions. Any decision to intervene in this manner is not only undertaken by a team – which includes parents – but is implemented for a short period of time in a mental health facility, not in a school.

- *Establishing eye contact.* This action is often considered a precursor to social interaction and communication. In this intervention, shaping strategies are used to reward successive approximations – turning the child's head toward the teacher, following a moving target about the face, and other subsequent gradual changes.

- *Reducing tantrum behavior.* Although the use of time-out procedures is associated with extinguishing tantrum behavior in children in more normal populations, in the case of Autistic individuals, the validity of the time-out strategies is seriously questioned. The reason is that, in this case, the behavior may not be a bid for attention. Other causes may include a response to an internal state of extreme anxiety triggered by a various factors – changes in the environment, new events, distorted perceptions, and other phenomena. As with other types of withdrawn children, the time-out procedure may serve only to create opportunity for engaging in additional withdrawal and/or self-stimulatory behavior, phenomena usually to be discouraged.

- *Reducing self-stimulatory behaviors.* Reducing behaviors such as hand-flapping, moving hand in and out of visual field, rocking, and other such actions – is an objective adopted for the purpose of increasing the student's sociability skills. Besides making the student appear "bizarre", such behaviors reduce opportunities for social contact, especially when the student appears to retreat inward. If these behaviors are self-stimulatory, that is, the student is deriving personal pleasure from them, teachers and workers will devise ingenious ways to circumvent their reinforcement value. For example, when a student habitually strokes a piece of carpet for tactile stimulation, that individual is fitted with suitable gloves.

- *Increasing tolerance for environmental change.* Raising tolerance for change is often an important feature of the intervention plan for an Autistic student. Typically, the sensitivity to change exhibited by these individuals will be expressed with anxiety-reducing behaviors similar to or even identical to those used for self-stimulation. In such cases, the teacher is required, first, to observe the pattern of antecedent events which might identify the source of the anxiety, and then to find ways to temper these. Very frequently, anxiety is a function of novelty, and, therefore, as the environment becomes more familiar and predictable for the student, it also becomes safer. In such circumstances, routine is necessary, meaning that change should be introduced in small doses. *cont'd*

- *Emphasizing language development.* In the structuring of an intervention plan, the development of language skills is often primary because Autistic students vary in their communication skills — some of them have none, while others, on a continuum, reach limited levels. In this connection, some jurisdictions classify Autism as a communication disorder.

- *Social skills.* Because the ability to interact socially is often lacking in these students — who sometimes appear oblivious to the people around them — social skills training becomes necessary. Not only their limited language skill but also their lack of interest in communicating means they are usually isolated, but their "bizarre" behavior patterns add to the isolation. In a few cases, Autistic children are treated as special pets in the school environment, especially if some of their behaviors are endearing rather than repulsive. At school, Knut is greeted and hugged by other children who find him an amusing distraction. His gentle disposition and ability to make eye contact, as well as to smile appropriately, allow a pleasant level of interaction with others.

Language Patterns that Warrant Intervention

Autistic children vary in three language domains; specifically:

- the amount of speech produced – from lack of speech, to a delay in speech, to limited speech
- the anomalous patterns contained in each individual's speech
- the overlap of contextualized language and behavior – pragmatics

Unlike other children with language disorders, Autistic children when they lack speech do not use gestures. Those who manifest a delay in speech – speech is present and then stops – may have it or lack it for brief amounts of time – months – or for long periods of time – years. Some Autistic children, having limited speech, may use "telegraphic" speech such as "Go eat" or "Go bus", and, in some cases, longer but still limited word patterns.

In many Autistic students, atypical patterns of speech are present; for example, echolalia — parrot-like repetition of words or phrases previously heard — can immediately follow every communicative attempt. When Ms. Wilcox asked Marlon, "What is your name?" he responds immediately with the words, "What is your name? What is your name? What is your name?" Eduardo, an Autistic student who has delayed echolalia, repeats in class either statements he may have heard on television the night before or others heard earlier the same day. Atypical speech characteristic of Autism also includes:

- pronomial reversals – "you" is mistakenly substituted for "I"

- neologisms – non-words are created for their auditory value; for example "higgle sniggle"

- metaphorical use of language – "the crying boat"; inappropriate remarks – "stinky-poo"

- articulation difficulties – the child is unable to pronounce certain sounds

Deficits in pragmatics include the autistic student's:

- difficulty in accepting turn-taking; when Gabriel wants a toy, he will grab it out of the hands of the student who is playing with it

- lack of motivation in communicating with adults or peers

- inability to use objects symbolically

- problems with inflection, especially in the areas of intonation and stress; utterances may sound "flat", meaning, for instance, that no differences are audible that would distinguish between statements and questions

- ineffective use of visual facial features — the affect may be "flat" or inappropriate, but is usually non-responsive

Interventions

In addition to programs that will promote pro-social behaviors and minimize those that interfere with learning activities, several programs exist that focus on developing language skills. First to be described and introduced in 1960s is Lovaas' Vocal Training program, followed by its offshoot, Applied Behavior Analysis. Somewhat later, attempts were made to develop communication skill relating to aspects of the teaching of American Sign Language. The Miller Method sets out to incorporate both spoken language and ASL, employing strategies that will focus the attention of the student. Finally, because parents are often intrigued by this intervention, the procedure known as Facilitative Communication is described.

Outline of Vocal Training Proposed by Lovaas et al.

As a radical behaviorist, Lovaas focused on the Autistic child's lack of communication, directing his intervention primarily to this topic. In order to promote vocal training, Lovaas used *shaping* procedure among a sample group of Autistic children lacking speech. Equipped with behavioral principles, Lovaas and his colleagues recorded their methodology in the film "Behavior Modification" (1969).

In the vocal training, two major stages were involved:

> - *Training Vocal Imitation.* Because their students were completely lacking in speech, the procedure first had to train them to imitate speech sounds
> - *Training Meaningful Speech.* At the second stage, the students were taught to understand the underlying meaning of groups of speech sounds

Training Vocal Imitation

In the *shaping* procedures adopted by Lovaas and his team, the training of vocal imitation involved using food as a reinforcer. Initially, to increase the vocal output of students, food reinforcement was employed any time a vocal sound was made. Once the objective was met, trainers became interested in exercising temporal control over vocalization instead of waiting for random sounds to be made. To accomplish this task, the schedule of reinforcement was changed from a continuous one to a pattern which reinforced vocalizations emitted within a five-second interval.

After reducing the waiting period between vocalizations, the researchers' next step was to train the students to imitate speech sounds. Of course, the first speech sounds to be attempted were those most easily learned, because their obvious differences in mouth movements provided additional visual and motor cues; for example, "aaah" and "mmmm". To access reinforcement, instructors expected that within six seconds the student would match the sound made by the trainer. Once a sound appeared easy to imitate, trainers introduced a new one. Using this procedure, teachers are able to help students to learn to imitate speech.

Training Meaningful Speech

During this phase, as the trainers focused primarily on the meaningfulness of spoken language, they attempted to establish expressive speech by reinforcing a student as soon as the appropriate word was emitted to describe an object. The sequence might involve the trainer's saying, first, "What is this?" while holding and pointing to an object, and then providing the answer: "An apple". In order to receive reinforcement, the words "An apple" must be imitated by the student. With this *prompt-and-fade* strategy, the student is initially cued, "An apple", but eventually, when the prompt is removed, the student provides the correct answer whenever the question posed.

The last step is to establish verbal comprehension by having the student carry out simple commands. Again, a *prompt-and-fade* strategy is used to encourage the student to respond to such statements as, "Close the door".

Criticism

Although Lovaas has produced a language intervention which, in its overall concept and practice, exemplifies good *Learning Theory*, his system overlooks the potential contributions of Psycholinguistic and Developmental theories. When observed in natural settings, children do not acquire language in the manner presented by Lovaas' procedure. In his far-reaching study of human language acquisition, Chomsky proposed that because the human brain – within social environments – is pre-wired for language, speech is acquired as a function of adequate language stimulation. When seen in terms of Chomsky's theories, Lovaas' artificial intervention will be likely to lose strength once reinforcement is no longer available. In fact, when they left residential care to go back to their homes, the children in the sample experienced this outcome. Subsequently, however, further experimentation showed that *spontaneous recovery* was obtained when the children returned to the residential setting where the earlier structure, along with the previous levels of reinforcement, could be re-introduced.

In fairness to Lovaas, his sample contained children with very severe language deficits. Because the *encoding specificity principle* in human memory predicts that information encoded in a context is best remembered when retrieved in the same context, Lovaas would have been wise to extend training to the children's homes, incorporating parallel conditions on a day-to-day basis. Regardless of such considerations, Lovaas' training does not appear to have produced, in any usually accepted sense of the idea, true language acquisition.

Applied Behavior Analysis (ABA)

An extension of the Lovaas Method, Applied Behavior Analysis, is an intervention model that continues to be applied to the treatment of Autistic individuals. As it is a program with roots in Behaviorism, many essential elements contained in an ABA program are predictable:

- *The target behavior is relevant to the student's functioning.* A choice is made about which behavior is central to the student's social functioning.

- *Behaviors are observable and recorded.* The target behavior is defined in such a way as to be recognizable by various observers who can easily record its frequency or duration.

- *Changes in behavior should be attributable to the behavior intervention.* When clear and precise data have been collected and analyzed, a cause-effect relationship – between the intervention and the subsequent change in behavior – is evident.

- *The procedures are thoroughly described.* The strategies are so well defined that various individuals, teachers, parents, and other interested parties are able to obtain the same outcomes when the intervention is specifically applied.

- *The interventions are based on sound principles based on Learning Theory.* Techniques such as differential reinforcements, extinction, and other relevant procedures are incorporated into the program to achieve the desired goal.

- *The program is continuously evaluated.* Based on the data collected, changes are implemented to obtain the greatest effectiveness.

- *The transfer of newly learned behavior to other contexts is planned.* Recognizing that context effects are to be expected, any ABA plan should incorporate strategies to maximize transfer of new behavior not only by conducting the program in various settings but also by relating it to similar behaviors.

Discrete Trial Training (DTT)

Although some consider Discrete Trial Training to be a teaching method under the umbrella of ABA, others believe the two to be quite different. With both rooted in the tradition of Behaviorism, DTT uses the idea of targeting a single cycle of an instructional routine which is consecutively repeated many times – several times a day, over many days – until the skill is mastered. In this procedure, then, the primary focus is the component parts of a single trial which contains the following elements:

- the discriminative stimulus (S^D) represents the instruction or cue that triggers the student to respond

- the optional prompting stimulus (S^P) is provided by the teacher to ensure that the student responds correctly; for example, whispering the correct response in the student's ear or mouthing the response. Once the correct response is established, the prompt is removed[8].

- the response (R) represents the skill or action which is the target of instruction

cont'd

- the reinforcing stimulus (S^R) designates the reward and/or feedback that serves to reinforce the making of the response as well as doing so correctly

- the inter-trial interval (^{TTI}) identifies the duration of a brief pause between consecutive trials

Within a teaching sequence, these elements are ordered in the following manner: the teacher's instruction (S^D) comes first. If a prompt is required to facilitate the student's correct response, the teacher provides a suitable cue; otherwise the student's response (R) is awaited. If the student responds incorrectly, the correct answer is provided, and a new trial follows immediately after a very short interval (^{TTI}). Again, the teacher's instruction (S^D) prompts the student to respond (R). Perhaps, the inclusion of a helping gesture (S^P) is warranted. When the student's response (R) is correct or a close approximation of the acceptable response, it is followed by a reward or praise (S^R). At this point, a longer interval (^{TTI}) is implemented to designate the successful completion of the set. Particularly relevant to Autistic students is the structure of DTT because it has the ability to circumvent some of their learning limitations. For example, the particular procedure allows the teacher to implement a program even with a student whose attention span lasts for just a few seconds. At the outset, it recognizes that such a student will be motivated primarily by concrete rewards. By pairing the expected rewards with social praise, however, the trainer expects that the student will eventually learn to complete tasks simply for social reinforcers – some praise, a smile, or another inducement. With the focus on a single trial, as well as on differential reinforcement, the student can learn to discriminate between the relevant cues – those that are part of the instructional routine – and to ignore any irrevelant stimuli in the environment: chairs moving, birds chirping. In planning programs, practitioners of DTT (similar to those who work with ABA) recognize the need to include activities that will maximize transfer of learning to new situations. Although DTT can be structured to teach not only communication skills (see Lovaas), but also skills related to perspective taking and social competence; other techniques have also proved to be very useful (see p. 379).

Because Autistic individuals have serious difficulties when attempting to extract the contingencies present in the environment or trying to learn from observing the behavior of others, DTT offers a structure that nonetheless promotes learning. Any reader who is interested in this form of intervention is encouraged to read a "how to" book on ABA, such as *Behavioral Intervention for Young Children With Autism: A Manual for Parents and Professionals*, edited by Maurice, Green, and Luce (1996)[9].

Use of American Sign Language (ASL)

Recognizing that many Autistic children demonstrate strong visual processing abilities, in contrast to their inferior spoken language accessing and responding skills, Konstantareas (1980s) studied the use of ASL in developing the communication skills of this special group. In her research, in which she evaluated three types of interventions – oral language training, ASL training, and a combination of ASL and oral language training – the three interventions were assessed according to the level of oral language produced by each. In the final analysis, the group who received both oral language and ASL training reached the highest level of oral-language skill.

When a student possesses an intact mode for processing information, which can be used to promote learning, it can be accessed as a fundamental remedial strategy, especially in the case of students with learning disabilities who present a broad array of strengths and weaknesses. For example, recognizing the student's visual memory strengths as a means of improving weak language skills appears to be an appropriate instructional practice.

Remedial Strategies

- Teach through the student's strengths

- Overcome the student's weaknesses

- Attempt both strategies

The Miller Method

In the Miller Method, (Miller & Eller-Miller, 1989) although communication is taught by means of both signed and spoken language, the process involves a sequence that mimics natural development. The process, which is initiated with motor movement in an environment two-to-four feet off the ground, is based on the idea that, in that locale, students are more focused, aware of their bodies, and responsive. Furthermore, within this method, meaning is acquired when an adult narrates, in both sign and spoken language, the actions of children negotiating obstacles placed in their paths. Although the Miller Method is not a *behavioral* intervention, *shaping* procedures are used to teach complex behaviors while special attention is given to any transfer of learning across settings, especially when it enables children to apply what is learned from one context to another.

In connection with their ingenious procedures, Arnold Miller and Eileen Eller-Miller, founders of The Language Cognitive Development Center, a treatment locus for children who have pervasive developmental disorders, offer courses to parents and professionals.

Facilitative Communication

For people unable to communicate directly, but especially for children so handicapped, this method proposes that an Autistic student, with the help of a facilitator who acts as a conduit, can transmit a personal message. Typically, both hold the writing instrument which produces the message believed to originate in the student's mind.

Although some parents have embraced this intervention, because it perceives Autism simply as a language-expressive problem, no empirical evidence exists to support the theory. In some cases, the process seems to demonstrate that a student's response may be dependent on the facilitator's knowledge rather than on what the student is thinking.

Perspective taking and social competence

More recently, proponents of the Theory of Mind perspective believe that an infant, by the age of 30 to 36 months, is aware that others have thoughts and feelings separate from the child's own mind set. When it exists, this set of thoughts — sometimes conveyed in the child's pretend play — is eventually expressed orally. In Autistic children, irrespective of their linguistic facility, the Theory of Mind does not appear to develop.

Difficult to define because of its abstract nature, Theory of Mind is easily conceptualized as perspective taking, a notion which, while it is important to the development of social competence, is generally absent in individuals with Autism. Some researchers, however, believe that perspective taking is teachable. To date, although recent attempts to teach perspective taking to Autistic individuals is fraught with problems of transfer – as expected, in this as in other contexts, skills acquired in certain contexts are not usually able to be applied to new situations.

In 2002, Charlop-Christy and Daneshvar employed the procedure known as video modeling to promote and facilitate transfer of skills. In this method – successfully used to teach and promote communication skills along with academic performance, not only by itself but also in conjunction with ABA training – the processes can be applied in the transfer of social and self-help skills. At the outset, its visual nature draws on the Autistic student's stronger modality. By watching others performing a series of behaviors, the Autistic individual is able to mimic and use the behavior in appropriate situations. For more information about this process, the reader is directed to consult *Visual Teaching Method for Children with Autism,* by Liisa Neumann (2000).

Other Treatment Interventions

In a range of contexts, several other interventions are used with Autistic children; for example, from a Psychodynamic perspective, Bettelheim believed that by establishing a warm, accepting environment, the teachers or institution could meet the basic needs of the student. In a further attempt to provide skills to Autistic children, Axline[10] offered play therapy as a way of dealing with, and learning about, the child's relationship with parents.

Especially in its attempt to deal with what happens to a family coping with a "challenged" child, the type of training called Family Therapy is recommended to address the many stressors that impact the overall family dynamic. By providing essential emotional outlets, a wide range of parent support groups and social agencies often helps to promote the socio-emotional well-being of the student and the family.

Asperger Syndrome

Although Hans Asperger, a Viennese physician, had first identified Asperger Syndrome in 1944, it was not until 1994 that AS began to be included in the DSM[11] (see Table 9-6). The controversy about whether AS should be in a separate category – or is possibly a learning disability of social communication with an autistic disorder – still rages (Freeman, Cronin, & Candela, 2002). Apparently, differences between those people with AS and high-functioning autistic persons (HFA) are not qualitative, but exist instead in the degree of intellectual and other functions possessed by the two groups (Meyer & Minshew, 2002). While the two types share what seems to be the same range of social dysfunction, persons with AS display impaired social judgment, while scoring higher on verbal tasks. On the other hand, those diagnosed as HFA may perform better on visio-spatial tasks such as the Block Design[12].

There is no doubt that because an overlap in symptoms exists in children and adolescents diagnosed with Autism and Asperger, some clinicians prefer to see the two conditions on a continuum. Nevertheless, this ambiguity poses a challenge for diagnosticians who compare the two groups according to their language and cognitive abilities. Also taken together are their symptoms of other disorders as well as their ability to function adaptively. In the meantime, students with AS are expected to be highly verbal, to possess intact cognitive abilities, and, on the negative side, to manifest major problems relating to social competence.

Myles and Simpson (2002) categorize AS primarily as a social disorder; but unlike most Autistics (AD) and despite the limited set of social skills at their disposable, young people diagnosed with Asperger Syndrome are motivated to interact socially. Thus, the teacher can expect students with AS:

- to appear stiff and awkward in social contexts
- to respond inappropriately to non-verbal social cues
- to appear self centered and inflexible
- to feel stressed and vulnerable in social situations

Aware of being different from their peers, they nevertheless lack the empathic skills that would allow them to recognize, understand, and respond to the feelings of others. As a result, they are readily rejected by peers and often become the targets of bullies.

Maturation does not guarantee an improvement in social awareness and skill. In the period when the child with AS is becoming an adolescent – without intensive teaching programs – these vulnerable individuals continue to experience social problems. As a result, the characteristic lack of skill creates stress, anxiety, and perhaps depression. In fact, as many as 80% of AS adolescents are ultimately prescribed antidepressants.

The manner in which the AS student is perceived varies according to who is questioned about the matter: parents, teachers, or the AS student. Whereas parents identify conduct problems, aggression, hyperactivity, and withdrawal as areas of concern, teachers report fewer deficits but focus on anxiety, depression, attention span, and withdrawal. Although the student does not perceive him/herself as "at risk", commonly, experiences of learned helplessness, as well as blame for social failure are reported. Moreover, the more self-blame is indicated, the more depressed the individual appears to be.

Academic performance

In the majority of cases, students with AS attend regular school programs, and, as a result, may not be in a position to access the specialized services they require. With average to above-average intellectual ability, in addition to good rote memory, extensive vocabulary, clear oral expression, reading recognition skills, and focused knowledge, these students often give the impression of knowing more than they actually do. Because of this aspect of AS, teachers are cautioned not to consider depth of knowledge of a restricted number of topics as evidence of general knowledge. While the AS student may obsess on a single topic, displaying a depth of knowledge that serves as fodder for conversation, at the same time, the student feels less anxious and, as a consequence, has the opportunity to receive feedback from others.

Characteristically, relative strength in oral language skills often overshadows many other language deficits experienced by AS students. As an example,

AS students may have difficulty understanding material presented verbally, that is, content typical of oral presentations or lectures. In addition, although these students may possess excellent word recognition skills, their overall comprehension of text is also impaired. Because they engage in concrete and literal thinking, abstractions, such as metaphors and idioms, are very challenging. A usual problem is their difficulty in distinguishing relevant from irrelevant information, an element that also impacts on concept formation. For these reasons, the teacher should not only expect written skills to be weaker than oral skills but also to anticipate trouble arising with math skills, especially those relating to equations, problem solving, and critical thinking.

At the outset, the teacher should not be surprised by the AS student's peculiar responses to sensory stimuli, along with poor motor coordination and balance problems. For this reason, the AS student is not expected to excel in areas such as Physical Education, Art, and/or Industrial Arts. On a final note, it should be remembered that, like many students with AD, the ones with AS will experience context effects; for example, new skills will be applied only in those situations identical to the ones in which they were learned. As a result, in order to encourage the student to engage in transfer of learning, teaching sequences must include steps that target applications of newly learned skills to varied settings.

Social competence

In the course of normal development, the role of social competence increases in significance as the student moves from childhood to adolescence – a stage dominated by the importance of the peer-group. Generally speaking, unless an intervention is planned, students with AS, whose social skills do not improve as a function of maturation, become more and more impaired. To promote an understanding of the scope of the problem, an outline of the implications is presented here as a review of the ideas associated with the normal development of social competence.

In an outline of the elements involved in social competence, three areas are deemed important (Gutstein & Witney, 2002):

1. *Secure attachment.* The third level in Maslow's hierarchy of needs, this concept refers to the sense of belonging that first develops between the infant and the parent and then branches out to connect with other adults and peers. In the model entitled *Creating a Positive Classroom Environment,* outlined in Chapter Four, attachment – especially in conjunction with needs of safety and control – is a necessary affective dimension.

2. *Instrumental social learning.* In most cases, many of the social behaviors learned in childhood are acquired on the basis of reward and punishment. At this time, the child

learns, for example, that saying "please" and "thank you", in communicating intentions, is expedient in what is desired or needed. Because of this cause-effect arrangement, the child learns about social conventions as representing a means to an end.

3.   *Experience-sharing relationships.* As a function of development, children abandon parallel play and turn to the chance to enter experience-sharing relationships. Unlike instrumental social learning, which allows the learning of social skills as predictable behavior sequences – rewarded or punished – the experience-sharing relationship, in the immediate situation, incorporates more sophisticated skills of spontaneous decision-making about the course of action deemed appropriate. Three important aspects are inherent in the experience-sharing relationship:

     • *Enthusiasm and shared enjoyment.* Inherent in the experience, motivating the child to engage in experience-relationship is the fun and joy that will be part of the interaction.

     • *Social and emotional coordination.* By the age of four years, children have developed sufficient skill to engage in a coordinated play situation in which both players are commonly focused on the shared experience. To achieve what is believed to be the first step in a reciprocal friendship, each child engaged in play with a second child acquires the ability to appreciate the perspective of the other. In this leap of understanding, although unconscious, a theory of mind is required. When the coordination successfully transpires, the two players are left with feelings of bonding and belonging.

     • *Ongoing relationship and repair.* Because, in the world of friendship and play, each event and/or contact represents a situation of flexible structure and rules, it is not surprising that misunderstanding as well as conflict can occur. When the two individuals have become friends, however, they are able not only to assess the damage but also to find ways of repairing the breach. When the process is operational, it is not unusual to observe children: first playing, then arguing, and, finally, playing again.

Usually, students with AS do not seem to experience difficulty in forming attachments or in learning instrumental skills – establishing eye contact, saying "please" and "thank you", learning various ways to greet people, responding to greetings, and engaging in other similar activities. Importantly, however, the greatest difficulty experienced by most AS students is evident in the more spontaneous domain of social competence, that of experience-sharing. Gutstein & Witney (2002) state, "It is the belief of the first author that one hall-mark of AS is a deficit in pure experience-sharing".

Interestingly, children with AS continue to demonstrate behavior typical of parallel rather than coordinated play. If they approach other children, it is not with the intention of sharing an interest or having fun. When a connection is made, it is with the intent of giving information, very probably from the source of their singular domain of knowledge. In areas of social and emotional coordination, the same problem is evident. For these children, a difficulty exists when they should be engaging in the back-and-forth dance of the interaction. Moreover, in rare situations when they manage to develop friendships, the usual emotional bonding is likely to be absent. Finally, when an interaction falters, a lack of strategies exists – on the part of the AS child – of the kind that might help to repair the situation. Not only children but also adolescents and adults with AS are unaware of the importance of ensuring that their words are understood. To complicate things further, they are insensitive to the feedback provided by listeners. In typical cases, the experience-sharing process is further sabotaged both by a lack of empathy for the ideas of the other person and by an unawareness of the need for concern.

Table 9-6. DSM-IV-TR Diagnostic Criteria of Asperger Disorder.

A. Qualitative impairment in social interaction, as manifested by at least two of the following:

   1. marked impairment in the use of multiple nonverbal behaviors such as eye-to-eye gaze, facial expression, body postures, and gestures to regulate social interaction

   2. failure to develop peer relationships appropriate to developmental level

   3. a lack of spontaneous seeking to share enjoyment, interests, or achievements with other people (e.g., by a lack of showing, bringing, or pointing out objects of interest to other people)

   4. lack of social or emotional reciprocity

B. Restricted repetitive and stereotyped patterns of behavior, interests, and activities, as manifested by at least one of the following:

   1. encompassing preoccupation with one or more stereotyped and restricted patterns of interest that is abnormal either in intensity or focus

   2. apparently inflexible adherence to specific, nonfunctional routines or rituals

   3. stereotyped and repetitive motor mannerisms (e.g., hand or finger flapping or twisting, or complex whole-body movements) persistent preoccupation with parts of objects

cont'd

C. The disturbance causes clinically significant impairment in social, occupational, or other important areas of functioning.

D. There is no clinically significant general delay in language (e.g., single words used by age 2 years, communicative phrases used by age 3 years).

E. There is no clinically significant delay in cognitive development or in the development of age-appropriate self-help skills, adaptive behavior (other than in social interaction), and curiosity about the environment in childhood.

F. Criteria are not met for another specific Pervasive Developmental Disorder or Schizophrenia.

Reprinted with permission from the Diagnostic and Statistical Manual of Mental Disorders, Fourth Edition, Text Revision, Washington, DC, American Psychiatric Association, 2000.

Intervention

In responding to this condition, teachers should devise interventions that target specific areas. Generally, these would be those that undermine the affective well-being of the AS student who complains: of feeling stressed, of having no control over life situations, and also of the inability to predict outcomes. In Chapter Seven, some of these techniques have already been outlined. In order to mentor predictable sequences of actions, teachers may use Applied Behavior Analysis and Discrete Trial Training; for example, among the possible choices would be: greetings, requests for help, questions about information, leads about directions, and queries about other such matters. By acquiring social competence in daily situations – especially ones that present themselves with a high degree of frequency and predictability – the AS student will be encouraged to interact with others.

In developing a program to target experience-sharing, the teacher must introduce a step-wise progression of capabilities, ensuring that pre-requisite skills are over-learned in order to construct a strong foundation for subsequent acquisition of new procedures. Although teaching sequences will involve regular guided situations with a coaching adult, when the fostering of self-regulation seems appropriate, the mentoring person can switch roles with students who have become able to coach themselves. Only then, is it wise to repeat the learning sequence, but, this time, employing peers. In another type of intervention, technology can be used to instigate communication with others. As a means of connecting with others, the AS student can be encouraged to write e-mails to penpals. By establishing strict guidelines, the teacher can control the process to ensure the student's safety and, at the same time, to form the basis for a social-skills program. In this new situation, the AS student is given coaching about appropriate ways of interacting with a pen pal.

Within this framework, it is also important to identify the novel aspects that vary from one situation to the next, and to make certain that the student is capable of learning to pick up on these subtle changes. Subsequently, it will be obvious that the student is beginning to implement the appropriate action sequence. Of course, it will appear, at the outset, that the learning of experience-sharing skills is occurring in very artificial and controlled conditions. In step with the student's progress, however, more distractions and variables can be introduced, with both teacher and student moving toward real-life situations, such as interaction with a cashier when paying for groceries.

Central to such a program is the necessity of bringing the student's attention to the importance of learning to deal with socially essential actions and communications. In some cases, such awareness can be learned by using techniques based on video modeling (Charlop-Christy & Daneshvar, 2002)[13]. Whenever possible, in addition to acquiring academic skills, the student will be moving towards the ultimate goal: skill acquisition that will allow adaptation in real-life circumstances.

Young Offenders

Unlike other special populations, young offenders are identified by the courts rather than by mental health professionals. Still in use is the traditional term "juvenile delinquency", a sociological label employed in contemporary professional literature to refer to young individuals who, when they commit criminal acts, are processed by the courts. In a subgroup are those whose criminal behavior has escaped notice. Consequently, if incarceration is not considered to be an excluding criterion, four groups of young people who may potentially form the focus of discussion are those:

- who are designated delinquent and have been incarcerated
- who are delinquent, known to the police, but have not been incarcerated
- who have committed illegal acts, are not known to the police, and have not been incarcerated
- who have been arrested but are not delinquent because they are not guilty of criminal acts

Because statistics – of necessity – are compiled, officially, only on the basis of incarceration, the actual incidence of delinquency is difficult to ascertain. Although two-to-four percent of minors commit criminal acts, anonymous self-reports indicate that more than 70% of adolescents claim to have committed at least one criminal act: the list of possible acts involves shoplifting, trespassing, and other such petty incidents.

According to media reports, generated to a credulous population, not only is delinquency on the rise but young offenders are responsible for more of the serious crimes than they were in the past.

Such are the widely believed impressions, that, whereas, previously, people associated mostly petty offenses with young people, now youth and even some children are perceived as capable of such crimes as rape, murder, assault with a weapon, and other violent crimes. In an attempt to find a scapegoat, the public – again with the help of the willing media – has condemned permissive parents, inadequate school systems, and lenient legislation as factors contributing to increasing delinquency.

Interestingly, the general public's perception is often inaccurate; for example, in cities whose crime rates have decreased, persons consulted on the street are still convinced that more crimes than in the past are being committed, a view partly the result of media bias. Because, characteristically, newspapers and magazines report primarily the unsociable behavior of children and adolescents, the public overlooks the volunteer work, scholarship, helpfulness, and even, in some cases, heroism, of young people. As a corollary, films, videos, and books portraying youth violence and gang warfare further encourage this biased attitude.

In times of social and economic crises, the hardship experienced by families contributes negatively to young individuals. Typically, children in some homes are left unsupervised as parents work longer hours while other young people experience increasing parental abuse and neglect, conditions which arise when families are in crisis. In difficult circumstances, some individuals seek the refuge and nurturing of a peer-group; others – who may choose to leave home – fall prey to unscrupulous people, often gangs, who may direct them to one or more of addiction, prostitution, cults, or crime.

Many people complain that a pattern of recently introduced lenient legislation is responsible for what seem to be increasing numbers of violent acts committed by young offenders. For example, in Canada, the Young Offenders Act (1986) attempts to establish guidelines appropriate to adolescent 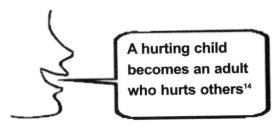 needs by replacing earlier legislation based on an adult formula (see Platt, 1994). Because this new act – whose goal is to hold the young person responsible for personal behavior – has increasingly been perceived as not sufficiently punitive, it is deemed to encourage young people to adopt lives of crime.

A hurting child becomes an adult who hurts others[14]

What changes should be made to the Young Offenders Act?

From a sociological point of view, many people are confused about the role which should or could be played by correctional institutions: should they rehabilitate their prisoners, punish them, or provide them with custodial care? Although society supports the ideal that criminals ought to be rehabilitated, many believe that at the very least they should be excluded from the mainstream. The correlation of this view is also held by many. Demonstrated in word and action, this is the idea that criminals should be punished to deter the unsociable behavior of others. When dealing with children and adolescents, workers and teachers find serious difficulty ridding themselves of the notion that punishment is the most expedient and effective way of handling any typical delinquency problem.

> ## What is the purpose of a correctional institution?
> ## How should it achieve its goals?

Systems have a tendency to search for simple ways to solve complex problems, but the reality is that problems with young offenders may require simultaneous action on several fronts. At the outset, potential courses of action may involve all or some of: parenting courses for adolescents and young adults, nutritious food and day care for toddlers, and early childhood education for a wide range of young children. In addition to these, comprehensive education programs could be made available for under-educated groups and parent-support groups could be organized for the many people without parenting experience. Add to these positive opportunities the founding of a regular structure of summer camps for disadvantaged children and youth, as well as the provision of adult role models from social service agencies. For those ready for them, scholarship and career programs could be introduced as could many other avenues of remediation and potential change. This list is a beginning of what is possible by way of prevention as opposed to the present system of penalties with its chronic lack of opportunity for change.

Conditions associated with Young Offenders

In the group called young offenders, a range of conditions is found that includes: depression, attention deficit disorder, conduct and oppositional defiance disorders, learning disabilities, and substance abuse. Although researchers are reluctant to promote single-cause or simplistic cause/effect explanations of delinquency, awareness of the range of accompanying conditions can provide a starting point when teachers are planning programs for these youths. For example, if a learning disability is involved, teaching the student to understand as well as accommodating the need for information processing skills will form at least a first step in providing assistance.

Depression in violent youth

Unlike those who act out, some juveniles react to the events in their lives with depression, anxiety, and withdrawal. Because depression and delinquency share common past histories – the same factors responsible for delinquency also cause depression – some youths succumb to both. Whereas, in childhood, rates of male and female depression are not only low but also equivalent, during adolescence, a sharp rise of depression's onset is seen in girls who, as result, may engage in antisocial behaviors. In this group of young women, persistent internalizing problems such as depressed mood, anxiety, shyness, or withdrawn behavior in middle-to-late childhood, predict the potential combination of subsequent substance use and delinquency (Loeber, Stouthammer-Loeber, & White, 1999).

Attention Deficit Disorder (ADHD)

Attention Deficit Disorder, previously described in this chapter (see Table 9-2), is closely associated with delinquency. Regarding incarcerated males between the ages of 12 and 18, reports suggest that the incidence of ADHD is between 42% (Chae, Jung, & Noh, 2001) and 68% (Dalteg & Levander, 1998). Although both male and female adolescents customarily engage in risky behavior, those with ADHD are more risk-tolerant – males moreso than females (Kaplan, 2001). Of course, this disregard for risk sometimes results in extreme cases of daring as well as in criminal activity.

By studying a group of 75 juvenile delinquents, ranging in age from six to 20, a group responsible for 12,000 crimes, Dalteg & Levander (1998) have examined the differences between those with ADHD and those without it. Although the hyperactive group appears to have better psychosocial background – when the incidence of family violence, broken homes, and mental health problems in the family is considered – they have experienced more pronounced school problems. In addition, a higher level of criminality is evident, becoming more pronounced as they grow older, leading to worse social outcomes, especially in the areas of relationships and employment. A great many teachers and psychiatric workers have come to believe that the hyperactive/impulsivity factor in individuals with ADHD causes them to be more vulnerable to the development of ODD behavior, that is Oppositional Defiant Disorder. (see below for further information about this condition).

Conduct Disorder (CD)

The condition known as Conduct Disorder, described in the DSM (see Table 9-7), is estimated to occur in approximately 6% of the student population. Of course, the incidence of Conduct Disorder figures more prominently in delinquent children and adolescents. In Dalteg and Levander's (1998) sample of 75 hard-core delinquents – all of whom were responsible for an estimated 1000 crimes per individual – each was believed to have a conduct disorder.

More common in boys than girls (4:1), CD may be accompanied by a number of other conditions – anxiety disorders, mood disorders, post-traumatic stress disorder, substance abuse, ADHD, and learning disabilities. In many children, some of these may become evident in childhood, gaining prominence in the adolescent years. For example, children with conduct disorders are likely to try illegal substances at quite early ages, but then to abuse them in their adolescent years (Armstrong & Costello, 2002)

Oppositional Defiant Disorder (ODD)

As it is described in the DSM (see Table 9-8), ODD is characterized by a defiant and oppositional stance with respect to those perceived to be controlling. Usually characterized as "You are not the boss of me", according to Hewitt (1999), this attitude is observable during three cycles of an individual's life: first, around age two, when establishing autonomy[15]; next, at the onset of adolescence when the child reaches puberty and demands more freedom; and, finally, in old age when the previously self-sufficient adult is forced to rely on others. In all three instances, the individual, who suffers a loss of control over the personal life situation, reacts by actively seeking to regain it. In most cases, this reaction is very different from the one expressed by the individual experiencing learned helplessness: that one fails entirely to react.

What kinds of environments are likely to trigger ODD? Although the answer is multi-faceted, situations involving the break-up of the family – as in the case of a divorce, or perhaps a placement of children in foster care – can cause the onset of ODD. In other cases, loss or disruption may occur when a significant person dies or when the family is forced to move frequently – the result of financial hardship, with the result that a young person is affected. In yet a different scenario, a parent is away in the armed forces, thus exacerbating the feeling of absence of control. On a regular basis, the teacher should be aware that many students in the normal stream will express isolated ODD symptoms. As this behavior can occur from time to time, by addressing affective needs as described in the model for Creating a positive classroom environment[16], the teacher will be able to decrease the need for opposition and defiance. From the point of view of peers in the classroom, the student with ODD is likely to be perceived as a leader. In some cases, the class, unwilling to suffer the individual consequences, will use the ODD student to act out on its behalf. Over-controlling teachers may find themselves the target of defiance readily condoned and encouraged by the rest of the class.

In middle childhood, juveniles with ODD are more likely to engage in delinquent acts, including substance abuse (Loeber, Stouthammer-Loeber, & White, 1999). Most children diagnosed with ODD do not, however, develop Conduct Disorder (CD).

Learning Disabilities

It is no secret that as many as 75% of young offenders are functionally illiterate – below a Grade Five-or-Six-reading level – or that many among the group have experienced difficulties at school. Although such evidence does not imply a cause/effect relationship, it nonetheless stresses the importance of providing effective services early in each student's career to ensure that both literacy and academic competence develop in step with their peers' skills.

Substance abuse

In their literature review of studies relating to substance use and abuse as well as drug dependence and the presence of psychiatric conditions, Armstrong and Costello (2002) suggest that in 60% of juvenile substance abusers, not only conduct and oppositional defiant disorders but also depression will probably be present. Children with conduct disorders, the two researchers point out, are likely to try illegal substances, and then, subsequently, to abuse the same or other ones in their adolescent years.

Subgroups of Delinquency

According to Quay (1979), young offenders do not represent a homogeneous group; instead, four main categories are proposed, each of which paints a different profile within the overall category.

Socialized Delinquent

In the group as a whole, those individuals who are designated *socialized delinquents* are victims of sociological causes – poverty, for example – and are likely to belong to a gang originating in the neighborhood or subculture. For these young persons, gang membership not only satisfies affective needs but also contributes to their survival. Usually, these individuals, although responsive to peer pressure inside the group, are psychologically healthy, even if they awaken late in the morning, go to bed in the small hours, and spend most of their time away from home. In this kind of group, gang membership may require specific behavioral repertoires that usually include criminal behavior, and, because their leaders demonstrate adaptive qualities, members learn a great deal about social structures.

Unsocialized Psychopathic

In this group – the young offenders of the *Unsocialized Psychopathic* type – are the solitary individuals who spend a large portion of their lives alone, usually away from their peers. Probably, such individuals have personality disorders: characteristically, they are defiant of authority[17], irritable, and aggressive, especially verbally. In addition, because some of them feel persecuted, they rarely have any remorse for their anti-social acts. Prototypical of *stimulus-reducers,* they engage in thrill-seeking behavior. From an educational perspective they are unlikely to benefit by learning from the consequences of their actions.

Disturbed Neurotic

Young offenders of the *Disturbed Neurotic* type – who are delinquent as a result of their emotional disturbance — are severely affected by stress in their pattern of delinquency. In this group, each person may be shy, timid, and remorseful. In addition, because, as a group, they are likely to be *Stimulus-augmenters,* they will usually have a tendency to over-react to the smallest incidents.

Incompetent Immature

In the group of juveniles classified as *Incompetent Immature,* most are expected to have "weak" personalities and to be motivated chiefly by self-gratification. Because such individuals characteristically feel inadequate, they are not only easily pushed around but can be readily set up and often manipulated by other offenders.

Grouping offenders by reaction to stimuli

Another attempt to categorize young offenders is related to their idiosyncratic reactions to stimuli. Because these groupings are based on the notion that each person has a unique threshold of stimulus perception, the manner in which stimuli are perceived by the individual affects action and reaction.

Stimulus-Augmenter

A *stimulus augmenter* is an individual likely to over-react to stimuli. Such persons are perceived as "making a big deal out of nothing" or "making a mountain out of a molehill".

Stimulus-Reducer

In contrast, a *stimulus reducer*, typically, is one who under-reacts to stimuli, usually pursuing activities that promise high arousal. As might be predicted, these thrill-seeking persons engage in daring and dangerous activities.

DSM-IV Classifications

In addition to *Attention Deficit Disorder* (see Table 9-2), two further DSM classifications which allude to conditions leading some children and adolescents to engage in delinquent behavior are: *Conduct Disorders* (see Table 9-7) and *Oppositional Defiant Disorders* (see Table 9-8).

Table 9-7. **DSM-IV-TR Diagnostic Criteria of Conduct Disorder.**

A. A repetitive and persistent pattern of behavior in which the basic rights of others or major age-appropriate social norms or rules are violated, as manifested by the presence of three (or more) of the following criteria in the past 12 months, with at least one criterion present in the past 6 months

Aggression to people and animals

1. often bullies, threatens or intimidates others
2. often initiates physical fights
3. has used a weapon that can cause serious physical harm to others (e.g., bat, brick, broken bottle, knife, gun)
4. has been physically cruel to people
5. has been physically cruel to animals
6. has stolen while confronting a victim (e.g., mugging, purse snatching, extortion and robbery)
7. has forced someone into sexual activity.

Destruction of property

8. has deliberately engaged in fire setting with the intention of causing serious damage
9. has deliberately destroyed others' property (other than by setting fire)

Deceitfulness or theft

10. has broken into someone else's house, building or car
11. often lies to obtain goods or favors or to avoid obligations (i.e., "cons" others)
12. has stolen items of trivial value without confronting a victim (e.g., shoplifting, but without breaking and entering; forgery)   *cont'd*

Serious violations of rules

   13. often stays out all night despite parental prohibitions, beginning before age 13 years

   14. has run away from home overnight at least twice while living in parental or parental surrogate home (or once without returning for a lengthy period)

   15. is often truant from school, beginning before age 13 years

B. The disturbance in behavior causes clinically significant impairment in social, academic, or occupational functioning.

C. If the individual is 18 years or older, criteria are not met for Antisocial Personality Disorder

Reprinted with permission from the Diagnostic and Statistical Manual of Mental Disorders, Fourth Edition, Text Revision, Washington, DC, American Psychiatric Association, 2000.

If these criteria are met before the age of 10 years, *Conduct Disorder* is considered to be of the *childhood-onset* type. After the age of 10 years, the *Conduct Disorder* is of the *adolescent-onset* type. In a range of cases, severity of the disorder may be defined as mild, moderate, or severe.

Table 9-8. **DSM-IV-TR Diagnostic Criteria of Oppositional Defiant Disorder.**

A. A pattern of negativism, hostile and defiant behavior lasting at least 6 months, during which four (or more) of the following are present:

   1. often loses temper

   2. often argues with adults

   3. often actively defies or refuses to comply with adults' requests or rules

   4. often deliberately annoys people

   5. often blames others for his or her mistakes or misbehavior

   6. is often touchy or easily annoyed by others

   7. is often angry and resentful

   8. is often spiteful and vindictive

Note: Consider a criterion met only if the behavior occurs more frequently than is typically observed in individuals of comparable age and developmental level.

B. The disturbance in behavior causes clinically significant impairment in social, academic, or occupational functioning.

C. The behaviors do not occur exclusively during the course of a Psychotic or Mood Disorder.   *cont'd*

D. Criteria are not met for Conduct Disorder, and, if the individual is age 18 years or older, criteria are not met for Antisocial Personality Disorder.

Reprinted with permission from the Diagnostic and Statistical Manual of Mental Disorders, Fourth Edition, Text Revision, Washington, DC, American Psychiatric Association, 2000.

In a case in which a student does not meet the criteria for *Conduct Disorder* or *Oppositional Disorder*, but nevertheless presents significant impairment, the classification made is *Disruptive Behavior Disorder, Not Otherwise Specified.*

Explaining Delinquency

The task of explaining the root cause of a phenomenon is, in every case, difficult because, as always, many potential explanations exist. Each theory hopes to describe why certain youths commit illegal acts – acts against society – and others do not. To offer clarification, the various theories are presented below in the context of the traditional paradigms.

Biological

As may be anticipated, biological theories attempt to explain delinquent behavior in terms of the genetic make-up of the individuals. If inherited anomalies are present, it is believed that the individual is predisposed to social wrongdoing. In its most extreme position, such a stance seems to predict that children of rapists will grow up to be rapists, because a "violent" gene is inherited.

In many reports, information obtained from studying identical and fraternal twins is normally used to support genetic or hereditary explanation. Whereas identical twins are the source of the greatest genetic similarity between individuals, fraternal twins share the same genetic distinctions as siblings. Interestingly, twice as many "identical" twins as "fraternal" twins can be found in the delinquent population. Although this evidence may suggest a correlation between delinquency and genetic make-up, an expectation exists that both twins in an identical pair will react in a similar way to stimuli. Alternatively, this ratio of "identical" to "fraternal" twins may be standard to all types of groupings, not just in the area of delinquency.

Because they are expected to be more aggressive and therefore to engage in anti-social behavior, individuals with chromosomal abnormalities have been the focus of some researchers. These subjects are the ones with with XYY or XYYY chromosomes, the "supermales". Although no reliable data to support this suggestion exists in the adult population, such research neither considers nor relates to juveniles.

Are there genotype or physical characteristics associated with delinquency? To respond to this query, scientists have made an attempt to examine the physical build of delinquent individuals residing in institutions. Although tall, thinner individuals with lower IQs stand out in the sample, no evidence available to date links these genotypes to criminal activity.

Because intelligence is considered to be a hereditary factor, lower IQ – in individuals who score in the lower IQ range on IQ tests – is a factor prominent in a biological explanation. Hirsch & Hindelang (1977) indicate that on the average, delinquents score eight IQ points lower than the norm. Not only do recent findings support the robustness of this finding but also this group is perceived as more likely to be used and exploited by criminals and also to engage in more property acts such as stealing, as well as to commit fewer crimes related to persons.

More recently, factors such as impulsivity – usually present in immature individuals and in those with ADHD – in addition to the high incidence of learning disabilities in the juvenile delinquent population, lend further support to a biological explanation.

Psychodynamic

In this view, delinquent behavior is attributed to difficulties in early developmental milestones, especially when these include repeated separation experiences as well as chronic loss of the chance to form associations of long duration.

Rational Choice Theory

Whereas biological theories reduce the degree of personal responsibility assigned to committing illegal acts, the Rational Choice theory holds the individual completely responsible for criminal actions. In this syndrome, the delinquent is perceived as calculating, and, after weighing the risks and potential rewards of the choices, is seen to be capable of making rational decisions about engaging in antisocial Id-like, pleasure-seeking activities.

In the case of juveniles, it is difficult to support this position because, along with the fact that their motives differ from those of adults, the actions of many of them are observed as impulsive – examples of acting before thinking. More likely is the possibility that behavior is directed against authority figures when these young persons rebel against cultural norms.

Control Theories

That human beings, left to their own resources, will commit criminal acts is one of the basic tenets of this view. To prevent this extreme result of total freedom, researchers believe, society's role is to create laws and institutions that will keep behavior in check. According to Control Theory, juveniles commit delinquent acts because normally deterring forces are absent or defective. Clearly, according to this theory, Freud's notion of personality would take over. His view is that, without a *Superego*, – the force that internalizes the morals and values of society – each human personality is dominated by its pleasure-seeking *Id*.

Factors that facilitate decisions to move away from delinquent acts include the strong bonds established between the individual and the significant people — parents, pro-social friends, churches, schools, teachers, and sports teams, to name the most effective ones. Because middle class norms (see Table 9-3) are promoted by these moderating representatives of society, when they are absent for any reason or when their controlling influence is reduced, the juvenile goes back to the original pleasure-seeking state.

As a result of a lack of commitment to the school as well as to school experiences, delinquent adolescents are likely to be low achievers, rarely participating in school. In those students with lower or no rates of delinquency, attachment to the school along with positive attitudes towards teachers seems obvious. Moreover, recent evidence indicates that variables such as regular school attendance – with the corollary of few behavior problems and consistent good grades – reduce the risk of delinquency among all youths including those who have been abused.

Behavioral

On the basis of Learning Theory, individuals learn to behave as a result both of the situations which they experience and the people with whom they associate. All learning models – classical, operant, and observational – are implicated in an explanation of delinquency.

Social Learning or Differential Association and Drift Theory

This theory of learning perspective promotes the notion that criminal behavior is learned in very much the same ways as social behavior is conditioned. In such a circumstance, the role of the peer group is central because, in the process of observation, the individual learns to be a part of collective behavior. It is through the delinquent peer group that the individual will internalize techniques for committing crimes and will embrace motives and rationalizations that make criminal activity more palatable.

Sutherland (1939)[18] suggests that the learning of delinquent behavior is based not only on the collective experience of the group but also on the basis of specific situational experiences. More specifically, Drift Theory focuses on the juveniles gliding in and out of delinquency, especially as they acquire skills that enable them to neutralize feelings of guilt. Some of these techniques consist of:

- denying any responsibility — "It's not my fault, my parents abused me".

- denying injury to the victim — "I took the money, but he slipped and hit his head; that's why he's bleeding".

- Denying the existence of a victim — "I stole from him because he's a crook".

- Condemning those who judge them — "Why do the police want to talk to me? They're the biggest crooks. They keep all that drug money for themselves, you know".

- Appealing to higher loyalties — "I did this because he was insulting my gang".

In the development of criminal tendencies, another consideration focuses on the child growing up in a family that espouses criminal values and behavior. In such circumstances, because the child may compare the family's values with traditional ones, perhaps the assumption follows that criminal acts are not as "wrong" as society or the law has defined them.

Interpersonal and Situational Theory

Like the differential association theory, the idea that criminal behavior is learned is supported by Matza (1964). According to this researcher, such behavior is not fixed but flexible, and, therefore, is subject to change. In this view, much of delinquent behavior is situational, resulting from association with delinquent peers and influenced by the factors present in a situation. To exemplify this, teachers will easily recognize the student who is reluctant, oppositional, and verbally abusive when classmates are around but friendly and agreeable when speaking one-to-one with the teacher. An appropriate conclusion in predicting behavior is: "It depends on the situation".

Sociological

As makes perfect sense, delinquency is often related to a young person's lack of opportunity to satisfy personal needs. While no society can satisfy the needs of all its members, some individuals will remain within the law's restraints and others will find anti-social means to sustain themselves.

What is socio-economic status?

Originally, when socio-economic status was tied to the relationship between income and personal values, the population was categorized as:

- Low SES

- Middle SES

- High SES

Today, in a heterogeneous milieu, in which the values of a group may no longer be tied solely to income level, socio-economic status refers more specifically to subcultures with values that vary in a range related to those of the dominant culture – middle SES.

Social Disorganization and Anomie

In this theory, which targets the environment as the primary explanatory factor in delinquency's causes, poverty, ignorance, and population density are influential variables. If it is true that delinquency is caused by this trio of environmental factors that leave the structure of social institutions in disarray, some individuals, particularly those in lower economic classes, are most vulnerable.

Once delinquency has gained a foothold in certain neighborhoods, children and adolescents are exposed to a gamut of conflicting values that may compete with those of the family and/or the dominant culture. When transmission of the criminal culture can be seen to occur not only in neighborhoods but also in prison, detention centers, and perhaps special education classes, the idea emerges that society itself generates groupings of like-minded individuals.

In the nineteeth century, a descriptive label, first introduced in the context of behavior by Émile Durkheim (1997)[19], is called anomie. This emotion embodies the feelings of frustration and alienation that result from a lack of economic opportunity. Although it has been suggested that anomie is associated with delinquency, evidence indicates a stronger link to suicide.

Lower-class based theories

In the literature, many theorists have noted the presence of delinquency in lower economic classes, particularly in males. Not only is this phenomenon described in many of Charles Dickens' (1812-1870) novels, but evidence is also displayed in films of the 1950s[20], in which juvenile gangs were tantamount to a delinquent subculture.

Although statistics of self-reported crimes, once analyzed, demonstrate no class differences, socio-economic class appears to dictate the type of crime as well as the manner in which various transgressions are perceived. Is it possible that individuals of lower SES are overly represented in the delinquent population because they are more visible when they commit their crimes? In fact, police records show differential rates of incarceration. In contrast, white-collar crime – as occurs in the defrauding of government and/or investors as well as in the more recent crimes of computer hacking and the spreading of viruses – is not as severely punished as are more common crimes. In fact, such illegal activities are often down-played.

Middle-class Measuring-rod Theory

On the basis of his study of delinquent boys, Cohen (1955) proposes a supposition of criminality on the basis of subculture. Because youth of the lower class have internalized some features of middle-class values, but, at the same time, do not have that class's economic opportunities, they are motivated to create a parallel culture of opposite values. Given the importance of the status of the family in the context of the social structure, Cohen hypothesizes that status frustration, along with strain[21], dictates whether the young person becomes a corner boy, a college boy, or a delinquent boy. Whereas corner boys make do with the hand that life deals them, the delinquent boy, by banding with other similar types, not only achieves status, but also accesses those desirable amenities not otherwise available.

Consider the dilemma facing a youth from a family of modest means who is induced to earn money in order to buy designer clothes like those worn by the school in-crowd. Should Thomas apply for the minimum-wage job at the fast food chain? The financial rewards resulting from selling drugs, burglarizing homes, and engaging in other such criminal acts are much more attractive.

Table 9-9. **Middle-class values according to Cohen (1955).**

- Drive and ambition
- Taking personal responsibility for actions
- The pursuit of achievement and success in all areas
- The willingness to delay the gratification of immediate desires and needs for the opportunity of future gain
- Long-range planning and budgeting
- The ability, in relation to others and strangers, to be courteous and to exercise self-control
- The habit, in all settings, both physical and verbal, to control violent and aggressive actions
- The regular participation in clean, constructive, and "wholesome" amusement, e.g., hobbies
- The acceptance of the idea of respect for the property of others

Differential Opportunity Structure

Along the same line as Cohen (1955), Cloward and Olin (1960) argue that economic success can be achieved through either legal or illegal means. Because there is unequal opportunity among the social classes, many individuals feel themselves to be forced to use criminal means. In the absence of positive adult role models and a stable family system that provides social control, the status-seeking adolescent, in neighborhoods where organized crime has roots, may choose to belong to one of three types of gangs: in the *criminal* gang the group may engage mainly in thefts; in the *conflict*[22] gang, turf wars and violence are dominant; in the *retreatist* gang are included not only members rejected from criminal gangs but also adherents who engage in drug abuse and drug-related behavior.

The Radical Theory

In another sociological position, the Radical Theory assumes that delinquency is an outcome of the struggle between economic classes, primarily in the context of a capitalist system. The lower and working class representatives commit criminal acts as a rebellion against the limits placed by the middle class; for example, this opposition occurs when the management class minimizes the value of a worker's labor by offering small wages. Of course, Karl Marx (1818-1883) also outlined and promulgated this notion of class conflict.

Labeling Theory

The sayings "Do the clothes make the man, or does the man make the clothes?" and/or "If the shoe fits, wear it" are both applicable to a labeling explanation of delinquent behavior. Not only is a young offender likely to be arrested on the basis of age (juveniles more so than adults), race (visible minorities), and social class (poor and homeless), but also may face processing by the court system and be branded. Once labeled, the youth or adolescent, when placed in detention, has closer access to the criminal element and also a much greater need to live up to the anti-social description: Young Offender.

Female Delinquency

Explanation of delinquency in girls and young women has largely been disregarded because the incidence of such behavior in females is relatively low. In the last thirty years, however, the increasing rate of delinquency in girls and the incidence of female gangs have brought attention to the problem. Thus, in addition to a biological explanation, other theories that attempt to explain delinquency in young females include: changes in gender roles resulting from the women's movement as well as feminism, in addition to power-control theory. Among others, these ideas are used to clarify the new emergence of criminality in adolescent girls.

A biological explanation focusing on the inherent differences between men and women suggests that girls – because they are less fool-hardy, aggressive, and territorial – are less likely to offend than boys.

Whereas a boy may be both the hero and the criminal, a girl may use sexual wiles and personality guile, first, to seek excitement and then to achieve personal goals. In this burgeoning field, some researchers go a step further to associate delinquency with menstruation – placing the entire matter on a scientific/hormonal basis.

Because girls in lower socio-economic classes are more likely to commit crimes, it is believed that the extent to which gender roles are enforced in their environments will either increase or decrease the incidence of delinquency. The stereotype[23] of the wayward and promiscuous girl, labeled in girls as a symptom of delinquency, but not in boys, is associated with disobedient girls who sometime run away from their families. Family violence is predictive of delinquency in girls, but not in boys.

Initially, crimes committed by women were often hidden and invisible – in some cases, having illegal abortions, in others, acting as accomplices. With changing gender roles resulting from the Women's Movement of the 1960s, not only is an increase in female delinquency reported – although the figure is still lower than that of males, but also a move toward property and drug-related crimes is noted. Freer to develop their potential, young women are demonstrating, some analysts believe, a desire to imitate their male counterparts when they engage in increased amounts of fighting and get caught up in gang activity. When confronted by the police, girls express more shame and guilt than do boys. As might be imagined, some researchers interpret this reaction to mean that girls are more thoroughly socialized than boys – more conforming and adopting of social values. As a corollary, those girls who are shown to be more attached to family and school commit fewer acts of delinquency.

In the school system, very few girls are placed in specialized classrooms for students with Behavioral Exceptionalities. Perhaps girls engage in behaviors that are less disruptive to the flow of the classroom than do boys. What is clear is that, in special classes, girls who are given such placements usually exhibit far more severe symptoms than do the boys.

In summary, the changing role of young women in the police files in industrialized society may be related to a number of alterations in parental roles, especially female parents, altogether: increased participation in the work force, the economic responsibility of heading single-parent families, and a range of other social stressors. Although such changes may create the climate that explains increases in youthful female delinquency, family violence still represents the greatest threat.

Summary

It is evident that, because many explanations of delinquency exist, the recent approach of researchers is to integrate these in their search for an encompassing and thorough explanation of the phenomenon. This new model attempts to explain not only why some youth become involved in criminal acts but also why some cease to find the delinquent world attractive as they get older.

Characteristics of Youth at risk of offending

As a means of consolidating the information about delinquency in a form relatively easy to decipher, the outline that follows uses language and categories meaningful to teachers.

- *Behavioral history.* When students are in conflict with the law, often they also have histories of disruptive behavior in childhood. If left unchecked, such behavior continues into adolescence and adulthood, but these students may eventually engage in criminal behavior. For this reason, in the Primary and Junior Divisions, resources must be available to the teacher and students as well as to the relevant families to curtail the range of problems at an early phase.

- *Early and current family conditions.* The existence of problems within the family – many of which lead to conditions of neglect and to the weakening of the bonds between its members – is a high-risk factor for delinquency. In situations of economic and/or emotional hardship, parental supervision decreases, creating, as a result, new opportunities for delinquency. For example, adolescents from families that move frequently from one place to another – as many as six to 13 locations – are shown to be less involved in extra-curricular school activities. In addition, in cases in which the mother experiences negative feelings regarding the relocation, this factor is correlated with student depression. In fact, the more often the mothers experience unhappy emotions, the more likely are their feelings to affect their school-age children's moods. (Norford & Medway, 2002).

   Also playing a major role in student dysfunctional behavior is family violence. Whereas this element has a direct effect on the delinquency of girls, it does not, however, place them at a higher risk level in later years. In contrast, although family violence appears not to account for delinquency in boys, any educational plan for the student should include an evaluation of the family circumstance. When such a focus is undertaken and details warrant a follow-up, strategies in conjunction with other agencies should be implemented by the school to bolster the function of the intervention. Moreover, forms of family support — parent training, career counseling, debt counseling, family counseling — should be made available.

- *Personal attitudes, values, beliefs, and feelings.* If students hold values and beliefs not consonant with those of their school, their classroom, their teachers, and their peers, a high risk exists that they will experience conflict in the classroom. Revealed in peer comments – "He's not like us" and "Are you kidding? I'm not inviting her to my birthday party" – the social ostracism of the student is obvious. Although Bradlee is suspected of stealing student lunches, gym shoes, school supplies, and even money, he always denies his involvement when confronted, even after he is observed selling some of the loot. Usually, when students engage in criminal behavior, they have acquired both divergent values and specialized skills by fraternizing with a delinquent

   cont'd

403

peer group. Also providing criminal direction to a young person is, sometimes, the culture of the surrounding neighborhood and even, occasionally, the family's own anti-social values. When, moreover, the student shares the values of the school but is treated by peers at school as an outcast, for physical preconceptions – "You're too fat"; academic biases – "You sure are dumb"; or racial and ethnic reasons – "We don't like your kind", the young person may seek refuge in a delinquent gang. In unfriendly circumstances like these, the victim may turn to a group of other youth who willingly respond to the young person's affective needs – safety, belonging, power-control.

- *Personal, educational, vocational, and/or socio-economic achievement.* In almost all cases, the student who is achieving well at school has considered career options that will allow the eventual earning of a good living. In addition, it is fair to say that any student who has attained this status – and who has been able, freely, to focus on other similar goals – is in a privileged position. Normally, students from families of low SES – social economic status – need support and encouragement necessary to the planning and the achievement of goals. In unique circumstances, on the other hand, certain of these students will find or make opportunities to build lucrative careers in such fields as athletics, music, and the performing arts.

- *Personal temperament.* When teachers are examining students in terms of temperament, one of two extremes is considered problematic. While some individuals readily externalize their emotions – by acting out, lashing out, and becoming verbally aggressive and abusive – others internalize, becoming sullen and morose, withdrawing themselves from social situations. Although students who act out are more likely to be recognized as requiring help, teachers should be especially aware of the withdrawn student, the one sitting quietly at the back of the classroom, or, alternatively, the truant one.

- *Emotional instability of parents.* Unfortunately, in any neighborhood, a young offender may be contending with a parent who either is emotionally unstable or is suffering from mental illness. In such circumstances, the young person is forced to cope alone, and, at times, to take responsibility for younger siblings. While the school may be willing and able to connect the household with appropriate social agencies, ones that will provide support to the family – teachers should not be surprised if the student, regardless of the level of abuse or neglect in the family, is unwilling to involve outside agencies because of fear that family members will be separated.

- *Parental transmission of values.* When there is good communication with the home, a teacher will often rely on the cooperation of parents in dealing with the problem behavior of their children. In some cases, however, a parent is unable or unwilling to lend support because the very behavior being questioned is one that is part of the parent's value system. For example, some parents may condone verbal and physical aggression against those who obstruct their goals. Perhaps they even approve of a young family member who displays no respect for authority. Accordingly, the student's education plan should reflect this lack of support. *cont'd*

- *School-based risk factors.* When students experience academic problems early in their school careers, they often develop negative feelings towards school, and, subsequently, as a result may resist forming attachments with teachers and peers. Notably, regular school attendance is one of the first markers. Clearly, unless present in class on a regular basis and participating in the flow of activity, the student is not able to develop relationships. Equally important is another variable: the development of literacy as well as academic skills essential to the personality's need for self-competence.

- *Psychopathy.* Obviously, the more there are complicating factors contributing to a student's delinquent behavior, the more considerable in scope will be the intervention. At the most serious level is the diagnosis termed "pyschopathy" or "sociopathy", first introduced in 1980 in DSM-III as an Antisocial Personality Disorder[24], an adult disorder with roots in adolescence (see Table 9-10). Responsible for about 50% of the crimes are about 20% of inmates, those who are twice as likely to re-offend as other convicts. Standing by themselves, these startling statistics reinforce the need for early, carefully planned, interventions.

- *Peer influence.* Hanging out with the wrong crowd can lead some students toward criminality. During adolescence, the draw of the peer group is so compelling that some students are elated to be accepted by any group. Recalling that the group meets affective needs, teachers will be aware that those things individuals may not do alone, they may venture with the support of their peers. Especially in the case of those students who are emotionally immature – or perhaps low-functioning – these will be used to do the group's bidding.

- *Lower-class origins.* In classrooms in most neighborhoods, each teacher has a balancing act to accomplish. When the teacher is, as most are, middle-class and espousing the values of the dominant culture, the question must constantly be asked: "Should lower-class values be denied?" While viewing behavior from the perspective of its legality is a good thing, often, teachers are unfamiliar with values other than those of their own families and educational milieus.

- *Interpersonal relationships.* Clearly, the opportunity for students to cultivate pro-social relationships with their normative peer group is an important factor in discouraging delinquency. Ideally, such relationships are formed in the context of the school or in local community centers, especially if a criminal culture exists in the neighborhood. Whereas it is easier in the elementary panel to foster such relationships – because students are together in classroom units for most of the day – the structure of the secondary school is less conducive to the formation of strong links. Here, not only is the student population much larger, but, conceivably, a student may initially be in various classes with peer groups comprising a range of near strangers. Considering the reluctance of adolescents to be embarrassed, and, even worse, to be rejected, the recently arrived or immigrant student is certainly capable of becoming anonymous. With the best habits learned in elementary school, this student may quickly lose any previous emotional attachment to the idea of school.

Table 9-10. **DSM-IV-TR Diagnostic Criteria of Antisocial Personality Disorder.**

A. There is a pervasive pattern of disregard for and violation of the rights of others occurring since age 18 years, as indicated by three (or more) of the following:

  1. failure to conform to social norms with respect to lawful behaviors as indicated by repeatedly performing acts that are grounds for arrest

  2. deceitfulness, as indicated by repeated lying, use of aliases, or conning others for personal profit or pleasure

  3. impulsivity or failure to plan ahead

  4. irritability and aggressiveness, as indicated by repeated physical fights or assaults

  5. reckless disregard for safety of self or others

  6. consistent irresponsibility, as indicated by repeated failure to sustain consistent work behavior or honor financial obligations

  7. lack of remorse, as indicated by being indifferent to or rationalizing having hurt, mistreated, or stolen from another

B. The individual is at least 18 years old (under 18, see Conduct Disorder)

C. There is evidence of Conduct Disorder with onset before age 15 years.

D. The occurrence of antisocial behavior is not exclusively during the course of Schizophrenia or a Manic Episode

Reprinted with permission from the Diagnostic and Statistical Manual of Mental Disorders, Fourth Edition, Text Revision, Washington, DC, American Psychiatric Association, 2000.

Interventions

Whether the delinquent is placed in a residential treatment center or in a correctional institution, or if the young person is in a special class or alternative placement in the school, several available modes of treatment can be accessed. Although an outline of fundamental information is presented here, the reader interested in supplementary detail is encouraged both to consult the references provided and to initiate further research in the field.

Psychodynamic

Traditional psychotherapy – one-on-one treatment – is found to be ineffective in most cases because individuals not only indicate they do not like it, but, in addition, they try to avoid it. Furthermore, teens often are unable and/or unwilling to engage in talk therapies. In many cases they possess neither the verbal skills nor the ability to reflect and to examine their behavior.

Biological

For conditions such as ADHD and for mood and anxiety disorders, medication is prescribed in cases where the delinquent individual needs to be normalized. In these circumstances, family doctors and psychiatrists play important roles in finding the medication with the fewest side effects, thereby permitting the young person to benefit from other types of interventions.

Behavioral

When coupled with work experience, approaches in this range – which include outlining contingencies and providing consequences for anti-social behavior – are more effective than if attempted only within the school context.

The REST (Real Economy System for Teens) program (Stein & Smith, 1990) shows positive results when professional researchers examine the effectiveness of a behavior method versus a talk therapy with a group of adolescents categorized as ODD. Given only food and shelter, these adolescents were required to pay money to cover the rest of their expenses. In the program, money could be earned if the young persons complied with the rules associated with keeping their rooms clean, maintaining personal hygiene, doing necessary chores, establishing proper interaction with others, and cultivating a safe environment. According to the results of the research, not only was the active group of adolescents more compliant in the target behaviors than the talk-therapy group, but they also reported being happier.

Cognitive

Because Cognitive Skills programs usually target such behaviors as self-control, interpersonal problem solving, cognitive style, social perspective-taking, values, and critical reasoning, students in these training activities learn to make changes. Often, by becoming aware of the existence of such skills, by examining them, and by finding ways to incorporate new processes in a personal repertoire, the individual is able to alter patterns of behavior.

When teachers are able to help a student to move from an impulsive to a reflective style and thence to thinking before making a response, the individual becomes capable of examining options, evaluating the consequence of each, and then deciding on a course of action. At the same time, learning the expectation that a consequence will follow an action helps to cement a cause/effect relationship between action and consequence. The ability to accomplish such a process is not only necessary for social learning but is also required by those who hope to develop a sense of self-control. For those readers who are interested in more specific details about applying cognitive techniques to reducing impulsivity, by using verbal mediation as well as and self-regulation and similar processes, Chapter Seven contains a range of details.

In the context of *Bibliotherapy*, along with films and videos, teachers will find it interesting to examine and discuss themes that relate to adolescent issues. With the use of such media, students can move the spotlight away from personal behavior, and, as a result, become more willing to scrutinize feelings, values, attitudes, and beliefs about imaginary characters. When school and popular culture merge, acting together, the curriculum becomes more relevant.

In looking at the range of problems facing students, teachers should turn their attention to an issue that warrants particular notice: violence. By defining it, determining its causes and consequences on individuals and families, classroom programs will not only acknowledge an actual a part of the young offender's life but will also force change in attitudes and beliefs about violence. When focusing on aspects of violence, students can be encouraged to write and then tape or act out creative stories.

In the same vein, many adolescent students with behavior problems will benefit from training in anger – and emotion-management. Incorporated in the student's individual plan should be a list of resource programs for teens that may exist in the community; this will include outreach programs provided by mental health facilities.

Many such programs, usually designed for young offenders, will target six main skill sets:

1. Empathizing with the victim's feelings
2. Distinguishing between aggressive and non-aggressive acts
3. Using self-statements to diffuse anger
4. Generating and evaluating alternatives to aggression
5. Identifying feelings underlying anger
6. Discerning opinions of others toward aggression

Because they are unable – or less able than most – to take the point of view of another person, aggressive children and teens have little awareness of their own feelings, a factor in most humans that normally inhibits cruel and hurtful acts towards others. When a social situation is ambiguous, or the aggressive person is lacking empathy, it is easy for such an individual to interpret hostile intent in another, in order to justify personal behavior; for example, a gaze in the direction of the angry student might be interpreted as a showdown.

In persons whose emotions are unexamined, underlying feelings of embarrassment, rejection, and anxiety are often the basis for angry reactions. By becoming aware of the subtleties behind these feelings, the young person is not only able to acknowledge them, but can begin to understand their origin as well as to create alternative ways of reacting emotionally and behaviorally. By recognizing that violent outbursts are associated with the embarrassment felt when the teacher requests homework assignments, Alleyn is able to seek the academic help required to raise the quality of his work to the standard of the class.

Lacking verbal skills, some aggressive students are unlikely to use verbal mediation to diffuse their anger, especially those that require self-statements such as "OK, calm down, count to ten". In addition, they need to learn the skill to generate non-aggressive options the better to achieve their objectives; for example, "Instead of punching Raul when he teases me, what else can I try?" Developing skills that promote assertiveness rather than aggressiveness will allow students to find ways to stand up for themselves.

Humanistic

Traditionally, one of the hallmarks of Humanism is its emphasis on personal responsibility. As Spider-Man put it, "With power comes great responsibility". Following is a series of programs that focus on making the student more responsible.

Contracts

Engaging in the making of contracts represents one of the ways for the teacher to establish an egalitarian position with the student. By negotiating the classroom work to be done in exchange for privileges or for free time to work on personal projects, the teacher attempts to circumvent oppositional and defiant behavior.

To achieve this structure, two frameworks for establishing contracts are provided – one, by Lloyd Homme (1970) in the book *Contingency Contracting*, and the second by William Glasser's (1975) *Reality Therapy*. In this pair, the first book provides a recipe-type format, outlining the duties of each party – the student and the adult – and detailing the outcome once the contract is fulfilled. The latter book, however, provides an additional component in which Glasser describes the necessary interactions that occur in a series of conferences – some for creating and monitoring and others for dealing with violations of the behavior parameters set out by the contract.

Victim Awareness Programs

Victim-Awareness Programs are designed to encourage an empathic understanding of the victim's perspective. Typically, juveniles rarely consider the feelings of victims, and, after the commission of a crime, will often engage in a variety of neutralizing activities in order to inhibit feelings of shame and remorse.

In a Victim-Awareness Program, normally functioning over the course of many weeks, the content will be organized to include a variety of guests – victims of crime, policemen, fire-fighters, health professionals, – as well as a range of activities: videos, films, story telling, and role-play activities. In each session, while the objective is to bring the student closer to adopting the perspective of the victim, the transference must be effected in a manner that involves neither anger nor moralizing, and that also ensures ample opportunity for discussion and interaction.

Reporting on an experiment comparing the participation of young offenders in three victim-awareness programs, Putnins (1997) reveals that participants in these experienced positive changes, in contrast to those young persons not involved in any programs. As a result of participation, an increase in understanding of a victim's perspective was noticed as were changes in attitudes known to reduce the rate of re-offending.

Moral Development Programs

Borba (2002) is one of several authors proposing the concept of moral intelligence in conceptualizing the types of social behavior to be encouraged. The inclusion of the word "intelligence" in a set of strategies that promote moral behavior is somewhat misleading, however, because it implies that morality is a fixed trait rather than the flexible adoption of set of values and norms.

Although programs can be effective when they target values-clarification and moral reasoning – because they engage students in solving moral dilemmas, thereby altering the attitudes and beliefs of young offenders – they are found to be unsuccessful with many chronic or more severe offenders. In particular, because these adolescents may possess poor verbal abilities as well as weak abstract reasoning skills, they consequently are more likely to benefit from the practical focus found in victim-awareness programs.

Sociological

Very often, Family Therapy is used to strengthen the organization and the bonds within the familial unit by improving communication and family interactions. Usually, this type of treatment is offered by psychologists and social workers who focus on the "sick family", although recognizing the possibility that at least some of its members – or perhaps all – may be "healthy". In line with *Control Theory,* this systems approach predicts that a stronger family is able to exercise greater control over the behavior of children and adolescents – that is, only through the healing of the family will·the individual members be healed.

Ecological

Milieu Therapies

Milieu Therapies address problems arising in the context of simulated situations that mimic real ones. For example, group homes give individuals the opportunity to acquire living experiences in an environment that attempts to simulate the lifestyle in a home. When a problem arises, the group's response is to use the difficulty as a learning opportunity to engage in the problem-solving process.

In programs such as Project Re-ED (see the description in Chapter Two), as well as in survival projects and boot camps, within environments that are very structured, individuals are offered unique chances to develop some sense of belonging by becoming interdependent with others in the respective groups.

Community programs

"Youth Bureaus" along with several other such community programs, may make available counseling services for neighborhood youth referred for delinquent and other problematic behavior. With a counselor caseload of 8-12 clients each, the overseers ensure that every young person has access to services – whose intention is to encourage bonding between parent and child – as well as to remedial education that deals with academic issues. Also provided is access to a mentor and, in addition, to programs that discourage association with delinquent peers. Hanlon *et al*. (2002) show that such a comprehensive program has a more positive impact on younger participants, and that, especially important to disadvantaged youth, the mentoring is presented in a culturally sensitive fashion, exploring needs particular to the group.

Another tack for dealing with youth in the community addresses leisure skills. Usually, this is done by occupying the young person's free time in constructive activity, as well as directly meeting the social and affective needs. Twemlow and Sacco (1998), for example, examine the effect of participating in a traditional martial arts program. Because such activities place emphasis on self-control, leadership, community service, and the responsibility of power, the training – at the same time as it exposes the young offender to a philosophy of nonviolence – will also boost self-confidence. It is also able to provide a sense of belonging and attachment opportunities in conjunction both with the teacher and with the other students. Results of Martial Arts training are recorded as they relate to three violent students: one in residential treatment, the second expelled from school for violent behavior, and the third enrolled in a special class. Subsequently, case studies of all three students demonstrate positive changes as a function of the features available in such a program.

Whether youth are taking music lessons, engaging in martial arts, doing volunteer work to help the elderly, or assisting the needy, it is clear that the more structured and supervised the effort, the more successful it will be. The organizer must not only keep in mind the level of need of the student but must also ensure that safety needs for everyone concerned are met.

Finally, in regard to those youths who are completing their respective periods of incarceration, Community Integration Programs are helpful in minimizing the risk of re-offending. In these procedures, the focus is on creating new opportunities, allowing the individual to circumvent the specific factors that have led to confinement.

Parenting Training Programs

In situations in which a lack of parenting skills is a main obstacle for the family, information can be very helpful when it is directed to all or some of: the structure of various types of families, the role of parents, the nature of child development, and the many needs of children. In fact, this type of program can be effective not only with parents of "at risk" children but also with adolescents. Because the young person has probably not had an opportunity to observe enough adequate models, the acquisition of healthy parent skills can break the negative cycle as well as forcing perspective-taking.

Parent training programs typically target skills dealing with:

- Communication between parents and between parents and children
- Problem-solving of normally occurring family challenges
- Affective management, including anger, and communication of positive emotions
- Effective discipline which requires having realistic expectations about children's behavior as well as about the parenting role
- Awareness of methods for seeking support from various services available in the community

Despite the effectiveness of many Parent Training programs, such systems cannot fill the needs of all families. Unless other community-support facilities are made available to the families suffering from a myriad of stressors, a Parent-Training program is likely to produce a negative outcome (Assemany & McIntosh, 2002).

Schools

Because the school is such an integral part of children's and adolescents' lives, it has an essential role to play in minimizing delinquent behavior. To some extent, this is accomplished by providing students:

- a safe environment that offers prizing opportunities – in some schools, it may be necessary to initiate procedures both to exclude weapons and intruders and to improve supervision. Although policy and procedures to deal with violence are in place in all schools, both the teachers and the student body should be made familiar with them, as well as observing their implementation in an expedient and judicious manner

- role models, real and imaginary, from a variety of ethnic and racial backgrounds, that are observed satisfying both general and personal needs in a socially appropriate manner

- opportunities for values clarification – chances to explore a personal value system while examining those belonging to peers as well as to the dominant culture

- moral reasoning – learning in contexts in which people think through potential situations – especially those examining moral behavior – and having access to skills that are able to resist peer pressure

- literacy development – chances to increase reading and writing abilities, focusing on those which lead to accessing knowledge of personal interest

- availability to use introspection, reflection, language – openings for the cognitive and language skills to grow in order to ameliorate and evaluate potential behavior

- the application of academic skill to real-life situations, particularly skills required in wage-paying jobs

- opportunities for Co-op education [25] – when applicable – at the secondary level in addition to supervised volunteer opportunities within the elementary panel; for example, reading once a week to the Grade 1 class

- specialized programming for needy students and their families, and especially for teachers who regularly work with students in special-needs groups

Sometimes, additional resources are required. The implementation of specialized programs may be necessary in the context of schools, for instance, the ones in need of violence prevention or requiring help for either underachieving students or those lacking social skills.

Student Programs

Usually, Social Competency Training can be achieved with the use of curricula and student training videos. For example, in Hazel et al. (1981), ASSET : A Social Skills Program for Adolescents the program includes eight training videos that provide vignettes, each one focusing on a particular social skill, including:

- thanking or complimenting others

- expressing criticism or disappointment in a calm, non-threatening manner

- listening calmly to criticism; asking permission to tell the other side of the story

- saying no; giving a personal reason; suggesting alternative activities

- identifying problems; considering consequences; determining possible solutions

- resolving conflicts with others; suggesting solutions; asking for alternative options; learning to compromise

- listening carefully; acknowledging; clarifying; following through

- Interacting with others; introducing oneself; initiating and maintaining a conversation

In the program called *Peacemaker* (Shapiro *et al.,* 2002) is outlined a violence-prevention presentation for students in Grades 4 to 8. Overall, the program involves 17 lessons, of 45 minutes each, delivered by teachers working from detailed lesson plans. In addition to targeting behaviors and attitudes related to violence, the unit incorporates an anger-management procedure as well as structures for conflict resolution. By providing a remedial portion led by counselors and the school psychologist, the program goes beyond the level of a classroom intervention, hoping to reach students referred by the teacher.

Tested on 2000 students, this unit boasts a 41% decrease in aggressive behavior as well as a 67% decrease in student suspensions following violent behavior. Unlike the results of other similar programs, these stronger positive outcomes are noted in the intermediate rather than in the junior division.

Initially produced by the nonprofit *Committee for Children* in the 1980s and rated an exemplary program by the U.S. Department of Education, the program *Second Step* is also a violence-prevention curriculum. Updated in 2002 to include more lessons and videotapes, a series of scripted lessons, based on interpersonal situations depicted in pictures and videos, is presented by the teacher. After this comes a period of discussion and skill practice. The pre-Kindergarten curriculum incorporates puppets and sing-along music, while homework assignments are provided to students in Grade 6 to high-school levels.

Designed for teachers in the elementary panel is the program known as PATHS – Promoting Alternative THinking Strategies. This curriculum, authored by Greenberg & Kusche (1993), was originally designed to help in the development of social competence among deaf students. Soon, its application to other students was very evident. Organized in a series of three major units, the curriculum not only is defined specifically but also offers sample lessons. Thoroughly evaluated in controlled studies, the program asserts a reduction in peer aggression and disruptive behavior as well as improvements in the climate of the classroom. Many other such prevention programs are widely available.

A good example of a Canadian initiative is The *Resolve Alberta* project, led by Leslie M. Tutty, who produced the *School-based Violence Prevention Programs: A Resource Manual*. This is a freely available[26] resource which schools and educators may use.

Teacher Training

An important aspect of any prevention program is the assurance that teachers are trained to deal with any situation expected to arise in the classroom as well as in the school at large. Not only must they feel competent in coping with problem behavior but they should also be comfortable when promoting pro-social behavior. An example of such a teacher-training program is *Teaching Prosocial Behavior to Antisocial Youth*. In this video series of six tapes produced and written by Goldstein (1999) are presented: *Skillstreaming, Aggression Replacement Training,* and *The Prepare Curriculum Programs*.

For those who want to reach out beyond these levels, teacher training is available on many platforms: face-to-face, as in additional-qualification courses; graduate programs; web-based courses on the Internet; programs at conferences and colloquia; learning through the reading of books and manuals; mentoring from a range of highly skilled teachers.

In an effective school, not only is provision made for teacher training, but also the necessary leadership is available for encouraging teachers to work together in resolving school-wide challenges.

In-school and Community Programs

In disadvantaged areas, in particular, schools must offer students the opportunity to participate in after-school recreational activities as well as in athletic programs. In addition, information programs about substance use, sexual matters, health issues, and various types of addiction, along with programs dealing with issues relating to youth employment, should be available. Finally, the implementation of a mentoring program is a very effective means to consolidate the attachment of a youth to the school.

Conclusion

When problems associated with young offenders are closely examined, it becomes evident that society as a whole should begin to re-think and re-assess goals and values. An interesting aspect, for example, is the difficulty law-abiding people have in understanding why young people break laws all the while knowing society will punish them. The Law of Effect[27] states, however, that if responses are likely to be followed by punishment, they will be weakened. Could it be that such miscreants intend to escape punishment? More recently, some commentators argue that at an even younger age than ever before, children are committing more crimes, apparently because the relevant laws are not sufficiently punitive.

An alternative explanation, offered by the sociological paradigm, assumes that offenders, like other people in society, have the same goals and values – the money, the fame, the glamour. Unlike others, however, they do not have the same capacity of achieving these goals through legal means. Thus, while more conventional people obtain education to realize personal goals, offenders choose illegal means. Although plausible, this explanation does not, however, account for people with access to legitimate means who nonetheless resort to illegal activities – for example, thieving "rich" kids or persons convicted of white-collar crimes. Nor does it explain the countless people from low-income households who quietly and doggedly work their way up into the middle and wealthy classes, without assistance from crime.

People who break laws perhaps justify their actions in order to make them personally acceptable: a method of rationalizing behavior involves relinquishing responsibility for the act. Possibly, the victim was ultimately responsible for the commission of the crime: "If he hadn't started the fight, I wouldn't have had to bash him".

Sometimes an offender may minimize the severity or the impact of an action by downplaying it; for example, the perpetrator may focus attention on the fact that no one got hurt. Another ploy involves suggesting that the ensuing damage was not as extreme as reported; a further evasive defense is that the victims were covered by insurance. Interestingly, some offenders may construe abusive actions as less extreme if directed towards undeserving individuals; for example, "This department store overcharges its customers anyway". There was also a drunk driver who blamed the people he injured after hitting them head-on in their own lane: "There shouldn't have been six people in that little Kharmann-Ghia".

In another vein, offenders may justify their behavior by claiming that many people engage in similar activities; for example, "I'm not the only one who cheats. Everybody cheats on income taxes, even my parents". or "I wasn't the only one drinking and driving. Everybody does it".

Finally, sociological theory considers that certain groups in society – the poor, the young, certain minorities – are held more accountable for law violations than are citizens in mainstream groups. Everyone, in the course of a normal life, is bound to violate a law. The dominant culture, however, invests a higher proportion of its resources in prosecuting certain target groups while selectively downgrading the offenses of others – such as perpetrators of white-collar crimes as well as violations by politicians and major corporations. It is possible, therefore, that because their behavior is more closely scrutinized, young offenders appear to commit more crimes than do other groups. Consequently, when statistics show that certain groups have a higher percentage of offenses, the data may reflect the pattern of scrutiny of law-enforcement agencies rather than itemizing a list of the true numbers.

If this concept is generalized to the classroom situation, a teacher may understand why several individuals appear continually to be in violation of either the classroom or the school rules. Consider the following questions:

- Are these students the only ones violating expectations?
- Why do the violations of this group captivate the teacher's attention?

Interestingly, this point of view may answer the question of why integration of students with behavioral difficulties is often a negative experience both for those students and for their teachers and classmates.

Summary

In overview, several special populations are targeted here for discussion, not only because they are encountered in the context of the classroom but also because each group requires appropriate intervention plans to address the unique behavioral needs of its members. At the same time, another point becomes clear: certain standard practices – such as *shaping* procedures – are usually independent of the individual, being more related to the pedagogical strategies of complex behaviors. For example, in the case of an "impulsive" student, or one unable to engage in "perspective-taking", similar procedures are used regardless of the diagnostic label – the impulsive student may have ADHD, Autism, Asperger, and so on, or perspective-taking may be lacking in the student with Asperger or the Young Offender. In both situations the procedure is independent of the student's condition.

In examining the phenomenon of juvenile delinquency, teachers should be aware that the classroom and the school can influence, to some degree, especially in earlier years, the ways in which protective and resilience factors assist students at risk. Some of the contexts in which such assistance can be useful are: ability level of the student, resources of the family, early intervention, strong interpersonal bonds, attachment to school and teachers, interest and achievement in high-school, interest and involvement in religious worship, participation in regulated or monitored social activities, interest and investment in the future[28]. When looking for ways of helping students, teachers may find it useful to begin with this partial list.

Although many effective prevention programs are available, several barriers exist that prevent major change. Included in these are: sources of money and adequate funding; resources to support teachers;

opposition to the lowering of the pupil-teacher ratio; denial of problems by administrators; and finally, the attitudes of many parents.

The reader is encouraged to take note of the many behaviors that have been outlined and promoted throughout the book and to compare them with the middle-class values presented in Table 9-3.

Endnotes

1   The Identification Placement and Review Committee

2   Students challenged by literacy difficulties fall further and further behind in their general knowledge. By the time, students reach the Intermediate Division (Grades 6, 7, and 8) a large part of this knowledge is accessed in print. Viewing documentaries and having access to information in non-print formats allow the student to acquire knowledge about the world.

3   This DSM classification is included and defined later in this chapter.

4   Refer to the notion of normal distribution presented in Chapter One.

5   Operant conditioning refers to learning as a consequence of reinforcement and/or punishment.

6   See Meichenbaum (1993) for a retrospective analysis.

7   The process of "shaping" a behavior involves the concept of differential reinforcement and is discussed in great detail in Chapter 7, p. 241.

8   This procedure is identical to the Prompt-and-Fade technique described in Chapter 7, p. 247.

9   See Bibliography for the full reference.

10   In the 1970s, the books of Virginia Axline were very popular. Published, by Ballantine, their titles are *Dibs in Search of Self* (1967) and *Play Therapy* (1969).

11   The *Diagnostic and Statistical Manual* published by the American Psychiatric Association.

12   The Block Design Subtest is one of the many Performance subtests on the Wechsler Intelligence Scale. Shown a two-dimension arrangement of while and red blocks, the individual is required to reproduce it in three dimensions using a set of plastics blocks.

13   See description in the section on Autism, in this Chapter.

14   From the video *Nine* produced by Harpo Productions.

15   A description of Erikson's "Eight Stages of Man" identifies Stage 2 in the second year of life as the quest for autonomy *vs.* self-doubt and shame. See Chapter Two.

16   A thorough description of the model is found in Chapter Four.

17   See diagnostic criteria for *Oppositional Defiant Disorder.*

18   This book was first published in 1924.

19   Originally published in French in 1897.

20   The 1955 movie *The Blackboard Jungle* was so disturbing in its depiction of racial and violent content that some cities initially banned it.

21   Strain theory suggests that because the attainment of success is restricted for people of the lower economic class, they are forced to either abandon the middle-class dream of success and prosperity or break the law to fulfill it.

22   This type of gang is depicted in the 1961 film of the Broadway musical *West Side Story.*

23   See White (2002).

24   More in-depth information about Antisocial Personality Disorder is featured in the books *Without Conscience,* by Hare (1999), and *Bad Boys, Bad Men,* by Black & Larson (1999).

25   Co-op education consists of integrating classroom study with internships in the business world.

26   A PDF file is downloadable from the following website: http://www.ucalgary.ca/resolve/violenceprevention/English/

27   See Chapter Two.

28   see Hanlon *et al.* (2002).

CHAPTER 10

Considerations, Organization, and Procedures of the Behavioral Class

In a behavioral classroom, practical decisions face the teacher at all times, and sometimes the same kinds of practical issues face a teacher in a regular class, especially when mainstreamed students have behavioral problems. The intention of this chapter is to consider all the classroom issues that play important roles in achieving the goals identified for these difficult-to-serve students.

Recently, school boards have begun to regard closed classrooms – specialized settings within the context of the school – as economically unfeasible. Such a policy may affect the placement of every student with behavioral difficulties. Often, administrators will defend this attitude by proposing that retaining students in the regular class circumvents the stigma of a special-class placement, at the same time encouraging modeling of normative behavior. It is true that in a class of eight to ten students with behavioral exceptionalities, as in detention centers and prisons, individuals may mimic and, in some circumstances, learn socially inappropriate as well as criminal behavior. But, as previously outlined in Chapter Four, (p. 104), students should be accommodated in a variety of settings because their immediate needs dictate varying structures. In U.S. Law 94-142, the term **least-restrictive environment** is used to describe this process.

For the same reasons that a small number of students may need to be placed in a residential setting, some school-aged children and adolescents cannot be served effectively in the context of the regular classroom. Of course, this statement assumes that the pupil-teacher ratio will stay at 30:1. In addition to the large classes, few, if any, resources are available to support the already-difficult work of the classroom teacher. Perhaps a case can be made for a regular program which begins with an 18:1 ratio, accepts no more than three students diagnosed with Behavioral Exceptionalities, and includes full-time support from a qualified Child Care Worker. But even if such ideal conditions were available, some students would need the segregation and safety of a program outside the mainstream.

Consider, for a moment, the student who is identified and placed in a segregated classroom either in a school or in a treatment center. Which important aspects of the process should the "receiving" teacher consider among the topics that are examined here?

- Admission
- Physical Organization of the Environment
- Curriculum: Academic and Social Skills
- Classroom Management
- Teaching Assistance
- The Role of Parents
- Supply Teachers
- Field Trips
- Mainstreaming
- School
- Mental Health

Awaiting Admissions

Whereas, in a regular class, students are immediately accepted as they transfer into the school, if placement is to be in a special education program, for each new student admitted into the class the teacher is required to undertake certain preparations. Why prepare for the admission of a new student? First is the task of ensuring that a specialized program is available – that curriculum, materials, and resources will be found. Yet another factor relates to the preparation needed to introduce a new individual into the existing class. Any change to the *status quo* is likely to disrupt the delicate balance of the classroom as well as to threaten the affective needs of class members.

To accomplish the groundwork before admitting a new student, the several stages that the teacher will find necessary include:

- collecting all available data on the student awaiting admission, a procedure which might include interviewing previous teachers, reading reports, and examining assessment documents (see Chapter Three, pp. 82-96).

- formulating a tentative short-term plan based on all the information gathered and including steps to be taken to introduce the student to the class and the school (see Chapter Three, pp. 97-101).

- admitting the student only when all preparations are completed. Sometimes, because placement in a closed class is a means of solving a crisis somewhere else, there are pressures to accept the student immediately. The extra time taken by the process, however, ensures that the student will begin a new placement on a positive note.

cont'd

- staggering admissions when more than one student is to be admitted, to assure that appropriate care is taken with each. When a new student arrives, there is always a temporary destabilization of the classroom environment.

- discussing the case with the special-education team, especially when severe behaviors are anticipated, so that they may engage in formulating the appropriate policies, procedures, or plans with the support of the school administration. Although preventive measures may require an initial investment of resources, the benefits to everyone concerned are immeasurable.

- meeting with parents prior to admission to explain expectations, routines, and policies. Parents must be enlisted as part of the treatment team to maximize treatment outcomes. When parents are unable or unwilling to participate, they might perhaps require either help from social workers or community support.

- having the child visit and tour the school to become familiar with the new environment – what to expect on the first day, the location of washrooms, and introduction to other procedures. At this time, also, the student meets with the class and personnel.

- Such measures are taken to allow a smooth transition for the incoming student and to ensure minimal disruption to the students already in the class. In addition to the list of procedures included here, the teacher should consider implementing any other actions suitable to the fulfilling of this goal.

The Honeymoon Period

Teachers experienced in working with newly enrolled students in a special class will attest to the fact that, at first, it is easy to answer the question of whether the student's placement is appropriate. For a period of several weeks the young person is so well behaved that the other students in the class will query: "Why is he here?" or "She's not anything like us!"

The incoming student, faced with a new and unfamiliar environment, adopts a position of observation as well as conformity, avoiding any behavior that might "rock the boat". Once the student feels safe enough to reveal the real person underneath the façade, however, then some of the anticipated problems will begin to surface. Having exercised so much self-control during the honeymoon period, the student will suddenly demonstrate explosive behavior that will be little cause for wonder during the release period that follows – not very different from attempts to suppress a sneeze.

When the teacher is anticipating the release phase, the best preparation is accomplished by first acknowledging that it is inevitable. Then the student's individualized education plan should be put into place because it incorporates the needs identified in the case study (see Chapter Three, pp. 81-101).

Fire setting

In this chapter – and specifically in this section – the topic of arson and fire setting is described because many special education programs are reluctant to admit those students who have histories of these activities. Given that fire is a major safety threat to both staff and students, the exclusion policy is not surprising. Before the problem is dismissed as occurring infrequently, however, teachers must be aware that juveniles are more involved in fire setting than are other age groups – anywhere from 50% to 55% of arson arrests involve juveniles; about one third of all arsonists are under the age of 15 years; and about 7% are below the age of 10 years (Garry, 1997).

Generally, fire setters fall, by age, into three major categories:

> - Children under the age of 7 years who are usually motivated by curiosity
>
> - Children between the ages of 8 and 12 years; although some of these are fascinated by fire, others are acting out psychological problems
>
> - Adolescents between the ages of 13 and 18 years: these young persons often have long histories of arson-related behavior that is worsened by psychological problems and criminal intention

Noting that statistics on arson are gathered from fire-department data, Wilcox (2000) predicts that the incidence of arson would be considerably greater if all fires – set and extinguished outside the knowledge of the authorities – were considered in the records. Because of his dismay, he draws attention to the dearth of research, a relatively small amount compared with the magnitude of the problem. Of interest to teachers is the work of Nishi-Strattner (2001), material that identifies several correlates of fire-setting behavior:

> - age – boys between the ages of 10 and 13 years
>
> - ADHD – Attention Deficit Hyperactivity Disorder
>
> - history of abuse – 27% had experienced physical abuse; 10.4% reported sexual abuse; 19% had sustained both types of abuse

Such information reinforces the need for early intervention in addition to the availability of appropriate treatment resources.

In regard to treatment, these three approaches are recommended:

- *Fire safety education.* Usually sponsored by Fire Departments, the presentation – that includes the topics of dangers of fire, fire prevention, and emergency procedures – is usually made by a uniformed firefighter.

- *Individual child therapy.* The child/juvenile is taught problem-solving strategies and social skills, as well as a range of alternate interests and recreational activities. In this approach, the aim is to reduce the motivation to use fire as entertainment or as a form of spite/anger response.

- *Parent training.* Parents are given management techniques to manage and promote pro-social behavior of the child/juvenile. Specific emphasis is focused on the consequences of fire-setting behavior as well as on the young person's responsibility for and involvement in the safety of the home.

Very useful, too, to teachers and other professionals working with students who exhibit fire-setting behavior, is Kolko's (2002) newly published handbook.

Classroom Set-up

New teachers in the field often find it hard to believe that the organization of the classroom can contribute to or hinder class management to the extent that it is sometimes capable of doing. When a student, for example, is unable to find materials, there can be a vague wandering off, an "off course" activity in which the individual perhaps becomes involved in mischief; as simple a detail as the wrong seating arrangement, moreover, can lead to repeated physical altercations between students.

For this reason, the following suggestions are offered:

- The physical organization of the classroom should be based on need and efficiency. Right from the outset, it is helpful to create sectors that warrant different seating arrangements – an area for independent work, one for cooperative work, one in which relaxation is encouraged, and others as they are needed. By setting up these separate areas, the teacher hopes students will develop strong associations between the delineated physical areas of the classroom and the specific activities expected to occur in them. Once these associations are strengthened, for instance, the minute the student enters the relaxation area there should be a feeling of stress reduction. Of course, the teacher can expect the same phenomenon to encourage working on assignments in work areas as well as quiet reflection in the independent[1] setting.

                                                        cont'd

- In any arrangement that encourages individualized instruction, a large quantity of curriculum material at various levels of difficulty and interest will be required.

  ° A filing system is set up to accommodate individualized plans, portfolios, and other gear. Over a period of time, it is important to keep different pieces of work which will chronicle the academic improvement of each student. Often, comparing pieces of work completed months apart can show striking transformation not evident on a day-to-day basis.

  ° Locations for storing and working with audiovisual materials, library materials, and high-interest low-vocabulary books[2] are included in one area. When a variety of resources containing an assortment of knowledge domains is available, students will be enriched and their learning stimulated. For example, having a microscope in the class to examine both pond water and melted snow can perhaps spark an interest in Biology, in the same manner that a trundle wheel[3] can incite curiosity in geometry.

  ° Computers with the appropriate assistive technology should be available to students. With the aid of a scanner linked to a personal computer, software packages can be accessed that will read any material to a reluctant reader. For students with reading levels below functional literacy, such equipment provides access to text material at their cognitive levels. Similarly, the student unable to write due to poor spelling skills is able to dictate to voice-activated software.

  ° Bulletin boards should always be attractively designed and decorated in such a manner as to make the room look like a classroom. Important to students, despite all their relevant problems, is the impression that they are attending a school. As alluded to throughout this book, maintaining a semblance of normality is important to the student's self-concept. Moving away from this idea by either labeling students or forcing them to engage in what appear to be non-school activities – seeing a counselor, psychologist, or psychiatrist – often causes rebellion, and/or, in some cases, the adoption of a "sick" **persona**.

  An interesting aside relates to the information placed on bulletin boards. Akin to information in ads posted on billboards across the city, although seemingly ignored by students, the information is nonetheless learned when unexpectedly it is incorporated in learning activities.

Curricula

The special class for students with behavioral exceptionalities is required to offer two types of curricula: an academic curriculum focusing on developing literacy and numeracy skills and a social-skills curriculum whose intent is to return the student to a normative setting, wiser about social expectations and able to interact with a range of people.

Academic Curriculum

Often, the teacher is charged not only with providing individualized programs for each class member but with providing teaching that will involve one-on-one interaction. In the special classroom, it is possible to have a span of four or five academic years differentiating the students' competence levels. As a result, the teacher must become familiar with the developmental sequence of literacy and numeracy skills, a task more difficult for secondary school teachers whose training and experience have been subject-oriented rather than skill-based. Another consideration involves the lack of general knowledge that results for a student who has not acquired the literacy skills needed to access print information. Even information on the Internet is composed primarily of text, which means that unless it is transmitted orally, knowledge about the world is difficult to access by the student unable to read. In this situation, the major drawback is that the less knowledge is acquired, the less likely the student will be able to comprehend new concepts. In most classrooms, teachers assume, sometimes erroneously, that students have acquired an entire level of implicit knowledge. That this kind of assumption is dangerous was made obvious when some children were asked where milk comes from. The first student answered, "from a pig", while another responded "from the refrigerator in the supermarket".

Because such a strong relationship exists between knowledge on the one hand and comprehension of new ideas on the other, older students who find certain subjects – social sciences, mathematics, and the like – difficult to grasp, have the option to remediate background knowledge by borrowing books on respective topics from the Children's section of the public library. By referring to such books, an older learner can identify central ideas and develop them in a fashion that is easily understood. At this stage, the student will be able to adapt the newly found knowledge to understand age-appropriate material.

Examples of books on non-fiction topics include:

Priceman, M. (2001). *It's me, Marva:* a story about color and optical illusions. New York: Alfred A. Knopf.

Worsick, D. (1994). *Henry's Gift: the Magic Eye.* Kansas City: Andrews and McMeel.

Brimner, L. D. (1998). *Mars.* New York: Children's Press.

Scagell, R. (1998). *Space: an accessible guide that really explains the universe.* London: Marshall Pub.

MacDonald, F. (2001). *The World in the Time of Tutankhaman.* Philadelphia, PA: Chelsea House.

Group Teaching

As a result of the diversity of academic competence among students, it will seem fitting to provide only one-on-one instruction. It is important, however, that the teacher strive to identify course subjects – like the social sciences and music – that can be taught to the entire group, with special modifications for certain students only when necessary. Group learning offers advantages not found in one-on-one situations:

- *To compare one's knowledge with the knowledge of others.* Hadley may be unaware that he is the resident expert on North American mammals. At the same time, Padma thinks, "If Magar can learn about prisms and stuff, so can I".

- *To learn from a peer's description of the manner in which a correct solution is obtained, as well as learning from mistakes made by others.* When Mr. Ashwini asks Victor to describe the procedure he used to find information on the historical contribution of the Black Loyalists[4], on the basis of Victor's explanation, Carinne finally makes made sense of the topic. In the same vein, using Colby's well polished report, Mr. Ashwini gently explains that a person's ideas should be acknowledged, through a citation of the original author's name, an idea that Hugo has never considered.

- *To participate without being the center of attention.* For many students who value the teacher attention of one-on-one situations, but who do not want to be centered in a large classroom, this set-up creates learning by leaps and bounds. For a few who want to avoid the spotlight at any cost, the group situation affords them the option of sitting back and learning vicariously. Luciano, the learning-disabled student described in Chapter Nine, (pp. 341-345), is such a candidate. His favorite response in a one-on-one situation, sometimes even before a question is posed to him, is "I don't know". In a small-group environment, Luciano always exerts more effort, and, from time to time, will volunteer a response, to guarantee the social approval of group members.

Physical Education, Music, and Visual Arts

Considered frill subjects by some teachers, for students in special classes, Physical Education, Music, and Visual Arts are no less important than academic subjects. Because the students enjoy them, these subjects can be used as a means to incorporate disguised academic skills. For example, number facts are best learned on a trampoline and word cards, inscribed with verbs, can be read as actions are completed on a variety of physical education equipment.

Knowing that these subjects have intrinsic value to the personal growth of students, the teacher should not make their study contingent on the completion of academic work. Never should they be used to punish or reward behavior, unless reading, writing, and arithmetic are employed in the same manner. Because all three subjects provide an alternative mode of expression to students who may normally experience academic failure, some members of the class may excel in them, while others will enjoy the activities associated with the three kinds of learning.

When possible, opportunities for physical education should be planned on a daily basis for short periods of time. Although many students appreciate the exercise after sitting for relatively long stretches, the physical education class is also an opportunity to practice social skills, like sharing, cooperation, and even perspective-taking.

Time Management

By organizing the day into small time slots and varying activities throughout the day, the teacher is able to create a fast-paced rhythm that maintains high student motivation. In such a schedule, skills that require practice can be re-visited several times throughout the day, for short intensive periods, concentrating on different contexts[5]. By employing graphs, charts, and other recording techniques, the student is encouraged to log personal progress. In this context, both the teacher and the student should remember that distributed practice is usually superior to massed practice: better pedagogy is involved in four 30-minute study periods than in a single two-hour period focused on one narrow task.

In school settings, many students claim to be procrastinators – work completion is left to the very last minute. Normally, the procrastinator feels motivated to undertake the task only when the stress level is high enough to trigger the action. When Ms. Machover assigns a task to be completed independently during a 45-minute time slot, Lloyd examines the task and estimates that it will take him only ten minutes to complete. "This is great! I can talk to Ben about last night's hockey game for the next half-hour". Following his usual pattern, Lloyd will settle down to work in the last fifteen minutes of the class because he has learned that he can always count on doing other more pleasurable activities before attempting responsibilities. By decreasing the amount of available time, Ms. Machover can indirectly encourage her students to begin work immediately if they have any hope of finishing on time, an attractive objective because a more preferred activity follows (for a discussion of the Premack principle, see Chapter Seven, p. 228).

The Social Skills Curriculum

Although, in the context of the classroom, social skills are learned vicariously, often in the special class these must be taught formally, using approaches and planning similar to those employed when teaching academic topics. (see Chapter Four, pp. 117-122). The teacher has the option of either working from a published program with scripted lessons or of developing lessons based on the needs of individual students. While some teachers might prefer to work initially with published materials – because they are easier to implement – eventually, they may want to develop specific units of instruction to target skills sets unique to individual students.

Among many published programs, here are some to consider:

Hazel *et al.* (1981), *ASSET : A Social Skills Program for Adolescents* (see Chapter 9, p. 413)

Shapiro *et al.,* 2002, *Peacemaker* (see Chapter 9, p. 414)

Committee for Children *(2002) Second Step* (see Chapter 9, p. 414)

Greenberg & Kusche (1993), *PATHS – Promoting Alternative THinking Strategies,* (see Chapter 9, p. 414)

Knoff, H. (2001), *Stop and Think Social Skills Program,* is organized into four grade-specific sets (PreK-1, 2-3, 4-5, 6-8), *Stop and Think Social Skills Program.* Longmont, CO: Sopris West.

Arise Foundation (2001) produces various titles known as *The ARISE Life-Management Skills Program*; for example, *Arise Brain Food Series,* designed for teens (ages 13-18) consists of six books plus a teacher's manual, that address topics such as: Peaceful Living, Creating a Positive Outlook, Supercharging Your System, Being Safe, The Right Stuff, and Money Matters.

Free resources for K-6, including lesson plans, are available on the website Assembly Program, Lifeskill4kids at the following URL: http://www.lifeskills4kids.com/

Using published materials should not discourage the teacher from continuing to utilize the Language Arts program as a means to integrate social skills' learning. To support the social skills curriculum, literature, drama, storytelling, and writing activities should continue to be encouraged. For the teacher who wants to learn about the teaching of social skills, the process may begin by consulting some of the following books:

Cartledge, G., & Milburn, J. F. (2002). *Teaching Social Skills to Children and Youth: Innovative Approaches* (Third ed.). Boston, MA: Allyn & Bacon.

Csóti, M. (2001). *Social Awareness Skills for Children.* Philadelphia, PA: Jessica Kingsley Pub.

Harkness, S., Raeff, C., & Super, C. M. (Ed.). (2000). *Variability in the Social Construction of the Child.* San Francisco: Jossey-Bass.

Gullotta, T. P., Adams, G. R., & Montemayor, R. (Ed.). (1990). *Developing Social Competency in Adolescence.* Newbury Park, CA: Sage.

Additional factors to be considered in the teaching of social skills are the phenomena of biculturalism and multiculturalism. In the classroom, these variables compel the teacher to pose such questions as: "Which social skills should be taught?" and "Is it important to encourage an ethnic identity?" In the following section, these delicate issues are looked at in some detail.

Cultural Diversity

Whereas some countries are relatively homogeneous in culture, for example, Greece and Japan, many have become heterogeneous, like Canada, the United States, Great Britain, and France, as well as several others. Even though such diversity is often associated with the New World, waves of immigration – linked to economic, religious, and political strife – are responsible for the diversity of people found in several countries known for their open immigration policies. Within these nations, often to their great advantage, several cultures that originally may have evolved worlds apart are able to co-exist, side by side, in the neighborhoods of their new countries.

While parents are the initial trainers of their progenies' social skills as they relate to their respective cultural affiliations, teachers, too, have a role in socializing each student in the context of the dominant culture. Sometimes, if the student is having difficulty relating to both peers and teachers – especially when social skills training is considered to be the appropriate intervention – several possibilities warrant consideration before a program is planned. The student has been:

> * socialized by parents in a culture other than the dominant surrounding one
> * socialized by parents in a process through which the student failed to acquire the needed skills
> * received no formal socialization; as a result of family break-down, the student has, subsequently, acquired "splintered[6]" skills

To address the first consideration, especially in a classroom, it is important to recognize that many students are present whose cultures differ from the dominant culture, including: minority groups, members of subcultures, new immigrants, refugees, and several others.

In examining issues that relate to culture and diversity among both students and teachers, the major focus must lie in the realization that when there are gaps there is a likelihood of conflict. If teachers have experienced a predominantly middle-class upbringing, usually in a White community, and have taught primarily in schools matching their backgrounds, it is startling for them when they suddenly become aware of the plight of students in the inner city. An example of the possibility of failing to understand is demonstrated by the reaction of a group of teachers who saw the film *Nine*. After viewing this very vivid portrayal of nine-year olds of different racial and socio-economic backgrounds, describing their personal experiences with sexual abuse, fear of bullies, homelessness, and other grim situations, without fail a small number of the teachers who watched the film refused to acknowledge the problems. Unwilling to credit the way of life presented in the video as a fair depiction of the experiences of some of their students, these teachers downplayed even the emotions portrayed by the nine-year-olds.

While it is often true that people are most attracted to others with similar experiences, values, and physical characteristics and it is common to hear the idea that "the more you remind me of myself, and the more I like you", the corollary is that the a lack of knowledge about others who are different leads to misconceptions about their behavior, as well as about their motives and intentions. When this cultural gap occurs among teachers, these misperceptions about the social behavior of students who are culturally different can lead to excessive punishment of their behavior.

When thinking in terms of punishment, teachers should always be aware that unless great care is taken to avoid this trap, the more a student's culture deviates from the teacher's, the greater the likelihood that negative feedback about the student's social actions will emerge. When there is a penalty, the student will usually interpret the negative response according to a personal frame of reference. For example, immigrant students with a history of corporal punishment – especially when it has been used to punish inappropriate behavior – may find it difficult to conform to the social conventions of the classroom, when only a set of clear expectations is given as a control mechanism. Accustomed to harsh punishment to signal disapproval of inappropriate behavior, these students habitually disregard rules as well as gentle reminders. In such cases, students are best served by a teacher who creates opportunities for explorations that employ various modalities: watching movies, reading stories, consulting books, interviewing relatives, discussing relevant topics, and viewing videos. In these varying media, issues are presented outlining a range of ways in which both people and cultures exercise control over erratic behaviors. By examining the similarities and differences that exist in people's attributions, the teacher hopes not only that some understanding will take place but also that students will recognize the necessity to move towards personal control of behavior. Eventually, students may even come to recognize this as the standard of adult behavior in a democratic society[7].

What is the value of recognizing a student's culture?

Across the world, each culture represents a people's way of life: their traditions, language, religion, family life, values, attributions, and, importantly, the manner in which their economic system is organized. When a process is developed and passed on to be shared with subsequent generations, it becomes a unique marker defining the identity of a representative individual. In the case of cultures with strong oral traditions, storytelling – of elaborate tales and sagas and myths – recounts the history of the people, increasing the bond that is established among the different age groups[8].

By recognizing the values, knowledge, and beliefs that affect behavior in the context of each different culture, the teacher will find it easier to understand and alter the suitability of a particular student's action. Because Ms. Trudelle is aware that Hiroshi, an East Asian student, has been socialized not to respond to an adult's scolding, she does not interpret as a defiant stance his lack of response to her question "Why is this task not finished?" Similarly, with his group of First Nations' students, Mr. Caulfield recognizes that planning a class debate on the pros and cons of recycling may not be the best choice of activities to explore the topic. Instead, he chooses to take the class on a field trip so that they may experience at first hand the waste-and-litter phenomenon. In evaluating the appropriateness of behavior as well as in identifying the need to remediate social skills, both Ms. Trudelle and Mr. Caulfield have tried to become familiar with the varying cultural backgrounds of their students.

What should be known about cultures?

Across the planet, an important feature of cultures is their continually changing characters. For immigrant cultures, this aspect may be problematic because, once they have left their country, a group or extended family may become culturally locked into a time continuum. In this syndrome, the culture brought to the new environment remains static, while, in the country of origin, the nation's varied culture continues to change, to replicate, and to evolve. Also true is the manner in which the process of acculturation changes attitudes, behavior, and values, especially when the traditional ethnic and the local cultures come into contact. Within their household, Mr. And Mrs. Shivan recognize the need to be flexible enough with Sakshi to permit her to entertain a couple of school friends at home. A range of influences exists, including the geographic alienation from the country of origin, the need to preserve the old culture and the awareness of the ongoing process of acculturation: all are responsible for the subtle differences that emerge between East Indian-Canadians and newcomers from Asia. A similar pattern may emerge in a family of East-Indian Americans, when a relative visiting from India might disagree with and/or condemn the Shivans' parenting practices. Mishu complains that her father's friends have pressured him successfully to insist that she quit her culturally liberating job at Wendy's, because, within the Bengali community, her working makes him look cheap. In addition, her grandparents visiting from Bangladesh believe she should be interested in helping her mother keep house until she marries, rejecting her plan to apprentice as a cosmetician.

For the larger proportion of students living in a multicultural society, group membership may extend to at least two sets of contacts, with the result that the task of developing an ethnic and/or racial identity within the context of a distinct dominant culture begins to pose problems. In these circumstances, several options open up for the individual who may feel:

- A strong identity with one culture and a weak one with the other. "I am so Canadian now that I don't care about being a Klingon – except at family parties"[9]. A strong identity with both cultures – the ethnic importation and the dominant culture. In this situation, the student has a bicultural existence in which each part is independent of the other; the individual is, for example, Ukrainian at home and Canadian at school

- No identification with either group. The existence of such a student would be a cause for concern, implying rejection or passivity   *cont'd*

> - An exclusive identification with the dominant culture – the result of a process of total assimilation. For example, some third- and fourth-generation Japanese[10] Canadians are incensed when asked to explain why they speak English so well. In fact, most of the young people already spoke accent-free Standard Canadian English in 1946 when they moved East from the camps in British Columbia.

Belonging to a cultural group not only implies a sharing of history, experiences, values, and many other elements but also, in everyday situations, represents an understanding of all that culture's tacit communications – a look, an idiomatic expression, and other recognizable cues.

New immigrants and refugees

When immigrant students first arrive in the new country, the dominant culture may appear more attractive and seductive than the customs of their former home countries, as they strive to learn the new language, acquire new expectations, and alter their clothing and gestures. In order to possess a sense of belonging, they begin to recognize that fitting in is an important goal. If several students from a single ethnic background attend the same school, they will sometimes have a feeling of safety when they are together. Often, however, individuals have to resist being placed in a pecking order established on the basis of the length of time each student has been in the new country. Of course, the immigrant student who arrived more than a year ago has more status than the one in the country for only a few months. Having taken root in the new land, however, the student may, eventually, re-assert an interest in the original ethnic identity while, in some contexts, fully embracing the dominant culture.

According to many accounts of the immigrant experience, refugee children have unique stories to tell because only rarely does the whole family leave the country of origin at the same time, arriving in the new land together. The emigration procedure often entails separation from the parent(s) either imprisoned in the place of origin or estranged in transit. Worse still, many family members may disappear entirely. In addition, some students will have also lost grandparents or siblings, often both. In many Canadian situations, refugee families are composed only of women and children, groups who have experienced traumatic events. In commenting on the war in Croatia, Zivcic (1993) reports that refugee children, more often than adults, experience depression and fear which impact on their emotional functioning. In summary, unlike the factual but less traumatizing accounts and stories common to immigrant students, the tales told by the children in refugee families will involve more harmful, long-term data. Not only will these young people need social-skills training; they will also require, at times, intensive emotional counseling[11].

The problem with sterotypes

In the same manner that ALL immigrant Italians were once suspected of having membership in The Mafia, currently, African-Canadians may find themselves unfairly associated with criminal behavior. Apparently, some racist individuals are disinclined to forego stereotypes even when contradictory evidence is available. When observing Asian class members, many teachers and even other adults expect them to be hard-working and high-achieving students, despite evidence compiled in New York City where 25% of Asian students not only drop out of school but also add to the increase in criminality. Whether positive or negative stereotypes are being applied by either teacher or students or both, the practice is not acceptable. On behalf of the dominant culture, the school's role is to dispel the use of stereotypes in social interactions, and, at the same time, to promote inclusiveness along with the pleasure of enjoying diversity.

In a typical school setting, an example can be shown of the way stereotypes play themselves out. According to his immigrant parents, Bushiri, a new Canadian from East Africa, is a good student who acts in a responsible manner, not only looking after his younger siblings after school but also helping them with their homework whenever he is able. Nevertheless, he has twice been suspended from school for incidents not supported by evidence. In one of these, as he was leaving the washroom, he noticed a group of students just near the washroom door, running at the sight of the vice-principal. Although he remained standing there, merely observing, as the incident unfolded, Ms. Vieira accused him of being part of the mischief. In the investigation, despite clear explanations by both Bushiri and his parents, no amount of supportive evidence could change the mind of the Vice Principal. In this case, a further telling element is that the two parents, both hard-working immigrants, do not want to rock the boat. Here, as they were in their home country, they behave passively towards institutions, withdrawing into themselves rather than demanding justice. In examining the Vice Principal's perception of the situation, an observing teacher might wonder whether Ms. Vieira's racial stereotyping prevented her from being objective in this situation. Or is this an example of an honest mistake of an overworked administrator? Negative expectations of a student's behavior – based solely on racial or ethnic stereotypes – are not helpful. Furthermore, the danger is that such profiling may, over time, encourage some of the less assertive members of visible minority groups to live up to this and similar distorted views of their cultures.

Cartledge and Milburn (1996) indicate that it is not unusual for some students to buy into the same stereotypes of their own racial group as others do. For example, some Black students may come to accept mischief as what defines them, and to think of being poor as either the cause or the outcome of being dumb and lazy. As a corollary, these same students may maintain stereotypical notions of other races – Whites and Asians are rich because they're smart. Often, the same kind of thinking is indulged in by First Nations' students who may believe that addiction is part of their make-up. When such negative stereotypes as these are practiced and received within the schools – notably from the feedback of others both in and out of the dominant culture – they are a testament to the necessity for encouraging the search for a set of positive cultural identities.

For this outward-looking change to occur, the dominant culture must be willing to embrace diversity, as well as to ensure that such variety is represented in all forms of media. Within the dominant culture, a need exists to have one's own ethnic group, racial subgroup, or religious sect endorsed by the power brokers. In order to achieve this external approbation, a student from a little-trusted minority must be able to observe representatives who symbolize the positive contributions made by persons of different origins. For example, the models that Black students honor should not be limited to leaders in the world of entertainment and athletics. Although Canadian Sports Hall of Fame inductee, Harry Jerome, was a powerful figure with his "never quit" attitude, students should also be given the chance to recognize the leadership and contributions of men and women in other fields: Martin Luther King, Condoleeza Rice, Desmond Tutu, Austin Clarke, Maya Angelou, Lincoln Alexander, Chinua Achebe, and Colin Powell[12]. Similarly, members of the many other cultural groups should be able not only to open a newspaper but also to listen to the radio and to watch television with a good chance of encountering a range of positive role models from their own ethnic groups. In all these forms of media, members of the different ethnic backgrounds, from all walks of life, should be depicted, with the hope that pride and a sense of identity will be felt by young members of their respective ethnic roots.

Generally, teachers can help the process, first of all by making students aware of these VIPs, but, equally important, by recognizing prominent or interesting local community members. Sometimes, small gestures are able to create far-reaching impact. In one instance, Petronelle was thrilled to see a photograph of her classroom teacher along with a Filipino friend. When Ms. Fairfax acknowledged that the person in the picture was not only Filipino but also a close personal friend, Petronelle whose parents, years before, had immigrated from the Philippines, made a point of showing the photo to her classmates as well as providing a commentary. In Petronelle's world, the special image focused on her cultural group, in a positive way, conveying a sense of importance and acknowledgement. Taking the long view, racial and ethnic identities established prior to adolescence will affect the behavior of young people. In the schools, especially, steps must be taken to guarantee that these identities are perceived and registered in a positive way. Traditionally, such identification is the result of teachers and other adults encouraging pride in cultural heritage, and, at the same time, fostering an understanding of the sense of belonging. Feeling a kinship with the dominant culture means that students know it belongs to everyone, comprising, as it does, the values and experiences that all its members share.

Culture and Learning Style

The teacher should take for granted the truism that children from every culture will be receptive to factors affecting learning in the classroom. Similarly, a student capable of noting the link between effort invested and positive outcomes is more likely to succeed than the apathetic and uncaring one. In 2002, Armbrister, McCallum, and Lee, when they compared American and Korean children, found that Korean children, although no different when measured according to social attributions, scored highest in their accounting of academic failure. To understand this result it is necessary to examine what Korean parents try to teach children – be modest in everything; it is a virtue to attribute the cause of failure to yourself rather than to others; effort will lead to success. Very commonly, Korean children complain about the insistence, on the part of their mothers, that they study.

One of the most demeaning classroom practices – particularly for students of modest ability – is the exclusive use of ability groupings. In any classroom, regardless of the labels on the reading groups, all class members are aware of each student's level of competence. For students with long histories of academic failure, an ability grouping serves chiefly to confirm a lack of control, perhaps even learned helplessness (see Chapter Eight, pp. 332-333, Chapter Nine, pp. 367-368). For others, a sense of shame is attached to being in a low-end group. Unforeseen, but inevitable, problems should be expected when shame and humiliation become incorporated into a young person's self-image or self-worth – "there is something wrong with me".

In many cases, especially among at-risk students, *Direct Instruction* is recommended as the pedagogical tool for teaching social skills. (Cartledge & Milburn, 1996, 2002). This highly structured approach targets an explicit set of skills, all of them presented in a fast-paced instructional sequence – from simple to complex – with a high level of teacher-student interaction aimed at student mastery. Because this teacher-direct method subdivides skills into manageable units, many tacit skills are made explicit for students unaware of the nuances of social situations. Originally designed for younger children, but extended and adapted, the program has also proved effective with secondary school students (Grossen, 2002).

At the outset, *Direct Instruction* methodology may require some adjustment for students from First Nations. Initially, gaining mastery involves a system of guided skill practice, a process incompatible with the private practice preferred by many First Nations' students. Dyami doesn't like to be singled out in class, either to receive praise or to accept criticism, a feature central to DI. Interestingly, too, his modesty prevents him from outperforming less able students, to the point of denying his achievement rather than bragging about it. Ultimately, Dyami values the small-group instruction in DI, especially because he prefers to be evaluated by his peers rather than by his teacher. An alternative method for teaching skills involves the creation of carefully designed activities with the expressed deductive purpose of allowing students to discover truths and processes. Equipped with problem-solving as well as trial-and-error strategies, the student, individually or as part of a small group, explores the theme of the lesson to uncover information and, in addition, to engage in mental processes. In a good example of this technique, a small group of adolescent students is directed to the Star Trek website at http://www.startrek.com/library/alien.asp. Then the assignment asks them to compare the Klingon and Borg cultures, especially to note similarities and differences. Eventually, the exercise can be extended to include comparisons of human cultures[13].

437

Planning of teaching units also warrants a choice of environments – a cooperative versus a competitive environment. Teachers have found that some students seem to thrive in a competitive environment, adolescent boys in general. In some cultural groups, however – First Nations, and also girls, particularly in Mathematics and Science courses (Pollina, 1995) – appear to prefer a cooperative environment. Regularly, this finding is evident in cultures that commonly reward the efforts of the team rather than those of the individual. In these cultures – East Indian, African, Asian, First Nations of North America – the collectivistic is emphasized, instead of the individualistic, represented by the so-called "Western" societies, the United States, Canada, Great Britain, Australia, and much of Europe.

Designing and presenting activities that will engender a high degree of verbal communication is almost always problematic for students with language problems and disabilities. In some cultures – East Indian, Native North American – a period of careful forethought is encouraged before speech, as is a greater use of non-verbal rhetoric, such as gestures. Because so much emphasis is placed on verbal communication in North American classrooms, some teachers may find it difficult to recognize that in some cultures, speaking – especially that of children – is not greatly valued or encouraged.

Culture also predisposes an individual to attend to or to disregard aspects of an experience; for example, Brant, as a result of his native culture, prefers a holistic rather than a sequential perspective, one that is supported by favoring the visual over the verbal modality. In addition, his time-recognition focus includes the past and the present, in contrast to the perceptions of his classmates, from different ethnic backgrounds, many of whom emphasize the present and future. In the stories Brant reads, these differences are expressed in his close attendance to setting, situation, and outcome of events, as he concurrently disregards the names of the characters, the time elements, and many of the specific, ephemeral details.

In overview, children of varied cultural backgrounds offer differential levels of attention to the variety of elements in the fictional situations. Across the world, children, adolescents, and even many adults enjoy listening to and telling stories. Being read to is also apparently a favorite pastime in many cultures, indicated by the wide range of books for parents to read to children and long lists of 'talking books' that many adults favor. In some cultures, storytelling is the main vehicle for transmitting knowledge and information between generations; as a result it is a device that can be used effectively in the context of the classroom[14]. McGuire (1997) describes the way that a storypath[15] easily combines social skills with the study of culture, time, and place, creating a memorable learning experience for students.

Finally, some child-rearing practices, unique to a particular culture, can be adapted to become of interest to the school. Here, a special focus is on the degrees of dependence, independence, or interdependence granted to children across cultures. Whereas, in one culture, a young child is given an amount of autonomy – with the understanding that natural consequences are the main learning vehicle – in another culture, the teacher may be protective of the youngster's every move, concluding that the child is incapable of dealing with the dangers all around. Is it possible that such differences in rearing practices predispose some children to prefer purposeful learning? "Show me how to make change because I often shop for my parents."

Summary

In the context of working with students who have behavioral problems, a social skills curriculum is a necessary accompaniment to the academic ones; this truism means that opportunities to integrate the two should be sought whenever it is possible[16].

Considering the wide range of content found in a typical social skills curriculum, the multicultural nature of the student population makes the task more difficult. Should the school be responsible for communicating the values as well as the behavior only of the dominant culture? By recognizing the merits of a strong cultural identity to the self-concept students, it is worthwhile that the social skills program acknowledge the strengths of each culture. Among other examples might be listed: the altruism of the North American First Nations; the esteem for mothers and grandmothers among African-Canadians; the Asian propensity for tranquility and reflection; the Latin reputation for enthusiasm and passion; and the traditional African regard for pride and leadership. By focusing on the positive aspects of various cultures, both newly arrived students and their fifth-generation classmates will learn to embrace their own, to respect the others, and, willingly, to adopt the values of the dominant culture.

Classroom Management

The strategies and procedures outlined in Chapters Four, Five, Six, and Seven are as applicable in the *closed* setting as in the regular class. Always, the teacher:

- should be clear about general goals for the classroom and the students – teaching persistence, cooperation, problem-solving, and other skills

- may examine the expectations of a variety of regular classrooms for the purpose of teaching students how to adapt to each different one

- will recognize that every time a behavior is reinforced, the student's name is used – to direct the attention of others – and the category of behavior is mentioned in a positive manner. For example, it is more appropriate to say "Corin, I'm glad to see that you used polite language when you spoke to Terence", rather than saying "I'm glad you weren't swearing" *cont'd*

- should enlist the cooperation and the input of the students in designing and implementing expectations

- will move from a very structured approach, at first, to a less structured method, as students become more effective in learning to handle new situations

- tries to make the environment as predictable as possible in order to highlight contingencies

- always employs language in a continuous manner, describing the events in the classroom, the rationale for action, each statement to be modeled by students, and other pertinent information

The Role of School-wide Policies and Procedures

All people involved in education agree that students should not injure each other or their teachers. For this reason, many school boards have developed policies regarding zero-tolerance for violence. It is important, however, for students to have the opportunity to discuss the purpose of such policies and also to become familiar with the procedures. It follows that, in the case of a student turning violent, the other students will expect the policy to be invoked. If the policy is ignored or neglected, the lack of action will not only undermine the safety needs of the class but will send the message that consequences are optionally implemented.

In addition to establishing the school policy, teachers and administrators may consider it necessary to incorporate further provisions for class members who are quick to anger. In most cases, this is achieved by identifying typical pre-cursors to aggressive behavior, so that intervention can be made well in advance of any occurrence of the violence itself.

Parents

In most situations, the input and cooperation of parents represent essential components in the student's program. Because parents may have negative interactions with the school – their child is always in trouble – they are often reluctant participants, and so it is important, immediately, to establish a positive relationship. This may be achieved by contacting them on a regular basis rather than speaking to them only in the event of a crisis. When Mr. Ketelaars telephones Mrs. Abernathy,

Leon's mother, Wednesday evening at 7:30 p.m., he initially discusses with her the importance of establishing a routine, and, as result, he makes sure that a similar call will be made at the same time each week. When he speaks regularly to Mrs. Abernathy, Mr. Ketelaars informs her of the different activities accomplished that week as well as giving her feedback on Leon's performance. At first, in particular, he makes sure, by writing comments in advance, always to speak of Leon's accomplishments before mentioning any downfalls. In the conversations, Mr. Ketelaars also encourages Mrs. Abernathy to describe to him anything noted at home about Leon's positive actions and gestures. By December, contact is reduced to a fortnightly call in which other topics of conversation are included:

- target behaviors and objectives for the coming week
- background information to help predict Leon's responses
- details which would explain and model ways to encourage Leon's behavior at home
- data about school policy – discussing and explaining class and school procedures, especially those regarding aggressive behavior, but also field trips, etc.
- assumptions stated and shared about Leon's home-related chores, responsibilities, crises, curfews, and other matters
- concerns about the importance of parental involvement in addition to mentions of the contributions from home made to Leon's progress

As parents begin to trust the teacher and the school, they become more willing to share sensitive information and to request help.

Teaching Assistants

In the best arrangement, the closed classroom is employed by professionals who acquire specific training in programs related to children who have behavior problems. To augment the work of the specially trained teacher, graduates of Community College training programs in Child Care Work – and sometimes in other similar courses of study – are very effective complements to the classroom teacher. For this reason, the teacher, if consulted, should voice a preference for a partner with such training, and, as soon as it is known that an additional adult will be in the classroom, certain steps must be taken, including:

- deciding ahead of time the scope of responsibility for each adult – in all such meetings, the resulting decisions should be noted in the form of minutes. Of course, these can be amended and altered as time passes, especially because something that seems reasonable in a conversation may appear quite different when presented in print. In regular meetings, classroom procedures should be evaluated and changed as needed, on the basis of discussion and joint observation

- presenting a cohesive strength in front of the students is important in satisfying their safety needs When students are able to manipulate the adult supervising people by pitting one against the other, the climate of the classroom is in jeopardy

Field Trips

Because students with behavioral difficulties are expected to behave in a socially inappropriate manner, they often miss going on outings in the community. In fact, however, as a result of their social ineptitude, they should have increased rather than decreased opportunities to learn socially acceptable behavior. For this reason, a behavioral class deserves instead to be exposed to various social milieus rather than become isolated in the classroom.

In spite of this goal, most students, initially, are unprepared to deal with field trips. Learning to behave in the community requires a solid plan from the teacher and from the Child Care Worker partner who will provide chances – in advance of the field trip – to model and *overlearn* behavior in the context of drama and creative imagery. Building awareness of appropriate behavior is accomplished cautiously by:

- going on field trips in the neighborhood – to the library, to the park, or to the street market

- graduating to longer and further trips

- evaluating the acquisition of a concept learned in the classroom by observing its application in a community setting – recess, cafeteria, library, supermarket, or bus, as well as other locales

- ensuring a minimal standard of behavior before a student is allowed to demonstrate an ability to transfer it into the community – working to guarantee the success of the student

- having the courage, at any stage, to abort a trip for an offending student if certain limits and boundaries are crossed; of course this means arranging for transportation to return a student to the school or home without dampening the enjoyment and accomplishments of the other students

For students, learning to behave in a socially appropriate manner in the community is a way of ensuring that they develop a sense of belonging and participation.

Supply teachers

From time to time, the classroom teacher will be absent and, it is expected in most schools, will be replaced by a supply teacher. On a day-to-day basis, managing the behavior of class members is difficult enough, but in the event that the regular teacher is not present, the task becomes even more difficult. In the same manner that introducing a new student usually destabilizes the class environment, the absence of the regular teacher causes disruption.

At the outset, students will be reluctant to take directions from another adult, and, perhaps, even from the Child Care Worker, who, if available, can act to stabilize the situation. In addition, it must be recognized that although Supply Teachers strive to fulfill a necessary role in the Educational System, their position is on the fringe of the school system. Facing different schools daily, in addition to new groups of children of different ages, they experience very little continuity of experience or sense of belonging.

Consider the typical day of supply teacher Ms. Clarica, that begins with a call to replace a teacher who will absent from duties. Rushing to gather her paraphernalia, she manages to reach the school before 9 o'clock by public transportation. Sometimes, however, supply teachers own cars. Once she arrives at the right school – on one occasion she arrived at a school with a very similar name – she hunts around for the office, but finds the secretary speaking on the telephone or doing what secretaries do before 9 o'clock, a busy time. Finally, she is given the room number of her class assignment and manages to arrive there (with some detours) to find the students quietly lined up at the door, with only one small scuffle in progress. The door is locked! Here is a safety question Ms. Clarica ponders over for a few moments. Should she return to the office for the key or dare she trust one of the students to get back with it before recess. Because she is usually in a generous mood in the morning, she sends a friendly-looking student who re-appears with the key.

Once everyone is inside the room, Ms. Clarica follows her first impulse: to track down a seating plan. She can't find one! Because they know who everybody is, classroom teachers rarely make seating plans. Next, she hunts for the daybook, but only a teacher who plans to be absent – at a meetings or a conference – or a teacher who is obsessive about daybooks leaves one[17]. In a very well run school, though, a standard lesson plan has been prepared for an emergency situation such as this one. Some supply teachers always carry sets of prepared lessons that can be pressed into service.

How different is Ms. Clarica's experience if called to replace a teacher of a Special Class? Many substitute teachers refuse the assignment. Some who have previously survived the experience, or who are familiar either with the school or with the particular class, will accept the challenge. For the future, a good strategy for the regular teacher is to befriend a visiting supply teacher, already in the school to oversee a regular class, and, as frequently as possible, to introduce this teacher to the special class. Many reasons may explain why supply teachers do not get the respect that is due to them, but some are:

> • Students see them strangers in the classroom. To minimize the impact of this factor, the classroom teachers might incorporate a unit dealing with the treatment of guests. In this manner, the supply teacher can be identified as a guest.
>
> • As far as students are concerned, these visitors are not REAL teachers. Again, the classroom teacher can provide information about the various setting in which teachers are employed along with some of the reasons they choose to work in those settings. A parallel can be made with other professions.

The supply teacher, too, can alleviate these factors, perhaps by describing other assignments in the school, mentioning children enrolled in the school, and relating to other local issues. A presentation about teacher training, former experience, and personal choice of profession will reinforce the idea that students are dealing with a REAL teacher.

The first step to establishing control requires learning the names of the students – this is a relatively easy feat in a special class of 8 to 10 students. To facilitate the process, however, the classroom teacher is encouraged to prepare a seating plan that includes pictures and names of students. When the supply teacher is addressing a student, the name of the student should always precede a request.

The supply teacher must be familiar with techniques to create a positive classroom environment (see Chapters Four to Seven). Particular emphasis should be given to:

> • enlisting the cooperation of the class in completing the activities and tasks assigned by the classroom teacher: avoidance of competition between students is always to be encouraged
>
> • ensuring that work periods are kept short, followed by more preferred activities (see p. 228); varying the mode of expression helps keep order – writing, drawing, speaking, watching (see p.121)
>
> • using visual aids to note the achievement of each task. The entire class can be enlisted to plan the day, with checkmarks being employed to indicate completed work
>
> • making the class aware of the pro-social behaviors that will be valued and acceptable
>
> *cont'd*

- giving each student an opportunity to earn a privilege – taking a note to the office, cleaning boards, and collecting assignments

- taking the time to speak to each student and finding out likes, dislikes, and important preferences (see Appendix: "What is your preference?"). When each party knows about the other and students no longer consider the supply teacher a stranger, the beginning of rapport can be established

Although these opening strategies may prove very difficult, the supply teacher must remain focused on the positive, hoping to reinforce appropriate behavior rather than using punitive measures to address disruptive actions.

Integration and Mainstreaming

Although great amounts of time and effort are involved in having a student with behavioral problems *identified* and then finally placed in a *closed* classroom, the process of deciding either to try mainstreaming or to attempt to move towards re-integrating is even more arduous. Usually, the momentum is in the direction of the special class, not the reverse. After such a transfer is completed and interventions are in place, when the students begin to thrive, teachers of regular classes are still reluctant to accept them back even for small amounts of time. In fact, students with behavioral problems are the hardest group to integrate, especially because their reputation not only follows but also precedes them everywhere.

When the process of mainstreaming is being undertaken, it will require careful consideration and planning on the part of the special education teacher and the CCW. In brief, the transition involves:

- choosing the *receiving* teacher carefully – a loving person, willing to accept the student. First of all, this teacher is chosen because of having devised a management system based in an explicit structure. When moving into the mainstream, some students fail to adapt because insufficient cues are available in the new environment to clarify the expectations

- integrating for short periods of time: initially, for under half an hour, the schedule is maintained until a pattern of success emerges. At the beginning, if changes are made at the first sign of success, these will possibly be soon regretted by everyone. A *honeymoon period* lasting days or weeks should be expected whenever a student is placed in a new setting; it is dangerous, however, to mistake an apparent leap forward for genuine achievement

cont'd

- ensuring that mainstreaming efforts begin with a subject area which the student enjoys or is proficient in. The more students can experience confidence about their ability to succeed, the more likely they will be to achieve actual success. Typically, students report that they abhor being perceived by their peers as limited or being called "stupid" by others

- teaching students the concepts to be encountered in the regular class. If the teacher of the behavioral class is able to maintain a close relationship with the *receiving* teacher, both can be aware of the curriculum content to be presented within a week's span. Again, the new student will feel confident when the material is encountered for a second time, now in the regular class. This strategy is helpful both to *anxious* students and to those who need to upgrade their skills

- teaching study skills and supporting the student by following up on homework assigned in the regular class

- discussing and anticipating social difficulties with peer relations in order to role-play appropriate ways of solving such problems

- making frequent informal and/or scheduled contacts with the *receiving* teacher to monitor progress. Sometimes regular teachers are reluctant to approach special education teachers for what may be perceived as insignificant problems. By taking the initiative to establish regular contact, the referring teacher can help to address problems before they interfere with the process of mainstreaming

- making arrangements to team-teach with the *receiving* teacher, not only to lighten the load, but:

  ° to be perceived by the class as a "teacher" rather than a "shrink" to provide assistance to students in the class

  ° to appeal to particular interests – photography, for example, or primates

  ° to serve as a model and mentor to the receiving teacher who will be able to model and pattern through observation

Problems Associated with Mainstreaming and Integration

When a process of mainstreaming and integration has been planned with insufficient care, it risks not only failing but also increasing the chances that subsequent attempts will also fail. By examining factors that undermine the process and setting out to avoid them, planners will find their success maximized. If they are anticipated, some pitfalls may be avoided:

- overloading the student by expecting participation in two separate programs in the same subject area – for example, a different reading program in each of the classes. A more suitable recommendation would be to streamline the individual student's program to minimize such conflicts

- setting up accidental miscommunication with *receiving* teachers; when a student is given verbal messages to impart to another teacher, invariably, unwarranted problems arise. Ms. Dupris' class was about to be treated to a video presentation of a popular movie, but the student, Kersten – who meant to carry the message – forgot and then, unwittingly, Mr. Tarsus, the special education teacher, planned a field trip during the same time slot. Of course, when last-minute decisions and changes had to be made, everyone was unpleasantly affected. To avoid such disruptions, regular, close contact with the *receiving* teacher will circumvent problems associated with using the student as an intermediary

- overlooking problems related to the student's move from one class to the other can easily undermine the goals of the integration: all types of mishaps can occur during that brief span – altercations, wandering, forgetfulness, and other drawbacks. If the journey between classes is expected to cause problems, these must be addressed in the intervention plan – scheduling practice, using a "buddy", or drawing a simple map

- shifting responsibility for discrete areas of the program to the *receiving* teacher may create new difficulties; until full integration is attained, the student who is transferring may be better served by having the special education teacher oversee the intervention plan. The *receiving* teacher, usually accountable for as many as 30 to 35 students, is almost certainly less able to coordinate new obligations

- reporting to parents is shifted to the *receiving* teacher who has not built up a pattern of continuity. Although comments obtained from the *receiving* teacher are used in the report, it is less disruptive when the special education teacher retains responsibility for reporting to parents. As the integration progresses, it may become appropriate for the two teachers and the CCW to arrange an interview in which to talk with parents

- neglecting to update and re-evaluate the integration plan allows for small obstacles to become large ones. Again, scheduled contacts with the *receiving* teacher will circumvent such difficulties

- creating continuous changes in procedures will be certain to undermine the stability of the program. Always, when planning a transition, the teachers should schedule the student in the regular class during a stable time slot. Characteristically, students with behavioral difficulties, especially those who are anxious, respond poorly to last-minute changes but do well with routine

In looking at ways to serve the integration process effectively, teachers should consider implementing a team approach that includes cooperation – in all directions – from teachers and CCW to student and with each other.

Planning Integration

To be re-integrated into the regular class is one of the cherished goals of most students who are being educated in a *closed* special-education classroom. For this reason, teachers are advised to consider the following questions in connection with each student:

- the purpose of the re-integration: is it academic or social?
- the student's academic and social strengths: are they of similar weight?
- the time slots available: what is appropriate?
- the amount of homework and range of practice activities required from the student: where does the student best fit?

Establishing an integration plan not only requires that certain conditions be created, with the cooperation of the *receiving* teacher, but also involves the student in the process. One effective way to accomplish this task is by implementing *Management by Objectives,* a procedure used in the business world. Based on the idea of identifying the purpose of the integration, the plan then, typically, outlines the means by which to achieve it:

- objectives are formulated by the teacher and student
- goals set are reviewed regularly
- strategies used to meet each objective are discussed, listed, and recorded
- consequences for meeting or not meeting objectives are outlined
- reference is made to the relevant objective prior to the start of each activity

The Purpose of Integration

Two types of integration that commonly rely on the individual competence of the student are the academic and the social. Although, for the teacher, both involve considerable investment in preparing students to behave appropriately in class, when academic integration is the type chosen by the plan, often the student has sufficient knowledge and skill to follow the regular class curriculum at an age-appropriate level. In social integration, on the other hand, academic skill-level is usually below age-appropriateness. Nevertheless, in both these situations, the student probably needs the chance to acquire social skills in the company of peers. To reiterate, keeping in mind that academic performance and social performance are linked, the target of mainstreaming in both conditions is the acquisition of social behavior.

Because academic proficiency creates the basic difference between the types of integration, the special-class teacher will take the initial steps differently for each move. When preparing for academic integration, the special class teacher determines the curricular level of the student and then matches the areas of skill, competence, and general interest to topics studied by certain regular classes. If Anthony is very knowledgeable about First Nations people, then placing him in an age-appropriate class which is engaged in doing projects on the topic will give him the opportunity not only to "shine" but also to assist the teacher – a new role for him. Similarly, his advanced skill in language arts will ensure placement in a core subject for part of the day.

When the impetus for integration is social, the teacher must show great discretion so that the child is placed in a regular classroom at a time when a modified program can be implemented. Instead of slotting the student into core subjects, it is more effective to handle these in the special class where an individualized program is feasible. The integration area should be more appropriately non-academic – including, perhaps, one of physical education, visual arts, and music. Here, the aim is to choose activities that make few or no academic demands while at the same time providing a social context for the student. Because such a fit may be difficult to find, the transfer may require some pre-planning on the part of the teacher. Aside from this major difference, the steps, which are very similar, will be the ones outlined in Table 10-1.

Table 10-1. **To do a checklist of a student integration into the regular class.**

A	**Meeting** with the *receiving* teacher to:
✔	provide background information
✔	outline the goals and objectives of the student's plan
✔	anticipate problems that may arise and then discuss potential solutions
✔	finalize the time slots
✔	keep initial integration short, increasing it as the student achieves success
✔	match the student with a peer-tutor in the class – preferably a student high in the pecking order *cont'd*

B	**Holding** a small conference with the classroom teacher and the student to ensure consensus. In this encounter, the group will
✔	discuss the goals and objectives
✔	clarify classroom expectations: the receiving teacher may explain what is done and expected during the class
✔	outline general classroom expectations; an instance here would be the way the peer-tutor will interact with the student; for example, the student may be required to speak initially to the tutor when novel or troubling situations occur
✔	predict the consequences of appropriate and inappropriate behavior including the effect on integration time. Consider different "What-happens-if" scenarios
✔	list the social skills to be taught in the special education classroom which will be carried over to the regular class
✔	pinpoint the follow-up activities to classroom instructional units expected to be undertaken in the special class

At this juncture, the special education teacher will provide learning opportunities for the anticipated classroom expectations: role-playing activities that mimic regular class conditions are the most appropriate.

Integration During Recess and Field Trips

When integration efforts are discussed, teachers rarely consider opening exercises, recess, lunchroom period, and field trips as target situations, but transferring special students with behavioral difficulties often results in such unstructured situations providing difficulties. If a student presents problems when operating in such situations, some hints would be:

- goals and objectives relating to integration in these settings become a part of the student's intervention plan, an outline which is being constantly revised

- time is set aside to teach the social skills required by the students who expect to participate in these chosen activities

- objectives concerning participation in recess or in the field trip should be discussed with all the teachers involved; in initial sessions, the special-education teacher or the CCW may be co-opted   *cont'd*

- all participating teachers will be briefed about expectations and the consequences associated with the student's misbehavior

- if an incident occurs, a follow-up with teachers will be coordinated by the special education teacher or the CCW to de-brief those returning from a field trip or a recess.

Following-up Integration Efforts

In any program of integration, a major pitfall can be a lack of follow-up. Once plans are put into place, priorities have a way of shifting. Integration plans must continue to be supported throughout the duration of the plan:

- daily evaluation by the special-education teacher, the CCW, the classroom teacher, and the student

- daily – and eventually weekly – contact with the classroom teachers to be scheduled or arranged informally

- when the student is successful for a pre-defined length of time, on-task integration time is increased slowly while new objectives are carefully implemented

The special-education teacher is the one responsible for the integration, follow-up, and evaluation of the student until the intervention team decides that responsibility for the student should be shifted to the regular-stream classroom teacher.

School

In many ways, special education teachers are in a privileged position. While, usually, regular-program teachers are envious of the low pupil-teacher ratio, they soon become more respectful of special-education teachers when witnessing the very demanding needs of the students. Teachers of Special Education also have the daily opportunity of interacting with and learning from many types of professional personnel. In addition, however, because certain perceptions should not be encouraged, in order to avoid some of these, the teacher should attempt to be seen as:

- another teacher in the school rather than the person who looks after the crazy kids
- a staff member who performs the role and duties assigned to other teachers; for example, supervision, committee work, and volunteer jobs should be part of the special-education teacher's responsibility
- an active participant in school life, who supervises extracurricular activities, coaches a sports team, assists the chess club, or helps with other functions
- a public-relations person who speaks out for the program as well as an advocate for special-class students and special education in general
- a consultant to teachers, providing help whenever it is feasible
- an integrated member of the school staff

Relationship to the Principal and/or Vice-Principal

Very often, administrative personnel are concerned with situations created by students who have behavioral problems. Because of their close involvement, they find it helpful to receive regular updates about objectives and intervention efforts related to special students. It is a professional courtesy to keep them informed and to draw their attention when the need arises for policy changes or specific interventions.

Making the Special Class a Positive Environment

The special-education classroom should be one to which its members are proud to invite other students in the school. For this and other obvious reasons, it should be attractive, comfortable, and tidy; but, foremost, it should look like a classroom – a place that encourages academic learning. Plants not only add to the building of a positive atmosphere but their care teaches students responsible behavior. Creating special themes or events several times a year – to encourage other students to spend time in this class – helps to de-stigmatize the environment.

The Mental Health Center

What makes the mental health center[18] a unique experience? Teachers transferred to positions in the mental health center face new circumstances which inevitably help to re-define the role of "teacher". When involved in such a transfer, the teacher is soon aware that:

- the educational unit resides in a treatment facility whose organizational structure varies somewhat from the school setting. In this context, the teacher becomes familiar with the policies and procedures of the treatment center in addition to those of the school board

- the teacher has to relinquish personal autonomy in the classroom because clinical decisions affecting each student's entire intervention program are made by an intervention team – of which, usually, the teacher is a member. In the classroom, a CCW may share – or may have exclusive responsibility for the behavior of – a designated student or a set of students

- the teacher, as a member of the intervention team, works with a multi-disciplinary team containing members who represent varying philosophies, use separate jargons, have varied goals, and promote disparate objectives. As a result, to function efficiently in the team, the teacher must acquire adequate knowledge of the other disciplines. If the thrust of the student's program is focused in the classroom, the teacher may be required to adopt a leadership role

- the educational component within the center consists of teachers hired by a school board, not usually by the center itself. As a result, the newly arrived teacher may experience antagonistic feelings from other members of the center's staff, arising not only from pay inequities but also from discrepancies in working conditions noted by the non-educational personnel. A sense of equality and intra-staff fellowship can be carefully achieved by the new teacher who is able to learn to promote cooperation among all staff members; to give treatment-staff full professional respect; and to use every opportunity to minimize professional barricades and obstacles that often exist between the two staffs

- some or all of the students attending the treatment center may be qualitatively different from those who attend special education classes in schools. Facing different student needs, the teacher must be prepared to implement a variety of pedagogical strategies

453

Some teachers find it challenging but rewarding to work in close contact with a multi-disciplinary team. Constantly, however, a hoped-for positive experience in this setting requires flexibility and cooperation on the part of the teacher. In a few instances, center staff intent on partitioning the various roles will insist that the teacher should be concerned solely with teaching academic skills. In a situation such as this, although more comfortable for the staff, the students will rarely be as well served as they might be with a more integrated staff. Because students are known to capitalize on any dissension that exists among their caregivers, all members of staff – treatment as well as educational – must be fully responsible for the "whole" child.

Strategies to Maximize Team Effectiveness

One of the ways in which mental health centers differ from school settings is in their greater access to intervention personnel. As a result, an intervention team will oversee a student's program, and, as a result, the effectiveness of the team becomes an important variable in working with students. Constant encouragement of team effectiveness is possible if the teacher:

> - becomes familiar with the focus and perspective of each member of the intervention team. In addition, the teacher will become aware of the type of information each requires about the student as well as the frame of reference and the potential contribution to be derived. In this way, the team will develop into a panel of active mentors and consultants
>
> - helps the team formulate ways to work efficiently: members must share a basic set of values, tenets, and ideas that all members hold in common. One of its initial responsibilities, upon inception, is to define these basic axioms with the intention of evaluating the means by which team action can coincide with the recognized values
>
> - cooperates to help clinical decisions to be team decisions. For this to happen, the team must meet regularly to plan student programs. At such meetings, an action plan is identified, describing what is to be done; in the outline, the name of the person nominated to do each separate task should appear. On a calendar, regular meetings should be scheduled, preferably in the form of dialogue-and-feedback sessions
>
> - is able, at the outset, to define the locus of personal contribution and then to make other team members aware of this role. For such a process to occur, the teacher is encouraged to take every opportunity to describe to the other members the various educational activities that may contribute to satisfying socio-emotional goals for the student; at the same time, the teacher will learn from the other team members their perceptions of the student's potential abilities, along with the goals that will help reach these

Because teachers are accustomed to being autonomous, working with a team can be overwhelming at first. By never relinquishing the best interest of the student, the teacher finds ways to maximize the effectiveness of the team that is responsible for the treatment.

Meetings

Teamwork invariably requires meetings for planning, discussing, evaluating, and other such activities, but no activity is as frustrating as a long meeting that does not generate useful outcomes. Traditionally, any meeting can be both time-consuming and relatively ineffective unless certain guidelines are respected. First, the group is working from a pre-arranged agenda. Prior to each meeting, a copy of the agenda should be received by all participants so that they may attend the meeting bearing the necessary data, records, information, and relevant materials. Although it should be a truism, chairpersons often forget that the number of items on the agenda should be able to be covered in appropriate depth within the time allotted.

Shorter meetings – those under 30 minutes – are more efficient than gatherings that run until all agenda items are discussed. If meetings are both short and begun on time, people make an effort to be punctual and ready to discuss agenda issues. Minutes taken by the meeting secretary, when printed and filed in a binder, serve as a record of approved actions, including a specific list of people named to carry out respective all directives. Without such accountability, meetings rarely are able to produce beneficial outcomes.

A meeting structure should focus on two queries:

- what is to be done?
- who is going to do it?

A narrow framework such as the one suggested will clarify the issues and give momentum to the process[19].

Conclusion

In the realm of education, the focus on children with behavioral difficulties is a tremendous challenge for all teachers. Throughout the ten chapters, it has been the intention of this book to demonstrate the necessity for cooperative involvement. By emphasizing the need for teachers, parents, and students to create opportunities for each child to acquire knowledge about social appropriateness, the book has not forgotten about helping the child to continue to grow as a person and to strive for academic success.

Teachers are not simply the promoters of academic skills but are also responsible for the personal growth and social development of students. Because the school is the major socializing agent of the dominant culture, in order to foster a sense of inclusiveness, teachers must continually recognize the value of encouraging a student identity that incorporates both the ethnic and dominant cultures.

The major challenge rests in investing community effort in the "total" education of children and adolescents. Without the consistent desire of the society to promote this ideal through education, most communities will be resigned to rehabilitating/punishing each adult who has failed to find an appropriate niche. When teachers, parents, and students are committed to creating positive environments, everyone benefits.

Endnotes

1 The study carrel, for use as an independent work station, is an ideal piece of furniture that encourages quiet, inward activities. Several of these units can be lined up along a wall in the Library area of the classroom.

2 See the listing in the Appendix.

3 A trundle wheel is a measuring apparatus consisting of a circular wheel that rolls along the ground, with a simple mechanism that clicks every time the wheel has traveled the entire circumference. Unlike a ruler, the wheel is able to measure squiggly lines.

4 To find more information on this topic, go to the following URL: http://collections.ic.gc.ca/blackloyalists/

5 For an outline of the idea of transfer of knowledge, see page 121.

6 "Splintered" skills is a term referring to an incomplete mastery of a domain of knowledge which leads to partial and/or misunderstood concepts.

7 A description of the interactive web-based module – *Share the Power: Applying Democratic Principles in the Classroom* – is available at the following URL: http://www.learncanada.org/e-showcase.html#cabd

8 First Nations are an excellent example of a people with a rich oral tradition.

9 The *Star Trek* website at http://www.startrek.com/library/alien.asp makes it possible for students to learn about Klingon and Borg cultures. As an introduction to comparative cultural study, this sector would form a motivational activity in a larger unit of study that could include human cultures, past and present.

10 Japanese Canadians, as well as Japanese Americans were placed in internment camps during the Second World War, a partial result being that they moved out of their enclaves and later, after the war, became assimilated into the dominant culture.

11 In the context of a multi-ethnic classroom, C. Rousseau & N. Heusch (2000) use drawing and storytelling to promote the psychological adjustment of refugee students.

12 Students might be directed to the website of the Schomburg Center for Research in Black Culture, The Harriet Tubman Resource Centre on the African Diaspora, The North American Black Historical Museum, and The Museum of Black History in Amherstberg, near the Canadian-American border.

13 An additional example involving perspective taking can be found in the Appendix.

14 Shepard, A., & San Souci, D. (Illustrator). (1995). *The Gifts of Wali Dad: A Tale of India and Pakistan*. New York: Simon & Schuster/Atheneum. – for ages four and older.

15 A storypath utilizes story elements, including setting, character, and plot, to capture a historical event or to portray the essence of a people.

16 Suggestions are available throughout Chapters Six, Seven, and Eight.

17 With access to new technology, it is now common for a teacher who is absent to send lesson plans to the school by e-mail or FAX

18 In Ontario, Canada, this type of center is referred to as a Section 25 facility. The reference is to the section number in the Education Act over time, however, the section number changes.

19 Meeting organizers may find it helpful to consult *Robert's Rules of Order* or to turn to page 273 of the present book to the remarks about the structure for a Discussion Group.

References

Achenbach, T. M., & Edelbrock, C. (1991). *Manual for the Child Behavior Checklist/4-18 and 1991 profile*. Burlington: University of Vermont, Department of Psychiatry.

Ainsworth, C., Waller, G., & Kennedy, F. (2002). Threat processing in women with bulimia. *Clinical Psychology Review, 22*(8), 1155-1178.

Albrecht, G., Veerman, J. W., Damen, H., Kroes, G. (2001). The Child Behavior Checklist for group care workers: A study regarding the factor structure. *Journal of Abnormal Child Psychology, 29*(1), 83-89.

Allen, R. E., & Allen, S. D. (1995). *Winnie-the-Pooh on Problem Solving: In which Pooh, Piglet and friends explore how to solve problems so you can too*. New York: Dutton.

Amdur, R. L. (1989). Testing causal models of delinquency. A methodological critique. *Criminal Justice and Behavior, 16*, 35-62.

Amos, J. (1993). *Angry*. Bath, Avon: Cherrytree Press Ltd.

Anderson, D. R., Huston, A. C.,Schmitt, K. L., Linebarger, D. L., & Wright, J. C. (2001). Early childhood television viewing and adolescent behavior: The recontact study - Introduction. *Monographs of the Society for Research in Child Development, 66*(1), 1-9

Anderson, H. C. (1955). *The Ugly Duckling*: Walt Disney Productions (video).

Armbrister, R. C., McCallum, R. S., & Lee, H. D. (2002). A cross-cultural comparison of student social attributions. *Psychology in the Schools, 39*(1), 39-49.

Armstrong, T. D., & Costello, E. J. (2002). Community studies on adolescent substance use, abuse, or dependence and psychiatric comorbidity. *Journal of Consulting and Clinical Psychology, 70*(6), 1224-1239.

Arise Foundation. (2001). *Arise Brain Food Series*. Arise Foundation: Arise Foundation.

Assemany, A. E., & McIntosh, D. E. (2002). Negative outcome of behavioral parent training programs. *Psychology in the Schools, 39*(2), 209-219.

Bandura, A. (1997). *Self-efficacy : the exercise of control*. New York: W.H. Freeman.

Bandura, A., & Walters, R. H. (1963). *Social learning and personality development*. New York: Holt Rinehart and Winston.

Barnes, L., & Grater, L. (1994). *The Story of the three little pigs*. Toronto: Sommerville House.

Bassett, L. (2001). *From Panic to Power: Proven Techniques to Calm Your Anxieties, Conquer Your Fears, and Put You in Control of Your Life*. New York: HarperCollins Pub.

Beck, C. M. (1971). *Moral Education in the Schools: Some practical suggestions*. Toronto: The Ontario Institute for Studies in Education.

Bellak, L. B., & Bellak, S. S. (1949). *Children's Apperception Test (CAT)*. New York: CPS.

Bender, W. N., Rosenkrans, C. B., & Crane, M. K. (1999). Stress, depression, and suicide among students with learning disabilities: Assessing the risk. *Learning Disability Quarterly, 22*(2), 143-156.

Berry, M., Gray, T., & Donnerstein, E. (1999). Cutting film violence: Effects on perceptions, enjoyment, and arousal. *Journal of Social Psychology, 139*(5), 567-582.

Biederman, J., Faraone, S. V., & Monuteaux, M. C. (2002). Differential effect of environmental adversity by gender: Rutter's Index of Adversity in a group of boys and girls with and without ADHD. *American Journal of Psychiatry, 159*(9), 1556-1562.

Biederman, J., Mick, E., Faraone, S. V., Braaten, E., Doyle, A., Spencer, T., Wilens, T. E., Frazier, E., & Johnson, M. (2002). Influence of gender on attention deficit hyperactivity disorder in children referred to a psychiatric clinic. *American Journal of Psychiatry, 159*(1), 36-42.

Black, D. W., Larson, L. C. (1999). *Bad Boys, Bad Men: Confronting Antisocial Personality Disorder*. Danver, MA: Oxford University Press.

Bloom, B. S. (Ed.). (1956). *Taxonomy of Educational Objectives: Handbook 1: Cognitive domain*. New York: David McKay.

Borba, M. (2002). *Building Moral Intelligence: The seven essential virtues that teach kids to do the right thing*. San Francisco: Jossey-Bass.

Borkowski, J. G., Peck, V. A., & Reid, M. (1983). Impulsivity and strategy transfer: Metamemory as mediation. *Child Development, 54*, 459-473.

Bowlby, J. (1998). *Attachment and Loss, Separation: Anxiety and Anger* (Vol. 2). London: Pimlico.

Brier, N. (1989). The relationship between learning disability and delinquency: A review and reappraisal. *Journal of Learning Disability, 22*, 546-553.

Brimner, L. D. (1998). *Mars*. New York: Children's Press.

Brody, L. R. (1985). Gender differences in emotional development: A review of theories and research. *Journal of Personality and Social Psychology, 53*(2), 102-149.

Brody, L. R. (2000). The socialization of gender differences in emotional expression: Display rules, infant termperament, and differentiation. In A. H. Fischer (Ed.), *Gender and emotion: Social psychological perspectives. Studies in emotion and social interaction* (pp. 24-47). New York: Cambridge University Press.

Burke, J., Loeber, R., & Birmaher, B. (2002). Oppositional defiant disorder and conduct disorder: a review of the past 10 years, part II. *Journal of the American Academy of Child and Adolescent Psychiatry, 41*(11), 1275-1294.

Buscaglia, L. (1982). *The Fall of Freddie the Leaf: A Story of All Ages*. New Jersey: Charles S. Black.

Canada. (1986). *The Young Offenders Act*. Ottawa: Library of Parliament, Research Branch.

Carkhuff, R. (2000). *The Art of Helping VIII*. Amherst, Mass: Human Resource Development Press.

Cartledge, G., & Milburn, J. F. (2002). *Teaching Social Skills to Children and Youth: Innovative Approaches* (Third ed.). Boston, MA: Allyn & Bacon.

Cartledge, G., & Milburn, J. F. (1996). *Cultural Diversity and Social Skills Instruction*. Champaign, IL: Research Press.

Chae, P., Jung,H., & Noh, K. (2001). Attention deficit hyperactivity disorder in Korean juvenile delinquents. *Adolescence, 36*(144), 707-725.

Chamberlain, P. (2000). What works in treatment foster care. In M. P. Kluger, Alexander, Gina, et al (Ed.), *What Works in Child Welfare* (pp. 157-162). Washington, DC, US: Child Welfare League of America, Inc.

Chance, P. (1986). *Thinking in the Classroom: A survey of programs*. New York: Teachers College Press.

Charlop-Christy, M. H., & Daneshvar, S. (2003). Using video modeling to teach perspective taking to children with autism. *Journal of Positive Behavior Interventions, 5*(1), 12-22.

Chase, W. G., & Simon, H. A. (1973). The mind's eye in chess. In W. G. Chase (Ed.), *Visual information processing*. Oxford, England: Academic.

Christophersen, E. R., Mortweet, Susan L. (2001). *Treatments that work with children: Empirically supported strategies for managing childhood problems*. Washington, DC, US: American Psychological Association.

Clarizio, H. F., & McCoy, G. F. (1976). *Behavior Disorders in Children*. New York: Crowell.

Cloward, R. A., & Olin, L. E. (1960). *Delinquency and Opportunity*. New York: Free Press.

Cohen, A. K. (1955). *Delinquent Boys: The culture of gangs*. Glencoe, IL: Free Press.

Colligan, R., Osborne, D., Swenson, W., & Offord, K. (1983). *The MMPI: A contemporary Normative Study*. New York: Praeger.

Committee for Children (2002). *Second Step*. Seattle, WA: Committee for Children.

Condry, J., & Condry, S. (1976). Sex differences: A study of the eye of the beholder. *Child Development, 47*, 812-819.

Crawford, R. P. (1954). *The Techniques of Creative Thinking*. New York: Hawthorn

Csóti, M. (2001). *Social Awareness Skills for Children*. Philadelphia, PA: Jessica Kingsley Pub.

Dalteg, A., & Levander, S. (1998). Twelve thousand crimes by 75 boys: A 20-year follow-up study of childhood hyperactivity. *Journal of Forensic Psychiatry, 9*(1), 39-57.

de Bono, E. (1985). The CoRT thinking program. In J. W. Segal, S. F. Chapman ,& R. Glaser (Ed.), *Thinking and Learning Skills: Vol. 1. Relating instruction to research*. Hillsdale, NJ: Erlbaum.

De Coster, S., &, & Heimer, K. (2001). The relationship between law violation and depression: An interactionist analysis. *Criminology, 39*(4), 799-836.

Diagnostic and Statistical Manual of Mental Disorders. (Fourth, Text Revision ed.)(2000). Washington, DC: Amrican Psychiatric Association.

Diener, C., & Dweck, C. (1980). An analysis of learned helplessness: The processing of success. *Journal of Personality and Social Psychology, 39*(5), 940-952.

Dollard, J., Doob, L. W., Miller, N. E., Mower, D. H., & Sears, R. R. (1939). *Frustration and Aggression*. New Haven: Yale University Press.

Doran, B., Bullis, M., & Benz, M. R. (1996). Predicting the arrest status of adolescents with disabilities in transition. *Journal of Special Education, 29*, 363-380.

Drawe, H. L. (2001). An animal-assisted therapy program for children and adolescents with emotional and behavioral disorders. *Dissertation Abstracts International, 61*(11-B), 6130.

Dreikurs, R., & Cassel, P. (1974). *Discipline Without Tears* (Second ed.). New York: Hawthorn Books.

Dube, P. (1995). *Sticks and Stones*. Richmond Hill, ON: Scholastic Canada.

Dunn, W., Saiter, J., & Rinner, L. (2002). Asperger syndrome and sensory processing: A conceptual model and guidance for intervention planning. *Focus on Autism and Other Developmental Disabilities, 17*(3), 172-185.

Durkheim, E. (1997). *Suicide: A study in Sociology*. New York: Free Press.

Dweck, C. (2002). The development of ability conceptions. In A. Wigfield, & J. S. Eccles (Ed.), *Development of achievement motivation. A volume in the educational psychology series.* (pp. 57-88). San Diego, CA, US: Academic Press.

Dworet, D. H. R., A. J. (1990). Provincial and Territorial Government Responses to Behaviorally Disordered Students in Canada — 1988. *Behavioral Disorders, 15*(4), 201-209.

Edwards, C. H. (2001). Student violence and the moral dimensions of education. *Psychology in the Schools, 38*(3), 249-257.

Eifert, G. H., Schulte, D., Zvolensky, M. J., Lejuez, C. W., & Lau, A. W. (1997). Manualized behavior therapy: Merits and challenges. *Behavior Therapy, 28*(4), 499-509.

Erikson, E. H. (1963). *Childhood and Society*. New York: Norton.

Evertson, C. M., & Emmer, E. T. (1982). Effective management at the beginning of the school year in junior high classes. *Journal of Educational Psychology, 74*(4), 485-498.

Exner, J. E. J. (1986). *The Rorschach: A Comprehensive System, Volume 1 (2nd ed.) : Basic Foundations*. New York: Wiley.

Eyberg, S. M., & Ross, A. W. (1978). Assessment of child behavior problems: The validation of a new inventory. *Journal of Clinical Child Psychology, 7*(2), 113-116.

Faraone, S. V., Biederman, J., Monuteaux, M. C., Doyle, A. E., & Seidman, L. J. (2001). A psychometric measure of learning disability predicts educational failure four years later in boys with attention-deficit/hyperactivity disorder. *Journal of Attention Disorders, 4*(4), 220-230.

Feingold, B. (1976). Hyperkinesis and learning disabilities linked to the ingestion of artificial food colors and flavors. *Journal of Learning Disabilities, 9*(9), 551-559.

Feng, H., & Cartledge, G. (1996). Social Skill Assessment of inner city Asian, African, and European American Students. *School Psychology Review, 25*, 227-238.

Feuerstein, R. (1980). *Instrumental Enrichment: An intervention program for cognitive modifiability*. Baltimore: University Park Press.

Fivush, R. (1989). Exploring sex differences in the emotional content of mother-child conversations about the past. *Sex Roles, 20*, 675-691.

Fraczek, A., Lubanska, D., & Zwolinski, M. (1999). TV violence viewing and aggression in childhood vs. psychosocial functioning in young adults. *Aggressive Behavior, 25*(1), 21-21.

Freeman, B. J., Cronin, P., & Candela, P. (2002). Asperger syndrome or autistic disorder? The diagnostic dilemma. *Focus on Autism and Other Developmental Disabilities, 17*(3), 145-152.

Gardiner, H. S., & Kosmitzki, C. (2002). *Lives Across Cultures: Cross-Cultural Human Development* (Second ed.): Allyn & Bacon.

Garry, E. (1997). *Juvenile Firesetting and Arson*: US Department of Justice, Office of Juvenile Justice and Delinquency Prevention.

Gatzke Kopp, L., Raine, A., Loeber, R., Stouthamer-Loeber, M., & Steinhauer, S. (2002). Serious delinquent behavior, sensation seeking, and electrodermal arousal. *Journal of Abnormal Child Psychology., 30*(5), 477-486.

Gilligan, C. (1977). In a different voice: Women's conception of self and morality. *Harvard Educational Review, 47*, 481-517.

Glasser, W. (1975). *Reality Therapy: A new approach to psychiatry*. New York, NY: Harper & Row.

Glasser, W. (1986). *Control Theory in the Classroom*. New York, NY: Perennial Library.

Godart, N. T., Flament, M. F., Perdereau, F., & Jeammet, P. (2002). Comorbidity between eating disorders and anxiety disorders: A review. *International Journal of Eating Disorders, 32*(3), 253-270.

Godfrey, A. W. (1987). Upward bound: Teaching Latin to disadvantaged inner-city students – Latin in an unlikely setting. *Classical World, 80*(3), 197-198.

Goffman, E. (1968). *Asylum: essays on the social situation of mental patients and other inmates*. Paris: Éditions de Minuit.

Gold, M. (1978). Scholastic experiences, self-esteem, and delinquent behavior: A theory for alternative schools. *Crime and Delinquency, 24*, 290-308.

Goldstein, A. P. (1999). *Teaching Prosocial Behavior to Antisocial Youth (Video)*. Champaign, IL: Research Press.

Gollobin, L. B., & Gruhn, L. A. (1991). Ellis Island: Coming to America: A Drama-in-Education Unit. *Drama Theatre Teacher, 3*(2), 18-24.

Gollobin, L. G., Laurie Ann. (1991). Ellis Island: Coming to America: A Drama-in-Education Unit. *Drama Theatre Teacher, 3*(2), 18-24.

Gordon, M. (1993). *I Would If I Could: A Teenagers's Guide to ADHD/Hyperactivity*. DeWitt, NY: GSI Publications.

Gordon, W. J. J. (1961). *Synectics*. New York: Harper & Row.

Grande, C. G. (1988). Delinquency: The learning disabled student's reaction to academic school failure? *Adolescence, 23*, 209-219.

Greenberg, M. T., & Kusche, C. A. (1993). *Promoting Social and Emotional Development in Deaf Children: The PATHS Project*. Seattle, WA: University of Washington Press.

Grossen, B. (2002). The BIG accommodation model: The direct instruction model for secondary schools. *Journal of Education for Students Placed at Risk, 7*(2), 241-263.

Guerrero, L. K. (1994). "I'm so mad I could scream:" The effects of anger expression on relational satisfaction and communication competence. *The Southern Communication Journal, 59*, 125-141.

Guerrero, L. K., & Reiter, R. L. (1998). Expressing emotion: Sex differences in social skills and communicative responses to anger, sadness, and jealousy. In D. J. Canary, & K. Dindia (Ed.), *Sex Differences and Similarities in Communication: Critical essays and empirical investigations of sex and gender in interaction* (pp. 321-350). Mahwah, N.J.: Lawrence Erlbaum Associates.

Guerrero, L. K., DeVito, J. A., & Hecht, M. L. (Ed.). (1999). *The Nonverbal Communication Reader: Classic and contemporary readings* (Second ed.). Prospect Heights, IL: Waveland Press, Inc.

Gutstein, S. E., & Whitney, T. (2002). Asperger syndrome and the development of social competence. *Focus on Autism and Other Developmental Disabilities, 17*(3), 161-171.

Hagan, J., McCarthy, B., & Foster, H. (2002). A gendered theory of delinquency and despair in the life course. *Acta Sociologica, 45*(1), 37-46.

Hall, K. (2000). *Asperger Syndrome, the Universe and Everything*. London and Philadelphia: Jessica Kingsley Publishers.

Hanlon, T. E., Bateman, R. W., Simon, B. D., O'Grady, K. E., & Carswell, S. B. (2002). An early community-based intervention for the prevention of substance abuse and other delinquent behavior. *Journal of Youth and Adolescence, 31*(6), 459-472.

Hare, R. (1999). *Without Conscience*. New York: Guilford Press.

Haughton, E. (1971). Great gains from small starts. *Teaching Exceptional Children, 3*(3), 141-146.

Hawkins, J. D., Jenson, J. M. & Catalano, R. F. (1988). Delinquency and drug abuse: Implications for social services. *Social Service Review, 62*, 258-284.

Hazel, J. S., Schumaker, J. B. , Sherman, J., & Sheldon, J. (1981). *ASSET: A Social Skills Program for Adolescents. [Video].* Champaign, IL: Research Press.

Heath, N., & Ross, S. (2000). Prevalence and expression of depressive symptomatology in students with and without learning disabilities. *Learning Disability Quarterly, 23*(1), 24-36.

Herpertz-Dahlmann, B. (2002). Outcome in adolescent anorexia nervosa. *Acta Neuropsychiatrica, 14*(2), 90-92.

Hewitt, M. B. (1999). The control game: Exploring oppositional behavior. *Reclaiming Children and Youth, 8*(1), 30-33.

Hirschi, T., & Hindelang, M. J. (1977). Intelligence and delinquency: A revisionist review. *American Sociological Review, 42*(4), 571-587.

Hobbs, N. (1966). Helping disturbed children: Psychological and ecological strategies. *American Psychologist, 21*, 1106-1115.

Hobbs, N. (1969). A brief history of project Re-ED. *Mind over Matter, 14*, 9-14.

Hogben, M. (1998). Factors moderating the effect of televised aggression on viewer behavior. *Communication Research, 25*(2), 220-247.

Homme, L. (1970). *How to Use Contingency Contracting in the Classroom.* Champaign, IL: Research Press.

Hommel, K. A., Chaney, J. M., Wagner, J. L., & McLaughlin, M. S. (2002). Asthma-specific quality of life in older adolescents and young adults with long-standing asthma: The role of anxiety and depression. *Journal of Clinical Psychology in Medical Settings, 9*(3), 185-192.

House, A. E. (2002). *The First Session with Children and Adolescents: Conducting a comprehensive mental health evaluation.* New York, NY, US: Guilford Press.

Houts, A. C. (2002). Discovery, invention, and the expansion of the modern Diagnostic and Statistical Manuals of Mental Disorders. In L. E. Beutler, & M. L. Malik (Ed.), *Rethinking the DSM: A psychological perspective. Decade of behavior.* (pp. 17-65). Washington, DC, US: American Psychological Association.

Hufford, M. R. (2000). Empirically supported treatments and comorbid psychopathology: Spelunking Plato's cave. *Professional Psychology: Research and Practice, 31*, 96-99.

Iwamasa, G. Y., & Orsillo, S. M. (1997). Individualizing treatment manuals as a challenge for the next generation - Manualized behavior therapy: Merits and challenges - Commentary. *Behavior Therapy, 28*(4), 511-515.

Jenesse, A. (1990). *Families, a Celebration of Diversity.* Boston, MA: Houghton Mifflin.

Johnson, D. W., & Johnson, F. P. (1997). *Joining Together: Group Theory and Group Skills* (Sixth ed.). Boston: Allyn and Bacon.

Johnson, J. G., Cohen, P., Kotler, L., Kasen, S., & Brook, J. S. (2002). Psychiatric disorders associated with risk for the development of eating disorders during adolescence and early adulthood. *Journal of Consulting and Clinical Psychology, 70*(5), 1119-1128.

Johnson, V., & Pandina, R. J. (1991a). Effects of the family environment on adolescent substance abus, delinquency, and coping styles. *American Journal of Drug and Alcohol Abuse, 17*, 71-88.

Johnson, V., & Pandina, R. J. (1991b). Effects of the family environment on adolescent substance abuse, delinquency, and coping styles. *American Journal of Drug and Alcohol Abuse, 17*, 71-88.

Kagan, J., & Lamb, Sharon. (1990). *The Emergence of Morality in Young Children*: University of Chicago Press.

Kandel, D., Simcha-Fagen, O., & Davies, M. (1986). Risk factors for delinquency and illicit drug use from adolescence to young adulthood. *The Journal of Drug Issues, 16*, 67-90.

Kaplan, B. (2001). A comparison of adolescents with and without attention deficit hyperactivity disorder on five 'wellbeing' variables. *Dissertation Abstracts International Section A: Humanities and Social Sciences, 61*(12A), 4672.

Keilitz, I., & Dunivant, N. (1986). The relationship between learning disability and juvenile delinquency: Current state of knowledge. *Remedial and Special Education, 7*, 18-26.

Kellogg, S. (1986). *Best Friends.* New York: Dial Books.

Kinsbourne, M. (1970). The analysis of learning deficits with special reference to selective attention. In D. Bakker, & P. Satz (Ed.), *Specific Reading Disability:Advances in Theory and Method* (pp. 115-122). Netherlands: Rotterdam University Press.

Klein, R. G., & Mannuzza, S. (2000). Children with uncomplicated reading disorders grown up: A prospective follow-up into adulthood. In L. L. Greenhill (Ed.), *Learning disabilities: Implications for psychiatric treatment.* (pp. 1-31). Washington, DC, US: American Psychiatric Publishing, Inc.

Knoff, H. (2001). *Stop and Think Social Skills Program.* Longmont, CO: Sopris West.

Kohlberg, L. (1969). Stage and sequence: The cognitive-developmental approach to socialization. In D. A. Goslin. (Ed.), *Handbook of Socialization Theory and research.* Chicago, IL: Rand McNally.

Kolko, D. J. (Ed.). (2002). *Handbook on Fire Setting in Children and Youth.* New York: Elsevier Academic Press.

Kolvin, I., & Fundudis, T. (1981). Elective mute children: Psychological development and background factors. *Journal of Child Psychology and Psychiatrry, 22*, 219-232.

Konstantareas, M., M. (1996). Communication training approaches in autistic disorder. In J. H. Beitchman, N. J. Cohen, M. Konstantareas, & R. Tannock (Ed.), *Language ,Learning, and Behavior Disorders: Developmental, biological, and clinical perspectives* (pp. 467-488). New York, NY: Cambridge University Press.

Konstantareas, M., M. (1987). Autistic children exposed to simultaneous communication training: A follow-up. *Journal of Autism and Developmental Disorders., 17*(1), 115-131.

Koppitz, E. M. (1968). *Psychological Evaluation of Children's Human Figure Drawings.* New York: Grune & Stratton.

Koppitz, E. M. (1984). *Psychological Evaluation of Human Figure Drawings by Middle School Pupils.* New York: Grune & Stratton.

Krupski, B. (1981). An interactional approach to the study of attentional problems in children with learning handicaps. *Exceptional Education Quarterly, 2*(3), 1-11.

Kuhn, T. S. (1970). *The Structure of the Scientific Revolution.* Chicago, IL: University of Chicago Press.

Kulling, M. (1992). *I Hate You, Marmalade.* Toronto: Penguin Books.

Lachar, D. (1982). *Personality Inventory for Children: Revised format manual supplement.* Los Angeles: Western Psychological Services.

Lachar, D. (1999). Personality Inventory for Children, Second Edition (PIC-2), Personality Inventory for Youth (PIY), and Student Behavior Survey (SBS). In M. E. Maruish (Ed.), *The use of psychological testing for treatment planning and outcomes assessment* (Second ed., pp. 399-427). Mahwah, NJ, US: Lawrence Erlbaum Associates, Inc.

Lachar, D., Godowski, C. L., & Snyder, D. K. (1984). External validation of the Personality Inventory for Children (PIC) profile and factor scales: Parent, teacher, and clinician ratings. *Journal of Consulting and Clinical Psychology, 52*, 155 164.

Lahey, B. B., Hratdagen, S. E., Frick, P. J., McBurnett, K., Connor, R, & Hynd, G. W. (1988). Conduct disorder: Parsing the confounded relation to parental divorce and antisocial personality. *Journal of Abnormal Psychology, 97*, 334-337.

Lamb, S. (2002). *The Secret Lives of Girls: Sex, Play, Aggression, and Their Guilt.* New York: Simon and Schuster.

Larson, K. A. (1988). A research review and alternative hypothesis explaining the link between learning disability and delinquency. *Journal of Learning Disability, 21*, 357-363,369.

Leone, P. E. (1994). Education services for youth with disabilities in a state operated juvenile correctional system: Case study and analysis. *Journal of Special Education, 28*, 43-58.

Lewis, D. O., Lovely, R., Yeager, C., Ferguson, G., Friedman, M., Sloane, G., Friedman, H., & Pinkus, J. H. (1988). Intrinsic and environmental characteristics of juvenile murderers. *Journal of the American Academy of Child and Adolescent Psychiatry, 27*, 43-58.

Lipschitz, D. S., Rasmusson, A. M., Anywan, W., Cromwell, P., & Southwick, S. M. (2000). Clinical and functional correlates of posttraumatic stress disorder in urban adolescent girls at a primary care clinic. *Journal of the American Academy of Child and Adolescent Psychiatry, 39*(September), 1104-1111.

Loeber, R., Stouthammer-Loeber, M., & White, H. (1999). Developmental aspects of delinquency and internalizing problems and their association with persistent juvenile substance use between ages 7 and 18. *Journal of Clinical Child Psychology, 28*(3), 322-332.

Lovaas, O. I. (1969). Behavior modification: teaching language to psychotic children (film). New York: Appleton-Century-Crofts.

Lozanov. (1978). *Suggestology and Outlines of Suggestopedy* (M. Hall-Pozharlieva, & K. Pashmakova, Trans.). New York: Gordon and Breach.

MacDonald, F. (2001). *The World in the Time of Tutankhamun*. Philadelphia, PA: Chelsea House.

Machover, K. (1949). *Personality Projection in the Drawing of Human Figure*. Springfield, IL: Charles C. Thomas.

Machover, K. (1960). *Sex Differences in the Developmental Pattern of Children as Seen in the Human Figures Drawings*. New York: Grune & Srtatton.

Manassis, K. (2000). Childhood Anxiety Disorders: Lessons from the literature. *The Canadian Journal of Psychiatry, 45*, 724-730.

Martin, R. P. (1988). *Assessment of Personality and Behavior Problems: Infancy through Adolescence*. New York: The Guilford Press.

Maruish, M. E. (Ed.). (1999). *The Use of Psychological Testing for Treatment Planning and Outcomes Assessment* (Second ed.). Mahwah, NJ: Lawrence Erlbaum Associates.

Mathews, J., (Dir.). (1987). *Frog and Toad are Friends/Frog and Toad Together*. Los Angeles, CA: Churchill Media (Video).

Matza, D. (1964). *Delinquency and Drift*. New York: Wiley.

Maurice, C., Green, G., & Luce, S. (Ed.). (1996). *Behavioral Intervention for Young Children With Autism: A Manual for Parents and Professionals*. Austin, TX: Pro-Ed.

Mayer, R. E. (1992). *Thinking, Problem Solving, Cognition*. New York, NY: W. H. Freeman.

McGuire, M. (1997). Taking a storypath into history. *Educational Leadership, 54*(6), 70-73.

Medley, P., & Russel, B (1994). Twitch and shout [videorecording]: a documentary about Tourette syndrome. (L. Chiten, Director).

Meichenbaum, D. (1993). Changing conceptions of cognitive behavior modification: Retrospect and prospect. Special Section: Recent developments in cognitive and constructivist psychotherapies. *Journal of Consulting and Clinical Psychology, 61*(2), 202-204.

Meichenbaum, D., & Burland, S. (1979). Cognitive behavior modification with children. *School Psychology Review, 8*(4), 426-433.

Mellonie, B., & Ingpen, R. (1983). *Lifetimes, The Beautiful Way to Explain Death to Children*. Toronto: Bantam Books.

Meltzer, L. J., Roditi, B. N., & Fenton, T. (1986). Cognitive and learning profiles of delinquent and learning disabled adolescents. *Adolescence, 21*, 581-591.

Meyer, J. A., & Minshew, N. J. (2002). An update on neurocognitive profiles in Asperger syndrome and high-functioning autism. *Focus on Autism and Other Developmental Disabilities, 17*(3), 152-161.

Miller, A., & Eller-Miller, E. (1989). *From Ritual to Repertoire*. New York: Wiley.

Molina, B. S. G., & Pelham, W. E. (2001). Substance use, substance abuse, and LD among adolescents with a childhood history of ADHD. *Journal of Learning Disabilities, 34*(4), 333-342.

Morgan, C. D., & Murray, H. H.,. (1935). A method for investigating fantasies: The Thematic Apperception Test. *Archives of Neurology and Psychiatry Chicago., 34*, 289-306.

Moss, D. (1989). *Shelley, the Hyperactive Turtle*. Bethesda, MD: Woodbine House.

Mower, O. H., & Mower, W. (1938). Enuresis: A method for its study and treatment. *American Journal of Orthopsychiatry, 8*, 436-459.

Munsch R. & Askar, S. (1996). *From Far Away*. Toronto: Annick Press Ltd.

Murray, H. H. (1943). *Thematic Apperception Test Manual*. Cambridge, MA: Harvard University Press.

Myles, B. S., & Simpson, R. L. (2002). Asperger syndrome: An overview of characteristics. *Focus on Autism and Other Developmental Disabilities, 17*(3), 132-137.

Neumann, L. (2000). *Visual Teaching Method for Children with Autism*. Crofton, MD: Willerik Publishing.

Newcomer, P. (1980). *Understanding and Teaching Emotionally Disturbed Children*. Boston: Allyn and Bacon, Inc.

Ng, E., & Bereiter, C. (1991). Three levels of goal orientation in learning. *Journal of the Learning Sciences, 1*(3-4), 243–271.

Nishi-Strattner, L. (2001). Abuse history and juvenile firesetting. *Hot Issues, 11*(3), 1-2.

Norford, B. C., & Medway, F. J. (2002). Adolescent's mobility histories and present social adjustment. *Psychology in the Schools, 39*(1), 51-62.

Olson, D. R. (1977). From utterance to text: The bias of language in speech and writing. *Harvard Educational Review, 47*(3), 257-291.

Ontario, Ministry of Education (1984). *Special Education Information Handbook*. Toronto: Ontario Ministry of Education.

Osborn, A. F. (1963). *Applied Imagination*. New York: Scribner's.

Osman, B. B. (2000). Learning disabilities and the risk of psychiatric disorders in children and adolescents. In L. L. Greenhill (Ed.), *Learning Disabilities: Implications for Psychiatric Treatment* (pp. 33-57). Washington, DC, US: American Psychiatric Press, Inc.

Osterman, K., Bjorkqvist, K, Lagerspetz, K, Charpentier, S., Caprara, G., & Pastorelli, C. (1999). Locus of control and three types of aggression. *Aggressive Behavior, 25*(61-65).

Pasternack, R., & Lyon, R. (1982). Clinical and empirical identification of learning diabled juvenile delinquents. *Journal of Correctional Education, 33*, 7-13.

Pazaratz, D. (2001). Theory and structure of a day treatment program for adolescents. *Residential Treatment for Children and Youth, 19*(1), 29-43.

Pelligrini, A. D., & Horvat, M. (1995). A developmental contextualist critique of attention deficit hyperactivity disorder. *Educational Researcher, 24*(1), 13-20.

Perlmutter, B. F. (1987). Delinquency and learning disabilies: Evidence for compensatory behaviors and adaptation. *Journal of Youth and Adolescence, 16*, 89-95.

Platt, P. (1991). *When Kids Get into Trouble with the Law and What to Do About It*. Toronto: Stoddard Publishing.

Pollard, R. R., Pollard, C. J., & Meers, G. D. (1995). A sociological, psychological, and educational profile of adjudicated youth with disabilities. *Journal for Vocational Special Needs Education, 17*, 56-61.

Pollina, A. (1995). Gender Balance: Lessons from girls in Science and Mathematics. *Educational Leadership, 53*(1), 30-33.

Pope, A., & Bogart, E. (1996). Extended attention span training system: Video game neurotherapy for attention deficit disorder. *Child Study Journal, 26*(1), 39-50.

Porter, N., & Taylor, N. (1972). *How to Assess the Moral reasoning of Students: A teacher's guide to the use of Lawrence Kohlberg's stage-development method*. Toronto: The Ontario Institute for Studies in Education.

Posner, M. B., S. (1971). Components of attention. *Psychological Review, 78*(5), 391-408.

Priceman, M. (2001). *It's me Marva: a story about color and optical illusions*. New York: Alfred A. Knopf.

Putnins, A. (1997). Victim awareness programs for delinquent youths: effects on moral reasoning maturity. *Adolescence, 32*(127), 709-715.

Quay, H., & Peterson, D. (1996). *Revised Problem Behavior Checklist: Professional Manual*. Odessa, FL: Psychological Assessment Resources.

Quay, H. C. (1979). Classification. In H. C. Quay, & J. S. Werry (Ed.), *Psychopathological Disorders of Childhood*. New York: Wiley.

Rapaport, J. L. (1989). *The Boy Who Couldn't Stop Washing: The experience and treatment of Obsessive Compulsive Disorder*. New York: Dutton.

Robinson, E. A., Eyberg, S. M., & Ross, A. W. (1980). The standardization of an inventory of child conduct problem behaviors. *Journal of Clinical Child Psychology, 9*(1), 22-29.

Rohner, R. P., & Britner, P. A. (2002). Worldwide mental health correlates of parental acceptance- rejection: Review of cross-cultural and intracultural evidence. *Cross-Cultural Research, 36*(1), 16-47.

Rorschach, H. (1951). *Psychodiagnostics: A diagnostic test based on perception (P. Lemkau & B. Kronrnberg, Trans.)*. New York: Grune & Stratton.

Rousseau, C., & Heusch, N. (2000). The trip: A creative expression project for refugee and immigrant children. *Art Therapy, 17*(1), 31-39.

Scagell, R. (1998). *Space: An accessible guide that really explains the universe.* London: Marshall Pub.

Scardamalia, M., & Bereiter, C. (1983). Child as coinvestigator: Helping children gain insight into their own mental processes. In S. Paris, G. Olson, & H. Stevenson (Ed.), *Learning and Motivation in the Classroom* (pp. 61-82). Hillsdale, NJ: Lawrence Erlbaum Associates.

Scardamalia, M., Bereiter, C. & Steinbach, M. (1984). Teachability of reflective processes in written composition. *Cognitive Science, 8*(2), 173-190.

Schachar, R., & Wachsmuth, R. (1990). Oppositional disorder in children: A validation study comparing conduct disorder, oppositional disorder and normal control children. *Journal of Child Psychology and Psychiatry and Allied Disciplines, 31*(7), 1089-1102.

Schonfeld, I. S., Shaffer, D., O'Connor, P., & Portnoy, S. (1988). Conduct disorder and cognitive functioning: Testing three causal hypotheses. *Child Development, 59*, 993-1007.

Scieszka, J., & Smith, L. (1989). *The True Story of the Three Little Pigs.* New York: Viking Kestrel.

Seifert, K. L. (1991). *Educational Psychology.* Boston: Houghton Mifflin Company.

Seixas, J. (1989). *Living with a Parent Who Takes Drugs.* New York: Greenwillow Books.

Selye, H. (1978). *The Stress of Life (Revised).*). New York, NY: McGraw Hill.

Shafii, M., & Shafii, S. L. (2001). Diagnostic assessment, management, and treatment of children and adolescents with potential for school violence. In M. Shafii, S. L. Shafii, (Ed.), *School Violence: Assessment, Management, Prevention* (pp. 87-116). Washington, DC, US: American Psychiatric Press, Inc.

Shapiro, F., & Maxfield, L. (2002). Eye Movement Desensitization and Reprocessing (EMDR): Information processing in the treatment of trauma. *Journal of Clinical Psychology, 58*(8), 933-946.

Shapiro, J. P., Burgoo, J. D., Welker, C. J., & Clough, J. B. (2002). Evaluation of the Peacemaker Program: School-based violence prevention for students in Grades Four through Eight. *Psychology in the Schools, 39*(1), 87-100.

Sheehan, J. A. (2001). Social skills training with children and adolescents: An overview and guidelines. *Dissertation Abstracts International, 62*(4-B), 2078.

Shepard, A., & San Souci, D. (Illustrator). (1995). *The Gifts of Wali Dad: A Tale of India and Pakistan.* New York: Simon & Schuster/Atheneum.

Shoemaker, D. J. (2000). *Theories of Delinquency.* New York: Oxford University Press.

Sikorski, J. B. (1991). Learning disorders and the juvenile justice system. *Psychiatric Annals, 21*, 742-747.

Simmons, R. (2002). *Odd Girl Out: The Hidden Culture of Aggression in Girls.* New York: Harcourt.

Simner, M. L. (1985). The warning signs of school failure: an updated profile of the at-risk kindergarten child. *Topics in Early Childhood Special Education, 4.*

Simon, N. (1976). *All Kinds of Families.* Chicago, IL: Albert Whitman & Company.

Simpson, S. B., Swanson, J. M., & Kunkel, K. (1992). The impact of an intensive multisensory reading program on a population of learning disabled delinquents. *Annals of Dyslexia, 42*, 54-66.

Skaret, D., & Wilgosh, L. (1989). Learning disabilities and juvenile delinquency: A causal relationship? *International Journal for the Advancement of Counselling, 12*, 113-129.

Smith Myles, B., & Simpson, R., L. (2002). Asperger syndrome: an overview of characteristics. *Focus on Autism and Other Developmental Disabilities, 17*(3), 132-138.

Smith, S. L., & Boyson, A. R. (2002). Violence in music videos: Examining the prevalence and context of physical aggression. *Journal of Communication, 52*(1), 61-83.

Smith, S. L., Nathanson, A. I., & Wilson, B. J. (2002). Prime-time television: Assessing violence during the most popular viewing hours. *Journal of Communication, 52*(1), 84-111.

Sobotowicz, W., Evans, J. F., & Laughlin, J. (1987). Neuropsychological function and social support in delinquency and learning disability. *The International Journal of Clinical Neuropsychology, 9*, 178-186.

Sprague, J. R., & Walker, Hill. (2000). Early identification and intervention for youth with antisocial and violent behavior. *Exceptional Children, 66*(3), 367-379.

Stein, D. B., & Smith, E. D. (1990). The "REST" program: a new treatment system for the oppositional defiant adolescent. *Adolescence, 25*(100), 891-905.

Sutherland, E. H. (1939). *Principles of Criminology* (Third ed.). Philadelphia: J. B. Lippincott Co.

Tavris, C. (2002). Are Girls Really as Mean as Books Say They Are? *The Chronicle of Higher Education: The Chronicle Review, July 5.*

Taylor, D. T., Berry, P. C., & Block, C. H. (1958). Does group participation when using brain-storming facilitate or inhibit creative thinking? *Administrator's Science Quarterly, 3,* 23-47.

Taylor, S. E. (2002). *The Tending Instinct: How Nurturing Is Essential for Who We Are and How We Live.* London: Times Books.

Thornburg, K. R. (2002). Exporting TV violence - What do we owe the world's children? *Young Children, 57*(2), 6-+.

Tiet, Q. Q., Bird, H. R., Hoven, C. W., Moore, R., Wu, P., Wicks, J., Jensen, P. S., Goodman, S., & Cohen, P. (2001). Relationship between specific adverse life events and psychiatric disorders. *Journal of Abnormal Child Psychology, 29*(2), 153-164.

Tolan, P. H., & Lorian, R. P. (1988). Multivariate approaches to the identification of delinquency proneness in adolescent males. *Amreican Journal of Community Psychology, 16,* 547-561.

Twemlow, S. W., & Sacco, F. C. (1998). Tha application of traditional martial arts practice and theory to treatment of violent adolescents. *Adolescence, 33*(131), 505-518.

Vessey, J. (1991). *Nine.* In O. Winfrey (Producer). Chicago, IL: Harpo Procuctions, Prime Time Oprah.

Wagner, K. D. (2000). Children who worry too much. *Psychiatric Times, 17*(9).

Warner, S., & Rogers, J. (1999). *Accidental Lily.* New York: Knopf.

Weisberg, R. W. (1986). *Creativity: Genius and other myths.* New York: Freeman.

Weisskopf-Joelson, E., & Eliseo, T. S. (1961). An experimental study of the effectiveness of brainstorming. *Journal of Applied Psychology, 45,* 45-49.

White, E. (2002). *Fast Girls: Teenage Tribes and the Myth of the Slut.* New York: Scribner.

Wiener, J. S., & Siegel, L. (1992). A Canadian perspective on learning disabilities. *Journal of Learning Disabilities, 25*(6), 340-350, 371.

Wiesner, D. (2001). *Three Little Pigs.* New York: Clarion Books.

Wilcox, D. K. (2000). How do we know what we know about fire setting behavior? *Hot Issues, 10*(4), 1-3.

Winzer, M. (1995). *Educational Psychology in the Canadian Classroom.* Scarborough, ON: Allyn & Bacon Canada.

Wiseman, R. (2002). *Queen Bees and Wannabes: A Parent's Guide to Helping Your Daughter Survive Cliques, Gossip, Boyfriends, and Other Realities of Adolescence.* New York: Crown Publishing.

Wolpe, J. (1990). *The Practice of Behavior Therapy.* New York: Pergamon Press.

Worsick, D. (1994). *Henry's gift: The Magic Eye.* Kansas City: Andrews and McMeel.

Yehuda, R. (1999). *Risk Factors for Posttraumatic Stress Disorder.* Washington, DC: American Psychiatric Pub.

Yehuda, R. (2002). *Treating Trauma Survivors with PTSD.* Washington, DC: American Psychiatric Pub.

Zentall, S. S., Zentall, T. R., & Barack, R. S. (1977). *Distraction as a function of with-in task stimulation for hyperactive and normal children.* Richmond, KY: S. S. Zentall

Zivcic, I. (1993). Emotional reactions of children to war stress in Croatia. *Journal of the American Academy of Child and Adolescent Psychiatry, 32*(4), 709-713.

Author Index

Index

477

478

482

inadequate 165
    interventions 50,76
    teaching 103
methylphenidate (see Rytalin)
MFT (see Matching Figures Test)
middle-class values 418
Milieu Therapies
    group homes 411
Miller, A. & Eller-Miller, E. (1989)
    Method 373,378
mind
    biological advances 48
    cognitive 147
    Cognitive View 53-6
    dog's 31
    separate from body 17
    study topic 16,18
minimization
    depression 334
Minnesota Multiphasic Personality Inventory, The (MMPI)
    testing 69,72
misbehavior
    behavioral classroom 106,110,117-8,123
    Dreikurs 44
    language issues 140
mischief (-chievous)
    gender variables 138
misconception(s)
    experiential 56
    media 168
    misbehavior 167
    social living 166
mistake (s)
    behavioral class 108,119
    classroom 44
    concept of 166
    consequences 46
mistrust
    stages 28
Mixed Episode
    Manic Depression 336
MMPI *(see Minnesota Multiphasic Personality Inventory, The)*
    testing 69,72
mobility
    case study 83,87
model (-ling)
    behavioral class 106-9,111,116
    case study 90
    classroom 173-217
    cognitive 148
    cultural group 436
    familiarity 162
    imitation 39
    individualized programs 128-9,195-6
    intervention 32,297
    language 440
    media 247
    Reversal Design 77
    school phobia 318,320-1
    teacher 247
    team-teaching 446
    ways to act 244-5
modification
    behavior 32,116,139
    case study 96,98,100
    language 141,144

    secondary causes 80
    student 2
    teacher 2
mood
    disorder (s) 303,331
moral (-ity)
    behavior 166
    case study 85
    development 168-9,410
    madness 15
    post-conventional 169
    superego 24-5
mores
    case study 91
motivation (-nal)
    behavioral class 107,109,111,117-8,120,122-3
    case study 82,84
    inadequacy 46
    intervention 185-9
    language 143
    letters 163
    meaningfulness 214
    needs 128,131
    novelty 191
    self-efficacy 40
    TV violence 293
    variable 192
motor
    case study 91
    excess 75
    skills disorder 64-5
movement
    disorders 329
    from school 166
    invading space 136
    stereotypic disorder 65
MRI (imaging) 48
multi-cultural (issues)
    behavior 10
    classroom 431-9
    media unit 166
    research centers 457
multi-discipline (-nary)
    socio-emotional 205
    team 81
Multiple Baseline Design, The
    case study 102
    described 76-9
Multiple Sclerosis
    mood disorders 331
muscle (s)
    control 28
    progressive reaction 326
    tension 73
music
    academic skills 428
    as relaxant 136
    social 449
    stress relief 327
Mutism
    selective 65-317-8
mysticism
    Greek 16
N
nail biting
    self-stimulatory 298-9

pecking order
    behavioral class 111
    case study 91
peer (s)
    ADHD 366
    behavioral class 108,126
    buddy 257
    case study 83-4,90-2,99
    criticism by 165
    helpers 46
    influence 405
    language 141,145
    secondary causes 80
    socio-economic 204
    status 73
    tutor 135
penalty (-ties)
    behavioral class 106,109
    classroom 45
    lack of 51
    motivation 168
    Reversal Design 77
perception (s)
    behavioral class 107,116
    case study 86,90,93,95
    Cognitive View 55
    faulty 22
    Gestaltists 147
    individualized programs 139
    language 141
    self 10,79,85
    student 40,105,132
    in testing 72
    thinking 153-4,158
    traditional role 164
performance
    conditions 47
    educational 14
    expectations 125
    experts 160
    language 143
    thinking 152
peri-natal
    problems 50
permission
    behavioral class 113
    parental 82
personal growth
    individual plan 194
personality (-ties)
    behavioral class 111
    conflicts 66
    drawings 69
    Erikson 29
    Freud 24-7
    problem-solving 162
Personality Inventory for Children, The (PIC-2)
    testing 69,72-3
Personality Inventory for Youth, The
    testing 69,72-4
personalization
    behavioral classroom 106-10,117,121,123,126
    case study 82,93
    cognitive 146
    individualized programs 128-9
    language 140-1,143
    modeling 39

monitoring 56
    problem-solving 163
    safety 166
    social training 151
personnel
    case study 101
perspective
    behavioral class 116
    case study 92
    Cognitive View 56
    ethics of care 169
    "talking" 417
    thinking 154
    universal 168
Pervasive Developmental Disorder 303,315-7
phallus (-lic)
    stage 27
    symbol 23
pharmacological
    substances 48
phenomenon (-na)
    behavioral class 110
    case study 84
    emotional expressiveness 138
    gang formation 176-7
    psychological 51
    thinking 154
philosophy
    behavioral class 105
    of Re-Ed 58
    Summary 456
phlegm
    element (as mucus) 16
phobia (s)
    assessment 63
    behaviorism 30
    case study 83
    testing 70
    treatment 34
phonological area
    disorder 64
phrenology
    role of 17,19
physical cause (s)
    behavioral class 107
    of behavior 49
    brain disturbances 50
    case study 84-5,92,96
    handicap 75
    jealousy 139
    language 141
    mental illness 16
    safety 174-5
physical education
    academic value 428-9
    social 449
physician
    case study 86,95
physiology (ical)
    brain 50
    case study 85
    concepts 51
    phenomena 132
PIC-2 (see Personality Inventory for Children, The)
Pica
    assessment 65

497

Appendix

What is your preference?

Directions:

Read the following ten activities and place a number from 1 to 10 next to each - 1 next to the activity you enjoy the most and 10 next to the one you enjoy the least.

_____ I enjoy working on any activity as long as it is on the computer.

_____ I enjoy activities that involve writing stories.

_____ I enjoy activities that involve numbers and arithmetic calculations.

_____ I enjoy activities that involve reading about science or history.

_____ I enjoy activities that involve playing games in the gym.

_____ I enjoy activities that involve watching videos and films on science and history topics.

_____ I enjoy activities that involve watching stories in films and videos.

_____ I enjoy activities that involve reading poetry.

_____ I enjoy activities that involve reading a series of good stories.

_____ I enjoy activities that involve working with other students.

Name three other things you enjoy doing in class.

1. ....
   ....
2. ....
   ....
3. ....
   ....

Name three things you enjoy doing at home.

1. ....
   ....
2. ....
   ....
3. ....
   ....

Resources for the classroom

High Interest/ Low Vocab Materials

STAR is a magazine of high interest/low vocabulary which prints stories about prominent figures in the adolescent subculture – in sports, Rock, films, videos, and other fields. The stories are at the Grade Three reading level, as measured by the Harris-Jacobson readability formula; helpfully, the publisher allows teachers to reproduce pages for classroom use.

Each issue contains about 15 biographies, each a page long, followed by a page of comprehension questions. The exercises consist of multiple choice and short answer questions of the following type:

- identifying the main idea

- vocabulary

- identifying cause-effect relationships

- time sequencing of events

- asking for opinion

- making inferences

- activities relating the information to a socio-political theme.

STAR is published every 6 weeks from September to April, its six issues – annually – being available for a reasonable price. It may be ordered at the following address:

Turman Publishing Company
200 West Mercer Street
Suite 508
Seattle, Washington, USA
98119

Other high-interest/low-vocabulary materials are available from many publishers.

Bibliography of Articles and Books relating to Culture

The *Beaver* Magazine is a very useful resource for Canadian History, past and present. The partial list of books and articles in *Beaver,* all relating to culture, is included here as an initial point of reference. A search of Libraries' references and Publishers' catalogues will generate a more complete list.

Arnold, A. (1994). The New Jerusalem: Jewish pioneers on the prairies. *The Beaver, 74*(1), 37-42.

Avery, D. (2000). Peopling Canada: Immigration defines the Nation. *The Beaver, 90*(1), 28-37.

Band, I. (1998). Power Serge: The complex relationship between Canada's First Nations and the RCMP. *The Beaver, 78*(3), 18-23.

Barman, J. (1998). Whatever Happened to the Kanakas? "They're alive and well in British Columbia." *The Beaver, 77*(6), 12-19.

Bell, H. (2000). *Songs of Power*. New York: Hyperion Books for Children.

Berry, J. (1987). *A Thief in the Village, and other stories of Jamaica*. Markham, ON: H. Hamilton.

Bode, P. (1993). Simcoe and the Slaves. *The Beaver, 73*(3), 17-19.

Brooks, M. (1997). *Bone Dance*. Vancouver: Douglas & McIntyre.

Brown, S. R. (2000). Cormack's Quest: In search of the elusive Beothuk. *The Beaver, 80*(2), 34-39.

Buck, R. M. (1992). In the Midst of Life: A young woman's letters evoke the Old West. *The Beaver, 7*(6), 33-46.

Bumsted, J. M. (1992). Home Sweet Suburb: The great post-war migration to suburbia. *The Beaver, 72*(5), 26-34.

Bumsted, J. M. (1995). Becoming Canadians: The forces that have shaped our national identity. *The Beaver, 74*(6), 54-69.

Cochrane, J. (1992). Children of the Farm: At work and play on the Canadian frontier. *The Beaver, 72*(4), 12-18.

Dempsey, H. A. (1993). The Tragedy of White Bird: A great Indian leader's lonely death and exile. *The Beaver, 73*(1), 23-29.

Dickason, O. P. (2000). Making Claim: First Nations Seek Redress. *The Beaver, 80*(1), 38-43.

Feder, H. K. (2001). *Death on Sacred Ground*. Minneapolis: Lerner Publications Co.

Gambrill, L., & Lewis-Weinberger, M. (1998). *A Boy Named Neville*. Kingston, Jamaica: Ian Randle Publishing.

Gilmore, R. (2001). *A Group of One*. New York: Henry Holt & Co.

Kelly, W. E. (1997). Canada's Black Defenders. *The Beaver, 77*(2), 31-34.

Killingsworth, M. (1994). *Circle Within a Circle*. Toronto: McMillan Canada.

Koppel, T. (1999). Catching the Saviour Fish: Enlachon light the way for B. C.'s Nisga'a. *The Beaver, 78*(6), 20-25.

Lasky, K. (1998). *Dreams in the golden country: the diary of Zipporah Feldman, a Jewish immigrant girl*. New York: Scolastic.

Lee-Whitting. (1992). Along the Opeongo Road: Memories of Canada's first Polish settlement. *The Beaver, 72*(1), 29-33.

Levin, B. (1997). *Island Bound*. New York: Greenwillow Books.

Lingard, J. (1991). *Between Two Worlds*. London: Hamish Hamilton.

Loewen, I., & Miller, G. (1993). *My Kokum Called Today*. Winnipeg: Pemmican Publishing.

London, J., & San Souci, D. (1998). *Ice Bear and Little Fox*. New York: Dutton Children Books.

Lyon, J. T. (1998). A Picturesque Lot: The Gypsies in Peterborough. *The Beaver, 78*(5), 25-30.

McGhee, R. (1992). Northern Approaches Before Columbus: Early European visitors to the New World. *The Beaver, 72*(3), 6-23.

McIntosh, D. (1993). Go West Young Woman, Wanted: Wives, Mothers, and female pioneers. *The Beaver, 7*(26), 38-39.

Mitic, T. V. (1995). Gateway to Canada: Pier 21, Halifax, was the golden door to millions seeking a new life. *The Beaver, 75*(1), 9-15.

Molnar-Fenton, S., & Flesher, V. (1998). *An Mei's strange and wondrous journey*. New York: DK Pub.

Na, A. (2001). *A Step from Heaven*. Ashville, NC: Front Street.

Nye, N. S. (1997). *Habibi*. New York: Simon and Shuster; for Young Readers.

Pomeranc, M. H., & DiSalvo-Ryan, D. (1998). *The American Wei*. Morton Grove, Ill: A. Whitman.

Raible, C. (1994). 999 Queen Street West: The Toronto Asylum Scandal. *The Beaver, 74*(1), 37-43.

Rees, J. (1998). The Surplus People: Uncertainty haunts a boat load of Irish Immigrants. *The Beaver, 78*(5), 5-11.

Simpkins, M. (2000). Spoken Word: One man's mission to preserve Cree storytelling. *The Beaver, 80*(2), 42-43.

Tippet, M. (2000). Expressing Identity: A culture finds its voice. *The Beaver, 80*(1), 18-27.

Waboose, J. B., & Reczuch, K. (1998). *Morning on the Lake*. Toronto: Kids Can Press.

Williams, G. (1983). The Hudson's Bay Company and the Fur Trade, 1670-1870: IV The Indians and the Bay Trade. *The Beaver, Reprinted 1991*(314:2), 26-34.

Woodruf, E. (1997). *The Orphans of Ellis Island: a time-travel adventure*. New York: Scholastic Press.

Canada's Digital Collection

"This Web site is one of the richest, most significant sources of Canadian content on the Internet. Visitors to this award-winning site are able to explore a vast array of multimedia resources celebrating Canada's history and culture, landscapes, technology, scientific discoveries, and Aboriginal communities."

http://collections.ic.gc.ca/

Perspective Taking

As good examples of the ways in which children's literature can be used to develop a social skill, the following materials are recommended to assist the teacher in introducing the idea of perspective taking. Although the tale of The Three Little Pigs is a children's story, it can nevertheless be used with older learners because activities can be structured to require complex cognitive skills.

The Three Little Pigs

The following website – http://www.vickiblackwell.com/lit/threepigs.html – introduces the book, *Three Little Pigs*, by David Wiesner, and provides the titles of other versions of the story. The site includes activities, bookmarks, and wonderful pictures to download. An exquisite tool available on this site is the Kidspiration template which features a visual map of the story.

The following site – http://teacher.scholastic.com/writewit/mff/fractured_fairy_true.htm – features the book, *The True Story of the Three Little Pigs*, by John Scieszka, the story told from the perspective of the wolf. A variety of activities is described.

For older students (Grades 6 and up), computer activities relating to the Scieszka book are provided at the following URL – http://olp.swlauriersb.qc.ca/webquest/true_story.htm – also associated with these activities is a rubric of skills across the curriculum that is provided for evaluation purposes. This final website – http://www.shol.com/agita/wolfside.htm – presents the trial of the Wolf.